ROCKING THE STATE

Rocking the State

Rock Music and Politics
in Eastern Europe
and Russia

edited by
Sabrina Petra Ramet

Westview Press
Boulder • San Francisco • Oxford

Published in 1994 in the United States of America by Westview Press, Inc., 5500 Central Avenue, Boulder, Colorado 80301-2877, and in the United Kingdom by Westview Press, 36 Lonsdale Road, Summertown, Oxford OX2 7EW

Library of Congress Cataloging-in-Publication Data
Rocking the state : rock music and politics in Eastern Europe and
    Russia / edited by Sabrina Petra Ramet.
        p.   cm.
    Includes bibliographical references and index.
    ISBN 0-8133-1762-2 (HC) — ISBN 0-8133-1763-0 (PB)
    1. Rock music—Soviet Union—History and criticism.   2. Rock
music—Europe, Eastern—History and criticism.   3. Music and state.
I. Ramet, Sabrina P., 1949–
ML3534.R6384   1994
781.66'0947—dc20   93-36067
                                                                          CIP
                                                                          MN

Printed and bound in the United States of America

The paper used in this publication meets the requirements
of the American National Standard for Permanence of Paper
for Printed Library Materials Z39.48-1984.

10   9   8   7   6   5   4   3   2   1

For my spouse, Chris,
her mother, Delores,
and in memory of her father,
Bob (1924–1973)

I am dancing in heaven forever more,
Dancing to endless love.
Great is the power of love!
Oh love dance! Great is the power of love!
Love dance of Oneness,
Dancing mysterious dreams,
Blissful, floating, dances of love.
We are the children of the Lady of Light,
Light of heaven, light of endless love,
Light of blissful, floating love, light of endless love,
We are dancing to the sun,
All are dancing, all are One.
I am dancing in heaven a dance of love and Oneness.
Great is the power of love!

—Alan Hovhaness, "Lady of Light"

Contents

TWO *The Soviet Union*

       *Sabrina Petra Ramet, Sergei Zamascikov,
       and Robert Bird*   181

10   Rock Music in Belarus
       Maria Paula Survilla   219

11   Rock Culture and Rock Music in Ukraine
       Romana Bahry   243

       About the Book   297
       About the Editor and Contributors   299
       Index   303

Preface

Most readers of this book will have had at most a fleeting acquaintance with the music of some of the groups described in this book. Groups such as Laibach (from Slovenia), Borghesia (Slovenia), Pankow (the GDR), and Gorky Park (USSR) have concentrated on the Western market and have acquired followings in the United States and Western Europe. Other artists and groups, such as Boris Grebenshikov and Aquarium (USSR), Sergei Kuryokhin (USSR), Goran Bregović and White Button (Yugoslavia), and Plastic People of the Universe (Czechoslovakia), have also seen some Western exposure. But for the most part, the rock music of that part of the world is terra incognita to Westerners. So too is the story of their uneasy coexistence with communist authorities from the time that rock first appeared until the collapse of communism in 1989. This book aims to fill that vacuum.

There have been other studies of rock music under communism before—notably, Timothy Ryback's 1990 volume, *Rock Around the Bloc*, and Artemy Troitsky's earlier popular treatment of the Soviet scene in *Back in the USSR*. But this is the first scholarly attempt to treat systematically all the countries and regions of the western USSR and Eastern Europe, including Yugoslavia, Ukraine, and Belarus.

The coverage in this book is comprehensive. Omitted are only Albania and Romania (except for brief mention in Chapter 1). In Albania, there is no rock scene of any importance, and in Romania, such promising beginnings as were evinced in the 1970s withered away under the cultural suppression and economic strangulation of the late Ceauşescu regime. All the other countries of Eastern Europe are treated in this book. In addition, there are separate chapters devoted to rock in Russia/the USSR, rock in Ukraine, and rock in Belarus. The fascinating rock scenes in Estonia and Latvia are discussed in the context of broader developments in Chapter 9.

Bringing this book to fruition has been a difficult task, and it could not have been accomplished without the help of certain individuals. I am indebted, in the first place, to Margaret Brown for translating the chapter on the GDR from German and to László Kürti for suggesting the title for the book. I would also like to thank Karen Walton, our program secretary, for her invaluable assistance in preparing the manuscript for publication.

Earlier incarnations of Chapters 5 and 6 were published in *East European Politics and Societies*. An earlier version of Chapter 9 was published in *Journal of Popular Culture*. I am indebted to these journals for permission to reprint the articles here. Thanks also to C. F. Peters Corporation for permission to quote the text by Alan Hovhaness in the epigraph.

Sabrina Petra Ramet
Seattle, Washington

SABRINA PETRA RAMET **1**

Rock: The Music of Revolution (and Political Conformity)

MUSIC IS NOT merely a cultural or diversionary phenomenon. It is also a political phenomenon. Its medium is suggestion. Its point of contact is the imagination. Its voice is that of the muse. All of this makes music an unexpectedly powerful force for social and political change. Music brings people together and evokes for them collective emotional experience to which common meanings are assigned (Woodstock is an obvious example of music bringing people together). It gives them common reference points, common idols, and often a common sense of "the enemy."

Every revolution has its music. The American Revolution, the French Revolution, and the Bolshevik Revolution all produced stirring and riveting music, usually marches. Political revolution, it seems, is a powerful progenitor of certain kinds of music. The uses of and role played by such music are clear enough. Indeed, one may go so far as to say that without music, there cannot be a revolution.

The East European revolution of 1989 likewise had its music, and that music was rock. Václav Havel, former president of Czechoslovakia, even maintains that the revolution *began* in the rock scene.[1] And with the triumph of the anticommunist revolution, local rock stars were swept to positions of political responsibility in Czechoslovakia, Bulgaria, and elsewhere, and Frank Zappa was invited to Prague as an official guest of the Czechoslovak government. In Yugoslavia in 1990, a political party called the Rock and Roll Party was formed, albeit largely in jest.

Rock music produced its share of revolutionaries. This was not surprising given the strong antiauthoritarian sentiment that researchers find to be commonly associated with rock fans.[2] A Hungarian rock group, Coitus Punk Group, voiced this sentiment succinctly in a 1984 song:

1

Rotten, stinking communist gang,
Why has nobody hanged them yet?[3]

Bora Djordjević, the self-styled Bob Dylan of the Yugoslav rock scene, once compared the government of his native Yugoslavia to the apartheid regime in South Africa.[4]

And in the Soviet Union, the Leningrad group Televizor shook up the authorities with a 1986 song in which it sang:

We were watched from the days of kindergarten.
Some nice men and kind women
Beat us up. They chose the most painful places
And treated us like animals on the farm.
So we grew up like a disciplined herd.
We sing what they want and live how they want.
And we look at them downside up as if we're trapped.
We just watch how they hit us.
Get out of control!
Get out of control!
And sing what you want,
And not just what is allowed.
We have a right to yell![5]

Thus rock musicians figured—in the Soviet and East European context of the 1980s—a bit like prophets. That is to say, they did not invent or create the ideas of revolution or the feelings of discontent and disaffection. But they were sensitive to the appearance and growth of these ideas and feelings and gave them articulation, and in this way they helped to reinforce the revolutionary tide.

The revolutionary destabilization of Eastern Europe and the Soviet Union had roots in economic discontent, the disaffection of the intellectuals, the spread of corruption at high levels, the loss of confidence within the elite, and so forth.[6] It was borne along by the sprouting of independent activist groups, the mobilization of churches into politics, and the transformation of the citizen's sense of self. Alongside these phenomena, rock music played a supportive role. The archetypal rock star became, symbolically, the muse of revolution. The decaying communist regimes (in Bulgaria, Czechoslovakia, and Romania especially) seemed to fear the electric guitar more than bombs or rifles.

This is a book about the politics of rock music, or perhaps the sociology of rock music, in the Soviet Union and Eastern Europe. Its starting point is that rock music has proven to be a political phenomenon because rock artists themselves often choose to make political statements through their music, lyrics, attire, or performances and because regimes often make even politically innocent music political simply by reacting politically: As soon as something is censored or banned by political authorities, it becomes ipso facto politically charged.

There are many experiences shared by the national environments described herein. In all of them, the earliest phase was imitative, as the bedazzled local youngsters struggled to master the new idiom. This was followed by a second phase, in which emergent rock 'n' roll bands wrote their own material but always sang in English—the supposed obligatory language of rock 'n' roll. Eventually, a third phase ensued, in which local rock groups began to sing in their own languages and to develop their own musical styles.[7] And more recently, there have been clear signs of a fourth phase, characterized by the turn to local and exotic folk idioms for material (the latter after the model of Paul Simon's "Graceland") and, perhaps ironically, by the return of some groups (such as Slovenia's Laibach and Borghesia, and Berlin's now-defunct Pankow) to English, in their quest for a world market.

In another pattern common to all of these national environments, rock music pitted the younger generation against the older generation, just as it did in the West—the difference being that in the East, the older generation was willing to go to greater lengths to use political power to repress the new contagion.

In all of these national environments—including even Yugoslavia—there were also experiences of censorship and politically motivated interference with the musical process.

But there were also differences from one national environment to another. In Yugoslavia, for example, the omnipresent "national question" exerted an influence even in rock music, resulting in the fragmentation of the rock scene into five regional rock markets. In Hungary, by contrast, the communist state in time warmed up to rock music and even allowed the staging of a mammoth rock opera, "Stephen the King," to commemorate the millennium of Stephen's coronation.

SYMBOLIC AMBIVALENCE
AND THE OPAQUENESS OF LYRICS

In a provocative essay published in 1979, Bernice Martin argued that "all culture simultaneously reinforces the existing order and offers alternative visions," and more specifically she suggested that rock music, reflecting both sides of this paradoxical formula, has routinely mixed ritualized symbols of "communitas" with those of "antistructure."[8] In her view, thus, the use of rock alternatively for rebellion and for panegyrics is sown into the very nature of culture itself, which is always and necessarily ambivalent. At times, one aspect or the other may prevail—but such tendencies are inherently transitory and unstable, she argued. Taking up the connection between working-class solidarity and rock as rebellion, Martin continued,

> What began as a symbiotic exchange between the tribal and the liberating elements in working class youth culture was stretched to an ultimately un-resolvable tension when the middle classes, especially the anarchic radicals, moved in to elaborate the symbols of freedom, immediacy, and hostility to structures, and even to add an element of conscious political protest. Nevertheless, for a brief period in the 1960s, the contradictions did work as a symbiosis and united working and middle class wings of youth culture, the Underground and Rock into a powerful culture force. Yet ultimately— the Beatles' "Sergeant Pepper" album was probably the symbolic turning point—both Pop and youth culture began to disintegrate back into constit-uent elements, into largely class homogeneous "markets" or groupings. ... The progressive middle classes [for example] took Rock through the logic of anti-structure until for many it ceased to be recognizable as Rock and be-came indistinguishable from "serious" avant-garde music.[9]

Some of the "antistructure" messages sung to the accompaniment of a rock beat have been extreme. Take, for example, a song from Mike and the Mechanics, popular in 1987:

> *Take the children and yourself,*
> *and hide out in the cellar.*
> *By now the fighting will be close at hand.*
> *Don't believe the Church and State,*
> *and everything they tell you.*
> *Believe me, I'm with the High Command.*[10]

Then again, there is Leonard Cohen's "insurrectionary" song:

> *I'm coming now, I'm coming to reward them;*
> *First we take Manhattan, then we take Berlin.*[11]

But it is quite another matter whether such messages are taken seriously. A 1987 study by James S. Leming found that only 12 percent of American young people polled said that they paid "a great deal of attention" to the lyrics, whereas 58 percent indicated that the content of the lyrics was, as far as they were concerned, irrelevant.[12] Moreover, even among those who paid attention to the lyrics, there was some disagreement as to what they meant. In a striking example, Leming found no consensus among the fifty-eight persons sampled as to the meaning of Olivia Newton-John's 1981 song "Physical":

> *Let's get physical, physical,*
> *Let me hear your body talk.*[13]

In Leming's sample, 36 percent interpreted the song to refer to sexual relations, whereas an equal percentage believed it referred to physical exercise and conditioning; fully 28 percent asserted that they were unsure as to the song's meaning.

Does this suggest that we should write off rock music as socially marginal after all, on the argument that the fans are either not listening to or not understanding what is being sung? My answer is no—for a rather simple reason: The social functions performed by rock music necessarily vary across social systems and over time. Certain societies have more deeply rooted traditions of bard poets, and these traditions can sometimes be translated into a rock idiom. But more particularly, there is a world of difference in the social needs that rock musicians have wanted to address in collectivist societies as opposed to the more restricted ambitions of rock musicians in pluralist societies. As Goran Bregović, the leader of the Sarajevo rock group White Button, put it to me in 1989,

> Rock 'n' roll in communist countries has much more importance than rock 'n' roll in the West. We can't have any alternative parties or any alternative organized politics. So there are not too many places where you can gather large groups of people and communicate ideas which are not official. Rock 'n' roll is one of the most important vehicles for helping people in communist countries to think in a different way.[14]

In collectivist systems, a symbiosis of alternative culture and alternative politics is inevitable anyway because such systems define culture in political terms. Moreover, some of those drawn to the rock scene in conditions of collectivism have in fact been motivated, in many instances, by a desire to find a serviceable vehicle for some form of opposition. One of the ironies of political vicissitudes is that in collectivist systems, even subtle lyrics may summon a storm. Mike and the Mechanics and Leonard Cohen need scarcely to have concerned themselves with political repercussions from ostensibly revolutionary songs. But when the legendary Soviet rock group Time Machine sang a new song, "The Calm," at the Sverdlovsk Rock Festival in 1978, officials went into shock and disqualified the band from the competition. The lyrics in question:

My ship is a creation of able hands,
My course is a total disaster.
But just let the wind pick up
And everything around will change,
Including the idiot who thinks otherwise.
An answer ready for every question,
Might has always made right,
But no one believes that there's no wind on earth,
Even if they've banned the wind.[15]

THE CULT OF THE PERSONALITY

A Yugoslav poll taken in late 1988 found that Eric Clapton, a rock guitarist, was one of the people most admired by young people and that he was more popular among the young than was Serbian party boss Slobodan Milošević. The result was revealing because it demonstrated the occasional ability of rock stars to establish a credibility or following that transcends mere appreciation of their musical abilities.

Various Western rock stars have made a dramatic impact on the young people of Eastern Europe and the Soviet Union. In recent years this number has certainly included Tina Turner, Elton John, Madonna, and (in Bulgaria, at least) Uriah Heep.

But there is one figure who casts a long shadow over the entire East European (and Russian) rock scene and who served as an inspiration to an entire generation: former Beatle John Lennon, who was gunned down in Manhattan in December 1980. The martyr's halo transformed the musical prophet into a kind of saint in the eyes of his admirers, and his song "Give Peace a Chance" became a surrogate anthem of many young people not just in Eastern Europe but throughout the world.

Of Lennon's many memorable songs, there is one in particular that seemed to address with especial poignancy the dilemmas of growing up in late socialism. First released in 1970, it sings the praises of the working-class hero:

> *They hurt you at home and they hit you at school*
> *They hate you if you're clever and they despise a fool*
> *Till you're so fucking crazy you can't follow their rules.*
> *A working class hero is something to be*
> *A working class hero is something to be.*[16]

These words had at least as much resonance in Eastern Europe as they did in the West.

In Bulgaria, Lennon's death was saluted by Radio Sofia with a two-hour tribute to the music of the Beatles. In Czechoslovakia, unofficial shrines to the late Beatle sprouted up around Prague, and a large section of wall near the Charles Bridge, appropriately decorated with Lennon-esque graffiti, came to be known as the "Lennon Wall" and became a pilgrimage site for Czechoslovak pacifists and rock fans. In the USSR, several hundred Russian students assembled on the Lenin Hills in Moscow in the wake of Lennon's murder, playing his songs and carrying pictures of the revered ex-Beatle.

East Germany's straight-laced newspaper *Neues Deutschland* tried to make propaganda out of Lennon's death with the headline "Singer John

Lennon Just One of 21,000 Murder Victims Annually."[17] But in subsequent years this tone was less common, and sincere tributes multiplied. A Budapest publishing house released a biography of Lennon in 1981, written by local rock critic Gabor Koltay. The Moscow band Avtograf dedicated its song "Requiem" to Lennon, and the Estonian rock group Raja wrote a song entitled simply "To Mr. Lennon."

Each year, thousands of Lennon fans commemorated his death; the Czechoslovak memorial was one of the best known. In 1985, for instance, some 600 Czechs assembled in central Prague to mark the fifth anniversary of the ex-Beatle's death, singing Beatle songs. Security forces monitored the event with watchful eyes. In death, Lennon became a powerful symbol of hope and the aspiration toward peace, and his lyrics perpetuated this message.

FROM TABOO TO CONFORMITY

Rock music, which no one born before World War II seemed capable of ever understanding, is the music of the new generation. One's acceptance or rejection of rock automatically brands one as "young" or "old" (perhaps not always entirely fairly). The generational gap was certainly a part of the authorities' early hostility toward rock. They simply didn't like this new music.

But the antagonism ran deeper. Rock wasn't "serious." It was too Western. It got young people thinking about LA, the Big Apple, Chicago. Next they will become psychological exiles impervious to communist socialization. A poll taken among Hungarian young people in 1979 seemed to bear out these fears. Surveying roughly one thousand members of the communist youth league, pollsters found that young Hungarians knew much more about the latest rock stars in England and the United States than they did about Lenin, Stalin, Khrushchev, or Marxism.[18] Moreover, as Bulgarian authorities claimed when banning the rock group Signal in 1982, rock music stirs its listeners to "excessive excitement."[19] In Czechoslovakia, antirock hysteria reached a peak in spring 1983 in the wake of the publication by the party weekly *Tribuna* of a violent attack on rock by writer Jan Kryzl. The writer reserved especial venom for Czechoslovakia's punk bands, which he said had not only copied Western punk music but had "entirely uncritically taken over from western punks also styles of dress and behavior, obscene gestures, with men performing in women's panty hose, colored stripes across their faces, equipped with heavy chains and locks, crosses and other shocking junk."[20]

Rock groups challenged political, social, and sexual taboos. The Polish rock group Budka Suflera, for example, described in a 1984 song the totalitarian face of real socialism:

Someone is watching your thoughts and dreams
Someone is trying to mold you like wax
Some, perhaps, had zeroed in on you long ago.

In Poland in the late 1980s, a time when society temporarily despaired of the possibility of triumph over its communist masters, Polish rock groups abandoned politics for pornography, satanism, and other forms of escapism.[21]

To take a particularly poignant example, the popular East German group Renft Combo got its start in the early 1970s by singing what the authorities wanted. In exchange, group members were allowed to grow beards, let their hair grow long, and wear disheveled and torn clothing. In 1973, they included a song with the politically suggestive title "The Chains Are Getting Tighter" on their *Amiga* album.[22] By 1974, the Renft Combo had sold more than 200,000 LPs and 30,000 singles and began to denounce not merely injustices in the "capitalist" world but also those at home. Its 1975 song "Doubts" called into question military conscription in the GDR. Another song, "The Rockaballad of Little Otto," lamented the division of the two Germanys. On 22 September 1975, the leader of the combo was summoned before the Leipzig Council of Culture and informed that the band would not be allowed to perform again.

Eventually, authorities came to the conclusion that if rock music could not be suppressed, perhaps it could be put to work for socialism. In Hungary, for instance, after the publication of the results of the aforementioned poll, the government turned to rock musicians for help. In a three-day conference held in the town of Tata, 23–25 March 1981, Hungarian cultural commissars asked rock musicians to help them to make socialism attractive to young people.

Similarly, in Romania in the early 1970s cultural watchdogs tightened the screws on local rock groups and advised them to sing supportive songs, not irrelevant songs. In 1975, Vasile Donose, music editor of Romanian Radio and Television, complained that rock songs concentrated far too much on love and bemoaned that because of "insufficient guidance" rock singers had neglected patriotic social and political themes.[23] Authorities in Romania decided to make the necessary corrections. The result was a series of patriotic rock songs with titles like "The Party, Ceaușescu, Romania," "Communist Years," and "Glory to Our First President." In one rock paean to Romanian socialism, the musicians sang:

In the days of struggle and hardship,
As they followed the party, the pathfinder,
Our young heroes dreamed of the spring—
Of the spring that now has come to pass.[24]

Or again, in the USSR in the era of Brezhnev, Andropov, and Chernenko, the Ministry of Culture adopted directives for the regulation of instrumental groups and discos, published lists of "unacceptable" bands, and mobilized "musical patrols" under the auspices of the Komsomol to inspect and supervise the adherence of discos to the ministry's regulations.[25] As a result of these patrols, various rock groups were disbanded and a significant number of discos were ordered to be shut down. Meanwhile, the authorities promoted their own preferred brand of rock music—a rock music brimming with love of socialism and optimism for the socialist future. Its best-known purveyors were the so-called (and aptly named) Happy Guys.

In several of these countries (e.g., the GDR, Czechoslovakia, and Yugoslavia), the socialist youth organization eventually started organizing rock concerts and rock dances. In Yugoslavia, once Tito passed on, the once solemn celebration of the Day of Youth became the occasion for an annual state-sponsored rock spectacle. And in East Germany, once the socialist regime got over its early distaste for rock music, rock musicians were generously rewarded for loyal service. East Germany's rock musicians were allowed to travel freely to the West (a privilege denied most East Germans until 1989), were pampered by the authorities, and received state awards. As a result, by the late 1980s rock musicians were counted among the top earners in the GDR. Singers like Tamara Danz and Frank Schobel lived in private homes, owned Western limousines, and drew six-digit incomes.[26]

Only Albania's authorities held back, apparently locked in deep dread of this dangerous plague. For years, the conventional wisdom was that rock music was all but unknown in Albania. Not quite. A questionnaire administered anonymously to university students in August 1989 revealed that 3 percent of respondents admitted to liking rock music. The organizers of the survey reflected on the "fact" that "this kind of music … is far from the values of true art" and talked of trying to uncover the identities of the rock fans; higher authorities eventually intervened.[27] Albanian young people were not being exposed to rock music through Radio Tirana, of course. Most of what they knew of Western rock they heard on Voice of America, the BBC, or other Western stations or obtained on cassettes on the ever-present black market. But even orthodox Albania was not able to dam up the rock tide entirely, and by late 1990 Tirana's Enver Hoxha University featured a disco playing rock music every Saturday night.[28]

By contrast with the kind of political conformity that elites in the USSR, Czechoslovakia, Bulgaria, and Romania cultivated, there have been occasional instances of spontaneous political enthusiasm. One of the most endearing (perhaps in part because of its simplicity) was a twenty-nine-year-old Hungarian singer's expression of the hopes that Gorbachev had kindled among the people of Hungary. Known only as "Eva," she sang (in 1988):

> *Clap your hands for Mikhail Gorbachev.*
> *Clap, clap, clap, clap your hands.*
> *His sexy smile has started to show.*
> *This man, he's captured my mind.*
> *Oh, Mr. Gorbachev, you are so different*
> *   from all the other boys.*
> *I think I'm falling in love with you.*[29]

ROCK IN TRANSITION

By the end of the 1980s, some East European rock groups had composed rock suites in honor of Che Guevara and other meritorious socialist causes, had played in officially sponsored "peace concerts,"[30] and had behaved as surrogate emissaries of socialism to the world outside. Other rock groups, by contrast, spurned conformity and held fast to the posture of rebellion. The ambivalent role of rock music was graphically reflected and symbolized in a kind of "battle of the rock groups" waged literally across the Berlin Wall in June 1988. West Berlin had scheduled a rock concert to be held next to the wall on 19 June. Topping the bill was none other than Michael Jackson. East Berlin's masters felt they had to compete, so they put together a rival rock concert that featured an array of rock groups from Great Britain, the GDR, the USSR, and Poland and was hosted by Olympic ice-skating champion Katerina Witt.[31] In so doing, East German authorities confessed their sensitivity to the propaganda uses of rock. (See Chapter 2 for more details.) Polish presidential candidate Tadeusz Mazowiecki showed the same sensitivity when he promised that, if elected president, he would bring the Rolling Stones to play in Warsaw.[32]

The 1980s were indeed a classic age for rock music in the USSR and Eastern Europe, and much of that has to do with the courage of some rock musicians to defy the authorities, to flout taboos, and to sing "dangerous" songs. But, ironically, the near-complete triumph over communism has taken the wind out of the sails of the region's politically engaged protest groups. Rock rebels who had drawn energy from the fight against communism and who had seemed capable of fighting forever seemed to have difficulty adjusting to victory. In Poland, some first-rate rock musicians gravitated to the Marriott Hotel to play lighter fare; one musician joined the circus. In East Germany, after the fall of Erich Honecker and Egon Krenz, an iconoclastic industrial band, Pankow, which had tackled taboo themes boldly with its hard-driving rhythms, disbanded. Vocalist Andre Herzberg, who had led the group, explained: "We are no longer relevant. I'm not sure what I'm going to do now. I'll take some time off. Maybe I'll go into acting."[33]

CONCLUSION

The politicization of rock music is not unique to the communist world. In the United States, for example, the 1980s have seen the lead singer of Twisted Sister hauled before a congressional committee to defend the group's lyrics and attire, controversies over Madonna's attire, and passage of a bill by the Pennsylvania House of Representatives requiring a "parental warning" label to be affixed to recordings that American cultural commissars judge to be too "dangerous" for young minds. In 1987 came the publication of the provocative *Closing of the American Mind*, in which author Alan Bloom argued that rock music was sapping young people's energy, drawing them away from high culture, and generally ruining their imaginative capacities. Among other things, Bloom called rock music "junk food for the soul" and objected that "rock music provides premature ecstasy and, in this respect, is like the drugs with which it is allied."[34] The differences—if any—between Bloom's arguments against rock music and those of Czechoslovak communist writer Jan Kryzl are not significant. Nor are East European rock stars the only musicians to stand trial for their art. In October 1990, a Florida court in Fort Lauderdale heard arguments on the arraignment of the rap group 2 Live Crew for obscenity.[35] The gap between accusations of "political obscenity" and charges of sexual obscenity is not as great as it might seem at first. The principle at stake is the same in both instances, even if the costs and benefits are dramatically different. Obviously, there are people in all societies who react with fear to the presentation of alternative values and ideas and react by trying to suppress the "deviants." But once a society grants that *some* forms of censorship are legitimate, then it must face the consequences of the results that will be created by persons who have a taste for censorship.

Nor is rock music without its supportive uses in the West. In October 1990, MTV aired a new video showing Madonna draped in an American flag, belting out the patriotic refrain,

Abe Lincoln, Jefferson Tom,
They didn't need the atomic bomb.
We need beauty, we need art,
We need government with a heart.
Don't give up your freedom of speech,
Power to the people is in our reach.[36]

Or—on the more visceral side—rock music played a role in persuading Panama City's Vatican Embassy to expel General Manuel Noriega from its compound and allow him to be taken into custody: When diplomacy failed, Americans simply turned up the volume and blasted the Vatican emissaries with loud rock music until they could bear it no longer.

The themes taken up in this book are thus not strangely unique developments relating to only a short period in the now defunct communist systems of the USSR and Eastern Europe. On the contrary, they are specific instances of a much broader, even universal phenomenon. Insofar as rock music is entertaining and compelling, it can be useful for the promotion of ideas. The control, manipulation, regulation, and censorship of music inevitably tempt the would-be cultural commissars of perhaps any society. This book stands as a warning to those who feel that freedom and toleration are too costly and as a tribute to all those who have had the courage to sing what they have felt. I quote again from the lyrics of the Soviet rock group Televizor:

Get out of control!
And sing what you want,
And not just what is allowed.
We have a right to yell!

NOTES

1. *Corriere della Sera* (Milan), 22 July 1990, p. 8.

2. See Anna Szemere, "Pop Music in Hungary," in *Communications Research* 12, no. 3 (July 1985), pp. 402–403; and Furio Radin, "O nekim stilovima života zagrebačke srednjo-školske omladine," in *Mlada generacija danas: Društveni položaj, uloga i perspektive mlade generacije Jugoslavije* (Belgrade: Mladost, 1982), p. 311. Also William S. Fox and James D. Williams, "Political Orientation and Music Preferences Among College Students," in *Public Opinion Quarterly* 38, no. 3 (Autumn 1974), pp. 362–371.

3. Song "Standing Youth," by Coitus Punk Group, quoted in Zsolt Krokovay, "Politics and Punk," in *Index on Censorship* 14, no. 2 (April 1985), p. 20.

4. Song "Južna Afrika 85 (Ja ću da pevam)," on Fish Soup, *Osmi nervni slom*, RTB PGP 2320355 (1985).

5. Quoted in Artemy Troitsky, *Back in the USSR: The True History of Rock in Russia* (Boston: Faber and Faber, 1987), p. 127.

6. For an elaboration, see Sabrina P. Ramet, *Social Currents in Eastern Europe: The Sources and Meaning of the Great Transformation* (Durham, N.C.: Duke University Press, 1991), chapter 1.

7. Local audiences did not always appreciate hearing rock sung in their native language because they considered their language inappropriate for rock. Troitsky recalls how the Leningrad group Nomads was often booed off the stage when its members tried to sing in Russian. Troitsky, *Back in the USSR,* p. 35.

8. Bernice Martin, "The Sacralization of Disorder: Symbolism in Rock Music," in *Sociological Analysis* 40, no. 2 (Summer 1979), p. 87.

9. Ibid., p. 102.

10. Quoted in the *Sun* (Baltimore), 24 March 1987, p. 9A.

11. Quoted in ibid.

12. James S. Leming, "Rock Music and the Socialization of Moral Values in Early Adolescence," in *Youth and Society* 18, no. 4 (June 1987), p. 375.

13. Song "Physical," on Olivia Newton-John, *Greatest Hits, Volume 2,* MCA RE-CORDS 5347 (1982).

14. Goran Bregović, leader of the Sarajevo rock group White Button, in interview with the author, Sarajevo, 14 September 1989.

15. Quoted in Troitsky, *Back in the USSR,* p. 42.

16. Song "Working Class Hero," on John Lennon, *Plastic Ono Band,* APPLE SW3372 (1970).

17. Timothy W. Ryback, *Rock Around the Bloc: A History of Rock Music in Eastern Europe and the Soviet Union* (New York: Oxford University Press, 1990), p. 193.

18. Ibid., pp. 170–171.

19. *Index on Censorship* 12, no. 2 (February 1983), p. 7.

20. Quoted in Ryback, *Rock Around the Bloc,* p. 200.

21. See *Sztandar Mlodych,* 9 April 1987, p. 3, trans. in Joint Publications Research Service (JPRS), *East Europe Report,* no. EER-87-122 (7 August 1987), pp. 33–35; and *Gósc Niedzielny,* 10 May 1987, pp. 1, 5, trans. in JPRS, *East Europe Report,* no. EER-87-120 (4 August 1987), pp. 119–121. Also *Wall Street Journal,* 23 July 1987, p. 1.

22. Song "Ketten werden knapper," on Klaus Renft Combo, *Klaus Renft Combo,* AMIGA 855326 (1973).

23. Romanian Situation Report, *Radio Free Europe Research,* 31 October 1975, p. 7.

24. Quoted in Ryback, *Rock Around the Bloc,* pp. 127–128.

25. "The Nature of Official Documents Concerning Control of Vocal/Instrumental Groups and Discotheques," in *Survey* 29, no. 2 (Summer 1985), pp. 172–177.

26. *MacLean's,* 14 September 1987, p. 17.

27. *Zeri i Rinise* (Tirana), 30 August 1989, pp. 1–2, trans. in Foreign Broadcast Information Service (FBIS), *Daily Report* (Eastern Europe), 7 September 1989, p. 2.

28. *New York Times,* 5 November 1990, p. A4; see also *Los Angeles Times,* 10 July 1990, p. H6.

29. Song "O.K. Gorbachev," by Eva, quoted in *Bloc* (April–May 1990), p. 5.

30. For one example, see *Neues Deutschland,* 12 June 1987, p. 3.

31. See reports in *Frankfurter Allgemeine,* 20 June 1988, p. 4; *Berliner Zeitung,* 20 June 1988, pp. 1–2; *Rheinische Post,* 21 June 1988, p. 8; *Neue Zeit* (Berlin), 21 June 1988, p. 8; and *Die Welt* (Bonn), 21 June 1988, p. 20.

32. *New York Times,* 24 November 1990, p. 3.

33. Quoted in the *Christian Science Monitor,* 31 May 1990, p. 10.

34. Quoted in the *New York Times,* 18 October 1987, p. 30.

35. *New York Times,* 17 October 1990, pp. A1, A11.

36. Quoted in the *New York Times,* 20 October 1990, p. 7.

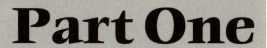

Part One

Eastern Europe

OLAF LEITNER **2**

Rock Music in the GDR:
An Epitaph

Life is like a lotto
or so I heard from Otto,
Though a functionary
crosses things out.
—**Renft Combo**
(Leipzig, 1975)

H ISTORICAL DEVELOPMENTS in the German Democratic Republic
(GDR) have decreed that this chapter shall serve both as a retrospective review and a swan song: The GDR is the only communist country that has had to pay for its successful and bloodless revolution, its
democratization, with its existence. East German rock has now fused
with the broader German cultural scene and, as a separate entity, has
passed into history.

For musicians in the GDR, rock was an art form that came from outside
and that had arisen under entirely different, even foreign, conditions,
namely, conditions of capitalism. Rock conveyed a feeling for life that
musicians in the "tutelary state,"[1] the GDR, took up and wanted to realize
for their public. One felt an emotional bond to that which pushed its way
into the GDR starting at the end of the 1950s. One discovered an identity
for one's own existence in the emotional state of the rest of the world. This
bound together the youth of the GDR and raised them out of their isolation.

Rock not only conveys capitalist ways of life. It also reflects the perceptions and problems of industrial mass society along with aspects that
were also found in socialism, even if they were not officially admitted—
isolation, brutality, drug abuse, homelessness, environmental catastro-

17

phes, hostility toward foreigners. These became themes that East German rock musicians transformed aesthetically, in their own way. But this development was constricted by state injunctions: The texts had to be in German, the music had to derive overwhelmingly from domestic composers. In public performances, concerts, radio and television broadcasts as well as in discotheques, the formula 60:40 was maintained, under which 60 percent of the music played had to come from socialist countries. Furthermore, DJs were instructed to "counter" the music of the "class enemy" with domestic songs that strictly followed the dictates of socialist realism.

But this precept was insufficient to generate an unmistakable GDR rock style, which in fact never emerged. Even though the cultural commissars of the GDR claimed to have pinpointed the nature of melodiousness (*Liedhaftigkeit*), this represented only one element of East German rock, which was also often found outside the GDR. This problem, totally understandable in light of the internationalism of popular music, was resolved by maintaining that the "socialist" aspect of music from GDR groups consisted in its conditions of production. Production *was* much more influenced by the limitations imposed by the state than by the creativity of the performers: through strict control, censorship, a state monopoly on the means of production, the existence of only one record company (VEB Deutsche Schallplatten, with the label Amiga), and, furthermore, an almost exclusively state-administered system of recording studios.

The authorities curbed and curtailed rock groups on every side, attempting to impose a set of socialist cultural norms, but the administration of cultural policy was uneven and uncertain. There was, in addition, a rather specific burden imposed on East German bands: Western bands were not allowed to give concerts in the GDR. Local GDR bands therefore felt the need to present the styles of specific Western bands to the GDR rock public. Thus, the Puhdys imitated the singing style of Uriah Heep, Elektra of Dresden ranked as the would-be Jethro Tull, the Modern Soul Band had many songs from Chicago or Blood, Sweat and Tears in its repertoire. A Beatles medley was considered a requisite in the concerts of every ambitious band.

Even though it was necessary to carry a breath of internationalism to the cities and towns of the GDR, this practice quickly yielded the criticism that GDR bands were mere imitators offering secondhand music. An additional drawback was the technological inferiority of the East German bands, which complicated their efforts to replicate and mimic the styles of Western bands. It is to their credit that they managed to produce excellent songs despite all these limitations and in the face of narrow-minded

and petty attacks by the censors and unnerving discussions with incom-
petent cultural functionaries.

Rock music was united with the other arts in the GDR through the self-
assigned task of compensating for the absence of critical media and for
the unrefined reporting in the daily press. The rock bands strove, at one
level, to condense the realities of "real existing socialism" (as the ruling
Socialist Unity Party, or SED, called its model) into an art form. However,
rock musicians stood out from other arts through their direct involvement in the process of bringing down the communist system in their
country.

ROCK AND THE REVOLUTION

It was a cool and sunny day that 17 May 1990. In the stuffy office of the
old proletarian cafe Berliner Prater, on the Prenzlauer Berg, a few dozen
musicians and journalists had come together. There they received copies of the first edition of *Neue Musik Information*, with the ink not quite
dry yet, from its editor, Jürgen Balitzki. The *NMI*, an ironic imitation of
the British trade journal *New Musical Express*, now came into competition with the solicitous music magazine *Melodie und Rhythmus*, which
had monopolistically reported on national and, on a limited basis, international rock music for decades, always upholding the aesthetic
values of the SED line.

And then there was a historic moment in GDR rock. Musicians Toni
Krahl and Fritz Puppel, singer and guitarist of City, one of the most important GDR bands, set up their own recording label, KPM—which
showed how much the scene had already changed. The Berlin rock
group Herbst in Peking (Autumn in Peking) was the first to release on
the KPM label. KPM of course had to confront the risks of the free market economy and the complicated strategies of advertising, marketing,
distribution, and sales. As long as musicians had recorded with Amiga,
the only question was whether one would be allowed to produce a halfway acceptable record on the short leash held by the cultural authorities. But given the small supply of records in the GDR, sales took off on
their own.

Nine months earlier, on 18 September 1989, the West Berlin *Tages-
zeitung* published a "Resolution of Rock Artists" that referred back to an
initiative of the rock section of the Committee for Entertainment Arts,
an organization representing the interests of professional artists and
musicians. The resolution was signed by the best-known artists of the
GDR and had been presented as a response to the wave of emigration

(mostly of young GDR citizens) to the West via Hungary. In the resolution, the musicians stated,

> We ... are concerned about the momentary situation in our country, about the massive exodus of many of our peers, about the breakdown in the meaning of this social alternative, and about the unbearable arrogance of the party and state leadership, which makes light of present contradictions and holds fast to a rigid course. ... This country badly needs individual action since the old structures are incapable of instigating necessary changes. We want to live in this country and it makes us sick to have to idly watch while attempts at democratization, attempts at social analysis, are criminalized and therefore ignored. We demand a public dialogue with the authorities. We demand changes in the present intolerable conditions.[2]

The resolution was read to the public before rock concerts or handed out as fliers (in small editions, as photocopiers were under strict state control). The leadership reacted in the usual manner: Many signatories were forbidden to perform, the newspapers were prohibited from publishing the manifesto (which happened only months later, after musicians had protested against the silence). And in internal circles of conversation, one tried to blackmail the signatories. In response to this, city leader Toni Krahl stated,

> They called me to the magistrate and wanted me to take back my signature. I asked, And what if I do not do it? Then it was indicated that they would have the opportunity to bring me down. I knew what they meant. My wife had just taken off to the West, which gave me a bad hand. Furthermore, they could get to my bank account. I told them, Take what you need, none of this interests me anymore![3]

Krahl, one of the most important personalities of GDR rock, had had his share of painful experiences in his dealings with the leadership earlier. In late summer 1968, he had naively but courageously handed out "small clumsily assembled fliers,"[4] on which he had tried to protest against the Warsaw Pact invasion of Czechoslovakia. He had been arrested and sentenced to three years of imprisonment; the sentence was later suspended. His father, a journalist by profession and a Jew, an old communist, and an antifascist, was made to suffer for his son's transgressions and "was not allowed to write another line. This broke him emotionally."[5] Ironically, the man responsible for the sentence became the minister of justice after the collapse of SED rule, in the first (and last) freely elected government in the GDR.

If Toni Krahl is particularly emphasized here, it is because he took an exemplary stand and showed how one might exploit the limited possibilities in state-censored rock to search for and spread truth via the medium of rock texts and music. This required cunning, courage, and intelligence.

A RETROSPECTIVE GLANCE

In earlier years, rock music was an official and therefore subsidized part of approved culture, located within the subcategory of "entertainment art." This subcategory was contrasted with "serious arts" (in which opera, for example, was to be found). East Germany's communist authorities classified everything.

Rock music, with all its various manifestations such as stage presentation, types of style and playing, attire and makeup, and the aesthetics of the instruments themselves, made it to the GDR via Western media at the beginning of the rock 'n' roll age and was imitated with enthusiasm. At first GDR rockers had only modest instruments at their disposal, but later they obtained better equipment from the West, which arrived in the GDR by complicated but reliable paths. In contrast to the situation of the other countries of the bloc, there was no language barrier between the Western media and their Eastern recipients—German on both sides. West German radio and television broadcasts were received without any problem by the East German public.[6]

In reference to the idols of the 1960s, such as the Rolling Stones and the Beatles, the group City sang

On the Dönhoffplatz, the clique met
with Jumping Jack and Lucy Sky.[7]

And the Blues musician Hansi Biebl remembered, in a song, how he once went home from school exhausted and depressed:

Suddenly a radio droned somewhere
And they played the rock 'n' roll music
of Chuck Berry.
Suddenly I was on my feet
and all at once there was something happening with me
I felt so big
My knees shook
My face started to glow
And the guy sang
"If you wanna dance with me."[8]

This seemingly superficial, rather anecdotal passage was recognized in its depth by a knowledgeable rock audience. A feeling for life that one had to borrow from Western culture could help one escape from the sadness of the daily grind of "real existing socialism."

After long procrastination and many individual battles, the cultural administrators had to accept rock music as a part of popular and youth culture. I will document this. Even if the new music of young people was considered at first to be a subversive agent with which the "class enemy"—the "imperialist warmongers of the North Atlantic Treaty Organization (NATO)"—wanted to destroy the minds and sensitivities of young people, it soon advanced to a courtly state art. Defiantly, the representative minister of culture, Werner Rackwitz, justified the change in attitude: "We will not give up jazz, beat, and folk music just because the imperialist mass culture has misused them as a manipulation of aesthetic judgment in the interest of maximizing profits."[9]

The basis for the change in attitude was pragmatic: On the one hand, the banishment of rock music would not be possible against the will of young people. On the other hand, after its antirock campaigns of the 1960s, the GDR wanted to appear to the international public as open to the world and tolerant. Hence in July and August 1973 East Berlin played host to the Tenth World Festival of Youth, with 25,646 guests from 140 countries. It did not seem opportune then, for example, to publicly cut off the hair of long-haired musicians, as the cruel custom had been. Now they needed rock bands to show off.

All musicians who performed publicly had to be in possession of a performance license, obtained when the musicians and their groups had successfully performed for a special state committee of cultural functionaries and artists. Their classification level determined the fee to be paid. Most professional musicians had formal musical training. New bands had the chance to introduce themselves at a variety of local and national competitions and workshops and were provided with forums in which to obtain advice from fellow musicians. The radio, acting as talent scout and as the largest producer of rock music, invited promising young bands to rehearsal recordings in the studio.

Many bands and artists were decorated with the GDR National Prize, a cash prize that also raised the recipient's performance fee and lifted travel restrictions. The idea, however, that rock musicians on capitalist terrain would ever adorn their T-shirts with medals from the socialist state seems absurd—rock musicians internationally consider their music to be an antiauthoritarian art form. But to the extent that these groups made "pacts" of a sort with the state, young people responded with scorn and derision.

State support, mostly via the culture fund of the Free German Youth organization (Freie Deutsche Jugend, or FDJ), flowed freely, unlike in the West, where the business of rock is left to private initiative. The price for acceptance was continuous control by the commissars of culture. They regulated everything from fees to record contracts, from concert repertoires to professional identification cards, from tour plans to passports. Passports were the highest of all ordinations for which a rock musician could hope, namely, the possibility of being allowed to travel in the West. But before the first trip to the West, a guest concert had to be completed in a fellow socialist country as a form of "service."

In the founding years of East German rock, the young combos and beat bands were persistently encouraged to sing in the German language. Lyricists and writers were assigned to them who were supposed to hammer out the verses for them. This offered a certain guarantee that cultural political dogma would be realized here as well. The head ideologist Kurt Hager was responsible for the implementation of the principles of socialist realism. As a member of the Politburo of the SED, he sat directly in the center of power. The goal of GDR cultural policies was supposed to be a "socialist-realist art, which enriches the intellectual world of the workers" through national solidarity and partiality, through realism and socialist content.[10] This was little more than a foundation of vacuous concepts, but it was useful all the same for interpreting daily politics and justifying policy decisions. In Hager's view, "the humanity of socialist culture" saw itself "opposing a rotten, anti-humanitarian culture of imperialism. ... Our cultural politics therefore have the additional task of supporting the political and ideological offensive of socialism with all cultural means."[11] The ideologue with a verifiable antifascist past fell into the language of his former enemy here! And this guiding principle could as well be traced to other authors. Hager also said, "Dance music [i.e., rock music] should aid even more effectively in encouraging the development of good taste and clean relationships between young people."[12]

Hager's text originates mainly from the specifically East German "song movement," which concentrated principally on politically motivated songs and ballads. In the October Club, upwardly mobile figures in the rock scene gathered. These personalities included Gisela Steineckert, who was later president of the Committee for Entertainment Art; Leipzig doctor Kurt Demmler, certainly the most productive and talented lyricist of various bands in the 1970s and 1980s; and Hartmut König, the author of the song "Tell Me Where You Stand," a signatory hymn of the GDR song movement. In 1970, König was allowed to sing songs by Greek composer Mikis Theodrakis in New York on the occasion of a meeting of the World Youth Organization of the United Nations (UN). He visited a performance of the musical "Hair" and found "a piece of dangerous forgetfulness and passivity ... [as well as] anarchy on stage."[13]

Regarding ideology, König always swayed in the wind. Later he became head of culture of the FDJ, and in the last SED government under
Egon Krenz he became representative of the minister of culture in the
subject area "entertainment art." He was an ambitious functionary who
was rather tough on his underlings, and he showed dogmatic, reaction-
ary tendencies. But under a pseudonym he wrote texts for several rock
groups in the GDR.

ROCK TEXTS

Only in recent years did continually more bands insist on writing their
own rock texts. Poetry and weak metaphor had competition through
this development because of the musicians' preference for increased
authenticity and realism (as in the case of the groups Pankow, City, and
Rockhaus). In the ideal case, a combination of high poetry and rough idiom was achieved, for example by the top group Silly and its text writers,
Werner Karma and Gerhard Gundermann. These professionals were ir-
replaceable for Silly.

Thus, language moved more and more from the everyday and was
taken from the body of speech of the "scene" and often transposed un-
worked and unbeautified into song verse. If one allows the products of
mass culture to be a valid indicator of atmosphere and the national state
of existence, pop lyrics provide a markedly clear view into the state of
emotion of GDR young people. Not infrequently, changes in the political
landscape were announced in pop songs:

> If I think of Germany, poems come to me
> Big names sound to me from dead stone
> And silence is in me as never known before
> I was born here, this is my country.
>
> . . . .
>
> If I think of Germany and you, my child,
> of all who were born in our times,
> If I think of the people over there and here
> Of those who overpower fear, together with us,
> I don't want to forget, I don't want to forget,
> I don't want to forget what once was.[14]

The use of the word "Germany" ("Deutschland") here was a small
sensation, taboo in the old GDR and generally allowed in only two
versions—in the phrase "Soviet troops in Germany" and in the name of
the SED's daily newspaper, *Neues Deutschland*. Elsewhere in the text,

the Puhdys sing, "If I think of Germany in the night, my sleep is taken from me"—a line that casts a retrospective glance toward poet Heinrich Heine (1779–1865).[15] For all that, the song was not prohibited, although its use in the media was restricted. The song was, for example, not permitted to be considered for the national hit parade. Even so, the demand to think about similarities between the two Germanys ("over there and here") had been raised—an initiative that the SED, with its need for *Abgrenzung* (demarcation), wanted to suppress.

In general, one can recognize a turn from art song to everyday song, from high expectations to arbitrariness in GDR popular music—a development that was strengthened many times over in the diverse media of the now capitalist-oriented GDR. Many taboo themes were treated in encoded form in the latter years of the GDR, hidden between the lines or veiled in metaphor. GDR citizens developed a fine sense for understated tone and hidden allusion. They guessed quickly what was not said. Getting around the lack of freedom of the press stimulated GDR rock to great poetic accomplishment, to a sculpted, nuance-filled language culture. By the closing months of the GDR's existence, one could sing whatever one wished, whether critical or supportive.

The rock songs were not political in the sense of a political party, as the SED certainly knew. Still, a song written in reference to an acute situation, communicating an opinion conforming to that of the government, was considered to be proof of social involvement and often meant, at the beginning of the 1980s, an invitation to the Rock for Peace Festival in the Palace of the Republic in East Berlin. This scheme was an attempt to get rock musicians involved in the concrete political demands of the SED, namely, opposing the stationing of U.S. Pershing II missiles in Europe or attacking U.S. policies in Latin America. During the festival, the concerts were interspersed with propaganda films that compared the "war-making" Americans and their NATO allies with the "peaceful Soviet people" and their East European partners, especially the GDR. A song title by the group Berluc in which the U.S. president was declared insane climbed high in the ratings in the GDR in 1983; its success was, however, probably more a result of its accessible rhythm and danceability rather than its lyrics:

Hey, Mr. President, of America!
Hey, Mr. President, he is a crazy star!
I am crazy, yet this much I still know
I won't get rid of this earth here
and if the earth is a big bomb hole
we will all fly to our deaths in its lap.
Hey! Mr. President of America!

Hey, Mr. President, he is a crazy star!
I am crazy but never ever so crazy
that I would gladly sit on a powder keg
I am crazy but never ever so crazy
that I would let myself be killed so easily
No bomb, no radioactivity,
No bomb, never Euroshima!
No bomb—but peace!
Hey, Mr. President of America!
Hey, Mr. President, he is a crazy star!
I am crazy and many also say
one like that has only music in his head
I have music in my head, I have music in my stomach,
and everything would be lost in the next war.
No bomb.[16]

Kurt Demmler, the lyricist responsible for "No Bomb," was one of the most important and lingually best-trained rock writers in the GDR. The song text falls far below the usual niveau achieved by its author. Shortly after the song's performance, it should be noted, the singer fled to the West, the sphere of influence of the very president reviled in the song.

The popular rock band Karussell (from Leipzig) also sang a Demmler text, a commentary on "imperialist politics":

An island lay dreamy in the south
yet not only dreamy, loved the palms,
loved the people, loved freedom,
Oh howdy, Grenada, the Ami [American] Armada has to go home!
When a people finally knows what it wants,
One can never get them down again![17]

Who knows?—maybe the last two lines were interpreted by GDR rock fans in the light of their own country. An early prophecy of what lay ahead?

ROCK AND THE GDR MEDIA

VEB Deutsche Schallplatten held the monopoly on the release of national and international popular music, issuing pop records on its Amiga label. Private and independent recordings were not allowed. Amiga presented a selection of the available GDR rock and also released, on license and in small editions, records by Western pop stars such as Michael Jackson, Santana, Madonna, Peter Gabriel, ZZ Top, Police, Van

Halen, Willie Nelson, and others. These concession records were especially popular with consumers and obtainable only through "connections." An LP cost M 16.10 (a 10 pfennig culture tax included in the price),
a high price in relationship to an apprentice's monthly salary of M 100–
200. A poll taken in the late 1970s found that 84 percent of young people
listened to rock music as their main leisure activity (between two and
four hours per day).[18] Thus, they invest a lot of energy into screening
and collecting primary and secondary information for their hobby. The
GDR media reacted to this and offered pop music on television programs such as "Hautnah," "Klik," "Logo," "Dramms," and "Elf 99"
(named after the zip code of the television station). Programs such as
"Bong" and "Stop! Rock" introduced national hit and rock parades.
Beginning in March 1986, there was also a youth channel on the radio,
Jugendradio DR 64, which broadcast twenty hours daily beginning in
winter 1987–1988. On special programs, international hits were offered
for taping. Through this venue, disc jockeys, with their mobile recording
equipment, got their hands on music that was otherwise not available.

East German youth wanted to dance. The 10,000 youth clubs of the
GDR drew some 120 million visitors annually. But the dance crowd
showed a disdain for domestic rock, preferring the music of the West.
The established rock musicians were suspected of being too close to
the powerful. Otherwise—so people said—they could scarcely have
achieved the prestige, media presence, and outright wealth they enjoyed, let alone be granted a passport.

As the example of City shows, this suspicion was not always justified.
Although the SED's practice of handing out privileges was a subtle
means of sowing conflict between artists and the public, the City musicians counter that "we often had to resort to blackmail to obtain privileges for ourselves."[19] On the basis of their great popularity, they could
threaten to turn to the Western public or even to conspicuously break
up—a risky procedure that required nerve and resoluteness.

The national and international pop scene was covered in music magazines such as *Unterhaltungskunst* and *Melodie und Rhythmus,* in the
youth magazine *Neues Leben,* in the radio and television magazine *FF
dabei,* as well as in the daily newspapers. The reviews of concerts and records were and are characterized by extensive knowledge and avoid the
brash arrogance with which West German critics like to cover up their
ineptitude with their own language.

And in terms of GDR rock music and cinema, the state film company
DEFA did succeed in finishing one documentary film about the GDR
rock scene, *Flüstern und schreien, Ein Rockreport* (Whispering and
screaming, A rock report), in 1988, under director Bernd Schumann. The
new aspect of this was the partially unedited presentation of rock fans,

punks, and skinheads who roamed train stations and open-air concerts. The long-present measures of censorship used by the SED for filming and editing were well known. This is not the place to list all the subtle techniques of film by which certain attitudes of the cinema-going public were supposed to be manipulated (to sow discontent with established bands with which the SED was having trouble, whitewashing the function of the police, and so on). Although the film was ultimately a product of the censor, it still was not aired on television before the revolution. The reason: At one point in the film, it became apparent that rock bands had been banned in the GDR from time to time since the 1960s. Everyone knew that anyway.

POLITICS AND CRISIS

If one takes the dance hall behavior of GDR youth as an indicator and follows music publications, East German rock had been stuck in a crisis since the mid-1980s. Record sales had decreased, and concerts were only marginally attended, except for gigs by top groups such as City, Silly, or Pankow. This situation could have resulted from the aging of many bands or the unattractive offerings of the new combos. At the Committee for Entertainment Art, the following questions were raised:

> What does the relationship between national identity and the search for international standards in artistic expression look like? Where do the borders between national identity and provinciality lie? At the moment, only a few salient leaders are able to bring in new faces and new ideas which will be accepted by the public, which is, in the meantime, markedly younger [than the musicians].[20]

The authorities criticized euphoria over Western rock entertainers. But later, when public pressure forced them to set aside their ideological prejudices, the authorities lurched in the opposite direction, showering even second-rate performances by Western artists with praise. After all, whatever was arranged by the state could not be bad! The experiences of GDR artists in the press, radio, and television was not even remotely comparable. "How productive and self assured it could appear," the *Presse-Telegram* mused, "if our own rock and pop music would be allowed as much space in the daily news as our foreign guests receive today. Much too often, our presence is limited to high points, occasionally to reports that we and our products exist."[21]

In comparison to Western rock music, with all of its technical know-how and spectacular forms of appearance, the GDR had little to offer. What Western television brought into the living rooms from Suhl to Rostok was favored by young people without fail.

Rock "made in the GDR" was always something political in the eyes of the state party as well as in the eyes of critical fans. The leadership demanded conformity, the fans opposition. The state had assigned rock the task "of formulating attitudes in which the social reality of everyday life in the GDR was reflected, encouraging involvement," as phrased in a handbook of popular music.[22] This music was said to possess "a social value that pushes it into the center of intellectual-cultural and ideological conflict, and in this way, opens up a new social dimension of reality."[23] The attempt to fully take advantage of these dimensions led to notable conflict during which groups and artists were often barred from performing. Many top stars left their country forever. Nonetheless, those responsible for culture occasionally admitted to having made mistakes and having wrongly assessed certain manifestations of pop culture. A characteristic example is the Beatles, who in the beginning were damned in the GDR—as elsewhere!—but who later were essentially canonized by GDR rock fans. Even so, the first licensed LP of the Beatles was released in 1965.[24] The opportunism of the SED-led cultural politics soon showed itself. Although officials made the lives of artists difficult through partially absurd individual measures (in the beginning, new musicians had to let their long sideburns be covered up with make-up), and even though they had the upper hand in daily business, in the long run they had to capitulate permanently to developments.

None of the other arts fought such spectacular battles with the state leadership as did rock music. In the following section, I provide details to document this.

THE STONES AND THE PLENARY SESSION

Even before the revolution of 1989, famous rock stars such as Bob Dylan, Bruce Springsteen, and Joe Cocker had performed in the GDR. In late summer 1990, the Rolling Stones were given the green light to come to the GDR, on public demand.

Ironically, the Stones, without realizing it, had exerted influence on GDR cultural politics a quarter of a century earlier. On 15 September 1965, their now legendary Waldbühnen Konzert (Forest Stage Concert) led to chaotic brawls and the destruction of the lovely open-air stage by rioters. The SED was frightened by what it believed to be a highly aggressive beat wave flowing over from the West. At the 11th Plenary Session of the Central Committee in December 1965, the SED began to place constraints on the disliked intellectuals of the country, the film directors, the songwriters, the poets, and also the rock musicians. Erich Honecker, a member of the SED Politburo, discovered at that time "that the opposition was using this music to ... stir up excess in the youth."[25]

The persecution of rock musicians began with this meeting. Harassment of rockers was stepped up, most pointedly in Leipzig, where the *Leipziger Volkszeitung* derided them as "degenerate, shaggy, [with] filthy manes [and] rumpled pants. They stink from 10 meters against the wind."[26] The music press found that "the most worthless Big Beat groups [were] spreading epidemically."[27] When beat groups came together in parks or marketplaces and drew crowds, the crowds were broken up by police with dogs and water cannon.[28]

Together with writers Stefan Heym and Christa Wolf, a young poet singer was reprimanded at the plenary session because of his "bombardment of complaints hidden in verse, 'spiced' with unflattering language and directed toward the party."[29] He fell from grace. The singer in question, Wolf Biermann, had been for many years the most important German songwriter; indeed, he may be said to have invented the tradition in Germany. Biermann, who schooled himself after Heinrich Heine and Bertold Brecht and who came from a communist working-class family, was forbidden to perform. His numerous home-recorded albums could be released only by CBS in the West. In 1977, he was expatriated from the GDR during his first appearance in the West. The withdrawal of his citizenship divided intellectuals and artists in the GDR. Many were forced by the SED to praise the measures taken against Biermann and to prove it with their signatures, which were then published in the news organ *Neues Deutschland.* Among the signatories was the song group Jahrgang '49, from which several members fled westward a few years later, and Dr. Rene Büttner, who would later become chief of the state label, Amiga. Those who refused to sign were publicly reprimanded and punished with sanctions.

Among those belonging to Biermann's circle of friends was dissident Robert Havemann as well as many musicians. Havemann had been in prison with Erich Honecker during the Nazi era. Among the musicians close to Biermann were the former members of the now defunct Renft Combo (a Leipzig group), who, inspired by Biermann, had been so daring in their song texts that their combo had been ordered to disband in 1975. The reason given was that "the working class [would be] hurt and the state and protection agencies would be brought into disrepute."[30] And the responsible cultural official made an immediate correction: The band was not "forbidden," he explained, "I told you that you do not exist for us anymore on the basis of these facts!"[31] In its song "Questions of Faith," the Renft Combo sang,

You, what does he believe in,
he who goes to the flag,
Swears to the glory of the flag,
Stands tall there?

You, what does he believe in,
He who does not take aim,
Who carries a sparrow
As a flag before him?
You, what does he believe in,
He who goes to the barge?
And turns his backside
Directly to the flag?[32]

The phrase "going to the flag," which refers to absolving one's military service, was contrasted here with the alternative offered in the GDR, namely, service with the construction brigades. The total objector could count on prison, however. Songs like this breached a basic taboo of the SED: the incontestability of the National People's Army (NVA) and all its rituals.

The Renft Combo was forced to break up, and most of its members were able to emigrate to West Berlin, though some had to spend six months in prison first. Only in 1990, after the revolution of 1989, were records of the band released in the GDR, and the remainder of Renft toured through its old homeland on a successful "revival" concert. Thomas "Monster" Schoppe, a Renft singer, remembers in retrospect, "It really was a damned nice time. It bugs me though that none of these 'gentlemen' who were in office and honor at that time have apologized to Renft."[33]

In the 1960s, Wolf Biermann lived with the actress Eva-Maria Hagen. As an actress, she brought a breeze of Marilyn Monroe into the DEFA films in the GDR of that time. And she had a daughter, Nina Hagen, who grew up with Biermann and became a hit singer a decade later. After following Biermann to the West with her mother, Nina Hagen evolved into a very original and extroverted rock singer who has left her mark in England, France, Japan, and even in the United States. The entertainment art scene in the old GDR was thus often a family business.

Let's stay in the year 1975 and go to East Berlin. The blues musician Günter Holwas (Holly Blues Band) refused the so-called honor service in the NVA on ethical-moral grounds and became a construction soldier. Through his close links with the church, he met the deacon of a home for disabled children who were being taken care of in the poorest of conditions. The GDR, a social state, provided the children with only M 1.36 per day for housing, food, and clothing. Holwas suggested to his pastor to hold blues services in the church and to make the profits available to the deaconate. After some initial difficulties, the first blues service took place in the East Berlin Samaritan Church on 3 June 1979. This blues music was enriched with excerpts from the Bible.

The number of visitors at this type of religious service rose from 450 in the beginning to 5,000 in 1980. The church, which was the only space not controllable by the state, had made itself into a podium for oppressed social groups on the periphery and for dissidents. Here critical texts could be read aloud or sung. Whoever left the church building, however, ran into the arms of the authorities, specifically the state security service. Thus Günter Holwas reported:

> In 1981 I was summoned to the Central House for Cultural Activity. ... There I was made to understand in a comradely way that I might wish to discontinue with the blues services, as it would not be of benefit for my further development. I had, for instance, always greeted the state security at each blues service. I said, have a nice evening gentlemen, those of you who have difficulties in remembering all that is said here. I informed the people that on every roof across from the exit and in every Barka [GDR small bus] was a member of the Stasi who had filmed everyone who came out of the church. I said, Please smile, in order to make a good impression. ... I received a summons for a clarification of a matter in the investigation prison. ... Yes, they said, we have here two witness statements against you because of illegal possession of a weapon. You have a pistol and have shot with it. But I was reassured by people from the church and two attorneys, I have to call them as soon as I get out [of prison] again.[34]

The pacifist is reduced to a hero of the revolver, a typical contribution from the Stasi's supply of tricks.

Günter Holwas is one of the many anonymous heroes in the history of sorrows in East German rock. He went to the West soon thereafter to emigrate to the land of his dreams—Canada.

The leadership started to increase its pressure on the church and to force it to stop the blues services. But the Samaritan Church, with its active congregation, became the center of the East Berlin opposition at the end of the 1980s, and its pastor, Rainer Eppelmann, was considered to be a symbolic figure of the resistance. After the first democratic elections in the GDR in March 1990, he of all people became minister of defense. "Swords into Plowshares!" had been the slogan of the East German pacifists. Would the plowshare now be hammered back into the shape of a sword?

HONECKER´S LEATHER JACKET

It is not known whether the chancellor of the Federal Republic of Germany, Helmut Kohl, ever had any difficulties with rock music. But for the governmental leader of the socialist GDR, things went quite differently. West German rock musician Udo Lindenberg, long denied an entry visa to perform in the GDR, had succeeded in blasting the division of Germany in terms readily palatable to the GDR's youth in sensitive songs:

> *I would like so much to sing there once . . .*
> *Yet the functionaries are still undecided,*
> *This Western "garbage culture" is nothing for comrades.*
> *When will the gentlemen finally see clearly,*
> *And build the rock 'n' roll arena in Jena?*
> *(Or will the GDR continue in matters of cultural exchange*
> *As the "German Disillusionment Republic"?)* [35]

The cultural administrators of the GDR were made uncertain by Lindenberg. Although he had on one hand taken a stance against the police establishment of the Federal Republic and signed demands against the NATO armament undertakings, which the SED always praised, he was still considered too spontaneous and hence not reliable in propaganda. To invite him for a guest concert in the GDR would have won points for the SED, and at first it adopted a wait-and-see stance. One song, in which Lindenberg described his situation as a Western border-crosser with a day visa who falls in love with a girl in East Berlin, was particularly touching and became popular with teens in the GDR. Fully armed for the "main battle of ideology," as was the common SED term for that area of entertainment art, a youth magazine snidely remarked, "At some point Udo Lindenberg seems to have missed that our focus here is still the border between imperialism and socialism."[36]

Annoyed by the delay tactics of the East Berlin artistic agency, which pulled the strings as organizers for a possible tour, Lindenberg wrote a text to the melody of the ever-popular "Chattanooga Choo-Choo" that rudely jostled the state council and SED leader Erich Honecker:

> *Oh, Erich hey, are you really such a dour imp?*
> *Why don't you let me sing in the workers' and peasants' state? . . .*
> *Honey, I think you are also actually totally loose*
> *I know that deep inside you are also actually a rocker.*
> *You secretly like to put on a leather jacket occasionally too*
> *And lock yourself up in the bathroom and listen to Western radio.*[37]

In an explanation to the press, the singer added apologetically to Honecker, "If I put a leather jacket on you in my song, it is the honorable piece of clothing of the real proletarian, the man on the street. Furthermore, even back then in the Saarland, you wore a leather jacket as a 'Street Fighting Man.' Also, so that you don't take it the wrong way, an 'imp' is a perfectly lovable entity in our terminology."[38]

The officious SED overreacted and was indignant. A top politician's private life had been shown, which broke a strong taboo. Lindenberg became an unperson; the radio locked his songs in the cabinet of evils. Even instrumental versions of the modest song "Chattanooga Choo-Choo" could no longer be played in public. East German young people were delighted, of course, by this duel and loved the singer from West Germany all the more.

Conciliation was celebrated nonetheless. On 25 October 1983, Udo Lindenberg performed in the Palace of the Republic in East Berlin. At the concert For World Peace he was once again welcomed as a propaganda medium, which did not keep him from criticizing the Soviet SS-20 rockets in front of high-ranking SED leaders. Later, after the revolution of 1989, he undertook a big tour through the revived country.

As the foregoing examples illustrate, in GDR history rock music was both a medium of politics and a medium against politics. A last example: In June 1987, the British pop star David Bowie and the Eurythmics had given a concert in front of the West Berlin Legislative Building (the Reichstag) near the Brandenburg Gate, drawing many GDR fans to the nearby wall to catch at least some sounds from the pop idols on the other side. The East Berlin police tried to prevent this and began using their clubs against the rock fans. There were arrests. Some young people shouted, "The wall has to go!" and "Gorbachev, Gorbachev!" The administration panicked. A year later, it became known that Michael Jackson and Pink Floyd were also going to perform in just this area near the wall. This time the SED reacted more efficiently and arranged a counterfestival on the occasion of the International Meeting for Nuclear Free Zones, at which many politicians from around the world were taking part. In the Weissensee district of East Berlin, world-renowned groups such as Big Country, Bryan Adams, Fisher Z, and Marillion performed alongside GDR rock bands such as City. The authorities hoped, in this way, to lure local rock fans away from the Western concert. The Eastern concert was moderated by ice skating world champion Katarina Witt.

The GDR groups had a tough position opposite the Western stars, and the audience reacted with derisive whistles. Still, the 120,000 rock fans best tolerated the band City. Toni Krahl of City recalled memories of the old GDR's unspeakable and ultimately trivial measures of censorship:

> At this concert, the highest level of security was in effect, it was attended by the cultural head of the FDJ, Hartmut König, and the leader of the FDJ, Eberhard Aurich. Egon Krenz was there too, at that time as "crown prince." I was just on my way to the stage when Hartmut König came up and took my arm like a comrade. We had been in school together, and were therefore on an informal basis from earlier times, although affection was never really

an issue on either side. He said to me, Toni, that "Half and Half," leave that out for once today, you won't sing that. And don't make any announcements, people don't want to hear that, that just brings unrest. I was already excited enough now and I replied, You go over to Heinz-Rudolf Kunze [a singer from the Federal Republic] and tell him something. To that König replied, I can't do that, he's our guest and Egon is here too. He made me appropriately nervous. Then he went away and I broodingly went the last three steps onto the stage. And in this instant the thought came to me, I said to Fritz, he [König] just talked to me, what shall we do now, we're walking into the lions' den. We won't play the song, I'll just say the words! This is what we did, and look, the effect of the text was so enhanced by this method that I would like to thank Hartmut König once again for this great part of the program which we subsequently always built in because the effect was really so immense.[39]

What König did not want to hear is presented here:

On some days I tell myself:
Half of it is over and you are still here
And not on the moon or under the grass,
Still half full in front of a half empty glass.
On such days it all comes out:
Half is over, what are you still waiting for?
Half and half.
Sometimes nothing is complete anymore:
Only half as much hair, and half of the bed,
And half loud it comes from the radio.
Half of humanity is dying somewhere.
Half-gods are dancing around the golden calf,
Thus is the half world—half and half.
Half and half.
In half a country and in a city cut apart,
halfway content with what one has.
Half and half.[40]

THE END AND THE BEGINNING

With the revolution of 1989, the renovation of East German rock history began. As Toni Krahl noted,

We recognize our complicity in the exit of thousands through our participation in the practice of suppressing problems in this country. Too often, too long and over all, we allowed ourselves to be used on the big stages of this country and in the media. We accepted insufficient artistic conditions, made compromises which were not even compromises anymore. We made statements about political problems in South Africa and Nicaragua, seldom about our own.[41]

The former FDJ mouthpiece *Junge Welt* published the first self-critical characterization of the rock history of the country in a weekly series in April 1990 under the title "Beat in the Grey Zone." The author was Michael Rauhut, a student of Peter Wicke, the leader of the Research Center for Popular Music at Humboldt University in East Berlin. Wicke himself, author of various publications on the subject of rock, had thus far kept out of this topic. Until April 1990, only one complete portrayal of GDR rock had come out anywhere in the world, namely, in the Federal Republic.[42] Although Wicke had reviewed this book in the GDR music journal *Unterhaltungskunst* and had shown due respect for the author ("He is excellent for an argument"),[43] he continued to suppress all mention of Western historical writings on GDR rock in the bibliographical appendixes of his own books on the subject.

Rock music in the GDR is a thing of the past, like the country from which it sprang. But the musicians, composers, writers, and singers continue to work—now under the unfamiliar capitalist circumstances with which they have had to become accustomed, albeit with difficulty. These new conditions meant an absence of state censorship and direction but also an absence of social certainty that could provide guarantees for life as an artist. Poet Volker Braun has said, "Now we have lost our chains. But there is something else: heavy lead wrists, crooked gait, soldered feet—What have they done to us? And now another question: What do we do now?"[44]

What unsettled the poets, the painters, the sculptors, and the theater people also worried the rock musicians: Would one be able to maintain an independent presence in a reunified Germany, to save that specific interpretation of culture that had become typical in the GDR? Capitalism was judged by many in the GDR to be overpoweringly inhuman. Its interests in art would be limited to its commercial aspects, in the opinion of many citizens of the former GDR. Their start in the new future began with frightened expectation, skepticism, and fear.

Just as the public now looks to the West unhindered and prefers to attend concerts and buy records there, the rock bands move West too, to try their luck with a new audience. This is difficult. On the one hand, opportunities to perform elsewhere are not readily or excessively available; on the other hand, only a few bands in the old GDR had become well known. And after the revolution of 1989, it was a stroke of good luck when a rock stylist was invited to other countries in the West. Rock singer Petra Zieger, for example, traveled to the Freedom Festival in Philadelphia to perform next to Crosby, Stills, Nash and Young; Bo

Diddley; and Ritchie Havens. Her contribution: the song "Break Down the Walls!"

Although the scene has changed radically, many of the old power structures are still standing. Once powerful leaders, the "turncoats," quickly started gathering their little sheep on dry land. Those who had once been responsible within the Central Committee of the FDJ for major events (for example, for the Festival of Political Song) capitalized on their positions and connections to launch new private careers, benefiting from their contacts with international artists. From something like that, money can be made.

The Committee for Entertainment Art dissolved itself. The rock musicians founded their own organization in February 1990, the Music Scene. A member of the umbrella organization Entertainment Artists, which was formed in March 1990, it represents artists, producers, and technicians and wants to maintain contact with international music organizations. It "works for the free development of all genres of popular music, ... for effective protection of accomplishments and copyright laws, for appropriate working and living conditions, for the development of a suitable infrastructure. ... *Musik Szene* offers its members workshops with national and international experts, and trade-specific legal advice."[45] The chair of the organization of Music Scene is City musician Toni Krahl.

In reference to the start of the new age for rock music, the band leader of Rockhaus said,

> Back then it was about being against pitiful egalitarianism which lamed initiative, didn't honor quality, where categorization mattered. Today, pure commercialism is necessary. Subsidies aren't flowing anymore, and the club house managers have a wait-and-see attitude. Don't want any risk, and would rather be safe with disco by numbers. It's actually understandable somehow. But now completely different systems are crashing into each other, and neither the old nor the future mechanisms are functioning. ... Many of us won't survive.[46]

But no one wants to go back to the dictatorship anymore. How did the rock band Pankow complain now?

> *Seen the same country too long*
> *Heard the same language too long*
> *Waited too long, hoped too long*
> *Honored the old men too long,*
> *I ran around*
> *ran around so much*
> *ran around so much*
> *and nothing happened anyway.*[47]

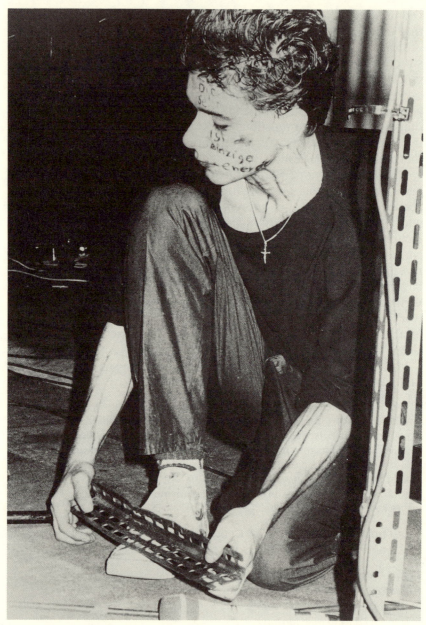

Pankow. Photo courtesy Wax Trax—Play It Again, Sam, USA.

Then something did happen. Some of the Germans had an effective revolution, free of violence. And the rock musicians of the GDR can say not only that they were there but also that they participated.

Translated from German by Margaret A. Brown

NOTES

1. This term comes from GDR lawyer and civil rights expert Rolf Henrich, who took it from Eduard Gans, the philosophy teacher of Karl Marx.

2. Cited from a copy of the original manuscript (in the possession of the author).

3. Toni Krahl, in interview with the author, Berlin, 15 June 1990.

4. Ibid.

5. Ibid.

6. Certain attempts on the part of the SED to keep East Germans from receiving Western broadcasts eventually failed. The viewing patterns of parents were researched by assigning schoolchildren to draw the TV clock shown on the screen at the end of the news broadcast. If the children drew a round clock, this indicated that Western TV was preferred at home. GDR television always showed an oval clock.

7. "z. B. Susann," on City, *Casablanca*, AMIGA 856 244 (1987).

8. "Für Chuck Berry," on Hansi Biebl, *Der lange Weg*, AMIGA 855 842 (1981).

9. Werner Rackwitz, "Wie entsteht unsere Tanzmusik?" Lecture on the occasion of the Dance Music Conference, Berlin, 24–25 April 1972, in Gisela Rüss (ed.), *Dokumente zur Kunst-, Literatur-, und Kulturpolitik der SED, 1971–1974* (Stuttgart: Seewald Verlag, 1976), p. 423.

10. Kurt Hager, "Zu Fragen der Kulturpolitik der SED," in *Beiträge zur Kulturpolitik* (Berlin: Dietz Verlag, 1981), p. 11.

11. Ibid.

12. Ibid., p. 48.

13. *Melodie und Rhythmus* 19 (1970), p. 6.

14. "Ich will nicht vergessen," on Puhdys, *Das Buch*, AMIGA 856 039 (1984).

15. "Nachtgedanken," from Heinrich Heine, *Sämtliche Schriften in zwölf Bänden*, ed. by Klaus Briegler (Munich and Vienna: Hanser Verlag, 1976), vol. 7, p. 432.

16. "No Bomb," on Berluc, *Rocker von der Küste*, AMIGA 856 090 (1984).

17. "Grüss dich, Grenada!" on Karussell, *Rock für den Frieden*, 1984 Live, AMIGA 856 038 (1984).

18. Helmut Hanke, *Freizeit in der DDR* (Berlin: Dietz Verlag, 1979), p. 90.

19. Interview with Toni Krahl.

20. *Presse-Telegram der Generaldirektion beim Komitee für Unterhaltungskunst der DDR*, no. 3 (1987), pp. 1–2.

21. Ibid., p. 4.

22. Peter Wicke and Wieland Ziegenrücker, *Rock-Pop-Jazz-Folk. Handbuch der populären Musik* (Leipzig: VEB Deutscher Verlag für Musik, 1985), p. 411.

23. Ibid., p. 410.

24. AMIGA 850 040.

25. Elimar Schubbe (ed.), *Dokumente zur Kunst-, Literatur-, und Kulturpolitik der SED* (Stuttgart: Seewald Verlag, 1972), p. 1077.

26. *Leipziger Volkszeitung* (Leipzig), 10 October 1965.

27. *Melodie und Rhythmus* 21 (1967), p. 26.

28. Erich Loest, *Es geht seinen Gang oder Mühen in unserer Ebene* (Stuttgart: Deutsche Verlagsanstalt, 1978), pp. 2off.

29. Schubbe, p. 1126.

30. Cited from an accidental recording during a rehearsal by the Renft Combo, Leipzig, 22 September 1975.

31. Ibid.

32. "Glaubensfragen," on Renft Combo, Private recording (1975).

33. *Junge Welt* (Berlin), 28 April 1990.

34. Interview with Günter Holwas, Berlin, 2 June 1982.

35. "Rock 'n' Roll Arena in Jena," on Udo Lindenberg, *Sister King Kong,* TELEFUNKEN 6.22609 (1976).

36. *Neues Leben* (Berlin) 8 (1977).

37. "Sonderzug nach Pankow," on Udo Lindenberg, *Odyssee,* POLYDOR 2371 171 (1983).

38. Cited from *Musik heute, Nachrichten aus dem Showbusiness,* no. 2 (21 March 1983).

39. Interview with Krahl and Fritz Puppel, Berlin, 15 June 1990.

40. "Halb und halb," on City, *Casablanca,* AMIGA 856 244 (1987).

41. *Der Morgen,* 7 November 1989.

42. Olaf Leitner, *Rockszene DDR—Aspekte einer Massenkultur im Sozialismus* (Hamburg: Rowohlt Verlag, 1983).

43. *Unterhaltungskunst. Zeitschrift für Bühne, Podium, und Manege* 5 (1984).

44. Volker Braun, "Wie es gekommen ist," in *Sinn und Form* (East Berlin) 3 (1990).

45. Cited from the flier of *Musik Szene,* e.V. (June 1990).

46. As quoted in *Berliner Zeitung,* 4 July 1990.

47. "Langeweile," on Pankow, *Aufruhr in den Augen,* AMIGA 856 294 (1988). Text from a typewritten copy, handed out by Pankow.

ALEX KAN
NICK HAYES

3

Big Beat in Poland

POLAND OCCUPIED A special niche in the range of the communist countries' approach to rock 'n' roll. Imagine a scale that would move from virtually complete repression to relative openness. Albania or North Korea, where rock was unknown, could probably claim the former, and the Soviet Union, with its illegal rock underground and occasional official acceptance, would hold the middle ground. In the 1960s and 1970s, Poland, like Hungary, would be on the other end of the scale, with a more or less open and flourishing rock scene. And of those two countries, Poland was home to probably the most developed pop and rock scene in the lands of the Warsaw Pact.

The Poles' advantage came as an indirect benefit of the de-Stalinization or Polish thaw that started in 1956. Polish anti-Stalinism escaped the tragedy of a similar movement in Hungary, as Władysław Gomułka took a more pragmatic approach. With it, there came into Poland new ideas on culture, art, and fashion that could not have entered other Warsaw Pact countries at the time.[1] Poland had opened the door a bit to Western ideas and through the backdoor came rock 'n' roll. But make no mistake about it—Polish rock may have enjoyed liberal conditions, but it was not free. The rules of this game were distinct and strict: no intrusion into politics.

This Polish deal between the rock community and the communist regime accounted for, on the one hand, the richness and variety of the scene—especially in the pre–martial law 1960s and 1970s—and, on the other, for its ideological sterility compared to its neighbors in both the East and the West. Only in the 1980s, during the martial law years, did Polish rock acquire the rough and hard political edge that shaped the rock culture in the other socialist countries.

MAKING BIG BEAT

Jazz and rock hit the Polish scene early. As early as 1956, Poland had a regular jazz newsletter. It came out first as the newsletter of the Culture Club in Gdánsk but then stayed on as a regular monthly magazine. As for rock, the first rock recordings reached Poland in 1956, the year in which Elvis had just begun to climb the charts with "Heartbreak Hotel" and "Blue Suede Shoes."

The Western airwaves brought the beat to all of Eastern Europe, including Poland, where audiences had a special fondness for rock 'n' roll on Radio Luxemburg and jazz brought by the venerable Willis Conover on Voice of America (VOA). Although he may be virtually unknown in the United States, Conover—not Leonard Feather or John Hammond—is *the* authority on jazz for any jazz musician or fan in Eastern Europe and the Soviet Union; his nightly "Jazz Hour" began on VOA in 1952 and is still on the air. His reputation cut across the borders of the Warsaw Pact, but only Poland officially acknowledged Conover with a state award in 1978 for his role in promoting cultural ties between Poland and the world. By the mid-1950s, Polish jazz was back with the performances of Andrzej Kurylewicz. When in 1954 the Bin Bon reopened in Gdánsk, other cabarets followed, and Polish cabaret started its comeback from the oblivion it experienced in the Stalinist years.

The first signs of the rock invasion appeared in 1957 when Drazek i pięciu (Drazek and His Five), a dixieland band from Kraków led by saxophonist Stanislaw ("Drazek") Kalwinski, advertised its shows as rock 'n' roll. Its concerts included a few Elvis Presley and Bill Haley hits. The group's soloist, a Canadian of Polish origin, Jenny Jaworske, took the stage name of Jenny Rogers, and Drazek i pięciu took its semidixie, semirock show on tour. The first genuine rock 'n' roll band came two years later.

Band manager Franciszek Walicki and pianist Leszek Bogdanowicz pulled together a group of musicians and singers, aptly called Rhythm and Blues, for its premier performance in the Red Cat Club in Gdánsk on 24 March 1959.[2] The concert opened with the American hit song "Rock Around the Clock." The lead singer, Bogusław Wyrobek, had credentials—but not in rock—he had a master's degree in economics. The concert, which lasted for only forty-five minutes, was a smash and had to be rebooked and repeated almost immediately. Overnight Wyrobek became the first star of Polish rock 'n' roll. At one of the concerts, he had to sing "All of Me" nine times in a row. His degree notwithstanding, Wyrobek was no different from the rockers he envied in the West. His high, shrill voice belted out the songs of Elvis Presley, Tommy Steel, and Paul Anka and soon made the band Rhythm and Blues a national favorite. In May 1959, Rhythm and Blues won the National Amateur Competition of Jazz and Rock Ensembles organized in Warsaw by the youth daily *Sztandar Mlodych*. The group also came up with Poland's first original rock 'n' roll song, "Big Boogie Woogie," written by the group's guitarist, Leszek Bogdanowicz (the first to play the electric guitar in Poland). The song was performed by Michaj Burano, who had joined the band shortly before and became an even bigger star than Wyrobek.

Burano, whose real name was Wasyl Michaj, was a gypsy. His life story was fed into the rumor and legend mills of the early Polish pop scene; Burano enjoyed all the noise. Some said he was a Romanian prince, others said he was a gypsy king from Bucharest. Maybe so, but the facts are that he joined Rhythm and Blues for the few last months of its existence when he was only fourteen, played the guitar, and somehow knew a few Presley songs. His career outlived the band that had given him his first gig. After Rhythm and Blues was gone, Burano went on, changing his stage name here and there. After "Michaj Burano" came the names "Steve Lucca," then "John Mike Arlow," and then simply "John," in a duo called John and Morgan that performed even in Paris.

Rhythm and Blues was so popular that its concerts turned into frenzy. The musicians were concerned—and as the near future showed, the group had good reason to be—that too hot a response would eventually jeopardize their concert careers. Their posters even appealed to their fans to behave, but in vain. In fall 1959, Rhythm and Blues was banned from performing. The group disbanded and never again played under its original name, although it did resurface sporadically in various guises.

Rhythm and Blues was the founding force in Polish rock. Its music, singing, and playing were amateurish, but it was the first, which counts a lot in the long run of rock history.

Franciszek Walicki followed that act with another project—Czerwono Czarni (Red and Black, as its name translates). Czerwono Czarni introduced the big-beat sound to Polish pop. In Poland the term *big beat* served as a euphemism for rock 'n' roll. Borrowed from the name of one the records of Art Blakey's Jazz Messenger, big beat sounded curt, precise, and sharp. It sounded cool and described the music but didn't have an obvious relationship to that subversive and suspect "rock 'n' roll." Invented as a musical term in Poland, big beat went no further than its native country, except perhaps to neighboring Czechoslovakia.

A renowned Polish music journalist and DJ, Roman Waschko, recalled later,

> The term "big beat" was born out of necessity: excesses and riots which in the opinion of some local authorities were an indispensable part of rock

concerts caused this unofficial discrimination against rock 'n' roll. There had to be a substitute for "rock 'n' roll" and "big beat" served as that substitute synonym. When the streets of Polish cities were covered with first posters advertising "seanse bigbitowe" (big-beat shows), only the select few knew what was up. The young knew ... even if they only recognized the names of their idols.[3]

Czerwono Czarni started touring the country in 1960 with *seanse bigbitowe*. In April 1961, its soloists were the first to record rock 'n' roll songs in Poland: Marek Tarnowski recorded "Elevator Rock," "Sweet Little Sixteen," and "Apron Strings." It also initiated the First Festival of Young Talents in Szczecin in 1962. The winner, among thousands of contestants, in the category of "ensemble" was a group called Niebesko Czarni, which would play an important role in the early 1960s.[4] This group brought the twist to Poland. Its soloist, Danuta Skorzynska, was Poland's Miss Twist, and the twist mania firmly reigned in the country's dance halls in 1962 and 1963.

Niebesko Czarni had another and more important initiative. By this time, the Polish press had found its characteristic voice on the subject of rock, sputtering in a range from irritation to impatience over the fact that most or all popular songs sung by Polish artists were in foreign languages, predominantly English. A few came to the defense with the claim that American hits could be a good vehicle for the young audiences to learn English. Although one could practice English by listening to rock, Michaj Burano or Danuta Skorzynska could hardly be passed off as instructors of English. Anyway, as the controversy grew it became clear that political survival would require Polish rock bands to sing in Polish.

Enter Niebesko Czarni with the slogan "Let's Sing in Polish." Easier said than done. There were not enough original Polish songs that could compete in popularity with the American rock 'n' roll standards. Niebesko Czarni reached for the obvious: Polish folklore. Young audiences were fed up with official pseudo folk ensembles, whose songs and dances for years were forced down their throats by cultural establishments, and thus were not likely to become folk enthusiasts overnight. Moreover, Niebesko Czarni's versions of Polish folk songs showed little innovation in the arrangements or little pizazz in performances. But the magic of electric guitars worked. Other pop artists followed suit into what became the trend toward Polish folk-rock. With the introduction of the Polish language into rock 'n' roll, original compositions followed. The pioneer here again was Niebesko Czarni or, to be more exact, the group's soloist, Czesław Niemen.

Niebesko Czarni was also the first to score foreign tours. From 1963 to 1965 it toured and played at festivals in Sweden, Hungary, and France. Its performance at the Song Festival in Rennes, France, in 1965 was a triumph for Niemen: He picked up the award as the best singer and composer and soon thereafter moved to the leading position in the group.

Niebesko Czarni had more going for it than just Niemen, although he certainly was the brightest and most talented personality in the group. Michaj Burano at certain points joined up with Niebesko Czarni and adeptly mixed its big beat with gypsy folklore. With Burano, the group won three major awards at the next 1966 Rennes Festival. And that was without Niemen, who had left the group by that time.

From 1962 to 1966, Niebesko Czarni was a laboratory for the future talent of Polish rock. It was for the next wave of Polish rock what the Yardbirds were for British blues-rock or what Miles Davis was for jazz rock fusion bands of the 1970s.

The next Polish wave came in 1965. Four important Polish bands of the 1960s made their debut: Polanie, Czerwone gitary, Blackout, and Skaldowie.

Polanie (The Poles) introduced blues rock and established its special place in the rock style in Poland. The group was inspired by the Animals, who had toured Poland in 1965 with Polanie on the bill as the opening act. From the outset it was the stuff of legends. Consider, for example, how the group was formed. It was born literally of an accident: Two trucks with two leading Polish bands of the time—Czerwono Czarni and Niebesko Czarni—collided on a highway. Some of the musicians decided to play together and form a new group. Or, take the story of how the group got its name. The famous Swedish actress Bibi Andersson suggested the name Polanie. The group liked the idea and, in gratitude, made Bibi its godmother. It could follow tough acts. In a 1966 German tour, it played in the famous Hamburg Star Club, which had been immortalized by a Beatles performances there in 1960. Polanie was a smash hit there and attracted the attention of Western impresarios of Polish rock. Polanie did not last long and broke up in 1968.

The inevitable influence of the Beatles appeared in Czerwone gitary (Red Guitars), a typical guitar group of the 1960s. Its tandem of leaders—Seweryn Krajewski and Krzystof Klenczon—penned the group's melodic and lyrical songs. Its slogan was "We are the loudest!" It had memorable melodies, harmonious singing, and exquisite taste—which soon made it the most popular band in the late 1960s. Unfortunately, the leading tandem did not last long. Klenczon quit to form his own band, Trzy korony (Three Crowns), and later left the country for good.

Skaldowie (The Skalds—named after the medieval Scandinavian wandering musicians and singers) came from Kraków and was formed by the Zielinsky brothers. Andrzej played keyboards and wrote all the songs. Jacek did vocals and played trumpet and violin. The conservatory-trained Andrzej enriched his songs and arrangements with classical baroque or romantic influences. Along with including guitars, he commonly added a cello solo, a jazz riff, or a string quartet arrangement. But most prominent in Skaldowie's move away from the mainstream was the inclusion of a Polish folk music element.

Folk-rock had developed into a separate and strong trend in Polish popular music by the end of the decade. Skaldowie took its main inspiration for folk-rock from the folk music of the Silesian mountains. Another group—Trubadurzy (the Troubadours)—used a broader approach. It made big-beat arrangements of East European folk melodies with strong rhythm and contemporary instrumentation. Band members wore pretentious and pompous costumes (resembling those of both the Three Musketeers and the Beatles in the *Sgt. Pepper* album inner sleeve) and expressed extreme exaltation in their singing. These two traits of Trubadurzy kept a few sarcastic snickers running through the critics' reviews.

No To Co (So What) was probably the most folklike of folk-rock groups. Unlike Trubadurzy, whose instrumentation was the standard big-beat formula of guitars, electric organ, and drums, No To Co added a violin (or rather, a fiddle), a banjo, a harmonica, and wooden flutes and whistles. The musicians' extensive use of both rural and urban folklore made them favorites not only with audiences but also with the authorities. The group thus picked up numerous awards from the state radio and television as well as from the ministry of culture. The members of No To Co were also the darlings of the Polish diaspora in the United States and recorded an album in English for release in Britain.

NIEMEN AND THE 1970S

The shift in style from the 1960s to the 1970s found expression in Poland. In 1968, the group Breakout started experimenting with the avant-garde. The expressive vocals of Stan Borys were backed by arrangements of leading Polish jazz saxophonist and flutist Wlodziemierz Nahorny. Their music and their look had the underground and psychedelic marks of late 1960s avant-garde. As with the style of many British or American heroes of the time, the style of Borys and Nahorny proved irreversible. It stuck. Tadeusz Nalepa's 1986 live recording brings back the music and the spirit of 1968.

By the 1970s, Polish rock was coming of age and Czesław Niemen had clearly emerged as the key figure and the most influential and significant artist of two decades of Polish rock.[5] Born Czelaw Juliusz Wydrzycki in 1939 in Grodno (in western Belorussia), Niemen sang in a church choir and started studying music at an early age. In 1958 the family returned to its native Poland. Czesław enrolled in a music school in Gdańsk, where his instrument was the bassoon. Soon thereafter, he began singing, first in a cabaret and then in concerts. His career in the early 1960s and even his first major successes with Niebesko Czarni were modest by comparison with his later status in Polish rock. His 1967 hit "Dziwny jest ten swiat" (Strange Is the World) was not just his major breakthrough to stardom as a singer/songwriter but was also a critical transition for the whole of Polish pop music and youth culture:

Strange is the world where there's still so much evil
Strange is the world where forever a man neglects another man.[6]

The song made the LP on which it was included the first ever "gold" album in the history of Polish rock and launched a huge controversy in the media as to the problems, needs, and views of young people. A "summer of love"—a brief phase of exaltation and expressiveness among young people—exploded in Poland as well and Czesław Niemen was the detonator of the explosion.

In 1967 and 1968, Niemen and his band Akwarele (Watercolors) toured, enjoyed international success, and made record after record. But in 1969 he made another sharp turn. He joined efforts with the outstanding Polish jazz saxophonist Zbigniew Namyslowski to form a new group, Niemen Enigmatic. With this group, Niemen parted with conventional song formats and tread into the worlds of experimental jazz, art rock, and avant-garde music. Here he came up with mind-blowing compositions and sophisticated, often electronic, arrangements to the accompaniment of the classical Polish poetry of Julian Tuwim, Cyprian Norwid, and Adam Asnyk. Every new record—*Niemen* (volumes 1 and 2), Niemen Aerolit, Katharsis, Idee Fixe—moved further and further away from popular music and into the realm of rock avant-garde.

Niemen proved himself not only an outstanding singer with a strong voice but also an inventive composer, arranger, and instrumentalist. Niemen's musical leap was similar to the move to "progressive rock" and jazz rock undertaken by Emerson Lake and Palmer, Pink Floyd, and Mahavishnu Orchestra at the same time. Obviously, not everyone was happy with the sudden change of teenage idol into serious rock composer, but Niemen certainly knew what he was doing. He resolutely and irreversibly detached himself from an image of *piosenkarz* (pop singer, hit maker). "One thing I know," he said in an interview, "is that I'm a composer. I want to concentrate on writing music for film, for theater. I don't know for how long I will continue singing. I am just bored by singing. This form of artistic expression seems quite exhausted for me. At least it does not excite me like it used to." His status as a thinking man's rock musician grew and soon he was offered a contract by CBS (Columbia Broadcasting System). The record *Mourner's Rhapsody* was recorded in 1974 in New York and featured, among others, the prominent American jazz rock stars John Abercrombie, Jan Hammer, and Rick Laird. It came out only in Britain and didn't live up to the expectations of Niemen fans in Poland. In fact, the whole Polish community had held its breath in anticipation of Niemen's success and recognition in the West. It experienced a disappointment not unlike that which befell the Russian scene fifteen years later when the love affair between rock star Boris Grebenshikov and CBS produced the underwhelming LP *Radio Silence.*

CBS may have been a pause in Niemen's career, but he nevertheless gave an enormous boost to the development of creative, noncommercial rock music in Poland. The nucleus of his Niemen Group formed the instrumental trio SBB, made up of three jazz rock virtuosi: Antymos Apostolis on guitar; Jozef Skrzek on bass, keyboards, and vocals; and Jerzy Piotrowski on drums. Another progressive rock artist, Marek Grechuta, whose "singing images" (the name of one of his records) poetic visions, evokes analogies with Van Morrison. Trio Ossian drew inspiration from Indian classical music.

Another line of progressive music came directly from the jazz milieu, an area equally well developed in Poland. Along with SBB, the most prominent artists moving in this direction were violinist Michaj Urbaniak and his wife, vocalist Ursula Dudziak. In the mid-1970s they left Poland for the United States. From there they fashioned a successful performing and recording career in the West. Their group was Novi Singers, a vocal quartet that sang both jazz and rock standards and was accepted and recognized equally in both communities.

But just as Yes, Genesis, and Pink Floyd were seen in Britain as dinosaurs of pomposity by the mid-1970s, Polish rockers were also tiring of the old stuff. Punk did not hit Poland as strong or as sharp as it hit Britain. But the dinosaurs of Polish rock had lost quite a bit of their momentum and fresh blood had to be poured into the midst of disco fever. In 1978, a group of musicians' managers and journalists formed an organization called Muzyka Mlodej Generaji (MMG) (Music of the Young Generation). A whole new wave of young bands arose; Exodus, Krzak (the Cry), Kombi, Lombard, Perfect, and Maanam were making the scene. These new groups, together with the MMG, had anything but uniformity of style: They were punk or heavy metal, new wave or rock. What they had in common was energy, guts, and drive.[7]

The center of the punk rock movement was a student club in Torun, Od Nowa (Again, Anew), where there were a few festivals of new wave. There were many groups on the Polish punk scene—De-Zerter, Brak,

Brygada kryzys, and the uncrowned king of the new Polish rock of the late 1970s, Perfect. Polish punk had its devoted fans and followers but did not exactly enjoy a mass triumph in its first season. At the first (and last) punk festival in Kolobrzeg in summer 1980 there was hardly any audience. The first MMG festival in 1979 in Jarocin was held comfortably in a small movie theater.[8] In summer 1980, punk had probably lost its audience to politics, but then in the next season politics would give Polish punk a role and an audience like no other in the history of Polish rock.

ANARCHY IN THE WRONa

"Do you ever feel like you've been cheated," Johnny Rotten screamed at the end of his last concert at the Winter Garden in 1977. Quite a few did in the West, and punk fed on the young's sense that they had no future. Well, maybe so, but much of Western youth just yuppied along into the 1980s. But if you wanted to feel young, cheated, and without a future, Poland was the place to be in the early 1980s.

The imposition of martial law in Poland on 13 December 1991 gave punk a new lease on life in Poland after its rather weak start a year or two before. Rock music was the exception to the rule of the otherwise uniform repression that martial law brought to Polish culture. Polish rockers had easy access to the radio airwaves, recording studios, and the concert stage even in the harshest years of the early 1980s. Perhaps General Wojciech Jaruzelski saw rock as a harmless safety valve for the release of adolescent frustrations or perhaps he calculated that the regime could tolerate a Polish rock scene that stuck to the old deal of rock without politics. He could have lived with the old-time Polish rock 'n' roll but he got punk anarchy in the WRONa.

The punk festival at Jarocin that began with only 600 fans in the summer of 1979 grew into an annual ritual of the Polish punk nation. By summer 1984 the Baltic town was bringing in 15,000 to 20,000 punk rockers. Reports in the official press described the event with horror, as if Jarocin had been taken over by an army of the worst of Polish society. In 1981, the Jarocin festival's founder, Grzegorz Brzozowicz, initiated what he called the Rock Front at Warsaw's Remont Club, which brought in punk bands from all across Poland. The house band SS-20 took its name in honor of the new generation of Soviet nuclear missiles. The rock of the old generation had been long on art and short on politics. Polish punk was long on politics, although most critics felt it came up short on the side of art. SS-20 gave antimilitary rock to a generation living under martial law. When officials objected to the name, the group switched to the title De-Zerter. Kult, another group, took shots at the other Polish establishment—the Catholic church. Brygada kryzys mixed punk and reggae with songs that described its society as brain-dead and suggested that ganja was Poland's only hope.[9]

Poland's punk revolution was led by three rock bands—Lady Pank, Manaam, and, above all others, Perfect. Manaam delivered two hit albums in the first two years of martial law: *Night Patrol,* which parodied the police, and *Totalski no problemski,* whose hit single "Stand! Stand!" played as a rally to the young to stand up and fight back. Manaam, however, owed much of its vitality to its lead female vocal, Kora. She was to Manaam what Debby Harry was to Blondie and, moreover, she took the band's sound beyond Poland. By 1984, she was wooing the critics and climbing the charts in West Germany. Lady Pank emerged as a cult phenomenon in the mid-1980s. It combined antigovernment songs with its own line of clothes, cosmetics, and accessories. Lady Pank seemed to suffer from a commercial itch that was worse than its political pains. In 1985, it made it to the United States and released a forgettable LP in English. Back in Poland, the band fell into a scandal when its bass player, Jan Borysewicz, took the liberty of exposing himself in concert. He ended up in court and in prison for three months while Lady Pank disappeared from the rock scene.

If any group was to Polish punk what the Sex Pistols were to the West, then that group was Perfect and the genius behind it was it Zbigniew (Zbiggy) Holdys.[10] A high-school dropout, he had been part of the Polish rock scene since the early 1970s. Hatched in Warsaw's Medyk Club at the end of the decade, Perfect was Zbiggy's third attempt at forming a band. In 1979 and early 1980, Zbiggy somehow managed to send the band on tour in the United States, where for the most part it made a living playing the repertoire appropriate for the Holiday Inn circuit.

Perfect's return to Poland in summer 1980 coincided with the spread of Solidarity's strike from Gdańsk to the rest of the nation. Perfect gave a concert for the workers engaged in a sitdown strike at the Ursus factory outside of Warsaw, and in March 1981 it marched and played with the strikers in the Crossroads Strike in the center of Warsaw. Perfect's 1981 hit "Autobiography" came across as the ballad of a generation raised on rock 'n' roll and finally standing behind Solidarity:

I was only a teenager, when the world first heard about him
Our club was in my basement
A buddy brought a radio, I heard "Blue Suede Shoes"
and I couldn't sleep at night.

A wind of renewal would blow
people were pardoned and you could laugh again
Jazz stormed into the cafe like a tornado
and I too wanted to play music

My father was working at a steel plant god knows where
I also roughed up my hands
I wore out my guitar and played millions of worthless tunes
I learnt about sex

Bootleg madness, all of us had hundreds of those
instead of a new pair of jeans
On Saturday nights we had digs, booze and Radio Luxembourg
We wanted to live so much

There were three of us, each different
Let's leave, the police are waiting for us,
even though others are busy stealing now

But, well . . .
This world is unbelievable
our music causes fear
our music causes fear.[11]

The lyrics celebrate in anger a generation raised in the Stalinist 1950s but liberated by rock and now certain that with a little more rock it could roll the WRONa.

After December 1981, Perfect played to the extreme its totally incongruous place in the new order of WRONa. The band was militantly antigovernment but had easy access to radio, concerts, and recordings. Its second LP came out on a newly formed private label in 1982 and sold a record 1.2 million. Few rock 'n' roll bands anywhere or anytime in the history of rock showed the political guts that packed Perfect's always sellout concerts. The group's pre–martial law hit "Pepe Come Back" was now sung in unison with the crowds as an obvious call for a return of Solidarity.[12] The sharpest political slap came in the song "We Want to Be Ourselves." With a slight alteration of accent, the song's refrain "We want to be ourselves" in concert came off as indistinguishable in Polish from "We want to beat up the zomos [riot police]." It worked for a while until spring 1983, when Perfect was banned from performances in most of the major Polish cities.

Punk, however, burns quickly. By 1984, Manaam was making big bucks in the West and Lady Pank would try to do the same. In 1984 Holdys delivered his last direct attack on the government with the recording of *Pigs* and then took to internal emigration. His next release, *I Ching,* was a bit too self-indulgent in introspection. Later in 1987, Perfect pulled off a musical and political comeback with sellout concerts in Warsaw and Gdańsk that rocked again with Zbiggy's hardest antigovernment songs. Then, Zbiggy sent a letter to the government that denied he had any political intent. The letter was published and

Perfect's image flipped from the hero to the embarrassment of the radical cause.

Perhaps the denouement of Polish punk was predictable. Thatcherism and the Reagan revolution had survived the Sex Pistols, and the WRONa had lived out the Polish punk revolution. But there was another point to Polish punk. Punk gave Polish rock something it had never had: political guts. What is more, the anger of Polish rock in the early 1980s revealed a cultural underground that could rebel as easily against the new Poland as it did against WRONa.

Since 1988 and 1989, the political and economic revolution of Poland has taken away what had been too easy of a political target for rock. Parts of Polish rock of the early 1990s reverted back to the let-them-have-fluff style that characterized much of Polish rock in the 1960s and 1970s. Other parts have floundered through the same economic woes that the market system has brought to every other facet of Polish culture. The challenge of Polish rock today is less like Manaam's call to "Stand! Stand!" in defiance of the government and more like a commercial push to stand up and buy records, concert tickets, and videos.

A few have noticed, complained, and hinted at a nostalgia for the days that may have had harder politics but certainly more vitality in its rock scene. Zygmunt Staszcyk, from the rock group T. Love, lamented in a recent issue of *Polityka:* "Rock is becoming a commodity. ... Technically, this music is much better when compared with what we used to play in the 1980s, but it lacks any drive. ... The new groups don't have anything to sing about. They have better instruments and they play better, but what they lack is inspiration so they end up just aping Western rock."[13] And it shows on the fans. The rock festival at Jarocin that had been the annual gathering of Polish punk in 1988 "looked like a communist youth gathering."

Is it over? Check out a release in 1990 by the group De Mono:

You no longer remember streets in flames.
Neither conversations until the dawn.
Nor stones thrown blindly.
You no longer remember what's fear and pain.

When you marched with others on the streets.
To fight for your rights.
Tired you'd come home late.
You were fighting until the dawn.
You no longer remember what's fear and pain.

It's not the same life.
It's not what it used to be.
You have new ideals.
Now it's all over.

You no longer remember the tears.
I know nobody's forever young
unless he wants to be.
You no longer remember what's fear and pain.

It's not the same life.
It's not what it used to be.
You have new ideals.
For you the revolution is over.[14]

The revolutionary age may be over as Polish rock has found its liberation in the age of commodity rock. If so, rock 'n' roll in Poland faces the same dilemma as in the rest of Eastern Europe and the former Soviet Union. Does anybody care if Poles can rock and roll with the best of Michael Bolton? Or, if that's all there is on the rock scene in the 1990s, maybe Polish punk of the 1980s left a few cues for what should be the next act.

NOTES

1. On the cultural politics of the Gomułka era, see Andrzej Albert, *Najnowsza historia polski, 1918–1980* (London: Polonia, 1989), pp. 77–79.

2. Timothy W. Ryback, *Rock Around the Bloc: A History of Rock Music in Eastern Europe and the Soviet Union* (New York: Oxford University Press, 1990), pp. 23–24.

3. LP *Czerwono Czarni* (Warsaw: Musa, 1964).

4. Ryback, *Rock Around the Bloc,* pp. 56–57.

5. Ibid., p. 130.

6. See LP *Akwarele* (Warsaw: Akwarele, 1967).

7. On the rock and punk scene in the 1970s, see "Zygmunt Staszczyk (Interview)," *Polityka,* 15 June 1991, p. 9; and Albert, *Najnowsza historia,* p. 1060.

8. On Jarocin rock festivals, see "Zygmunt Staszczyk."

9. Ryback, *Rock Around the Bloc,* pp. 183–190.

10. Jefferson Morley, "Zbiggy Meets the New Boss (Interview with Zbigniew Holdys)," *Spin* 6, no. 10 (January 1991), pp. 62–66, 83.

11. From LP *Perfect* (Warsaw: Tonpress, 1981/82).

12. Morley, "Zbiggy Meets."

13. "Zygmunt Staszczyk."

14. From LP *Oh Yeah* (Warsaw: De Mono, 1990).

SABRINA PETRA RAMET **4**

Rock Music in Czechoslovakia

I T WAS AN UNFORGETTABLE moment. Here was Frank Zappa, the creator of the Mothers of Invention, sitting down for a one-on-one with Václav Havel, the new president of Czechoslovakia. The two men discussed investment prospects for the country, culture in general, and, of course, the music of Frank Zappa.[1] Havel, who served as president from late 1989 until summer 1992, presided over a government with a heavy representation of rock musicians, DJs, and rock writers, including singers Pavel Kantor (head of protocol) and Michal Kocab (member of Parliament [MP]), and former Jazz Section collaborator Jarda Koran (the mayor of Prague). Under communism, rock rebellion had boosted the morale of a society living in protest. Political revolution signified, thus, a triumph in which rock artists could rejoice both as citizens and as long-time advocates of aesthetic and social freedom.

Rock made its entry as a foreign import, and it took time for rock music to establish its Czechoslovak autochthony. Even as late as 1987, Prague's House of Culture was promoting polkas and waltzes, arguing that the polka was an authentic Czech dance (a claim obviously denied to rock). Besides, as Jansa Jirmanova, director of the House of Culture, believed, "Those discotheques don't teach cultivated behavior. At our balls [by contrast], the children are well behaved."[2]

THE EARLY YEARS

Rock music in Czechoslovakia got its start much the way it did elsewhere in Eastern Europe—through exposure to Bill Haley and the Comets, Chubby Checker and the twist, Elvis Presley, and the Beatles. One of the first public exposures to rock 'n' roll came in 1956 at a singing competition for young people. Most of the young people dutifully intoned songs in praise of steel production or communism. But young Pavel Sedlacek chose, instead, to perform his rendition of "Rock Around the Clock"—a choice the jury clearly did not appreciate. Rock 'n' roll bands soon proliferated, and, in the late 1950s, the Reduta Club, near Prague's Wenceslaus Square, emerged as an early venue for the new genre. At the beginning of the 1960s, the twist hit Czechoslovakia with the songwriting team of Jiri Suchy and Jiri Slitr serving as the chief advocates of the new dance. They produced a number of popular songs, including "Mr. Rock, Mr. Roll" and "Life Is a Dog."

The first major rock 'n' roll concert in Czechoslovakia was put on by the band Komety (Comets) in spring 1962, in Prague's Lucerna Hall. The well-known band Olympic, which is still playing today, was also created in 1962; at that time it was an amateur band. This was followed, in 1963, by the launching of *Melodie*, Czechoslovakia's first rock 'n' roll magazine. In 1964, Petr Kaplan and Karel Svoboda launched Czechoslovakia's first professional rock group, under the name Mefisto.[3] By then, there were some 115 amateur rock 'n' roll bands in Prague alone, with such names as Hell's Devils, Crazy Boys (with Miki Volek), Strangers, Buttons, Shakers, and Beatmen. Even the Czechoslovak army had a rock 'n' roll band—a group called Big Beat VOJ, whose lead singer, Karel Cernoch, wore his uniform and regulation haircut while performing.[4] As of 1965, there were some 15 professional rock groups in the country (including Olympic, which had gone professional with its second album) and more than a thousand amateur rock 'n' roll bands in Czechoslovakia overall. Rock music had arrived. *Mlady svet*, the youth magazine, sponsored the release of five rock singles in 1964—Czechoslovakia's first—and within a year had sold a total of 400,000 copies.

Beatlemania gripped Czechoslovakia beginning in 1964. A local Czech reporter captured the spirit of Czechoslovak Beatle fans: "They wriggled, they fell off the platform and crawled back onto it, they gasped for air hysterically. I expected them to bite each other any minute. And then the destruction began."[5] Fans rushed onstage, seized chairs, hurled them and smashed them up, and broke windows. Czechoslovakia had its first taste of rock-inclined frenzy.

Catering to the young public's demonstrated craving for Beatles' music, Petr Janda's group, Olympic, got its start playing Beatles songs and quickly established itself as the number one group in Prague. But by 1966, Olympic was playing a large amount of original material, although it continued to play covers on Beatle songs; even its original material was consciously composed in the Beatles style. Accordingly, when the Beatles released their album *Sgt. Pepper's Lonely Hearts Club Band*, Olympic members appeared in brightly colored uniforms that closely resembled those worn by the Beatles on the *Sgt. Pepper* album jacket.

Until now, Czechoslovak rock had largely been restricted to Prague. But in the mid-1960s, rock spread outside the capital. Bands playing outside Prague included Pavel Novak's Synkopa (in Prerov, Moravia), a Beach Boys–style band known as Synkopy 61 (in Brno, Moravia), and Vulkan (also in Brno). One of Bratislava's earliest groups was the Beatmen (created in 1964), who performed a combination of Beatles covers and original music. One of the top groups at that time was the Rebels. Popularized through radio exposure, the Rebels reached the peak of their popularity in 1967. That rock had become a mass phenomenon was proven in December 1967 when Czechoslovakia held its first national big-beat festival. Some 12,000 fans attended the three-day event. By then a network of rock clubs had emerged to cater to the new fashion.

Up to now, rock 'n' roll had been about dancing, fun, being young, and, perhaps, about rebelling against the "oldsters." Some time in the late 1960s, rock came to be about art as well. A pioneer in this development was Milan Knizak, a Czech artist who viewed himself as a Czechoslovak John Cage. Together with his rock group, Actual, he put on aesthetic "happenings" that blended music, sculpture, and "being there" in an outdoor setting.[6] Authorities didn't like these happenings and were not sure whether they approved of "being there." They repeatedly sent the police to arrest Knizak, to interrogate him, and to shave his head. In June 1967, after a happening in Marianske Lazne, Knizak was sentenced to prison for ten months.

Until the late 1960s, Czechoslovak rockers had taken it for granted that rock songs had to be sung in English. Canadian journalist Paul Wilson, for example, was brought into the group Plastic People of the Universe in part because the other members wanted him to translate their Czech lyrics into English. But in the late 1960s, a number of rock singers started to challenge that custom, giving rise to inevitable controversy. Olympic played a role here, with the 1967 release of its album *Zelva* (Tortoise), in which it sang exclusively in Czech. Aficionados of the Czech rock scene consider this album to have been Olympic's biggest achievement out of its twenty-five to thirty albums. *Zelva* raised Beatlemania to its pinnacle and was the purest and most refined expression of Beatle-style music; after the release of that album, there was a gradual drift away from Beatlemania to other styles.

FROM DUBČEK TO HUSÁK

With the arrival of the Dubček era and the accompanying liberalization, rock bands started to perform in local propaganda centers. The Dubček era was a time of exultation, of tolerance, of cultural experimentation. It was a time strained by excitement and filled with fearful hope.

The most sensational group of the Dubček era was a band called the Primitives. It achieved a special reputation for its celebrations of the four elements—water, air, fire, and earth. These became, in practice, "animal happenings." First, there was the celebration of water, which became known as the Fish Fest: Band members hurled buckets of water onto the audience and then threw live fish over them. It followed this up with a celebration of air—the Bird Bash: This featured shapely young girls clad in little besides feathers, and of course there were plenty of live birds. It ended with everyone knee deep in feathers. The Primitives dressed extravagantly, painted their faces with loud and garish makeup, routinely tried to incorporate one of the four elements into their concerts, and played psychedelic compositions that showed the influence of Jimi Hendrix, Eric Burdon, the Grateful Dead, Pretty Things, the Doors, Frank Zappa's Mothers of Invention, and the Fugs.[7]

Equally exciting, though in a different way, was the group the Cardinals. The Cardinals played covers of Rolling Stones hits—something that had not been possible while Antonin Novotný was in charge.

This period of excitement and experimentation was cut short by the August 1968 Soviet invasion of Czechoslovakia, which had a paralyzing effect on all of Czechoslovak society, including the rock scene. *Tribuna,* the cultural journal, sounded the theme of cultural "normalization" in writing, "We will cultivate, water, and protect only one flower, the red rose of Marxism."[8] "Normalization" did not produce its full effect immediately. On 22 and 23 December 1968, for example, the second beat festival was allowed to proceed, at Prague's Lucerna Hall. The festival featured some twenty domestic groups and three foreign groups and was preserved on a live recording for the Prague recording company Supraphon.

Later, however—particularly after Gustáv Husák became general secretary in April 1969—conditions for the arts deteriorated, and many musicians emigrated to the West. About this time, hippie culture reached Czechoslovakia. Czech hippies called themselves *manicky* (literally, little Marys—the Czech equivalent of the English word "hippies"). The police would apprehend them and, as they did with Knizak, take them in and give them haircuts. Beginning in January 1970, Prague officials closed the leading rock clubs in the city, including Arena, Slunicko, Olympik, Play Club, F Club, and others, and the Orfeus Club was converted into a venue for folk music and renamed the Rubin Club.

The communist regime, now headed by the dogmatic party secretary Gustáv Husák, decided on tough "corrective" measures. Bands were forbidden to take English names, sing the songs of British or American groups, or wear long hair or exotic attire. Government censors were assigned to approve repertoires, and bands that wouldn't cooperate were deprived of their professional licenses. Some rock musicians gave in and cooperated. Others, like L. Hajnis and J. Erno Sedivy, both of the Primitives, simply left the country. Other groups, such as the Rebels and the Framus Five, folded. Olympic survived but adopted a more pop-oriented sound, and many Czechoslovak fans felt the band had sold out. Many groups felt the weight of censorship so heavily that they stopped singing altogether and became purely instrumental groups.

In 1972, the government issued regulation no. 212 (valid until 1989), which mandated the reorganization of professional agencies to tighten the authorities' control of the rock scene. Henceforth, rock musicians who wanted to perform professionally had to pass a written exam on Marxism-Leninism: Among other things, they had to know the elements of the ideology, how the government was structured, the nature of the federal system, the organization of the federal assembly, the names of key officials in the communist party, and the organization and policy of the party's cultural apparatus. These exams were administered for all entertainment categories. At first, many rock musicians refused to take these exams and immediately lost their professional licenses. But rock musicians later came to accept the exam as a necessary evil and by the 1980s they all routinely took, and passed, the exam.[9] Between 1968 and 1974, more than 3,000 rock and jazz musicians were expelled from the artistic agencies to which they needed to belong to work profession-ally.[10]

The authorities went to comical lengths in the vain effort to calm their boundless (and humorless) paranoia. In 1970, for example, pop singer Karel Gott came out with the song "Hey, Councilman!" which playfully told of a confused and bedazzled young lover who petitioned local authorities for a bit of "heaven on earth." Party leader Husák did not consider it beneath the dignity of his office to lambast the song for supposedly fostering "irresponsible illusions" among the young. The song was attacked in the press and banned from radio broadcast. Later, Gott wrote another song about a troubled lover who was worried about the uncertain affections of the object of his desire. "I may as well flip a coin," Gott sang, "when I ask you if you're sincere when you say you love me." Gott ran into trouble again; the song was said to insult the value of Czechoslovak currency.[11]

Faced with Orwellian regulation, rock musicians reacted with defiance. In the early 1970s, a number of underground rock groups were formed, including DG 307 (named for a psychiatric disorder), Umela Hmota, Bile svetlo, the Hever, Vazelina, Extempore, and Stehlik, which now took their place alongside the previously established Plastic People of the Universe as muses of an alternative counterculture.[12] The mood of this period was aptly expressed by Umela Hmota in its song "Living Corpses":

We live in a strange world
our hearts squeezed by invisible pliers.

. . . .

The sun is pale
the rivers full of dirt.
Creeping terror
is taking hold of us.

Along the streets
the sky is scraped away by steel towers.
There
the living corpses crawl.
They don't look left
they don't look right
All the time they are rushing after something.

We're sorry for them
We're sick of them
We know we don't belong to them
at all.

Sometimes we feel like flying to the sky
Sometimes like burrowing into the bowels of the earth.
How naive and mad we are
in this atomic world.
We don't want to be here
and yet
here we are.[13]

These groups were often pleased to poke fun at self-important persons and institutions that expected others to pay homage to their "magnificence." Although the targets of these barbs were never spelled out—why should they be?—such songs made the authorities nervous. DG 307, in its song "Similarities," sang the following:

What are you like
in your magnificence?
Are you a touch of a star
or the remnants of bone?

What are you like
in your magnificence?

Are you a savior,
something special,
or a flame?

What are you like
in your magnificence?

Are you truth,
God,
or a ton of vanity?

What are you like
in your magnificence?

shit shit shit shit shit shit shit shit shit shit shit [14]

The Czech underground acquired some theoretical foundation through the writings of philosopher-poet Egon Bondy, many of whose texts came to serve as lyrics for the songs of diverse underground groups, and through Ivan Jirous, manager of Plastic People of the Universe, who in 1975 brought out a samizdat study of underground rock entitled *A Report on the Third Musical Revival.*

PLASTIC PEOPLE OF THE UNIVERSE

Of all the groups to which Czechoslovakia has given birth, only one can claim to have achieved worldwide acclaim—Plastic People of the Universe. Created soon after the Soviet invasion, the psychedelic Plastic People briefly enjoyed professional status until fall 1970, when the authorities withdrew its professional license. The long hair and extravagant attire of the members had as much to do with this turn in fortune as anything else. The band adjusted to the changed conditions and began to play underground. Two of its members—Premysl Stevich and Michal Jernek—now left the group, and Paul Wilson of Canada joined the group as a vocalist. Since the Plastic People wanted to sing in English, Wilson translated its texts into English.

In 1972, the group invited Vratislav Brabenec, a saxophonist, to join its ranks. Brabenec agreed on the condition that the band stop playing covers and play only its own material.[15] The members agreed, and now that they were no longer playing Western songs, they decided to reapply for professional status. They went before a jury composed of music critics and professional musicians, who restored the group's professional license. But the state booking agency overturned the jury's decision only two weeks later, offering, as an explanation, its opinion that the music of the Plastic People was "morbid."

In fact, the group's music was becoming "darker, more dissonant, and more convoluted."[16] Lyrics were culled from various sources, including the poems of William Blake (1757–1827), the song texts to the opera *Fairy Queen* by Henry Purcell (1659–1695), texts by Jiri Kolar (a Czech poet of the interwar era), and, above all, the poems of Egon Bondy. Bondy himself had once explained his philosophy in this way: "Once and for all, you have to stamp out the Christian-Pauline lies, that people don't piss and don't shit and don't fuck, and the great silence about these things."[17]

In the early 1970s, Plastic People of the Universe recorded a series of songs and smuggled the tapes out of the country to be compiled onto an LP. The result was a lavish album—*Egon Bondy's Happy Hearts Club Banned*, which came with the sixty-page booklet *The Merry Ghetto.* One of the texts included in the album is "February 1975," by Egon Bondy:

It's got nothing to do with us!
We belong to ourselves alone.
As long as there is no world revolution
but only piddling pseudo-marxism
it's got nothing to do with us!

Who cares about the masturbations of the fascist socialist states
of the Third World?
Who cares about Trotskyism gone snobbish?
It's got nothing to do with us.

Make young Gulag socialisms
establish yourselves as a social elite
make yourselves a phoney culture—
—it's got nothing to do with us.

. . . .

Fear of us breeds hatred of us
the hatred of the idiot for the normal person
the hatred of the fascist for culture
the hatred of the jailer for the jailed.[18]

Because the group lived in a society permeated by fear, fear was understandably a poignant theme for it. In its song "One Hundred Points," it sang of the fears of the authorities:

They are afraid of the old for their memory.
They are afraid of the young for their innocence.
They are afraid even of schoolchildren.
They are afraid of the dead …

They are afraid of workers.
They are afraid of party members.
They are afraid of those who are not in the party.
They are afraid of science.
They are afraid of art.
They are afraid of books and poems ...
They are afraid of typewriters ...
They are afraid of telephones.
They are afraid to let people out.
They are afraid to let people in ...
They are afraid of Santa Claus ...
They are afraid of archives ...
They are afraid of their families.
They are afraid of their relatives.
They are afraid of their former friends and comrades.
They are afraid of their present friends and comrades.
They are afraid of each other ...
They are afraid of jokes.
They are afraid of the upright.
They are afraid of the honest.
They are afraid of the educated.
They are afraid of the talented.
They are afraid of Marx.
They are afraid of Lenin ...
They are afraid of truth.
They are afraid of freedom.
They are afraid of democracy.
They are afraid of the Human Rights' Charter.
They are afraid of socialism.
So why the hell are WE afraid of THEM?[19]

On 21 February 1976, the Plastic People organized a large rock concert, together with several other rock bands, in the town of Bojanovice. Authorities took no immediate action, but a month later—on 17 March—security forces raided various apartments, arresting twenty-two persons, including the members of Plastic People, DG-307, Umela Hmota, Hever, and Vazelina. Most of those arrested were ultimately released. But four musicians were put on trial in September 1976: Ivan Jirous and Vratislav Brabenec of Plastic People, Pavel Zajicek of DG 307, and singer Svatopluk Karasek. The official indictment charged that "their texts contain extreme vulgarity with an anti-socialist and an anti-social impact, most of them extolling nihilism, decadence, and clericalism."[20] The defense did not try to refute the charge of vulgarity but

pointed instead to the hallowed position that vulgarity had always enjoyed in Czech culture, whether in the writings of theologian Jan
Comenius (1592–1670) or in *The Good Soldier Švajk* by Jaroslav Hasek.
The defense also cited Lenin's indulgence in occasional vulgarity, quoting in particular his 1922 observation, "Bureaucracy is shit."[21] The court,
however, found that the lyrics and concerts were "highly dangerous"
and sentenced the musicians to terms of eight to eighteen months in
prison.

The trial of the Plastic People attracted international attention. But
there was also trouble brewing at home. The Prague cultural underground was quite diverse, and, basically, anybody who was anybody
knew everybody. Among its friends was playwright Václav Havel (the
current president of the Czech Republic), whose works were banned by
the communist regime. Havel characterized the Plastic People simply, as
"unknown young people who wanted no more than to be able to live
within the truth."[22] As the trial got under way, friends of the Plastic
People met and talked. They decided to do something, to draw up a protest. The result was the drafting of a document that called on the regime
to respect the constitution and the law. This document, which was
made public on 6 January 1977 and bore 243 signatures, came to be
known as Charter 77.[23] After that, the ensemble was unable to play in
public. That did not prevent it from smuggling its tapes abroad (released
on three albums: *Passion Play, Leading Horses*, and *Midnight Mouse*) or
from building and maintaining its legendary status.

Finally, in 1988, bassist Milan Hlavsa sundered the old group and put
together a new ensemble, giving it the name Pulnoć (Midnight). Jirous
and drummer Jan Brabec refused to go along with what they viewed as a
compromise, but keyboardist Josef Janicek and guitarist Jiri Kabes
agreed to join Hlavsa, and they brought in four new musicians. Offering
a new, lighter musical fare, Pulnoć quickly obtained official accredita-
tion from the communists.[24] By April 1989, Pulnoć was touring New
York, San Francisco, and Seattle. But whatever its charms, Pulnoć could
not fill Plastic People's shoes.

THE LATE HUSÁK PERIOD

After the trial of Plastic People in September 1976, cultural policy entered into a dark period. Meanwhile, Czechoslovak rock began to experiment with new musical forms that dispensed with conventions in melody and rhythm. The new direction befuddled the authorities, and some
rock musicians ran into trouble only because their music was considered "too inventive and interesting."[25] A new punk scene developed,

giving birth to dozens of underground punk magazines and a string of punk rock bands such as Jasna paka (You Bet), Letadlo (Airplane), Zaba (Frog), Zluty pes (Yellow Dog), Elektrobus, Extempore, and Prazsky vyber (Prague Selection). These bands were able to find sponsors with local communist youth organizations and trade unions, where there were sympathetic persons. Patent, a popular punk band in the early 1980s, watched its political Ps and Qs but ignored decibel level regulations and wore torn clothing.

Toward the end of the 1970s, blues, jazz, and jazz-rock (fusion) took off in Czechoslovakia. Recording companies started putting out LPs of fusion and, albeit timidly, returned to producing LPs of mainstream rock. Groups such as Energit, Jazz Q, Bohemia, Combo FH, Prazsky Big Band, Katapult, and Prazsky vyber achieved fame at that time. For a while, thus, the bands seemed to have found a modus vivendi and to have worked out a solution. Then, on 23 March 1983, the Prague cultural paper *Tribuna* published a lengthy article signed by Jan Kryzl. The article savagely attacked rock music, claiming that Western "capitalists" and "subversive centers" were promoting punk rock to spread alienation among East European young people. Kryzl imagined that punk rock figured into some grand conspiratorial plan. In Kryzl's view of things, "Young people were to conform to the life which capitalism prepared for them. Be indifferent to the life around you, do not go with anyone and be against anything! Nothing has any meaning! This should become the creed of the young generation. The enforcement of this creed was, and is, to be aided by the so-called punk rock."[26]

This proved to be the clarion call for a renewed official campaign against rock: Dozens of rock bands (including Patent and Prazsky vyber) lost their licenses, and others had to change their names and reshape their repertoires. Blacklists were drawn up and distributed to local functionaries. On 11 June 1983, the authorities canceled a rock concert that was to have taken place at Zabrice, near Brno, so the fans (roughly a thousand) moved to a nearby park in Brno to sing songs, play soccer, and drink beer. Around 6 P.M., police arrived and started checking IDs. Someone objected and was arrested. The crowd then became upset and started to chant, "We want peace, we want freedom." The police replied with tear gas, attack dogs, and clubs.[27]

These were difficult times for rock groups, and only the very careful would survive. Olympic, which in its 1979 album, *Holiday on Earth*,[28] had explicitly pleaded for environmental concern, now had to treat its chosen themes more delicately. Its 1984 album, *Laboratory*,[29] took up the theme of mechanization and warned that work was transforming people into robots. In the song "Robots" on this album, the group sang,

Don't teach robots to play with a gun
Don't teach robots mental telepathy
Don't teach robots to eavesdrop
So they don't become like us.[30]

The harassment of punk musicians continued until 1986 when, under the influence of Gorbachev's liberalization in the USSR, Prague authorities adopted a softer line. In June 1986, in a remarkable token of change, Prague's House of Culture played host to sixty rock bands for a three-day gala music festival that became an annual event. Even *Rudé pravo* seemed to have mellowed, and in its reportage of the concert it commented that "with only two or three exceptions, the level of performance was truly good."[31]

The Socialist Youth Union followed, in December 1987, by organizing a rock concert for peace. However, there continued to be police actions against rock concerts (for example, in September 1987 in Trutnov). And when the satanic rock band Törr gave a concert in Bratislava in August 1988 at which fans waved their arms and shouted "Hej!" (Hey! or more idiomatically, Ya!),[32] the party paper *Rudé pravo* provided a report of the concert. But in *Rudé pravo*'s account, the fans were described as thrusting clenched fists into the air and shouting "Heil! Heil! Heil!" *Rudé pravo* also characterized the band as "long-haired fanatics leaping around to the deranged noise of vibrating loudspeakers."[33]

All the same, by the closing years of the Husák era there were prominent voices calling for a change of policy. In an interview with *Mlada Fronta* in 1986, Josef Trnka, director of the Institute for Cultural and Educational Activities, described the past policy toward rock music as "an administrative path solving nothing." Trnka criticized authorities for their delay in responding "to the great interest of young people in this type of music." And he called for authorities to treat the subject more seriously and more *competently.*[34]

Even before Husák was finally retired in December 1988, performance and recording possibilities for rock musicians expanded dramatically. But if the communist apparatus seemed to be liberalizing somewhat, it was, all the same, still fundamentally intact. The state-controlled professional agencies maintained their control of the entertainment industry. Aspiring rock musicians were still required to take "qualifying exams" in Marxism-Leninism. And the state thought in terms of prophylactic measures to prevent rock from getting "out of control" as it had in the 1970s. The state therefore strove to identify "inconvenient" developments in music at their inception and to snuff them out then and there before they could take hold or do any damage. Approved groups would be rewarded. In an ironic twist, one of the new groups that won the state's favor at the close of the communist era and was even given permission to tour the United States (in spring 1989) was the rock group Pulnoć (Midnight), which was composed, in part, of some former members of Plastic People but which took a more accommodating stance toward the communist culture apparatus than the old Plastic People ever did.

The Husák regime did not get very far with its new line on rock music. By the end of 1987, Husák had been booted upstairs to a ceremonial post, and Miloš Jakeš had been installed as general secretary of the party. Two years later, the communists fell from power altogether and a new democratic government took office.

TOWARD THE VELVET REVOLUTION

One of the most interesting rock groups of the early 1980s in both musical and lyrical terms had been the Prague hard rock group Prazsky vyber. Its two leading musicians were Michal Kocab and Michal Pavlíček. The latter established his own group, Stromboli, in 1985 as a purely instrumental group, naming the group after an Italian volcanic island off the coast of Sicily. In 1986, the regime caved in to strong pressure from rock fans and allowed Prazsky vyber to regroup. As before, Kocab led the band, which Pavlíček now also joined. The coexistence of these two groups was a source of personal tension between Kocab and Pavlíček, and eventually, in 1990, Pavlíček agreed to disband Stromboli.

In June 1988 and March and April 1989, Stromboli had recorded its last album, *Shutdown*. The album included the politically daring and implicitly prophetic song "Back in the Castle" (a reference to Prague's Presidential Palace, which Czechs commonly call "the Castle" much in the way that Americans refer to the White House). Set against a recurrent rhythm, the song addresses the themes of regime lies and political conformity, swinging between despair ("What's the use?") and blind hope ("Hope against hope") and making it clear in numerous ways that the barbs are directed at communist rule:

Do you cherish proper wishes?
Do you carry proper cards?
Do you play the proper music?
Back in the Castle
Going forward
Do you take a proper stand?
Do you read the daily papers?
Do you make the proper faces?

Do you fully understand?
Do you sing [what you're supposed to]?
Caught in the back
Take my hand
Hold me tight and we shall fall in stride.
Welcome back
Take my hand
Hold me tight and we shall fall in stride.
Back in the Castle,
Made of concrete
Back in the Castle,
Made of rotten promises
Back in the Castle,
Made of fruitless successes
Back in the Castle
Made of better humans
One two, hope against hope
Back in the Castle
You will fall inside
What's the use?
Hoping against hope
Back in the Castle
You will fall inside
Back in the Castle.[35]

With the collapse of communism in late 1989, the cultural sphere, including rock, was freed from political controls. Although this was welcomed by rock musicians, the depoliticization of rock was accompanied by a general drift, on the part of the public, away from cultural events, especially music. People were enjoying new freedoms and possibilities and no longer needed rock groups to serve as prophets and mouthpieces of discontent. The worsening economic picture no doubt also contributed to a decline in ticket sales for rock concerts after 1989.

However, the recording industry has quickly been privatized, with the establishment of a number of new recording companies, such as Multisonic, Monitor, Tommü (created in 1990), Globus, and Orion. Supraphon, known for its productions of the Czech Philharmonic, is also trying to break into rock music. By early 1991, there were about seventy recording companies in Czechoslovakia (not all of them dealing with rock music). Tommü is the best label for rock music, chiefly because it is the most effective company where marketing is concerned. As a result, Tommü has sold about 250,000 copies of each album it has produced, in a country where a typical rock album sells 40,000 to 100,000 copies. One of the best-selling groups was Elan, which sold 750,000 copies of a 1984 album. During 1990, about fifty rock records from domestic groups were produced. Distribution has become a difficult problem for record companies, however, and the costs of effective distribution and promotion have been prohibitive for most companies. Sales of American and British rock records are limited, because they cost three to four times as much as domestic rock albums.

Television stations have expressed interest in producing music shows, but the substantial cut in government subsidies to Czechoslovak television had, in and of itself, a dramatic impact on programming possibilities. In early 1991, Czechoslovak TV began broadcasting "Top 20," giving play to Czechoslovakia's most commercially successful bands. Czechoslovak television also began broadcasting Music Television (MTV) in early 1990, shortly after the Velvet Revolution, and so far no domestic producer either in the Czech Republic or in Slovakia has been able to provide the capital sufficient to match MTV in quality. The Slovak monthly program "Triangel" presently gives the best television coverage (of either republic) to domestic rock; the Slovak program "Rhythmic" plays Western rock videos. The most popular rock show on radio is called "Gung-Ho." It comes on the air only one hour per week and plays both domestic and foreign rock.

At present there are no rock magazines in either the Czech Republic or Slovakia, although the youth magazine *Mlady svet* devotes some of its attention to rock music and also publishes a regular rating of the top rock and pop groups. The music magazines *Melodie* and *Rock 'n' Pop* also devote a considerable part of their contents to the rock scene.

After the revolution, the Czech and Slovak rock scenes, which had always been distinct, drifted further apart. They presently function more or less independently of each other. With the decision, by the respective prime ministers of the two republics in summer 1992, to split the country in two, the Czech and Slovak rock scenes appear likely to become even more isolated from each other. Prague has obviously been the rock capital of Czechoslovakia, and it is also, more particularly, the heart of the Czech rock scene. Ostrava, in Moravia, is actually a more important center for rock music than Bratislava, and most foreign rock groups (e.g., Deep Purple in January 1991) perform in Ostrava if anywhere. Brno also has a visible rock scene. The most important center for Slovak rock is of course Bratislava. Aside from the punk scene in Teplice, there are no other cities in either of the two republics with any particular rock presence. Other cities do not have the financial wherewithal and entertainment infrastructure to support lively rock scenes.

On 5 January 1991, a nostalgia rock concert was held in Lucerna Hall in Prague, bringing together many of the best rock bands from the period prior to 1970. Many of these musicians had since moved to other countries. Among these were the members of the Primitives, who reassembled from dispersion across the Netherlands, Denmark, and other countries. Komety, Blue Effect, and Flamingo were among other old groups on the program.

The top Czech new wave rock groups as of 1991 were Zentour, Lucie, Kreyson, Kern, and Nova ruze. All of these groups have released albums, Kreyson having done so in cooperation with a Western recording company. The top Slovak new wave groups are Metalinda, Tublatanka, Team, and Elan. The top Czech heavy metal rock groups are Arakain, Vitacit (literally, Lemonade, releasing its first album in 1990 after twelve years in rather mutable existence), Törr, and Motorband. There were no professional heavy metal bands in Slovakia as of 1991. Two all-female rock groups also deserve mention: Loretta and Lochness.[36] Loretta plays soft rock, whereas Lochness prefers heavy metal in the style of Slayer.

Czechoslovakia did not absorb all available rock currents. There is, for example, no rockabilly to be found in either republic; nor is fusion popular. But punk has had a presence since the early 1980s, centered in Prague and Teplice. The latter city has long had one of the worst environmental problems in the country, and punk seemed to respond to the disgust of the young for communist policy. There is also a strong punk movement in Slovakia. Satanic rock is represented chiefly by Törr (in Prague) and Root (in Brno). There are also bands playing various stripes of metal, including trash metal and death metal. Rock music now functions under politically "normal" conditions, without the macabre interference by the authorities in questions of haircuts, attire, lyrics, and so forth—forms of censorship and control more appropriate to a military institution than to musical entertainment. Czech and Slovak rock music should, under these circumstances, experience a revival and with time be put on normal commercial footing.

CONCLUSION

As in the other countries surveyed in this book, communist rule in Czechoslovakia narrowed organizational and ideological options to one monochromatic alternative. Underground culture thus became a vital channel through which alternative ideas could be nourished and expressed. In conditions of ideological monopoly, the protest song has much greater weight: It conveys courage, honesty, and the determination to struggle. In this way, forty years of communism left a deep impression on rock music. A 1973 song by Plastic People of the Universe captures some of the weight of protest in such conditions:

Bring your kilogram of paranoia into balance!
Throw off the horrible dictatorship!
Quickly! Live, drink, puke!
The bottle, the Beat!
Shit in your hand![37]

NOTES

I could not have written this chapter without the assistance of one of Czechoslovakia's top rock musicians, who graciously provided considerable material and information for this chapter, and of a graduate student of Czech descent studying at the University of Washington. Both of them requested anonymity.

1. Their meeting took place on 21 January 1990.

2. Quoted in the *Christian Science Monitor,* 19 November 1987, p. 25.

3. A useful treatment of the early years of Czechoslovak rock can be found in Ondrej Konrad and Vojtech Lindaur, "Zivot v tahu aneb tricet roku rocku" (1990, typescript).

4. Timothy W. Ryback, *Rock Around the Bloc: A History of Rock Music in Eastern Europe and the Soviet Union* (New York: Oxford University Press, 1990), p. 59.

5. Quoted in ibid., p. 58.

6. "Pop im Prager Untergrund. Brief eines Fans," translated from Czech into German by Lida Rakusan, in *Kontinent* (1976: special issue), p. 98.

7. Ibid., p. 95; and Ryback, *Rock Around the Bloc,* pp. 76–77.

8. Quoted in Ryback, *Rock Around the Bloc,* p. 141.

9. Interview with a Czech rock musician visiting the United States, Seattle, 11 June 1991.

10. Czechoslovak Situation Report, *Radio Free Europe Research,* 7 December 1988, p. 19.

11. These anecdotes about Gott are recounted in Ryback, *Rock Around the Bloc,* p. 142.

12. "Tschechische Rockmusik als Seismograph für gesellschaftliche Alternativen," in *Osteuropa* 35, nos. 7–8 (July–August 1985), p. A400; and Czechoslovak Situation Report, p. 19.

13. English text provided as part of the "Merry Ghetto" booklet that accompanied the Plastic People of the Universe's album *Egon Bondy's Happy Hearts' Club Banned.*

14. Ibid.

15. *New York Times,* 24 April 1989, p. 15.

16. Ibid.

17. Quoted in "Pop im Prager Untergrund," p. 100.

18. English text provided as part of the "Merry Ghetto" booklet.

19. Lyrics from "One Hundred Points," by the Plastic People of the Universe, as given in *Across Frontiers* (Spring 1986).

20. Quoted in Ryback, *Rock Around the Bloc,* p. 147.

21. Quoted in Ibid.

22. Quoted in the *Christian Science Monitor,* 10 August 1987, p. 20.

23. Janusz Bugajski, *Czechoslovakia: Charter 77's* Decade of Dissent, Washington Papers no. 125 (New York: Praeger, 1987), pp. 10–11.

24. *Christian Science Monitor,* 11 May 1989, p. 11.

25. *Gegenstimmen* (Vienna), Winter 1983, pp. 2–6, translated in JPRS, *East Europe Report,* no. EPS-84-023 (10 February 1984), p. 2.

26. *Tribuna* (Prague), 23 March 1983, p. 5, translated in JPRS, *East Europe Report,* no. 83438 (10 May 1983), p. 22.

27. Ryback, *Rock Around the Bloc,* p. 201.

28. Olympic, *Prazdiny na zemi* (1979), recording data not available.

29. Olympic, *Laborator* (1984), recording data not available.

30. Translated from Czech by Paul Perich.

31. *Rudé pravo,* 3 July 1986, p. 5, translated in JPRS, *East Europe Report,* no. EER-86-127 (19 August 1986), p. 104.

32. Interview with a Czech rock musician visiting the United States, Seattle, 11 June 1991.

33. *Rudé pravo,* 30 August 1988, p. 5, translated in FBIS, *Daily Report* (Eastern Europe), 7 September 1988, p. 6.

34. *Mlada Fronta* (22 July 1986), p. 4, as excerpted in Czechoslovak Situation Report, *Radio Free Europe Research,* 5 September 1986, p. 17.

35. Stromboli, *Shutdown* (Panton 81-0811-1311, 1989), recorded and mixed at the Smetana Theatre Studio and Hrncire Studio in June 1988 and March–April 1989; lyrics sung in English.

36. List derived, in part, from *Mlady svet* (Prague), 3–7 January 1991, p. 8.

37. Quoted in Ryback, *Rock Around the Bloc,* p. 129.

"How Can I Be a Human Being?" Culture, Youth, and Musical Opposition in Hungary

E AST EUROPEAN societies of the 1980s have often been described as beset by political turmoil, cultural ferment, and economic crises. This characterization is perhaps nowhere better demonstrated than in the emergence of alternative youth and rock music cultures in East Germany, Poland, Czechoslovakia, Hungary, Yugoslavia, and the Soviet Union.[1] For, unlike its mainstream popular counterpart, the new rock music scene has been inextricably bound up with politics.[2]

In this chapter I explore two contentions with regard to the dynamic interplay between this music and the ideological contexts in which it is both created and consumed: first, that the emergence of an oppositional musical culture helped paved the way for the East European revolutions of 1989 in general and that of Hungary in particular, and second, that the alternative music was a vital component in redefining the nature of the music industry and the political structure it served. I focus this discussion on the musical scene in Hungary since the late 1970s and early 1980s.[3]

STATE AND MUSIC

Let me first clarify what is meant by "new political music." In his essay *Musica Practica*, Roland Barthes states that "there are two musics (at least so I have always thought): the music one listens to, the music one plays."[4] Although Barthes's concept may be applied to the wider experience of listening to music, it will require modification to account more completely for the specifically political context of state socialism. Given the nature of the music industry for thirty years in Eastern Europe—the state as sole agent of bands and singers and sole producer and distributor of concerts and records—Barthes's proposition needs to be changed slightly. There were in fact two kinds of music: state-controlled (the music one is meant to listen to and play) and antistate (the music one is forbidden to listen to or play—"unofficial music," as Sabrina Ramet has called it).[5]

In other words, in Eastern Europe, all show business of the musical sort was intended to be state business. Whereas mainstream popular music and popular culture played an essential role in securing the political legitimation of the government, the alternative new music served another function—that of questioning the very existence and operations of the state while simultaneously providing a vehicle for critical expression by the subculture.[6] These two kinds of musical expressions, furthermore, represented different and opposing interests. Popular music under statism operated by appropriating elements sanctioned by the state and transforming them into a commodity to support the ruling party's hegemony. Anything antithetical to such a goal either lacked governmental support or, in certain cases, was suppressed entirely.

As argued by various Western theorists of the counterculture, anarchic music, or "rough music," is seen as expressing the voices of the masses.[7] In the case of Hungary during much of the 1970s and 1980s, "rough music" was the culture's unofficial music. The new political music that emerged in the late 1970s and early 1980s represented the voices of those unable to identify with the aims of the communist state leadership. To fully understand and appreciate its power, we must place it in its proper context, in the perspective of what preceded and what followed its flowering. As in other East European countries, the state-controlled music industry in Hungary provided no outlet for the music of the generations coming of age. It allowed and promoted only those bands and singers that adapted themselves to the political structure and conformed to the standards of ossified popular music. Quite the contrary, this music expressed attitudes critical of the state and its legitimate culture: antiparty, antistate, antipolice, and antibureaucratic themes lay at its heart. The popular Hungarian group Hobo Blues Band, for instance, implicitly indicted the state leadership by asking in one of its characteristic songs: "What have you done to this earth?"

THE OLD AND THE NEW

For almost two decades, Hungarian rock music, with few exceptions, was a plagiarized version of fashionable Western European popular music, copied relentlessly. Since the early 1960s, only the "Big Four" bands achieved national acclaim—Illés, Omega, Metro, and Locomotiv GT.[8] Eccentric though they may have been, these bands nevertheless represented a generation less dissatisfied and radical than that of the 1980s. Although there were typical problems such as fighting, drunkenness, and vandalism during their concerts, none of these bands exemplified the youthful restlessness of the early 1980s. Not only did they represent the establishment, but they also embodied it.[9]

Their songs and texts spoke in a neutral voice and utilized stereotypes typical of Hungary's "light-music" industry (the Hungarian term is *könnyűzene*, as opposed to *komolyzene*, which refers to "serious music," including compositions from Bach to Bartok).[10] The following examples from the early 1970s are telling:

Omega
There was a girl,
Whose hair was pearl
Was it really true, or
Did I only dream about her?

Illés
Sarah's a silly girl,
Her heart's open for me
I said: I can't live alone
But she doesn't listen to me.

Omega
When we sing, the world is different,
Freddie, the trumpeter came to sing,
He's like he always used to be,
Hey, you sleepyheads, wake up,
Freddie is here.

Illés
There never was and never will be, Rock and Roll without him,
On black shiny records, Little Richard sings for me.

Locomotiv GT
I'm shivering, I'm afraid, The trees are shaking:
Where are all the silver trees, The silver summers?

The decade between the mid-1960s and the late 1970s may be characterized, in the singer-songwriter János Bródy's phrase, as lukewarm. During that period, Hungarian pop music offered uncontroversial texts and images (boy loves girl, girl leaves boy, much homework and bad grades, party on Saturday night), which coalesced to form the stereotypes of "socio-pop," a distinct configuration of Euro-pop.[11] A comparison of the songs produced by the Big Four and of those by lesser-known counterparts in the 1960s and 1970s yields the same characteristics. The portrayal of love relations between men and women, often set in a "syrupy and mellow-tuned milieu" that was questioned by the singer *himself,* was perhaps the quintessential feature of early pop music. Although this overt romanticism was a recurring formula, even in the more rebellious and often scandalous heavy metal and folk genres, its resemblance to everyday life in Hungary was negligible. Yet on records and in concert, the music of the Big Four and its cohorts reinforced these stereotypes of the establishment.

Pop music stars dominated most major forms of media, including recordings by Hungaroton (the Hungarian version of the Soviet Melodiya or the Yugoslav Jugoton), concert tours arranged by the ORI (National Management Bureau) or the IRI (Youth Management Bureau), and radio and TV programs, representing Hungary at international festivals.[12] These institutions of state-supported pop music were indispensable to any group attempting to maintain professional status.[13] However, in the mid-1970s the Hungarian popular music industry faced three massive crises: (1) the impact of emerging Western youth subcultures and their music, as signaled by such new genres as skag, reggae, punk, rap, and heavy metal; (2) the instigation of technological advances that revolutionized the music industry, including the advent of music video; and (3) the decline of disco in the West and, ultimately, in Hungary as well. These changes paralleled wider social and economic developments taking place in the country. A maturing generation faced growing inflation, the difficulty of obtaining secure employment, inadequate housing, and other socioeconomic problems.[14] According to Dénes Csengey, a whole generation stood at the door, presenting itself and demanding its well-deserved place in society.[15]

In contrast to the 1960s, during which Hungary remained unshaken by social upheavals comparable to the 1968 events in France or Prague, by the late 1970s a new, more expressive generation was in the making. A large segment of the maturing generation associated itself with the re-emerging populist movement, the *táncház,* which was a folkloristic revival movement aimed at teaching peasant folk music and dance to a generation that lacked such traditions.[16] Another segment supported the new music that emerged from the troubled years after the "economic miracle" of the 1968 reforms. It is tempting to speculate whether the formation of this new generation and its radical *Weltanschauung* might have taken place had the economic and political processes of liberalization and democratization of the mid-1980s been introduced.

Yet as it happened, the late 1970s unleashed social and cultural conflicts that had lain dormant in the 1960s, intensifying the spontaneity and aggression of the new generation. Fonograf, the popular band from the late 1970s that was led by Hungary's outspoken singer-songwriter János Bródy, put it this way:

In 1958 we danced the rock and roll,
In 1968 we waited for a new roll,
In 1978 we can't find anyone waiting
And say, What will happen in 1988?

The state-run music business acknowledged the nature of the emerging crisis by resorting somewhat desperately to the rejuvenation of old stars and the reinvention of new ones. It is perhaps no accident that the late 1970s were marked by the particular resurgence of the "nostalgic wave," a music genre associated with singers of the 1960s and even those of the presocialist time. By 1980, the traditional chanson, American country, folk-rock, heavy metal, dixie, and rhythm and blues became big business for the state recording studio. Although the pop music industry created new faces such as the bands Kft, Dolly Roll, R-Go, and New Hungaria and the heavy metal bands Edda Works, P. Mobil, P. Box, VM Band, Piramis, and several vocalists, these bands and singers were nonetheless fashioned after West European pop music patterns and styles.[17]

THE POLITICAL ECONOMY OF THE NEW MUSIC

Contrary to state-supported popular music, the emerging new political music drew its source material from social malaise and its contradictions, from the family, and from the political system. For many, the new music was represented first and foremost by the bands appearing in the late 1970s such as the Vágtázó Halottkémek (Galloping Morticians, or, as abbreviated in Hungarian, VHK), the Spions (Spies), Albert Einstein Bizottsag (Albert Einstein Committee), Európa Kiadó (European Publishers), URH (Ultra Rock New Agency or Ultra Radical Wave), Kontroll Csoport (Control Group), Balaton, Trabant, the radical wing CPG (Coitus Punk Group), Mos-oi (Smile), ETA (the name of the Basque separatist group), T-34 (serial number of a Russian tank).[18] The emergence and success of these groups captured the pivotal spirit of the late 1970s and early 1980s and the convergence of the new music's aesthetic and ideological underpinnings.

The concerts in 1976 by the Spions and in 1978 by the Galloping Morticians were the first attempts "to come out of the closet" by Hungarian bands representing the new music.[19] Official reaction, however, was immediate and devastating: Spions was disbanded, and its leader, Gergely Molnar, opted for defection to the West rather than face harsh consequences. Members of the Galloping Morticians were branded as "bourgeois" and "decadent" punk rockers and, consequently, the band was temporarily forced into a marginal existence.

The shock of the new music that followed helped to strip Hungarian society of many obsolescent institutions and redundant ideas—remnants of 1950s Stalinism—and allowed popular masses of youth to think the unthinkable. Whereas most pop music protagonists lacked a sense of strategy for serious criticism of the János Kádár government, the new music dared to express its generation's feelings of alienation. At a 1978 concert, Attila Grandpierre, the lead singer of the Galloping Morticians, announced to his audience: "We are not here to entertain you. Don't even think that you'll be having a good time at this concert. If you want to have a good time, get lost. Go home and watch TV. Now you'll have something different." Later, in a candid interview, he expressed his views on alienation: "Just because I'm long and my color is pink and because I have these long and hanging extremities attached to my body, I shouldn't sit home all day watching TV, producing nothing but brain fat. What reasons do I have to feel happy and satisfied at the present?"[20]

In 1980, a concert aptly titled "Black Sheep" opened a new chapter in the history of music in Hungary, coinciding with the coming of age of a generation, the collapse of the economic miracle of 1968, and the general effervescence of sociopolitical change. These events signaled the rebirth of a radical antistate movement in the heartland of statism. At a semi-illegal (unapproved) concert in the rural city of Debrecen in 1981, a local band mocked the state-controlled media by smashing a television set to smithereens while the audience looked on, awestruck. Another singer threw stinking cheese at the spectators, yelling, "Is this what you want? Is this what you work for?"[21] At a 1982 concert in the School of Economics, the minimalist group Neoprimitiv, composed of university students, sang its famous "Condomfields," set to the tune of the popular American song "Cotton Fields":

And during my drunken nights I dream of the Stone Age
When there are no consumer goods, and no money,
In the Neanderthal Valley everything is so good.

One of the many problems musicians confronted was the ubiquitous relationship between rock music and political structure. The first attempts of the Spions and the Galloping Morticians attacked not only the state of the music industry in Hungary but also the very internal political structure that had for so long suppressed genuine musical experiments. The Spions song "Anna Frank" surpassed all boundaries commonly respected by artists with its overt racist-sexist and fascist message:

> *A little forced intercourse / before they come and take you away. / Anna Frank! / Make love to me! / Anna Frank! / Cry, you bitch! / Anna Frank! / Otherwise I'll give you up! / Anna Frank—the boys are waiting for you!*

A song by the Galloping Morticians, written in 1980, expressed the confinement forced upon musical life by politics:

> *Before you / there's the artificial life, / the sterile madness sizzles / but you don't see it / because you live an artifical life here, / this life is only enough / to strangle you. What we are saying / might even sound artificial / because we are forced to speak artificially.*

Later, the song rejects this world in its repeated chanting:

> *Other world ... nether world ... neither world.*

The band Galloping Morticians, with its nihilistic visions, was a rare phenomenon in an age influenced by mainstream pop music and limited to mild symbolic criticism.

The years 1981 and 1982 may be seen as a turning point in many respects, for Hungarians experienced the pressures of growing inflation, trade deficits, international debt, and external economic shocks. Agricultural and consumer prices accelerated in their downward slide and affected Hungarian export earnings.[22] Budapest sought various means of liberalizing a tight, centrally controlled economy in a half-hearted attempt of the Kádárist elite following the death of Leonid Brezhnev and the collapse of the Brezhnev doctrine.[23] A new system of management (elected company councils) together with various forms of second or informal economies, as well as private businesses, were legalized.[24] Hungary's socioeconomic foundation was once again under direct attack, just as in the late 1960s, when the New Economic Mechanism was implemented. One of the most striking features of the early 1980s was the relative well-being of the population, with its expanded spending on leisure activities. Publications and magazines multiplied, Western consumer goods flooded the country, private businesses thrived, rural entrepreneurs benefited from the new policies, and travel to the West increased.[25] Yet, these developments notwithstanding, one could not help noting the edge of hostility that defined this new, politically charged musical subculture. The reason for this, I believe, is twofold: Excluded from thriving private businesses, informal economies, and decisionmaking positions, and aware of the growing gap between themselves and the establishment, young people in Hungary realized full well that they were not the beneficiaries of these changes.[26]

The second aspect of this generational conflict was based on the oligarchic, bureaucratic nature of industrial organization. An authoritarian system based on a local party leadership that exercised monopolistic power over young workers—the apparatchik system so eloquently described by Miklós Haraszti and Elemér Hankiss among others—had become the norm after the 1970s.[27] This apparatchik ideology (or *kaderpolitika,* in the Hungarian expression) was such a powerful system of control that even with the introduction of semidemocratic informal economies after 1982, both white-collar and blue-collar youth were totally at the mercy of these bureaucrats. Pay raises, vacations, housing and bank-loan applications, job advancement, and a host of other possibilities that were needed to cope with the changing political economy were beyond their reach without the blessing of these cadres. This system was by no means defunct in the mid-1980s, when it became more subtle; thus competition among young workers for these benefits became more acute. The Hobo Blues Band song "Let's Drink to the New Gods" became an ironic slogan, epitomizing its criticism of these changes.

These and other events inaugurated a period of intense social struggle and acute political crises in the early 1980s, rendering palpable both the reality and potential of a new generational conflict. Together with new democratic and antistate movements emerged an articulate intellectual opposition and voice of democratic dissent. Following upon this sociocultural ferment, new bands, many with outrageous names (mostly Hungarian) and songs, appeared on the scene and demanded attention. As these bands performed in illegal or semilegal concerts, they produced illegal cassettes, attracting new followers on a daily basis. Gatherings at concerts were occasions for revelry that fostered generational alliances, but screams and curses also made their mark.

The resurgence of the radical new music in 1982, represented by the groups CPG, T-34, Mos-oi, and ETA, emphasized the depiction of a world fraught with difficulty, injustice, and corruption, peopled by rotten bureaucrats, feeble-minded policemen, and others "who don't care" and "who don't count." In short, in this music the totalitarian state—in the true Orwellian sense—became a reality in Eastern Europe. In a song using a Russian folk melody, the CPG members screamed:

> *You dirty, rotten communist gang,*
> *How come you aren't hanged yet,*
> *Hey hey on the meadow.*

And ETA went a step further in describing the fragile international climate:

You are white or you are red,
The streets are flooded with blood,
American or Russkie,
A total asshole anarchy.

The group T-34 took its critique to a yet higher plane:

They demand and want equality—the jerks!
All they do is yap all day, they feed on canned food,
Horse's prick to them, this is a senile gang,
I'll flush the toilet and the magic is over.

During a long musical number recorded at an unofficial concert in early 1983, T-34 indulged in incessant screaming and noisemaking, elements traditionally associated with rebellion, masked demonstrations, and anti-establishment protest.[28] Another group, Falatrax (Wall Builder), performed to a deafening din of scratching, hammering, and other nonmusical sounds that were antithetical to mainstream popular music aesthetics.

The songs of CPG, ETA, and Mos-oi subverted the cultural and ideological superstructure that had become indispensable to the maintenance and legitimization of power of the Kádárist single-party state. The lyrics of these groups, and to a lesser degree those of the less alienated groups such as Európa Kiadó, Trabant, and Sziami-Sziami (Siamese-Siamese), were angry and self-righteous. Alternately ecstatic and disillusioned, they were unabashedly pornographic and anarchist in their articulation of suppressed desire. But most important—and most threatening—was their unmitigated denial of the old and their assertion of the new. Their relentless, ruthless repudiation of official pop music culture, their spontaneous and determined new voice, made these bands outright radicals, and they were feared critics of the political hierarchy.

The group Kontroll Csoport sang of the devaluation of human life in the existing system:

This species is dead already
This kind of man is no more,
Evolution has caught up with you
But I want to be different,
You can't change me!
Control, control, control.[29]

To them this world was one where

All the jails are full,
The cemetery is full,

Even the insane asylum is full,
People's heads are totally full.

What they saw was a new generation in the wrong place at the wrong time, a notion made explicit in the song of the URH:

I'll count to ten and then I'll die,
Or freeze or at an institute I'll fry,
Too much talk and not enough action,
You are here too soon, we'll bury you, bye-bye
Idle tales, and not enough percussion, Bye!

The value systems of these bands were not grounded in a happy world of careless love and a bright future usually associated with youthful exuberance (and noticeable in the texts of the 1960s and 1970s). Instead, their words and performances addressed a real, unglamorized world in all its complexity. Kontroll Csoport sang:

I hate to work, I hate the policemen,
I love to work, I love the policemen.

The URH put it thus:

It's a very very hard world,
Too many cops, too many informers,
Not enough pimps, not enough whores,
Not enough cops, not enough informers,
Too many pimps, too many whores.

No other Hungarian music groups represented such intense criticism more insistently than ETA, CPG, and Mos-oi. Members of CPG openly attacked the socialist state and its leader, János Kádár, for creating the situation in which they found themselves:

We have a puppet for a king,
His legs and arms jerk on a string,
We're the people, we bow and scrape,
We're really humble.

In ETA's famous song "The International Situation Escalates," the group described the world, past and present, as a power struggle from the nationalistic viewpoint of East Central European youth:

Yankee, Yankee, so what? Russkie, Russkie, so what?
Persian, Persian, so what? German, German, so what?
English, English, so what? Basques, Basques, so what?
Polish, Polish, so poor? Romanian, Romanian, horse's cock.
Reagan, Reagan, so what? Dzhugashvili, so what?

Khomeini, so what? Hitler, Hitler, so what?
Churchill, Churchill, so what? USA so good!
Bow, wow, ETA. Ceauşescu, a dog!
An A-bomb, so what? One A-bomb, not enough?
Our clothing, not enough, our cock not enough,
Our freedom, not enough, even the food's not enough.
The Magyar word, not enough,
Newspapers, TV, not enough, power not enough.
Courage, not enough, self-distraction, not enough.
We'll start, we'll live, don't worry,
Even if this song's not enough, painfully,
Believe me, you'll be living in your own Hungary!

In 1982, after martial law was declared in Poland, Kontroll Csoport created a song recalling the popular rhyme espousing Hungarian-Polish historical friendship:

Tak, tak, tak. Gdańsk! Gdańsk!
Polak wenger dwa bratanki,
I dosabli, i dosklani.[30]

The group Trabant (originally the name of the much-maligned East German passenger car) mocked the state in its 1984 parody of socialist holidays:

January 1, April 4, Easter and May Day, half a year is gone,
August 20, November 7, Christmas and New Year,
And now the whole year is done.[31]

The band Neurotic focused on the alienation and hopelessness of Hungarian youth in the following song:

I'm a zero, one is my name,
Don't know much math, to me all's the same,
Sometimes they kick me, sometimes they kiss me,
Sometimes they show me off, sometimes they hide me,
What's left for me are a few more years,
The left-overs, but I take my share,
What I am I learned well: zero, zero, zero.
Your future is a page in a yearbook,
From my lot a cornerhouse, that's all I took,
I ate, I drank, I fucked,
In vain weird music I plucked.

The lyrics of Dr. Ujhajnal (Dr. Newdawn), a group formed in 1985, leave little doubt of their targets:

Animals were made into humans because of work,
Monday, Tuesday, Wednesday, Thursday, Friday,
I worked like a dog,
The whole damn week I worked like an animal,
How can I be a human being?

In general, Hungarian bands and musicians of the political music of the 1980s singled out the state for interrogation, attack, and criticism. This focus was evident in extremist groups exhibiting neo-Nazi tendencies such as ETA, Mos-oi, and CPG and equally so for such borderline groups as Európa Kiadó, AE Bizottsag, Kontroll Csoport, and Sziami Sziami. These bands were preoccupied with the meaning of words and the critical weight of their texts. For them, the communist party (the Hungarian MSZMP, reorganized in 1989 as a miniscule Hungarian Socialist Party, or MSZP) was more than simply a political organization: It penetrated the very core of private and social life in Hungarian society. These groups lamented the lawlessness and amorality of the most important tool of the state, the police; CPG, for example, bemoaned its oppressive power:

The Soviet atom is also an atom,
I can't stand this totalitarianism,
The police is always hassling me,
We have SS-20s in the East,
They have the neutron bomb in the West,
SS-20, SS-20, SS-20 in the East
In the East and in the West,
The almighty power is the test.

And when Mos-oi sang "I serve the working people," the group expressed anger toward the "police-state mentality" evident in certain bureaucratic circles:

I'm a good guy, but nobody likes me,
With my billy club I won't leave marks on your kidney,
You are a friend only that much I know,
This way I serve the working people.

For its part, CPG went so far as to name the chief manager of the Hungarian state recording company, thereby attacking personally Peter Erdos, one of the most powerful men in the state hierarchy:

I'd like to rip your ears off,
I'd like to poke your eyes out,

I'd like to tear your guts out,
I'd like to bash your head in,
Peter Erdos, you son of a bitch!

No other Hungarian group of the new music era, however, carried its messages to such extremes as Mos-oi. Its openness and simplicity and emphasis on the skinhead subculture—as exhibited in its (in)famous "Skinhead Marching Song," its rough music, and the "oi" of its name in reference to the well-known scream of the international punk scene—soon found devoted supporters among blue-collar vocational students, nationalists, and disenchanted intellectuals.[32] In the "Immigrants' Share" the musicians sang:

We'll get rid of everyone whom we don't need,
Including the garbage immigrants.
The immigrants' share can only be death,
We'll have to chase away all of the blacks,
For the Arabs—to be sure—machine-guns are waiting,
Over Palestine atomic clouds are gathering.

This racist, neo-Nazi, and xenophobic message also permeated a song about the Gypsy minority in Hungary:

The flamethrower is the only weapon I need to win,
All Gypsy adults and children we'll exterminate,
But we can kill all of them at once in unison,
When it's done we can advertise: Gypsy-free zone.[33]

And this message was equally evident in the lyrics about Hungary's neighbor, Romania, which was then ruled by dictator Nicolae Ceauşescu:

Collapsing house of cards; it's a real dirty slum,
Death to the hairy-legged lazy scum,
The mercenaries of Ceauşescu want to kill us, too,
There's no law there, there's no truth.
Transylvania and its people as a gift they got,
They chased the Hungarians away, decency they've not,
They don't like to work, that's why there's no food,
All the Romanians will die of hunger and that's good.
They're pest, men and women, we have to kill them all,
Ceauşescu's Romania will have to fall,
Just showing their teeth they hate the Hungarians,
They bark but don't bite, slaves of the Hungarians.
Romania! He-he-he![34]

The political and cultural turmoil that these bands caused can be explained not only by what these anarchist bands said but also by how they said it. Through criticism and sardonic wit, in their use of new rhythms and screamed chants, this micromusical culture asserted a mode of discourse that thumbed its nose at the pop music industry and the bureaucratic infrastructure. Although the songs played by AE Bizottsag, for instance, betrayed the influence of other mainstream musicians in their irony and offbeat sentimentality, they were also punctuated by black humor, dramatic asides, and contrived pauses, suggesting similarity to other East European, especially Polish and Czechoslovak, experiments.[35]

One important—if complex—aspect of the more acceptable variants of this music must not be overlooked: its ridiculousness or seemingly innocent absurdity. Breaking a television set in front of a live audience in communist Hungary (or in the Soviet Union and communist Poland, where both television and radio were likewise run by the state and therefore susceptible to censorship) meant something quite different from the same gesture performed, let us say, in Western Europe or the United States. Some Hungarian bands may have sounded childish or primitive to certain ears—and surely there were such aspects in this music, just as in other experimental art—their "absurdity" and "ridiculousness" both enriched and strengthened the genre.

AE Bizottsag, a much remarked-upon group since its formation in the early 1980s, serves to illustrate this point. Composed of university-educated writers, filmmakers, painters, and musicians, it offered a repertoire consisting of eccentrically staged happenings combined with an acute sense of the perverse alchemy of words and images. This combination was perhaps most evident in two of its LPs, "Up for an Adventure" (1983) and "Ice-Cream Ballet" (the latter was used as the title of a feature film produced and directed by the group in 1986). Here for the first time in Hungarian music history was a fully developed musical and literary configuration that fit comfortably into a mature avant-garde genre. Publication of AE Bizottsag's two albums—with their spontaneous association of images, absence of romanticized feelings, use of human sounds to indicate emotional intensity, and complete abandonment of formal music—contributed substantially to the acceptance of the new music in Hungary.[36]

MUSIC AND SEXUALITY

An analysis of the new music would be incomplete without an examination of its recurrent images of asexuality and its denial of romantic love. AE Bizottsag sang,

Love has come to me again, my palm's sweating again,
What for? What for?
I'm forced to think of her again, I want to screw her again,
What for? What for?
Love, Love, Love,
It makes me puke. Boo, boo, boo!

This kind of image also incontestably distinguishes the new music from its mainstream popular counterpart. In these songs, the hatred and rejection of romantic love is quite explicit. Crucial to this genre is the motif of the disinterested woman without a sexual aura. The heavy metal band P. Mobil sang tonelessly: "My old chick, finally, I had to marry," whereas in a song by the Európa Kiadó we hear: "If there is nothing better to do, why don't you just love me instead." The URH delivered the same message with greater vehemence in the song "I'm Finished with Sex":

I'm finished, I'm bored with sex,
Women are not beautiful, they're not ugly.
They're outdated, unexploded sex bombs.
I'll spend my sex vacation in a psychiatric ward.

The unusually literate URH deepened this theme in "Everything Is Still the Same in the East":

I'd prefer masturbation to sex,
But even my own hands shock me,
Everything is still the same in the East.

The more radical wing of the new music, such as Agydaganat (Braintumor), also degraded women and heterosexual relationships.[37] In the unabashedly sexist ETA song "In the Space Disco a Radar Penis Is Dancing," sexuality reached a pornographic apex:

In the space disco a radar penis is dancing,
Among the chicks he's really loafing,
Come on, little sissy, come on down,
Let me pull your panties down.
In the space disco tanned pussies are working,
To grab a penis for the night, they're really trying,
I pulled her panties down when I caught her finally,
And amazed I watched her birdie.

At this point, it is useful to ask why these songs revealed such an aggressive stance toward sexuality, especially on the part of a generation coming of age in the 1980s. The answer, I believe, lies in the difference between the culture of the 1980s, with its open availability of Western fashion, X-rated videos, and public nudity, and a value system inherited from preceding decades.[38] As I have shown, a generation ago several influential rock groups in Hungary sang of love, hate, jealousy, and dating—themes that sounded ridiculous and naive to teenagers coming of age in the 1980s. The male-centered point of view espoused in these songs further distinguished them from their predecessors. For it is certain that the most intriguing aspect of the new bands was their near-total composition of male performers and singers.

Like their pop music counterparts of the late 1960s and early 1970s—the Big Four, Hungaria, Kex, Syrius, Solaris, Skorpio, and others of lesser fame—these male groups became inextricably linked to gender stereotypes and, in particular, the all-too-common misogyny of contemporary Hungary. Attila Grandpierre of the Galloping Morticians, with his strong and convincing hallucinatory, even shamanistic, presence, became a model for Hungarian musicians. Unlike other singers, he cut himself on stage, boasted a police record, and managed all the while to maintain his intellectual life-style as an astronomer.

In contrast to this visionary shaman-hero were other anarchist types fashioned after the militant group Spions or the lead singer Feró Nagy of Beatrice, the prototype of an opinionated, macho character. T-34, Mosoi, CPG, and ETA all imitated and even surpassed these other bands in stage presence. These two major masculine role models—the visionary, agonized cult figure and the radical enfant terrible—were conventional figures of the new music of the 1980s. By comparison, the few women who appeared on the scene were marginalized by the industry. Koko, the female lead vocalist of AE Bizottsag, diasappeared soon after the group disbanded in 1986. In the same year, the rise of Orchestra Luna, a band composed mostly of women, was short lived. It would seem that, for all its radical apparel and "revolutionary" program, the new music was not influential enough to change the gender bias that typifies Hungarian rock music and, for that matter, Hungarian society as a whole.[39]

OFFICIAL REACTIONS

Initial reactions to the new political music were mixed. Some dismissed it as nonsensical or a mere joke. But by 1983, as the new music became more openly anarchist and critical of the political system, the government retaliated. The leaders of the Kádár government—obviously unnerved by the confusion following Brezhnev's death—claimed that many new bands and their peers manifested anarchistic and even petty bourgeois tendencies antagonistic to socialism and socialist ethics.

Károly Németh, a Stalinist on the Hungarian Central Committee, expressed this concern the following way:

> We know well that our youth, primarily because of lack of experience, are vulnerable; they are even more helpless before bourgeois propaganda and ideologies counter to socialism. We cannot dismiss the fact that bourgeois propaganda is successful in influencing a segment of our youth. Some of them are uncritical of the dominant lifestyles of developed capitalism and its harmful side effects. Our important task is to respond in depth and convincingly to the problems of our youth, disseminate our ideology, combat detrimental influences, and expose the intention of the enemy.[40]

These words reflected the official point of view emanating from Moscow as exemplified by the statements of hard-liners such as CPSU general secretary Konstantin Chernenko, who said in 1983 that "through rock, the enemy is trying to exploit youthful psychology," and as shown in *Pravda*'s declaration in 1986 that "rock and roll has a right to exist but only if it is melodious, meaningful, and well-performed."[41]

To be sure, with the economy in tatters and the draconian Muscovite prescriptions of János Kádár, the Hungarian government was not hospitable to the proponents of the new music, especially those with a strong political and nationalistic message.[42] Hard-core new music bands, namely ETA, CPG, and Mos-oi, were compelled to realize fairly early in their careers that their outspokenness and criticism would not be tolerated. In early 1983, Mos-oi and Eta were banned from public performances, and members faced court trials for their "crimes against the state." Harsh sentences were meted out to members of CPG—mostly jail terms, fines, and police surveillance—and lesser sentences to members of ETA and Mos-oi. A leader of the group CPG, Zoltán Benkő, was jailed for two years on 7 February 1984 but released in October 1985, just before the Hungarian government was prepared to host the Cultural Forum of the Helsinki Agreement.[43]

The latest of these show trials was held in 1985, when members of two groups, Kőzellenség (Public Enemy) and Auróra Cirkáló (Aurora Cruiser), received fines for trumped-up charges of "public indecency" and "enticing against the state."[44] The following year, marking the ascendancy of Mikhail Gorbachev to power, the Galloping Morticians faced the harsh reality of having been temporarily forbidden to appear in public performance, a sanction not without precedence.[45] Other groups out of favor with the establishment still found it difficult to rent equipment from state agencies, to receive permits required for concerts, and to stage concerts in certain towns and counties.

These extraordinary, if not extravagant, episodes demonstrated the frustrated sense of being young in Hungary in a time of difficulties and also revealed fundamental flaws and weaknesses in a state-controlled music industry. What should be stressed, however, is that pressure from below was mildly successful in forcing state machinery to make concessions.[46]

Although most of the protagonists of the new music never had the opportunity to cut their own records or appear in national tours arranged and promoted by the industry, some nevertheless were able to emerge on the official music scene. Such was the case of the more artistically oriented Európa Kiadó and Sziami Sziami. The former was allowed to record and cut LPs in late 1986, but the songs and sound had lost their originality and critical edge.[47] The latter, a group whose predecessor was the pioneering URH, also produced two songs for the film *Moziklip* (Movie Clip), a 1987 film directed by Peter Timar that resembles a rock video.[48] The Sziami songs were far removed from the venomous and overtly antistate texts of the URH, although the band preserved in a perhaps more symbolic and subtle way its sarcastic edge. It would appear that the only band that remained faithful to its original credo was the Galloping Morticians, as exemplified in its albums *Teach Death a Lesson,* produced and released in West Germany in 1988, and *To Break Down Nothing's Wall,* released in 1992.[49]

However, the majority of the bands of the new music genre continued to receive no state support and lacked recording contracts. Some attempted to maintain their repertoire through independently produced cassettes, performing in small clubs—such as the Black Hole in Budapest—and artistic circles that operated in semilegality. That the oppositional music continued to be held in official disfavor well into the late 1980s was evident from the fact that major national festivals and rock concerts were organized without the presence of these bands. Charity rock festivals (those held for the Hungarian earthquake victims in 1985, for the Ethiopian famine victims in 1986, the Stay with Us antidrug concert, and the Amnesty International Human Rights tour concert in Budapest in 1988) were censored, and mainstream popular music bands were instead featured as the main attraction.[50]

Exclusion, in fact, has been a powerful tool manipulated by the music industry. In 1986, the now-defunct Hungarian Communist Youth League (KISZ) and the Hungarian Radio hosted a nationwide talent search for promising bands of various musical persuasions. The contest was named "Aorta," but none of the prizewinners worked in a style that could be fully associated with the new music. Another instance occurred in summer 1988 when Hungary hosted the Interpop '88 international music festival in Siofok. Then, too, only state-supported, or "light," music was present on stage. New faces, aside from pop singers and revamped bands, were missing among the singers and bands representing Hungary on the international scene.[51] A sad feature of post-1989 Hungarian musical life, in fact, was that it remained controlled by radio and television and, in their service, the former concert agencies. Many of the stars of Illés, Omega, LGT, Tolcsvay, and Metro continue to enjoy the benefits of their stardom and the economic securities of their private recording studies, agencies, clubs, and networks that they established throughout the 1980s under the protection of what many scholars referred to as "existing state socialism." Thus under the new government of Prime Minister József Antall, the monopoly of the state music industry and the hegemony of popular music in a sense continue to go unchallenged, with minor concessions.[52]

NEW MUSIC AND THE WEST

At first glance, it might well appear that the political new music, with its more overtly—and perhaps even naively—nihilistic social and political concerns, was only a copy of early punk as exemplified by groups such as the Sex Pistols, the Beat, and the Clash.[53] It is worth noting, however, that the emergence of the new music was not wholly an outgrowth of the Western punk movement of the late 1970s. Although there was a strong kinship between the two, their differences outweighed their similarities.[54]

In any case, the important hard rock bands such as Beatrice and Piramis began to imitate music of the Sex Pistols, the Clash, and the Ramones only after they had become fashionable in Hungary in the early 1980s.[55] Many earlier attempts—for example, those of the Galloping Morticians and the Spions and to a lesser extent the Kex happenings in the late 1970s—were unique, isolated activities. They evolved in part because of vicious competition between the centrally controlled entertainment industry and the alternative music of the emerging youth subcultures. The late 1970s and early 1980s saw the proletarianization of large masses of youth, as exemplified by groups such as the Csöves (Hobo), Narkós (Narcotics), and Szipós (Glue Sniffers). Beatrice and its idolized but somewhat overrated leader, Feró Nagy (self-titled as "the nation's cockroach"), for example, identified themselves with such outcast groups existing on the periphery of Hungarian society by singing about their lives and fate.[56]

In what sense, then, can one say that the Hungarian new music of the 1980s was more political than its Western counterpart? Hungarian musicians of the avant-garde as well as members of the radical underground new music scene were more directly involved in the political struggle to create improved relations between the industry and the state than comparable groups in Western Europe or the United States. Although both Eastern and Western bands were, to a certain extent, extremists and even outright radicals, at the same time both had to conform to the exigencies of the music industry. Only a few Hungarian bands did so, though. Yet unlike Western punk rockers, who felt obliged to denounce capitalism, Hungarian bands of the radical persuasion created powerful, enduring images of communist statesmen, bureaucrats, police, and other detested symbols of state power.[57] For members of Mos-oi or CPG, it was clear that to celebrate in song the "beauty of police work," the expulsion of the "garbage immigrants," or the "son-of-a-bitch" manager of the Hungarian state recording company was to condemn themselves to criminal charges and jail terms.

Hungarian new music was politicized from its very inception, if only because mainstream pop music, too, was always under the political sway of the state. By refusing to adhere to the standards of "light music," the bands and their followers associated themselves implicitly with an attack on the state and its machinery.[58]

Another aspect of the indigenous development of new music concerned the fact that the majority of Hungarian rock musicians were isolated from Western European punk subculture. Most musicians were largely ignorant of the features of Western punk until 1980, when the first Hungarian bands began to assert punk status for themselves. Moreover, concerts and performances by Western rock bands were carefully screened by censors in Budapest. Needless to say, groups believed to be "detrimental" or "not expressing basic, positive human values and ideas" to young people were deprived of the blessing of organizers and promoters in Hungary. Santana, Queen, Paco de Lucia, Three Mustaphas, Tangerine Dream, Depeche Mode, and other major Western bands performed before Hungarian audiences in the mid-1980s. The list is long and impressive, but one should not lose sight of the fact that most of these were mainstream bands of established reputation. These groups seemed to have had virtually no effect on the direction in which Hungarian oppositional music had been evolving.[59] Their presence— like Music Television's overarching influence in Europe in the 1990s— appeared rather to reinforce boundaries between popular music and the new music.

It might be argued that Hungarian music changed during the early 1980s primarily through a process of internal development.[60] At first there appeared on the scene only a handful of bands that were aware, however marginally, of Western punk. Later, through their concerts and adamant "punkish" presence, groups around the country followed suit. By the early 1980s, Hungarian critics were reporting that these seemingly nihilistic punks had somehow struck a chord—an "ominous" chord—among Hungarian youth. They were scorned by the "Illés generation," who, even after having spent their college years wearing bell-bottom jeans and long hair and listening to country and disco, still took the screaming, the stinking cheese, and the dirty message quite literally.

A determining factor in shaping their style and success was the nature of local audience response. For example, the heavy metal formation from Miskolc known as Edda Muvek (Edda Works) emerged as a major force on the rock music scene by asserting its blue-collar origins and identity as a positive value.[61] Similarly, Hobo Blues Band's 1986 hit song, "Kőbánya Blues," identified with a particular working-class district of Budapest:

I was born and raised in Kőbánya,
I know that there's a nicer and better town,
But it's Kőbánya that pulls me down.

The more radical wing, such as Galloping Morticians, Mos-oi, and ETA, followed their example, drawing large numbers of followers from working-class neighborhoods and disenchanted intellectuals as well as students from the capital and other major cities. Although most of the groups came from urban and intellectual backgrounds, this new music was a dimension of a subculture that united a generation against the unfulfilled promises of the Marxist-Leninist state. A vox populi, then, linked blue- and white-collar youth in a political mode of discourse previously lacking in Hungary.

As the rock music world experienced diversification, the emergence of extreme groups such as CPG, Mos-oi, and ETA was essential to the success of the more antiauthoritarian, democratic new music. From a more progressive point of view, though, many of the songs by these groups were highly controversial—replete as they were with racist, chauvinist, and even authoritarian overtones ("Gypsy-Free Zone," "Immigrants' Share," "Anarchy," and others)—the reasons for which many performers faced legal consequences. However, their very unacceptability to the Kádár regime and the state-run pop music industry made them all the more desirable to the disillusioned generation for remaining the cynosure of Hungarian youth. The early 1980s were times of experimentation and euphoria, which may account in part for the convergence of so many different musical styles, not only on stage and during semilegal concerts but often in prisons as well.

CONCLUSION

In my view, the primary cause of the emergence of political new wave music was the stagnation and eventual collapse of the East European governments whose economic and political structures failed to pass the test of time.[62] At first, the ideas presented by the protagonists of the new music were unthinkable, but by 1985, when Mikhail Gorbachev announced his new policy of glasnost and perestroika, the changing climate found them not only acceptable but in certain cases welcome. In 1983, when Mos-oi mocked Nicolae Ceauşescu by singing of the atrocities committed by the Romanian state against ethnic Hungarians living in Romania, its members could hardly have foreseen that five years later, in 1988, the short-lived Grósz government of Hungary would do likewise or that the Ceauşescus would be executed following the Christmas uprising of 1989.[63]

The new musical opposition emerged from the quiet madness and myopia that had come to characterize Hungarian society after the late 1970s. It was not a state-controlled and state-run industry; on the contrary, it enjoyed popular support precisely because it existed outside the state sphere, representing ideas close to the hearts of everyday citizens. This oppositional music culture enacted a rebellion of both the semi-intelligentsia, which was a group composed largely of university-educated and white-collar workers, and frustrated blue-collar youth against party cadres and apparatchiks incapable of reforming the system.[64]

The beginning of the 1980s signaled the end of an era: Disco and mellow rock lost their appeal as a haven for ideological and political expression, and their adherents, though they lingered on for some time, eventually found their way to other musical styles. One such style was the fusion of rock and revitalized peasant folk music (*táncház*), which became a genre of musical based upon historical events.[65] It culminated in the 1984 "national rock musical" *István, a király* (Stephen the King). This production was succeeded by other successful adaptations of historical themes such as the 1988 *Bestia* ("The Beast," describing the life of sixteenth-century princess Elizabeth Bathory) and *Költő visszatér* ("The Poet Returns," concerning the death of nineteenth-century national poet Sándor Petöfi).[66] Whereas a great many Hungarians enjoyed such mixtures of folk and rock music, filled with overt nationalistic messages—historical injustices, St. Stephen's glorious thousand-year-old empire, religious revitalism, the fate of minorities in the successor states—others, turning to the new music, were more critical of the established order.

To the radical wing of the new political music, however, the changes of the early 1980s were not sufficient. Blue- and white-collar youth, fast on the heels of the collapse of the new economic mechanism and the rise of "goulash communism," were turning anxiously outward. The rage and energy—and the venom—of Hungarian youth who saw no place for themselves in the Hungarian communist caste system spewed forth. The new music became a dangerous music, unlike "light" pop music, or "serious" Bartok but instead a politically dynamic music with new ideas and a challenging program. It is perhaps regrettable that the post-1989 Hungarian musical life seems to have forgotten its own genesis in the 1980s. The political tone, the musical experimentations, and the critical stance are absent from the political agenda of the 1990s generation, whose preoccupation is to watch MTV and copy fashions from the pages of Western magazines.

In conclusion, I suggest that the new music emerged as the explicit agenda of a generation coming of age. In fact, these musical texts bespeak the fusion of two generations: Culturally and politically, the generation of the 1970s was only beginning to awaken, whereas that of the 1980s was already in the process of maturation. The results have been achieved thanks to the latter generation's persistent rejection of the old and desire for change.[67] By virtue of their experimentation with new musical forms of criticism, rebellious Hungarian youth of the 1980s, like their counterparts in East Germany in 1975, Czechoslovakia in 1968 and 1977, and Poland in 1980–1981 and 1988, gave Hungary a new vision.

This vision embodied new ideas and values and challenging possibilities for an alternative culture and future, the fruit of which was felt during 1989 and 1990 as witnessed by the abolition of the communist party, the establishment of a multiparty system, and the founding of a democratic civil society. The appearance of the new music may have helped pave the way for this more democratic liberalization process currently unfolding.[68] A cultural epiphenomenon, it was the music of a youthful generation that was particularly affected by the evolving crisis of strong party control of both economy and society. Finally, I would conclude that the stagnation of the Kádár government was both an essential precondition of and a powerful stimulus for the emergence of political new wave music. Its youthful practitioners gave hope to their peers and warning to their elders by anticipating these necessary changes, even though the most daring of its artists were condemned to oblivion.

NOTES

This chapter is a revised version of my "Rocking the State: Youth and Rock Music Culture in Hungary, 1976–1990," in *East European Politics and Societies* 5, no. 3 (Fall 1991), pp. 483–513. I would like to express my sincere appreciation to Mark Slobin, Daniel Warner, Catherine Portuges, Zdenek Salzmann, the two anonymous reviewers of *Eastern European Politics and Societies,* and Sabrina P. Ramet for reading and commenting on an earlier version of the manuscript. I am indebted to Attila Grandpierre for his information on the Galloping Morticians and the musical scene in Hungary in the 1980s. All translations of lyrics from Hungarian to English are mine.

1. Although it does not take up Eastern Europe per se, Pamela A. Myers-Moro's essay "Songs for Life: Leftist Thai Popular Music in the 1970s," *Journal of Popular Culture* 20, no. 3 (Winter 1986), pp. 145–158, describes well the nature of antagonism between state ideology and rock music.

2. James Lull, "Popular Music and Communication: An Introduction," *Popular Music and Communication* (Newbury Park: Sage, 1989), pp. 29–30. For material concerning the ideological struggles as they relate to music in the Stalinist era in the Soviet Union see Robert A. Rothstein, "The Quiet Rehabilitation of the Brick Factory: Early Soviet Popular Music and Its Critics," *Slavic Review* 39, no. 3 (September 1980), pp. 373–388; and for a useful summary of the "mass song" or socialist song tradition in Hungary in the 1950s, see the fine study by Andras Tokaji, *Mozgalom és hivatal a tomegdal Magyarorszagon 1945–1956* (Budapest: Zenemukiado, 1983).

3. The history and nature of Hungarian rock are described in several excellent studies in Hungarian, especially in Agnes Losonczi, *Zene Ifjusag Mozgalom* (Budapest: Zenemukiado, 1974); and János Sebok, *Rock evkonyv 1981* (Budapest: Zenemukiado, 1982); János Sebok, *Magya-rock* (Budapest: Zenemukiado, 1983–1984); and János Sebok, *A daltulajdonos* (Budapest: Muzsak, 1988). In English, important insights are provided by Anna Szemere, "Some Institutional Aspects of Pop and Rock Music in Hungary," *Popular Music* 3 (1983), pp. 120–142; and Anna Szemere, "Pop Music in Hungary," *Communication Research* 12, no. 3 (July 1985), pp. 401–411.

4. Roland Barthes, *Image-Text-Music* (New York: Hill and Wang, 1977), p. 149.

5. Pedro Ramet [Sabrina Petra Ramet], "Rock Counterculture in Eastern Europe and the Soviet Union," *Survey* 29, no. 2 (Summer 1985), p. 151.

6. The nature of rock music and its relation to the political and cultural milieu of the youth movements of the 1960s are discussed by Simon Frith, *Sound Effects: Youth, Leisure, and the Politics of Rock* (London: Constable, 1983), and "Rock and the Politics of Memory," in Sohnya Sayres et al. (eds.), *The 60s Without Apology* (Minneapolis: University of Minnesota Press, 1984), pp. 59–69.

7. Mary Russo and Daniel Warner, "Rough Music, Futurism and Postpunk Industrial Noise Bands," *Discourse* 10, no. 1 (1987–1988), pp. 55–76. Western youth movements and their musical expressions have been described by S. Hall and T. Jefferson (eds.), *Resistance Through Rituals* (London: Hutchinson, 1976), and more recently by Dick Hebdige, *Cut 'N' Mix Culture: Identity and Caribbean Music* (London: Methuen, 1987). Michael Blanch, "Imperialism, Nationalism and Organized Youth," in John Clarke, Charles Critcher, and Richard Johnson (eds.), *Working-Class Culture: Studies in History and Theory* (New York: St. Martin's Press, 1979), pp. 102–120; and Jean Woodall, "The Dilemma of Youth Unemployment: Trade Union Response in the Federal Republic of Germany, the UK and France," *West European Politics* 9, no. 3 (July 1986), pp. 429–447, also provide important information concerning the political economy of Western youth subcultures.

8. Sebok, *Magya-rock*, pp. 100–150; Peter Szanto, *És ilyen a boksz: Az LGT sztori* (Budapest: LGT); and Timothy W. Ryback, *Rock Around the Bloc: A History of Rock*

in Eastern Europe and the Soviet Union (New York: Oxford University Press, 1990), pp. 167–168.

9. Júlia Lévai, "Tanulságok a hetvenes évek poptörténetéből," *Valóság*, no. 4 (1984), p. 70.

10. The Hungarian taxonomy of musical genres is, of course, much more complex than this. "Serious music" would include not only classical but opera, operetta, and, depending on the critics' point of view, jazz. The category "light music" groups together musical styles as diverse as pop, *schlager* (light pop music hits), chanson, film music, and disco. The third large category is referred to simply as folk music; it includes traditional peasant music, urban-style folk songs (*magyar nóta*), gypsy music, and the recently popular revival "dance-house" (*táncház*) music. In Hungarian television, recording industry, and radio, the distinction between "art music" and "entertainment music" is also evident. For more detailed treatment see Losonczi, *Zene*, Sebok, *Magya-rock*, and Szemere, "Some Institutional Aspects."

11. Here I subscribe to the distinction between "pop" and "serious" music articulated by Theodor Adorno, *Introduction to the Sociology of Music* (New York: Seabury Press, 1976), p. 25.

12. There are several East European and European festivals in which Hungarian singers and bands are present: the Intervision, Eurovision, and Interpop festivals, held every year in a different city, among which Sofia and San Remo are the most important.

13. Levai, "Tanulsagok," p. 70; and Szemere, "Pop Music in Hungary," p. 407.

14. Istvan Szabo, "Historical Personalities, Political Symbols and the Hungarian Youth," *International Journal of Political Education* 5 (1982), pp. 339–353; Ferenc Gazsó (ed.), *Társadalmi folyamatok az ifjúság körében* (Budapest: MSZMP Társadalomtudományi Intézet, 1987); and Ferenc Kovács (ed.), *Az ipari dolgozók rétegződése. Magyar-Lengyel összehasonlítás* (Budapest: Társadalomtudományi Intézet, 1984). Compare these works on Hungarian youth, its economic (dis)position, values, and ideas, with János Kádár's remarks. At the 12th Congress of the MSZMP, he said: "Our young people grumble about many things, sometimes even when they are not right. This is natural, a concomitant of their age. ... Our young people must be provided with a guiding ideal, with a goal in life. However, we cannot offer a more noble goal than socialism. ... Young people must be given tasks in accordance with their age, because then they will be satisfied" (quoted in János Kádár, *Selected Speeches and Interviews* [Oxford: Pergamon Press, 1985], pp. 453–454.

15. Dénes Csengey, *És mi most itt vagyunk* (Budapest: Magvető, 1986).

16. Ferenc Bodor (ed.), *Nomadic Generation: Youth and Folk Art in Hungary, 1970–1980* (Budapest: Nepmuvelesi Intezet, 1981); and Laszlo Siklós, *Táncház* (Budapest: Zeneműkiadó, 1977).

17. If we compare the number of records produced in 1980 with that of 1988, the nature of this crisis becomes axiomatic. In 1980, 7.7 million records were produced in Hungary, of which 18 percent were arts (classical, jazz, opera), 72 percent pop music, and 1.2 percent folk; in 1988, only 4.9 million records were produced, and the percentages were 30.9 percent, 60.8 percent, and 2.1 percent, respec-

tively; see Kozponti Statisztikai Hivatal, *Budapest Statisztikai Zsebkonyve* (Budapest: KSH, 1989), p. 194.

18. Compare these names, for example, to those of the Russian groups, which include Television Set, Gulliver, Zigzag, DDT, Centre, Urfin Juice, Time Machine, Vabank, Aquarium, Kino, Alisa, and Strange Games; to the Czechoslovak Patent, Frog, Prague Selection; to the Polish SS 20, Fifth Column, Lady Pank, Verdict, Shortage, Protest, WC; to the East German Karat, City, Zebra, Pankow, Silly, Berluc; or to the Yugoslav Laibach, No Smoking, Fish Soup, and others. See also Sabrina P. Ramet, *Social Currents in Eastern Europe: The Sources and Meaning of the Great Transformation* (Durham, N.C.: Duke University Press, 1991), Chapter 9 ("Rock Music and Counterculture"); and Sabrina Petra Ramet, Sergei Zamascikov, and Robert Bird, "The Soviet Rock Scene," published in this volume.

19. These events coincided with Wolf Biermann's expulsion from East Germany to West Germany and the trial and subsequent jailing of the Prague-based Plastic People of the Universe and DG 307 in Czechoslovakia.

20. Ágnes Seszták, "Hová vágtáznak a halottkémek? Beszélgetés dr. Grandpierre Attilával," *Mozgó Világ*, no. 7 (1985), pp. 86–93.

21. Sebok, *Magya-rock*, vol. 2.

22. Bela Csikos-Nagy, *Szocializmus, piac, gazdasag* (Budapest: Kossuth, 1987), pp. 100–115.

23. See the discussion by sociologist Elemér Hankiss about the "confusion" and "hybridization" during these years. See his "In Search of a Paradigm," *Dædalus* 119, no. 1 (Winter 1990).

24. Tamás Bauer, "Perfecting or Reforming the Economic Mechanism?" *Eastern European Economics* 26, no. 2 (Winter 1987–1988), pp. 5–34.

25. Some of these changes are described in English in detail in J. F. Brown, *Eastern Europe and Communist Rule* (Durham, N.C.: Duke University Press, 1988); Ivan Szelenyi, *Socialist Entrepreneurs: Embourgeoisment in Rural Hungary* (Madison: University of Wisconsin Press, 1988); and Peter A. Toma, *Socialist Authority: The Hungarian Experience* (New York: Praeger, 1988). See also Elemér Hankiss, *Diagnozisok 2* (Budapest: Magvető, 1986).

26. For analyses on youth problems in Hungary, see, for example, Zoltan Bekes and Peter Havas (eds.), *Ifjusag, tarsadalom, ideologia i Nemetkozi Tanacs* (Budapest: Tarsadalomtudomanyi Intezete, 1986); Tibor Huszar (ed.), *A magyar ertelmiseg a 80-as evekben* (Budapest: Kossuth, 1986); Gabor Torok, "Dolgozo fiatalok szocializacioja és ertekorientacioja," *Politika-Tudomany* 1–2 (1986), pp. 23–38; and my "Red Csepel: Working Youth in a Socialist Firm," *East European Quarterly* 23, no. 4 (Winter 1989), pp. 445–468.

27. Miklos Haraszti, *A Worker in the Worker's State* (New York: Universe Books, 1978). See also *Annamaria Inzelt: Rendellenessegek az ipar szervezeteben* (Budapest: Kozgazdasagi és Jogi Konyvkiado, 1988); and Hankiss, *Diagnozisok 2*.

28. Russo and Warner, "Rough Music," p. 71.

29. The Leningrad group Television Set sings as follows: "They monitor us from birth, / Our kind 'uncles' and 'aunts,' / We grow up an obedient breed, / We sing what they want, / We live how they want."

30. For "Solidarity" themes in Yugoslav rock music, see also Pedro Ramet, "The Rock Scene in Yugoslavia," *Eastern European Politics and Societies* 2, no. 2 (Spring 1988), pp. 405–406.

31. For present purposes, I do not discuss the demise of these "socialist" state rituals and the rise of new nationalist and religious ones that occurred with the reconstitution of the Hungarian Republic in 1989. See my article "People vs. the State: Political Rituals in Contemporary Hungary," *Anthropology Today* 6, no. 2 (April 1990).

32. Compare the Hungarian skinhead subculture, as epitomized by Mos-oi, to the nationalist Russian skinheads Liuberis in Moscow, who, according to *Punch* magazine, "take pride in wearing ugly local plaid coats, go in for bodybuilding, reject drink and alcohol, and get their kicks by beating up the punks and Metallisti" (Martin Walker, "A Chip Off the Old Bloc," *Punch*, 18 March 1987, pp. 8–9).

33. In August 1992 I was still able to observe the graffiti "Gypsy-Free Zone" in various districts of Budapest. Ethnocentrism and racism concerning Hungary's half-million Gypsy minority population are yet to be addressed by policymakers and concerned individuals; see László Levendel, "A ciganysag gondja-mindannyiunk gondja," *Valosag*, no. 12 (1988), pp. 28–36; and Katie Trumpener, "The Time of the Gypsies: A 'People Without History' in the Narratives of the West," *Cultural Inquiry* 18, no. 4 (1992), pp. 843–884.

34. In spite of the disinterest manifested by the Kádar government with regard to the fate of ethnic Hungarians outside of Hungary, the nationalistic movement from below was successful enough that by 1988 programs such as "cultural unity of all Hungarians," "the thousand-year-old empire of St. Stephen," and "genocide of the Hungarian minority in Romania" had became an agenda for the Grosz government as well as the U.S. Senate. See Pal Koteles, "Nemzet és Hagyomany—Magyarsag és a Kisebbsegek," *Hitel*, no. 3 (1989), pp. 10–14; Zoltan Palotas, "50 eve tortent az elso becsi dontes," *Kapu* 2, no. 1 (January 1989), pp. 18–24; "Senate Adopts Lautenberg Resolution (93–0) Condemning Rumania for Its Human Rights Abuses, Particularly Its Plan to Raze Agricultural Villages in Traditionally Hungarian Areas" and "Expressing Support for H. Res. 505, House Members Condemn Rumania's Planned Destruction of 8,000 Villages and Its Persecution of Ethnic Minorities," 3, 4, 5, and 11 August 1988, *Congressional Record*. My disagreements with these and other views of the origins and evolution of nationalist tension and the hostile relationship between Hungary and Romania until the outbreak of the Romanian revolution, during Christmas 1989, are profound and extensive. Readers may turn to my "Transylvania, Land Beyond Reason: Toward an Anthropological Analysis of a Contested Terrain," *Dialectical Anthropology* 14, no. 1 (1989), pp. 21–52.

35. Although East European rock musicians are isolated from each other—willingly or not—further parallels are discernible between Hungarian and other East European musical cultures. Among these are the high regard in which classic British and U.S. bands and singers (Velvet Underground, Beatles, Rolling Stones) are held, the presence of rock operas and rock feature films, and concerts for world peace in Eastern Europe.

36. See Károly Szikszai, "Onelettan-Beszelgetes ef Zambo Istvannal," *Elet és irodalom*, 19 January 1990, p. 6.

37. The Agydaganat song "Our Teacher on the Toilet Seat" is too pornographic to quote here; I shall spare the reader such obscenity. In Hungary, however, these songs have been reprinted in various journals and books; see Sebok, *Magya-rock*, pp. 197–200.

38. For an analysis of gender bias and asymmetry in Hungarian society see Judit H. Sas, *Noies nokes ferfias ferfiak* (Budapest: Akademiai Kiado, 1984); also Torok, "Dolgozo fiatalok," pp. 30–38; and my article "Red Csepel," pp. 445–468.

39. I found the gossipy autobiography by the pop singer Sarolta Zalatnay, *I Am Not a Nun*, extremely interesting (as well as perverse) in describing the intricacies and hidden politicking that characterize the Hungarian music industry. See Sarolta Zalatnay, *Nem vagyok en apaca* (Budapest: A Szerzo, 1985).

40. Károly Németh, *Part, allam, politika* (Budapest: Kossuth, 1986), p. 20.

41. First statement quoted in Ramet, "Rock Counterculture," p. 155, and second statement quoted in *Boston Globe*, 21 October 1986, p. 4.

42. No doubt this had to do, in part, with the ideology of "socialist realism" and "socialist ethic" legitimating the bureaucratic structure of the Hungarian music industry; see Janos Marothy, *Music and Bourgeois. Music and Proletariat* (Budapest: Akademiai Kiado, 1974); and Geza Molnar, "A zene a szocialista tarsadalomban," *Magyar Zene* 24, no. 1 (1974, originally published in 1919), pp. 3–18.

43. "The Limits of Liberalization," *PEN American Center Report on Hungary*, April 1986, p. 11.

44. Similar attacks on musicians also occurred at the same time in Czechoslovakia and Poland. In October 1984, the Jazz Music Section of the Czech Music Union was ordered by officials to disband. Later, on 10 March 1987, five jazz musicians were sentenced to jail terms by the Prague court. See Martin Palouš et al., "Charter 77 Demands Space for Czechoslovak Youth," *East European Reporter* 2, no. 1 (Spring 1986), p. 28; and the *New York Times*, 9 March 1987, p. 3; for Poland, see "Polish Youth: We Don't Give A Damn … ," *East European Reporter* 2, no. 1 (Spring 1986), pp. 35–36; and "Opposition Rocks?" *Voice of Solidarity*, August–September 1986.

45. For Soviet parallels see Boris Kagarlitsky, "The Intelligentsia and the Changes," *New Left Review*, no. 164 (July–August 1987), pp. 5–19; and the *New York Times*, 9 April 1987, pp. 1, 26–27.

46. Szikszai, "Onelettan," p. 6.

47. Anna Szemere, "A jovo itt van és sose lesz vege: Ter és idokepzetek az Európa Kiadó egyuttes zene-és szovegvilagaban," *Magyar Zene* 1 (1985), pp. 70–74.

48. Another rock group, Neurotic, led by Tamas Pajor, has been featured in Janos Xantus's 1988 full-length film *A Rock terito*; for a critical review see Zoltan Szentgali, "Rock terito," *Kapu* 2, no. 1 (January 1989), pp. 58–59.

49. Among the Polish bands, Lady Pank was the most successful outside of Poland as a result, no doubt, of its released album. In Czechoslovakia, Plastic People of the Universe also recorded several albums and samizdat cassettes. Several Russian bands, including Alisa, Kino, Aquarium, and Strange Games, were featured on the album *Red Waves*, which was produced and released in 1986 by Stingray Productions in Los Angeles. Perhaps one of the most unique and ear-

liest independent labels featuring Eastern and Western groups was Fixed Planet, produced in West Germany in 1983.

50. Charity rock festivals are a recent development in Eastern Europe. The idea was borrowed from Western practice. The Amnesty International "Human Rights Now!" tour, in Budapest, featured János Bródy and the Hobo Blues Band; see James Henke, "Chimes of Freedom: Amnesty International's Superstar Human Rights Now! Tour Hits Road," *Rolling Stone*, 20 October 1988, pp. 15–18. For a critical evaluation of the Western charity rock phenomenon, see Robert Allan, "Bob's Not Your Uncle," *Capital and Class*, no. 30 (Winter 1986), pp. 31–37; Stuart Hall and Martin Jacques, "People Aid: A New Politics Sweeps the Land," *Marxism Today* 31, no. 7 (July 1986), pp. 10–14; and Robert Keating, "Sympathy for the Devil," *Spin* 2, no. 6 (1986), pp. 65–72.

51. For a short interview in English with the department head of the Interconcert (International Concert Management) that explains why, for example, pop music groups such as the Neoton Family are marketable in the West, see "Is Hungarian Pop Music Marketable?" *Hungarian Digest*, no. 5 (1981), pp. 27–28.

52. On the problems facing Hungarian musical life in the 1990s, see Attila Bozay, "A magyar zenei elet jovoerol," *Hitel* 2 (1990), pp. 34–36.

53. Dick Hebdige, *Subculture: The Meaning of Style* (London: Methuen, 1979).

54. Some of the similarities are evident in the study by A. Burr, "The Ideologies of Despair: A Symbolic Interpretation of Punks' and Skinheads' Usage of Barbiturates," *Social Science and Medicine* 9 (1984), pp. 929–938.

55. Sebok, *Magya-rock*, p. 235.

56. Gazsó, *Társadalmi*, pp. 50–75; and Tamas Fricz, "Ifjusag és civil tarsadalom," *Valosag* 11 (1988), pp. 34–45. For a different interpretation of the Csöves subculture see Ryback, *Rock Around the Bloc*, p. 171.

57. In the words of the anthropologist John Blacking, "Music is not a language that describes the way society seems to be, but a metaphorical expression of feelings associated with the way society really is. It is a reflection of and response to social forces, and particularly to the consequences of the division of labor in society." See John Blacking, *How Musical Is Man?* (Seattle: University of Washington Press, 1973), p. 104.

58. See Brown, *Eastern Europe*, pp. 399–403. For another symbolic form of popular resistance and protest see my article "The Politics of Joking: Popular Response to Chernobyl," *Journal of American Folklore* 101, no. 401 (July–September 1988), pp. 324–334.

59. The small number of records imported from the West also confirms that interest on the part of Hungarian youth to buy them has been decreasing since the beginning of the 1980s, a trend paralleling the general decline in the standard of living and the rising prices, including that of records. In 1980, 1.13 million records were imported to Hungary; by 1988, this number decreased to 986,000. See Kozponti Statisztikai Hivatal, *Magyar Statisztikai Zsebkonyv* (Budapest: KSH, 1989), p. 83.

60. Attila Grandpierre of the Galloping Morticians, for example, rejects any identification with Western punk by claiming, "We don't play fashionable punk, but something akin to it, a vital and more original music ... modern folk music"; see Seszták, "Beszélgetés," pp. 89–90, and Szemere, "A jovo," p. 71.

61. The history of Edda Muvek (Edda Works) is instructive on this matter; see Geza Risko, *Edda Muvek, Miskolc* (Budapest: Ifjusagi, 1984).

62. For thorough discussions on the economic and political problems of Hungary in the 1980s, see Tamás Bauer, "Hungarian Economic Reform in East European Perspective," *Eastern European Politics and Society* 2, no. 3 (Fall 1988), pp. 418–432; Charles Gati, *Hungary and the Soviet Bloc* (Durham, N.C.: Duke University Press, 1986), pp. 199–205; Katalin Koncz, *Nok a munkaeropiacon* (Budapest: Kozgazdasagi és Jogi Konyvkiado, 1987); and Peter Galasi and György Sziraczki (eds.), *Labour Market and Second Economy in Hungary* (New York: Campus, 1985).

63. In February 1989, at the United Nations Human Rights Commission in Geneva, the Hungarian government accused the Romanian government of "persecuting its ethnic Hungarian minority and forcing some 20,000 to flee for safety across the Hungarian border"; *New York Times*, 7 March 1989, p. A15; and *New York Times*, 19 February 1989, p. 14. As a result of this intervention, the commission "called for an investigation by an independent expert into abuses by the Rumanian Government of Nicolae Ceaușescu, the first such investigation by an outside expert it has ordered in five years." See the *New York Times*, 11 March 1989, p. 5.

64. The histories of Edda Works and the university group Neoprimitiv are instructive on this matter; see Laszlo Szentirmay (ed.), *Tizeves a Neoprimitiv* (Budapest: Marx Karoly Kozgazdasagtudomanyi Egyetem KISZ Bizottsaga, 1985). There is also informative material on the musical tastes of working-class youth by Janos Havasi, *Miert nem dalol a kalapacs?* (Budapest: Zenemukiado, 1985).

65. Gabor Koltay, *István, a király* (Budapest: Ifjusagi, 1984).

66. It is perhaps ironic that in 1989 attempts were made by several intellectuals to resurrect symbolically the poet Sándor Petőfi. One group of nationalists, for example, claimed that the hero poet had not been slain in 1849 at the battle of Sigishoara but rather had been taken to Siberia as a Russian prisoner of war. A highly dubious "scientific expedition" was launched to exhume, repatriate, and reinter the purported remains; however, for obvious reasons, this funerary project was doomed from its inception.

67. For example, URH sings in "An Awful Place": "This is the last place where I've yet to commit anything, / This city makes me rotten, I'm dying of decaying: / This is an awful place." Or in the CPG text: "The sky is always blue here, / The grass is always green here, / There're no problems here, / 'Cause everyone is a leech. / Riot, riot that's what we want, / Scandal, scandal that's what we want." Compare these songs to the Leningrad-based Kino, which sings: " 'Change!' our hearts demand. / 'Change!' our eyes demand. / 'Change!' We want change" (quoted in Kagarlitsky, "The Intelligentsia," p. 18).

68. For details on the formation of associations, independent parties, and agendas for political change during 1988 and 1989 and thereafter see Tamás Kolosi, "Eselyeink," *Valosag*, no. 1 (1989), pp. 22–33; Hankiss, "In Search"; and László Bruszt and David Stark, "Remaking the Political Field in Hungary: From Politics of Confrontation to the Politics of Competition," in Ivo Banac (ed.), *Eastern Europe in Revolution* (Ithaca, N.Y.: Cornell University Press, 1992), pp. 13–55.

SABRINA PETRA RAMET **6**

Shake, Rattle, and Self-Management: Making the Scene in Yugoslavia

This is a fact: people prefer to dance than to fight wars.
—**Mick Jones** of the Clash

ROCK MUSIC, ignored at first by social scientists, has lately become the object of increasingly frequent scholarly analysis. There are a number of general studies of a sociological nature,[1] complemented recently by a small literature on rock music under communism.[2] As John Orman has noted, rock is a political phenomenon both because rock artists sometimes take positions on controversial issues (or on the elites themselves) in their songs and because political elites may use legislative or coercive force to suppress, inhibit, or regulate rock performers, regardless of the political intent or content of their songs.[3]

Rock is also political insofar as it is part of a cultural or subcultural milieu that may exalt specific social values. In the late 1960s and early 1970s, rock music was closely linked with the hippie culture, which propounded a leisure ethic in opposition to the Protestant work ethic.[4] Indeed, one observer writing in 1971 concluded that "the only really new feature in the lives of the young is the intensity and resolution of their devotion to pleasure, a commitment to enjoyment and consumption."[5] And beginning in the 1980s, especially in the United States, much of rock music has celebrated dance, love, and the pursuit of ephemeral pleasure—values that, when contrasted with the protest rock of 1967 to 1971, seem to encourage political apathy and resignation. By the end of the 1980s, a new kind of rock had appeared: rap music. This new strain, originating among American blacks, was characterized by an emphatically monotonous tone, fast pace, and lyrics laced with ill-focused anger.

Rock music in Yugoslavia, and in the successor states of Yugoslavia, has reflected rock trends worldwide. But there have also been some characteristics peculiar to the Yugoslav context. In musical terms,the folk traditions from which Yugoslav musicians have drawn are very different from, say, those of the United States and Britain. In terms of the audience, whereas a study published in 1972 found that American youngsters at that time did not take lyrics too seriously and more often than not either had only the vaguest notion about what a song's message was about or completely misconstrued the message,[6] Yugoslav youngsters have tended to take the lyrics very seriously and in any case listen more attentively.

And finally, in political terms, American authorities banned songs and harassed rock performers in the early years (1955–1970) essentially because of their personal disgust with the rhythmic sensuality of the music or because of language they found obscene,[7] and in the 1990s they are still concerned about obscenity, as shown in the October 1990 trial of the rap music group 2 Live Crew in Fort Lauderdale, Florida, and in accusations in 1992 that the rap songs "Cop Killer" and "Apocalypse Now" had inspired fans to kill police.[8] Nor should one forget that the Pennsylvania House of Representatives passed a bill in 1990 that requires "parental warning" labels on certain records offering "lewd" or "provocative" lyrics.[9] In this context, Allan Bloom's claim, in his 1987 book *The Closing of the American Mind,* that "nobody thought to control it [rock], and now it is too late,"[10] sounds laughable. In communist Yugoslavia, by contrast, rock performers had to deal not only with a parallel reaction from their own parents and elders[11] but also with problems of specifically political censorship.

Originally highly imitative of American trends, Yugoslav rock has come of age and now boasts a broad range of styles—protest rock, punk, new wave, orthodox rock, and various kinds of revivals and syntheses.

There are groups like Bora Djordjević's Fish Soup (Riblja čorba), which see themselves as social critics and accordingly have been attacked regularly in the party press. Other groups are bored by politics and sing of romance almost exclusively—as was the case with the Zagreb-based Steamroller (Parni valjak) until the outbreak of war between Serbia and Croatia in 1991.[12] Still others, like the Belgrade combo of Vlada Divljan and Saša Šandorov, have been experimenting with "noninstrumental music." From heavy metal to hard core to soul to breakdancing to rap,[13] all the genres known in the West have appeared in Yugoslavia, sometimes with local variations. There was even a group in Ljubljana in the 1980s (Borghesia) whose members incorporated elements of sadomasochism into their songs and attire. There is also a specifically homegrown genre called "šogor rock,"[14] which developed in

Hungary and in the Hungarian community in the Yugoslav province of Vojvodina and which generously blends local folk music with rock.

Yugoslav rock groups borrowed from the West but produced their own blend, often crossing genres and blending elements not previously blended. In fact, there has been so much experimentation and borrowing that the boundaries between genres and subgenres have become fuzzy. Some of the music of the Macedonian group Bread and Salt (Leb i sol), illustrates this, blending rhythmic patterns of the Turkish Orient with rock melodies and interspersing country sounds straight out of Nashville.[15] Along similar lines, although pure punk is all but dead in the successor states of Yugoslavia today, the Slovenian group Bastards (Pankrti), which enjoyed popularity in the 1980s, blended elements of punk with more mainstream rock, and Tonny Montano, a kind of latter-day Elvis Presley who sang of terrorism and drugs, the Mafia, and comic-book fantasies, talked to me (in 1987) of infusing the rhythms of the late 1950s with the energy of punk.[16]

Rock music remains in a certain sense a phenomenon of the cities. The major rock clubs are naturally in the larger cities—Kulušić, Lapidarija, and Jabuka in Zagreb, Akademija and the Drugi Novi Klub in Belgrade, and in an earlier day (1982–1985) the F.V. Club in Ljubljana.[17] Later, with the closure of the F.V. Club, the Ljubljana alternative scene moved to the Disco Amerikanec, in the Old Town. New wave, hard rock, and alternative music find their supporters in the cities. Heavy metal, however, is much more a phenomenon of the smaller towns. Novi Sad, a quiet town with a provincial atmosphere, became one of the big centers for heavy metal in the mid-1980s, with several heavy metal clubs and Yugoslavia's only heavy metal magazine.[18]

More generally, there have long been some important regional differences in musical trends, differences that may be accentuated now that the country has fragmented. In the years prior to the Serbian Insurrectionary War, which broke out in June 1991, the major centers for "Yugorock" were Belgrade (in Serbia), Ljubljana (in Slovenia), and Sarajevo (in Bosnia). But with the virtual destruction of Sarajevo in the course of months-long bombardment in 1992, many of Sarajevo's top rock performers fled (some to Paris) and its once lively rock scene came to a sudden end. Aside from these three cities, Zagreb (in Croatia) and to some extent Skopje (in Macedonia) have also been important, the latter chiefly because of the accomplished group Bread and Salt. But musical tastes differ widely. In Serbia, for instance, folk music remains more popular than rock music, even among the young, and rock must compete for its share of the market; moreover, with the rise of Slobodan Milošević there was a rash of folk groups issuing recordings along a nationalist nature, thus intensifying the competition offered to rock.

Serbian rock groups tend to be orthodox in their approach to rock. In Bosnia-Herzegovina, in contrast, White Button (Bijelo dugme), long the most popular and most influential group in Yugoslavia ("the Yugoslav Beatles," as one music critic put it,[19] but a casualty of the war), sometimes used folk music as an introduction to its songs; another Sarajevo group, Blue Orchestra (Plavi orkestar), built its name by fashioning its own successful mix of folk and rock. Folk music is part of the old Slavic soul, and the temptation to draw upon it is very strong. Fiery Kiss (Vatreni poljubac, 1977–1987) also brought folk elements into its music and favored a syncopation that is native to Balkan folk music, not to rock.[20]

Again, Slovenia, the most developed and most Western of Yugoslavia's republics and long renowned for its more liberal political and social attitudes, saw the sprouting of Yugoslavia's only important hard-core punk scene in the early 1980s. Bands like Demolition Group, Epidemic, UBR, Tožibabe, the Third Category, and the Trash of Civilization all played during the heyday of punk in the early 1980s.[21]

As Marshal Tito and his comrades looked on, rock music spread to every corner of Yugoslavia—even to economically and socially underdeveloped Kosovo, where the ethnic separation of Serbs and Albanians has been reflected in two parallel rock scenes that were divided by language, ethnicity, and, of course, politics. Serbian groups in Kosovo sing in Serbo-Croatian for local Serbs, and Albanian rock groups sing in Albanian for local Albanians.[22]

INFLUENCES FROM THE WEST

Almost all Yugoslav rock musicians speak English. The reason is very simple: Yugoslav rock has grown and developed under the influence of American and British rock, and no other country comes close in influence. English remains, in this sense, the language of rock. Asked (in 1987) which Western rock performers impressed them the most, the rock musicians I met in Yugoslavia repeatedly mentioned Deep Purple, Billy Idol, Brian Adams, Bruce Springsteen, Lou Reed, the Rolling Stones, the Kinks, and U-2. Also mentioned—though less frequently—were the Beatles, Cream, Frank Zappa, Led Zeppelin, and Van Halen.

Most Yugoslav rock groups either have performed in the West or dream of doing so. Bora Djordjević boasts, among other things, of having had a video aired on MTV, and Goran Bregović, the leader of White Button, was interviewed at one time on MTV. Pop singer Djordje Balašević is the exception, singing on his 1987 album, *Bezdan,* of his lack of interest in either America or the Soviet Union.

Bijelo dugme (White Button), Sajam Hall 1, end of 1986 in Belgrade. Photo courtesy of Vladimir Bajac.

But where Russia is concerned—whether Soviet or post-Soviet—disinterest has been widespread. Russian rock records are nowhere to be found. No one listens to Russian rock music, and most Yugoslavs are unable to name a single Russian (or Soviet) rock group. In fact, aside from the special relationship between Hungarian rock and Hungarian-language rock in Vojvodina, essentially the only foreign countries whose rock performers have exerted any influence on the Yugoslav rock scene are the United States, Britain, and Ireland. The same pattern would no doubt hold true for the other countries of Eastern Europe, with the two Germanys as a special case.

ORIGINS AND GROWTH

As was the case everywhere, when rock 'n' roll first came to Yugoslavia it was considered impossible to sing in any language other than English. Yugoslavia's first genuine rock star, Karlo Metikoš, not only sang exclusively in English and French but also took the stage name "Matt Collins" to seem less exotic. He recorded various records for Philips under this name from 1960 to 1963, spent a few years touring Hilton hotels in

Athens, Tehran, and Africa, and then, toward the end of the 1960s, retired from performing to write his own songs.[23]

In the 1960s, rock music was, by definition, "alternative" culture. Zagreb was an early center for rock culture in Yugoslavia. Many Zagreb groups would listen to the top twenty on Radio Luxemburg on Saturday night and by Monday be playing the songs locally. Some Croatian groups specialized in soul (such as We from Šibenik and Robots from Zagreb). In fact, soul music was quite big in Yugoslavia in the 1960s, with Wilson Pickett, Otis Redding, and Aretha Franklin among the favorites. Yugoslav soul bands would sing in English, trying to copy the style of the original. Later they started to write their own soul, singing it in Croatian, but by and large this was not successful.[24]

Yugoslavia had its "Woodstock" in the mid-1960s, when Belgrade played host to the country's first rock festival. Fifteen thousand young people turned out to hear the bands—which was more than anyone had believed possible until then.[25] Rock music had come of age in Yugoslavia.

The year 1967 registered another important watershed when Index became the first Yugoslav group to play its own songs. After that, gradually more and more groups started writing their own material and singing it in Serbo-Croatian, Slovenian, or any of the other languages of this multiethnic country.

Gradually rock took hold in Yugoslavia and gained access to the media. A string of specialty magazines started to cater to the new taste—first *Ritam* in Novi Sad, then *Džuboks* and *Pop ekspres* in Zagreb, *ITD* in Belgrade, and in 1982 Belgrade's *Rock* magazine. All of these early endeavors are now defunct.

In 1974, a new group was created in Sarajevo, the aforementioned Bijelo Dugme (White Button), led by Goran Bregović. The group would in time establish itself as the number one rock group in the country. White Button changed the rules of the game, singing eloquently about the issues and problems confronting Yugoslavs and looking to local, Bosnian musical traditions for inspiration. In both lyrics and music, White Button was "Yugoslavicizing" rock music. At one point, White Button was subjected to a series of attacks in the weekly magazine *NIN*. But the group ignored the attacks and the affair blew over.[26]

The 1970s was a decade of consolidation in the Yugoslav rock scene in which a handful of groups established themselves as the leading rock voices of the day. Aside from White Button, two other major rock groups were founded in the 1970s: Bora Djordjević's Fish Soup (in Belgrade) and the Macedonian group Bread and Salt—both of them in 1978.[27] These three groups shared center stage with Azra (a group that did not survive into the 1980s) and Index. The hitherto renowned Belgrade group Korni Group folded in 1974. Aside from these groups, the Slovenian group

Bijelo dugme. Photo courtesy of Vladimir Bajac.

Bulldozer (Buldožer) won a large audience by taking up political themes and singing in Serbo-Croatian.

The 1970s were also the years of the Boom rock festivals in Yugoslavia, which attracted thousands of fans to annual spectacles held variously in Ljubljana, Novi Sad, and finally Belgrade.

The end of the 1970s brought new trends to Yugoslavia, when new wave (*Novi val* or *Novi talas*) and punk arrived, almost simultaneously. The new fashions seemed to be personified in the vaguely punkish covergirl Sladjana Milošević, a rock singer in her own right who produced three albums[28] and a number of singles. Her outlandish new fashions and sexually explicit language offended the conservative politicians and there were repeated articles in the party-supervised press warning that Milošević and others were "corrupting" the youth.[29] Punk took hold only in Slovenia, and it remained strictly "alternative." The arrival of punk, however, stirred heated controversies in the daily press.[30]

But despite the authorities' lack of enthusiasm, rock flourished in Yugoslavia. In 1982, *Rock* magazine tried to come up with a tally of how many rock groups were playing in Yugoslavia and asked the groups to inform the magazine of their existence; some 2,874 professional and amateur groups responded. Petar Popović, an international label manager for RTB PGP Records in Belgrade, estimated (in 1987) that there were, at that time, 30 to 50 professional rock groups in Yugoslavia and perhaps 5,000 amateur groups. There were by then more than 200 amateur groups in Belgrade alone.

Bajaga somewhere in Serbia, 1986. Photo courtesy of Vladimir Bajac.

Several important new groups were formed in Yugoslavia in the 1980s: Ljubljana's Laibach (formed in 1980), Belgrade's Bajaga and the Instructors (formed in 1984), and Ljubljana's Falcons (Sokoli, formed in summer 1989). These groups, together with the Belgrade groups Fish Soup and Yu-Group, Skopje's Bread and Salt, and Zagreb's long-lasting bands Steamroller and Haustor (briefly enjoying a reincarnation as the satirical Dee Dee Mellow in 1988 before returning to a more "serious" presentation once again as Haustor) dominated the Yugoslav rock scene in the late 1980s. Zagreb's Dirty Theater (Prljavo kazalište) gradually built its reputation as a strong band, and by 1990–1991 it was widely considered Zagreb's top rock band. Other top bands of the 1980s included Belgrade's Electric Orgasm (Električni orgazam), which disappeared from public view in 1988, Partibrejkers (another Belgrade band), and two all-female acts: Cacadou Look (Opatija) and Boja (Novi Sad).[31] The only well-known band to sing in Macedonian was Mizar, which wove Byzantine liturgical characteristics into its music. The top female soloists as of 1992 are Snežana Mišković Viktorija (in Belgrade) and a new entry, Kasandra (in Zagreb).[32] The top male vocalists as of 1992 are the erratically original Rambo Amadeus (in Belgrade) and Oliver Mandić (also in Belgrade).

COEXISTING WITH THE AUTHORITIES

Rock music came to the attention of the authorities very soon, and, as rock journalist Dušan Vesić has revealed, Tito and Kardelj personally discussed this genre in order to decide what posture to adopt toward it. In contrast to the other communist elites of Eastern Europe, Tito and Kardelj opted for a policy of toleration.[33] Tito was sensitive to rock's potential for rebelliousness but hoped that by showing toleration he could win the rock scene over to a supportive stance. His gamble paid off, and the 1960s in particular saw a rash of panegyric rock ballads praising him and his program of self-management.[34]

Yugoslav rock musicians would sometimes say that the communist authorities never banned a rock song in their country. That was not entirely true. Release of an album by the Sarajevo rock group Smoking Forbidden (Zabranjeno pušenje), for example, was held up in spring 1987 because of official disapproval of one of the songs included on the album.[35] The group was criticized for singing of people wanting to leave the country, and although the incriminated song remained on the album, the record directors had grey ink printed over the relevant passage in an attempt to render it illegible.[36] The problem was that the lyrics could quite easily be read through the "censor's" ink, which looked

Dr. Nele Karaljić of Zabranjeno Pušenje (Smoking Forbidden), 1986.
Photo by Milan Rašić.

rather more like highlighting than obliteration. When the album was released in June 1987, the inefficient "censorship" drew attention to the unwanted passage:

> *It bothers me that some people think*
> *that life is somewhere different,*
> *and that people there do not dream the old dream,*
> *and wait for their passports so they can leave.*[37]

But it is clear that the political atmosphere was fairly relaxed when it came to rock when one considers that the market has seen songs comparing the Yugoslav communist party to the Mafia, portraying Naziism in an ambiguous and hence possibly favorable light, and blasting East and West and of course highly pessimistic and cynical songs—none of which were banned.

Even so, rock groups occasionally encountered roadblocks. For instance, whenever a record was being taped, the group always had to submit in advance its song texts and its proposed jacket design to the recording company for approval. But when difficulties arose, there was usually a way to get around them—Yugoslav style. Fish Soup (Riblja čorba), for example, had recorded its sixth album with the Zagreb company Jugoton, but when it submitted the texts for its seventh album, Jugoton grumbled. So Fish Soup left Jugoton and went back to its earlier recording company and recorded the original texts without alteration.[38]

*Bora Djordjević of Riblja Čorba (Fish Soup), 1987. Photo courtesy of
Vladimir Bajac.*

The Slovenian group Bastards (Pankrti) had similar experiences. In 1982, the group wanted to call its second album "The Bastards in Collaboration with the State" and to adorn the cover with a photo of a band member kissing a memorial to the partisan struggle. This was too much for the company—and surely for the authorities as well—and the group was advised to come up with an alternative. So the Bastards submitted a nearly identical photo using a monument from World War I and suggested the transparently sarcastic title "Lovers of the State." It passed. And between songs dealing with sexual relations between the state apparatus and the individual citizen, the listener can hear excerpts from a speech by Stalin.[39] But I heard few such stories, although Divljan noted the obvious when he told me, "It is not clever to sing against Tito of course."[40]

A classic case involved singer Esad Babačić-Car, whose 1981 song "Proletarian" seemed to train its guns on the self-proclaimed protectors of the proletariat:

> *Where are you now, proletarian?*
> *Where's your gun now?*
> *Where are your fists now,*
> *proletarian?*
> *We're raising our flags*
> *in honor of your fight,*
> *lead us now, proletarian!*
> *Never mind blood,*
> *never mind lives,*
> *our thoughts will be with you,*
> *proletarian!*
> *Proletarian, proletarian,*
> *you're just an idol hewn in stone,*
> *proletarian!*[41]

The song was banned.

All the performers I talked to agreed that in Yugoslavia the lyrics were more important than the music, and some Yugoslav singers—Slovenia's Jani Kovačič, for instance—owed their popularity almost exclusively to their ability to verbalize the concerns and preoccupations of the current generation.

Many of the groups have been willing to tackle political subjects. For example, Hungry Frank (Lačni franc), a popular band from the provincial town of Maribor, satirized one-candidate elections. The group sings in Slovenian, but its song "White Shirts and Ties" deliberately plays on a double meaning associated with the Croatian: "Kandidati volimo,"

Lačni franc (Hungry Frank) performing in Ljubljana, 1987. Photo by Sabrina Petra Ramet.

which means "we choose/vote for the candidates" in Slovenian, means "we love the candidates" in Croatian. This word game only doubles the sarcastic effect:

White shirts and ties
We vote for you [We love you.]
Golden watches and wise thoughts,
We vote for you. [We love you.]
You fight for our clear heart and mind.
We vote for you. [We love you.]
Conductors of our happiness,
We vote for you. [We love you.][42]

Azra, a mainstream rock group active in the early 1970s, took up an even more sensitive subject in a 1982 song called "Weekly Commentary." In the song, the group calls attention to the media practice of attacking people with different political ideas and alludes to the Yugoslav presumption to be "the center of the world" in some usually ill-defined sense:

I read the weekly commentary
which says publicly
who doesn't think this way.
People without caliber or ideas
slander it and lie ...
Everywhere people are gripped with paranoia,
and would like to be the center
of the world ...
It is forbidden to answer.
Sluggards have an easy life today.[43]

The general, pervasive disillusionment with the communist party is reflected in other songs too. Bora Djordjević, for example, in his 1987 song "Member of the Mafia," compares the party to the Mafia. Against a Harry Belafonte–style calypso rhythm, he sings:

I don't want to be a member of the mafia.
It's the wrong step.
I don't need a piece of paper
where it's written that I am a member
of the mafia.
Even if they put me in jail,
I don't want to be a member.[44]

Nor were religious themes taboo in communist Yugoslavia. The Bosnian group Blue Orchestra, in its 1986 album (*Death to Fascism*), evoked the spirit of a revival in the song "That's the Shock." The song deals with the alleged miraculous appearances of the Madonna at Medjugorje, and in one passage it calls on the audience:

Brothers and sisters,
We are here to celebrate
the birth of the new Lord,
Appearance of the Holy Ghost.
So hand in hand, eyes in eyes,
Pray to Jesus,
Jesus is Our Savior.[45]

The emergence of the independent trade union Solidarity in Poland in 1980 stirred widespread sympathy in Yugoslavia, and inevitably the theme found its way into the rock idiom. Azra produced a musically striking song, "Poland in My Heart," in 1981:

Gdańsk 1980
when Autumn said
   no ...
Gdańsk 1980
the factories were aflame.
Twice they did not send
tanks against the workers.
They did not dare.
We won,
   all of us.
Poland
in my heart.
   Mazurka.
Poland
never had a quisling.
Every day
   a polonaise
plays in my house ...
Pope Wojtyła
   and I.
Gdańsk 1980,
lines for newspapers
Independent trade unions
Defense committees.
Gdańsk 1980
the factories were aflame.
Twice they did not send
tanks against the workers
tanks against the workers
tanks against us.[46]

DOMINATION AND THE LIBIDO (IN SLOVENIA)

Domination has, one might say, compelling power, and that power, as psychologists know, has libidinal connections.[47] Two Slovenian groups of the 1980s played on that connection between domination and the libido to tap into the energy and intensity experienced in "the psychic space where the libido comes into contact with the superego."[48] But whereas Laibach, a pop totalitarian band created in 1980, explores what we might call "social domination," staging totalitarian-style pageants and singing music that derives as much from fascist traditions as it does from industrial rock trends, Borghesia, a Ljubljana group that folded in 1988, preferred the "private domination" of S&M. Both bands had trouble booking performances and marketing their videos domestically. But both have targeted primarily the foreign market, producing their records in Britain, Belgium, and Germany and marketing them in the United States through Wax Trax Records of Chicago.

Laibach was created in Trbovlje around 1 June 1980, coinciding with the anniversary of the town's antifascist uprising in 1924. An industrial town of 20,000 inhabitants, located about 60 kilometers (36 miles) from Ljubljana, Trbovlje has a strong revolutionary tradition, which fed and nurtured Laibach. The first exhibition-concert by the new group was planned for 27 September 1980, but the authorities didn't like the posters and, in anxiety, quashed the concert.[49] The group's posters stirred trouble again in 1983, when Dušan Mandić produced a poster showing a heterosexual couple who looked like they had been wrenched out of an Annette Funicello movie. The male wore a suspicious-looking armband with the "approved" star and the words "Disko FV" and the woman had two badges on her dress, with the inscriptions "Crazy Governments" and "Nazi Punks Fuck Off."[50] The authorities did not like the poster if only because one of the badges depicted had been banned and had already put Laibach collaborator Igor Vidmar in jail for its alleged fascist overtones. But Laibach seemed to relish in provocation and advertised its satirical attitude with the declaration "Our freedom is the freedom of those who think alike."[51]

In 1983, Laibach was banned from appearing publicly under its name. It responded by forming a mock political superstructure, calling it Neue Slowenische Kunst (New Slovenian Art, but always referred to either in the German or by the initials NSK). It passed "statutes" for NSK, requiring that "a[n] NSK member must be diligent, respectful towards the tradition and history of the NSK, obedient and cooperative in carrying out common decisions and irreproachable in living up to the universal and secret, legal and moral norms of the NSK."[52] In a later manifesto, "Ten Points of the Convent" (1983), Laibach declared, under Point One: "Laibach works as a team (team spirit), in the fashion of industrial production and totalitarianism, which means the individual does not speak out—the organization does. Our work is industrial, our language political."[53]

Aside from Laibach, there were three other component parts of NSK: the New Collectivism (its "propaganda" division), the Irwin Painting Group, which did the artwork for the band, and the Theater of the Sisters of Scipio Nasica, which developed the stage presentation of Laibach rock pageants. The artwork and stage presentations followed the music in drawing inspiration from Nazi art and totalitarian art in

Laibach at Victory Monument at Kalamegdan Park, 1986. Photo by Zoran Jovanović.

general. The Irwin group, for its part, took to ironic mimicry of the paintings of old socialist realism (the official art form decreed by Stalin in the Soviet Union in the 1930s). The group worked underground during these years, from 1983 to 1987: Its 1984 concert in Ljubljana, for example, was announced only by a wordless poster marked with the familiar Laibach cross by Malevich and the date. Laibach would be restored to legal status only in 1987, with its concert Birds of a Feather staged in the Festival Hall in Ljubljana.[54]

Laibach quickly stirred controversy across Yugoslavia. Some people felt that Laibach sympathized with Naziism, others thought the members were suggesting that communism was the same as Naziism, and still others thought they were using Nazi imagery as an energized medium in which to communicate their ideas about culture and politics. People in the party were nervous and unable to shake the suspicion that the group was equating them with the Nazis. NSK members have always been rather tight-lipped about their intentions: One member told me, for instance, only that "art has to be frightening. It cannot be comfortable," and he offered that what Laibach was doing was waging "psychophysical terror" on its listeners.[55]

It is too simplistic to view Laibach as either pro-Nazi or anti-Nazi, although its members are, for that matter, fiercely antitotalitarian—but that is not the point. Fascism, thanks to the persistent drumbeating of the communist press, remained part of the political mythology of Yugoslavia, and the communists never stopped recalling their days of glory in the struggle against fascism in World War II. Thus, although the fascist motif would be an energized medium in any society, it acquired additional energies in the Yugoslav context. Laibach's "official" thinking about individualism and individual rights/needs was captured in a 1988 exchange between *Rockpool* and one of Laibach's members:

Q: "What is your definition of an individual?"
A: "A multitude of one million divided by one million."[56]

The tone of Laibach's "ideology" can be read in the text of "The Laibach Apologia" (a 1982 text by Laibach member Tomaž Hostnik):

Sons of the truth, since when have you been the brothers of the night?
What's making your hands red with blood, what blight?
The explosion in the night is a rose of pain,
there is nothing to justify by it or explain.
You cannot break the altar, the altar of lie[s],
that makes forms multiply.
An immaculate picture and painless lights,
the only refuge from terrifying nights.

We children of the spirit, brothers of might,
whose promises are still nowhere in sight.
We ate the black specters of this world below,
we are singing of this mad picture of woe.
The explanation is a whip, and you bleed.
Break the mirror of the world a hundred times;
it is all in vain. We have vanquished
the night; our debt has been paid,
and the light is ours.[57]

Every concert that Laibach did became the vehicle for political provocation. A 1989 concert in Slobodan Milošević's Belgrade was no exception. In this concert, Laibach showed *The Bombing of Belgrade,* a documentary German propaganda film from 1941, together with a section of a later (Tito-era) film entitled *First Official Meeting of the Nonaligned Countries in Belgrade,* in which the political leaders of the nonaligned states were shown dancing with their wives. Before the concert began, Laibach members read a text, mixing Serbian and German, with the intention of warning Serbs of the totalitarian proclivities of Serbian party boss Slobodan Milošević. In a prescient warning, the text read, "Brother Serbs, we are not going to let anyone rape you any more. We understand your problems." This was an allusion to Milošević's later-broken promise (of early 1987) that he would not let anyone "beat you any more."

By contrast with Laibach, Borghesia makes a rather different impression. This can be gathered already from the text of its 1988 song "Am I?":

Am I a man machine?
Am I a sex machine?
Am I a fuck machine?
Am I a dream machine?
Am I a killing machine?
Am I a space machine?
Am I a soft machine?
Am I a mad machine?
Am I a life machine?
Am I … am I … am I …[58]

Borghesia's music was industrial, making use of many noninstrumental sounds, and its videos featured everything from S&M scenes to film clips of the partisan struggle to shots of Tito. The S&M motif recurs in its art, as indicated by the album *Surveillance and Punishment*[59] and song titles such as "Discipline! (Punish Them)" and "Disciple."[60] In the 1988 song "Beat and Scream," Borghesia sings,

I care for my slave
sometimes I even feed him
would you?
yes ... captain
that's a good boy
please, sir
master I worship you.
I love your boots
yes, stomp and kick ...
you, wonderful boots
yes, you can beat me and whip me
beat me!
beat me!
beat me!
you can piss in my mouth
And I'll suck you
let me serve you, master
destroy me master
destroy!
destroy!
destroy!
why screaming?
I love those screams
screams?
screams?
screams?
just a part of me to use
and command.[61]

At times, as in the case of Laibach, Borghesia has turned its sights toward social criticism, as in the song "Police Hour":

Everything is under control
Streets are empty
Night is cold
Headhunt!
Patrols are everywhere
Special divisions
and civil agents
Rhythm of metal drum
Broken windows
Smashed cars
Everything is under control
There is no matinee today.[62]

Videosex, 1986. Photo by Jane Štravs.

Borghesia was even more explicit in its 1986 record *Their Laws, Our Lives*, which showed a well-armed "lawman" against a backdrop of number 133 written over and over again. Article 133 of the federal penal code provided for legal penalities for "verbal offenses."

Borghesia had links to the gay, lesbian, and pacifist movements in Slovenia, and its members gave firm support to all forms of sexual liberation. Goran Lisica, rock critic and manager of the Ljubljana group Videosex, offered that Borghesia systematically pursued the "subversion of traditional sexuality by negation of the classical family, in order to have a clean slate on which to reexamine the nature of sensuality, formulate new meanings and establish the reasons of sexual deviation."[63]

Laibach and Borghesia both inspired cult followings within Yugoslavia and in the West, and Laibach conducted very successful tours of a number of U.S. cities in 1989 and 1993. Inevitably musical clones appeared, especially of Laibach, such as the groups Children of Socialism, Ciao, Cunts, O! Cult, and Abbildungen Variete, all of which played at the New Rock festivals of 1982 and 1983.[64]

ROCK AS BUSINESS

A 1985–1986 survey conducted by Zagreb's Institute for Social Research found that about half of Yugoslavia's young people reported "high interest" in rock music. Interest was highest in Bosnia and Croatia, where more than 60 percent of young people surveyed reported "high interest," and lowest in the economically less developed province of Kosovo, where the figure was only 28 percent.[65] Overall, this amounts to a fairly dependable market for rock music, even if traditional folk music has remained more popular among young people in some regions, chiefly Serbia and Kosovo.

Of the twelve record and cassette companies that operated in pre-1991 Yugoslavia, all but one produced at least some rock. In all, they marketed about 100 new rock titles every year. Jugoton of Zagreb and RTB PGP of Belgrade were (and are) by far the largest companies, with Jugoton alone accounting, in the late 1980s, for about 30 percent of all rock titles and 70 to 80 percent of total production of rock records. In general, rock records accounted for about a fifth of annual Jugoton production of popular music (or about 1 to 1.5 million rock records and cassettes produced by Jugoton in 1986).[66]

A best-selling rock album (such as albums by Blue Orchestra, Fish Soup, or White Button) might sell between 200,000 and 500,000 copies. Less commanding groups have had to be happy to sell perhaps 6,000 records. It is interesting to note that at the time of the punk euphoria (in the early 1980s), punk groups were known to sell 20,000 to 50,000 copies and the first album of the popular heavy metal band Wild Strawberries (Divlje Jagode) sold around 200,000 copies within a short time.

With the exception of Laibach and Borghesia, Yugoslav (and post-Yugoslav) rock bands have played to a domestic audience. Many groups are interested in traveling to the West on tour, but for most groups the possibilities are very restricted.

Where the rock media are concerned, the early magazines catering to this sector did not survive. Even Petar Popović's pioneering *Rock* magazine, later reincarnated under the name *Pop-Rock,* was dead by 1990. But new magazines appeared to take their place, such as Peter Lovšin's *Gram* (Ljubljana, in Slovenian), *Heroina* (Zagreb, in Croatian), *Ritam* (Belgrade, in Serbo-Croatian), *Disko selektor* (Skopje, in Macedonian), and *Ćao* (Belgrade, in Serbo-Croatian, focusing on foreign rock). *Gram* and *Heroina* lasted only a few issues.[67] But by October 1992, yet another scene magazine, *Pop* (Zagreb, in Croatian), hit the stands.[68]

Aside from these magazines, there have been various television and radio programs featuring Yugo-rock (as well as foreign rock videos on television, mostly of American origin) and regular or semiregular rock columns and coverage in various newspapers.[69]

ROCK AND THE WAR

In my *Balkan Babel*, I sketched out the multivarious connections between Yugoslav rock and the famed "national question," which was ultimately allowed to tear the country apart.[70] These connections made it clear that the bands were in a position to comment on, reflect, and even to some extent affect interethnic behavior, especially at local levels.

As the political tensions boiled over into war, rock bands in the republics of what was once Yugoslavia took differing positions on whether and how to respond to the new situation. Some favored advocacy, such as Zagreb's Psihomodo pop, whose 1991 album *Maxi Single za Gardiste* featured four "patriotic" songs, including the strident "Croatia Must Win."[71] Certain Croatian punk groups began singing obscene anti-Milošević lyrics in early 1992. Others, such as Belgrade's Rimtutituki (an obscure band), urged pacifism, as in this group's song "Peace."[72] The town of Zaječar, for example, played host to rock groups from across the war-torn former republics of Yugoslavia, 29–31 August 1991. Bands from Belgrade, Pula (in Croatia), Skopje, Zagreb, and Sarajevo played to a crowd of 20,000 fans, promoting the old Beatles' message "All you need is love."[73] About a month later, several pacifist-minded bands got together on 4 October 1991 for a Rock for Peace festival in Ljubljana. The participating groups were Falcons (from Ljubljana), Steamroller (Zagreb), Hungry Frank (Maribor), Martinka Krpan (Ljubljana), Šank Rock (Velenja, Slovenia), and Automobili (Gorica).[74] Belgrade likewise saw its own Peace Concert, on 22 April 1992, with a crowd of some 50,000 people. Among the groups and artists singing for peace in Belgrade were Boye, Colored Program (Obojeni program), Rambo Amadeus, Ekaterina Velika, Electric Orgasm, Rimtutituki, Rade Šerbedžija, and Mira Karanović.[75] Yet another Peace Concert, this one dedicated to the city of Dubrovnik, was held in Pula on 22 August 1992. Artists from Croatia, Slovenia, and Bosnia-Herzegovina performed at this event, with some 6,000 fans in attendance.[76]

Still other groups, such as Belgrade's self-styled "anarcho-rocker" Rambo Amadeus, have declared themselves to be in "opposition."[77] Belgrade's rock bard Bora Djordjević actually registered a political party, half in jest, calling it the Party of Ordinary Drinkers (Partija običnih pijanaca, or POP). Soon he had recruited 1,100 members, so he decided to run as his party's candidate for the Federal Assembly, finishing second in his district.[78] Djordjević, an early supporter of Milošević, had in fact turned against Milošević before the end of 1991 because of the Serbian leader's decision to go to war. In any case, he would seem incongruous in any role other than permanent rebel.

For some musicians, such as Nele Karaljić, who saw the dangers of war three or more years before it finally broke out, the start of the war meant only a new phase in their activism for peace.[79]

The war has gutted Bosnia altogether and obliterated its indigenous culture, and many of the republic's best-known rock stars have now fled abroad. But rock music continues unabated elsewhere, war or no war. In Croatia, in particular, a number of new groups were formed between 1990 and 1992.[80]

CONCLUSION

Howard Becker once remarked that deviance is a category conjured into existence by persons who function, in some sense, as rule makers.

> Social groups create deviance by making the rules whose infraction constitutes deviance, and by applying these rules to particular people and labeling them as outsiders. ... Deviance is not a quality of the act a person commits, but rather a consequence of the application by others of rules and sanctions to an "offender." The deviant is one to whom that label has been successfully applied.[81]

The same holds true for dissidence, which may be viewed, in this context, as a kind of political deviance. It follows that the same behavior may be viewed as normal (if perhaps critical) in one system and dissident in another. The broad leeway allowed in communist Yugoslavia meant in effect that rock music was *not* viewed for the most part as a dissident force; this contrasts, for instance, with Czechoslovakia, where rock music was widely viewed as dissident activity by the country's hardline communist regime.[82]

In one sense, to the extent that the communist regime left rock music alone, rock music in Yugoslavia remained "depoliticized." But on other levels, rock in Yugoslavia was political, too. For one thing, certain rock groups took it upon themselves to try to actively mobilize people to support the ecology movement and other grass-roots movements.[83] Second, as amply illustrated, Yugoslav (and post-Yugoslav) rock performers have, from time to time, addressed central political concerns, sometimes taking risks in the process. And third, rock, as a component of youth culture (even if no longer appealing exclusively to youth), may be seen as a potential vehicle of socialization, even if the ideas reflected in rock music do not happen to originate with the particular rock performers. In this regard, Shmuel Eisenstadt comments that youth culture may serve as a medium of transitional socialism that detaches young people from their families and contributes to their integration into social roles.[84] As Simon Frith argues,

> Rock culture is not confined to ceremonial occasions but enters people's lives without aura, taking on a meaning there independent of the intentions of its original creators. The rock audience is not a passive mass, consuming records like cornflakes, but an active community, making music into a symbol of solidarity and an inspiration for action [even if only an inspiration to dance]. … The rock audience is not always manipulated but can make real choices; the music doesn't always impose an ideology but can, in [Greil] Marcus's phrase, "absorb events," absorb its listeners' concerns and values.[85]

NOTES

This chapter is a revised and updated version of the author's "The Rock Scene in Yugoslavia," which appeared originally in *Eastern European Politics and Societies* 2, no. 2 (Spring 1988). At the time of original publication, the author still used the name "Pedro Ramet." Reprinted by permission of the editor of *Eastern European Politics and Societies.*

1. Dieter Baacke, *Jugend und Subkultur* (Munich: Juventa Verlag, 1972); Simon Frith, *The Sociology of Rock* (London: Constable, 1978); Tibor Kneif, *Einführung in die Rockmusik: Entwürfe und Unterlagen für Studium und Unterricht* (Wilhelms-haven: Heinrichshofen's Verlag, 1979); John Orman, *The Politics of Rock Music* (Chicago: Nelson-Hall, 1984); William S. Fox and James D. Williams, "Political Orientation and Music Preferences Among College Students," *Public Opinion Quarterly* 38, no. 3 (Autumn 1974); Philip Lamy and Jack Levin, "Punk and Middle-Class Values: A Content Analysis," *Youth and Society* 17, no. 2 (December 1985); James J. Leming, "Rock Music and the Socialization of Moral Values in Early Adolescence," *Youth and Society* 18, no. 4 (June 1987); Harold G. Levin and Steven H. Stumpf, "Statements of Fear Through Cultural Symbols: Punk Rock as a Reflective Subculture," *Youth and Society* 14, no. 4 (June 1983); Karen Beth Mashkin and Thomas J. Volgy, "Socio-political Attitudes and Musical Preferences," *Social Science Quarterly* 56, no. 3 (December 1975); Lorraine E. Prinsky and Jill Leslie Rosenbaum, "'Leer-ics' or Lyrics: Teenage Impressions of Rock 'n' Roll," *Youth and Society* 18, no. 4 (June 1987); S. Lee Seaton and Karen Ann Watson, "Counterculture and Rock: A Cantometric Analysis of Retribalization," *Youth and Society* 4, no. 1 (September 1972); and John Stratton, "What Is 'Popular Music'?" *Sociological Review* 31, no. 2 (May 1983).

2. Christoph Dieckmann, "'Rock'n Roll Is Here to Stay'—Jugendkultur in der DDR," *Kirche im Sozialismus* 12, no. 3 (June 1986); Rainer Erd, "Musikalische Praxis und sozialer Protest: Überlegungen zur Funktion von Rock and Roll, Jazz und Oper," *German Politics and Society,* no. 18 (Fall 1989); Volker Gransow, "The Political Culture of Pop-Music in the GDR," *GDR Monitor,* no. 17 (Summer 1987);

Y.H., "Rock-and-Roll in Hungary," *Cross Currents* 7 (1988); Zsolt Krokovay, "Politics and Punk [in Hungary]," *Index on Censorship* 14, no. 2 (April 1985); Olaf Leitner, *Rockszene DDR: Aspekte einer Massenkultur im Sozialismus* (Hamburg: Rowohlt Verlag, 1983); Günter Mayer, "Popular Music in the GDR," *Journal of Popular Culture* 18, no. 3 (Winter 1984); Sabrina P. Ramet, *Social Currents in Eastern Europe: The Sources and Meaning of the Great Transformation* (Durham, N.C.: Duke University Press, 1991), chapter 9 ("Rock Music and Counterculture"); Sabrina Petra Ramet, *Balkan Babel: Politics, Culture, and Religion in Yugoslavia* (Boulder, Colo.: Westview Press, 1992), chapter 5 ("Rock Music"); Timothy W. Ryback, *Rock Around the Bloc* (Oxford: Oxford University Press, 1990); S. Frederick Starr, "The Rock Inundation [in the USSR]," *Wilson Quarterly* 7, no. 4 (Autumn 1983); Anna Szemere, "Pop Music in Hungary," *Communication Research* 12, no. 3 (July 1985); Anna Szemere, "Some Institutional Aspects of Pop and Rock in Hungary," *Popular Music* 3 (1983); Artemy Troitsky, *Back in the USSR: The True Story of Rock in Russia* (Boston: Faber & Faber, 1987); Peter Wicke, *Anatomie des Rock* (Leipzig: VEB Deutscher Verlag für Musik, 1987); Peter Wicke, *Rockmusik* (Leipzig: Verlag Philipp Reclam Jun., 1987); Peter Wicke, "Young People and Popular Music in East Germany: Focus on a Scene," *Communication Research* 12, no. 3 (July 1985); and "Pop im Prager Untergrund: Brief eines Fans," *Kontinent*, Special issue (1976). Also relevant are Donna Buchanan, "Popular Music in a Time of Glasnost: The Politics of Musical Transition in Bulgaria, 1988–90" (Paper presented at the Twenty-fourth Annual Convention of the American Association for the Advancement of Slavic Studies, Phoenix, Ariz., November 1992); and "The Nature of Official Documents Concerning Control of Vocal/Instrumental Groups and Discotheques," *Survey* 29, no. 2 (Summer 1985).

3. Orman, *The Politics of Rock Music,* p. x.

4. Frith, *The Sociology of Rock,* p. 54; also Loyd Grossman, *A Social History of Rock Music* (New York: David McKay, 1976).

5. Jeremy Seabrook, *City Close-up* (London, 1971), as quoted in Frith, *The Sociology of Rock,* p. 20.

6. R. Serge Denisoff, in *Sing a Song of Social Significance* (Bowling Green, Ohio: Bowling Green State University Popular Press, 1972), reported a study he conducted among 180 students when a pessimistic, nihilistic song titled "Eve of Destruction" was the number one record. Only 36 percent of those surveyed understood the lyrics as the composer had intended, and 23 percent completely misconstrued them. Denisoff concluded that "the protest song is primarily seen as an entertainment item rather than one of political significance." Quoted in Orman, *The Politics of Rock Music,* p. 150.

7. For example, in the mid-1950s the Juvenile Delinquency and Crime Commission of Houston, Texas, banned more than fifty rock 'n' roll songs within the space of a single week. This and other cases are discussed in Orman, *The Politics of Rock Music,* pp. 3–8.

8. *New York Times,* 17 October 1990, pp. A1–A11; and *Neue Zürcher Zeitung,* 22 September 1992, p. 5.

9. *New York Times,* 5 February 1990, p. A15.

10. Quoted in the *Seattle Post-Intelligencer,* 1 November 1987, p. F-1. See also the *New York Times,* 18 October 1987, p. 30.

11. *Vjesnik* (Zagreb), 8 December 1984, p. 11, called Bora Djordjević's album *The Truth* "ethically unacceptable."

12. Interview with Husein Hasanefendić, member of Steamroller, Zagreb, 24 June 1987.

13. Such as the Croatian rap group Ugly Leaders. See *Mladina* (Ljubljana), 17 March 1992, p. 40.

14. Literally "brother-in-law rock" but probably best understood as a home-grown equivalent of country rock.

15. See, in particular, the album *Zvučni zid: Musika za teatar, film i TV,* JUGOTON LSY-63249 (1986).

16. Interview with Tonny Montano, Zagreb, 24 June 1987. See also Snežana Golubović, "Čovek koji je ubio i taličnog tema" [interview with Tonny Montano], *Rock* (Belgrade), July 1987, pp. 26–28.

17. See Dragan Ambrozić, "FV založba," *Rock* (August 1987), p. 48; also *Novi Vjesnik* (Zagreb), 5 October 1992, p. 24C.

18. Interview with Petar Popović, International Label Manager for RTB PGP and founder of *Rock* magazine, Belgrade, 16 June 1987. See also Jadranka Janković, "Ja sam obićan mali lajava" [interview with Zlatan Stipišić-Džibo of the heavy metal group Osmi putnik], in *Rock,* June 1987, pp. 26–27. For a discussion of this era, together with sample rock lyrics, see *Drugom stranam: Almanak novog talasa u SFRJ* (Belgrade: SSO Srbije, 1983).

19. Interview with Petar Popović. The definitive study of White Button is Darko Glavan and Dražen Vrdoljak, *Ništa mudro–Bijelo dugme: Autorizirana biografija* (Zagreb: Polet Rock, 1981).

20. Interview with Mimo Hajrić, former member of Fiery Kiss (Vatreni poljubac), Sarajevo, 15 September 1989.

21. Interview with Zemira Alajbegović, manager of Borghesia, Ljubljana, 3 July 1987.

22. The Kosovo rock scene is discussed in Darko Hudelist, *Kosovo: Bitka bez iluzija* (Zagreb: Dnevnik, 1989), pp. 109–129.

23. Interview with Dražen Vrdoljak, music director of Radio Zagreb, Zagreb, 22 June 1987.

24. For an excellent account of the early years of Yugoslav rock, see Ljuba Trifunović, *Vibracije* (Belgrade: SSO Srbije, 1986).

25. Interview with Aleksandar Tijanić, *NIN* music critic, Belgrade, 18 June 1987.

26. As reported in Dušan Vesić, "Dvadeset taktova za Tita," *ITD* (Belgrade), May 1987, p. 9.

27. Re Bread and Salt, see *Oko,* 7–21 September 1989, p. 27.

28. Her third album was a collaborative effort with Darko Kraljić: *Alexandra Sladjana Milošević & Darko Kraljić,* RTB PGP 210382 (1989).

29. For example, in *Sarajevske novine* (Sarajevo), 22 March 1979. Also, inter-views with Sladjana Milošević, rock singer, Belgrade, 19 June and 5 July 1987; and interview with Dragan Todorović, rock journalist and editor of *NON* magazine, Belgrade, 10 July 1987.

30. For a detailed analysis and documentation of this trend, see *Punk pod Slovenci* (Ljubljana: Univerzitetna Konferenca ZSMS, 1985).

31. For more detail about the 1980s, see Ramet, *Balkan Babel,* pp. 88–100.

32. Re Viktorija, see *Pop Rock,* 3 May 1989, p. 20; re Kasandra, see *Novi Vjesnik,* 27 September 1992, p. 16B, and *Vreme* (Belgrade), 16 March 1992, p. 52.

33. Dušan Vesić, "Novi prilozi za istoriju Jugoslovenskog rock'n rolla": Part 1, "Josip Broz i rock'n roll," *Pop Rock* (Belgrade), 10 May 1990, p. 2.

34. For details, see Ramet, *Balkan Babel,* pp. 85–86.

35. *Danas,* 7 April 1987, as cited in *Bulletin* of the Democratic International Committee to Aid Democratic Dissidents in Yugoslavia (New York), July 1987, p. 18.

36. Aleksandra Marković, "Tragično smo odrasli" [interview with Nele Karaljić of "Zabranjeno pušenje"], *ITD,* June 1987, p. 5; and interview with Nele Karaljić, leader of Smoking Forbidden, Sarajevo, 14 September 1989.

37. Song "Dan Republike" ("Republic Day") on Smoking Forbidden, *Pozdrav iz zemlje Safari,* DISKOTON LP-8248 (1987). See also the report in *Glas Istre,* 28 June 1987, p. 17.

38. Interview with Bora Djordjević, lead singer of Fish Soup, Belgrade, 18 June 1987.

39. Interview with Peter Lovšin, lead singer of the Bastards, Ljubljana, 30 June 1987.

40. Interview with Vlado Divljan, Belgrade, 17 June 1987.

41. Song "Proletarian" by Esad Babačić-Car, banned, quoted in Aleš Erjavec and Marina Gržinić (eds.), *Ljubljana: The Eighties in Slovene Art and Culture* (Ljubljana: Mladinska knjiga, 1991), p. 43.

42. Interview with Zoran Predin, lead singer of Hungry Frank, Ljubljana, 1987.

43. Song "Poljubi me," on Azra, *Ravno do dna,* JUGOTON LSY-61661/2/3 (1982).

44. Song "Član mafije," on Fish Soup, *Ujed za dušu,* RTB PGP 2320436 (1987).

45. Song "To je šok," on Blue Orchestra, *Smrt Fašizmu!* JUGOTON LSY-63262 (1986).

46. Song "Poljska u mome srcu," on Azra, *Ravno do dna.*

47. See, for example, Robert J. Stoller, *Pain and Passion: A Psychoanalyst Explores the World of S&M* (New York: Plenum Press, 1991).

48. As I put it in my *Social Currents,* p. 229.

49. Interview with Ivan Novak, member of Laibach, Ljubljana, 21–22 March 1992. This interview was conducted in the hotel lobby of Hotel Slon, between 2 and 4 A.M.

50. The poster is reproduced in Erjavec and Gržinić, *Ljubljana: The Eighties,* p. 58.

51. Quoted in ibid., p. 88.

52. Quoted in ibid., p. 89.

53. Quoted in ibid., p. 89.

54. Ibid., p. 100.

55. Interview with Ivan Novak.

56. From material assembled by NSK for its project *NSK Embassy Moscow* in 1992.

57. Song "The Laibach Apologia," on *Germania* (1982), as quoted in Erjavec and Gržinić, *Ljubljana: The Eighties,* p. 115.

58. Song "Am I" [text in English], on Borghesia, *Escorts and Models*, PLAY IT AGAIN SAM RECORDS BIUS-1014 (1988).

59. Borghesia, *Surveillance and Punishment*, PLAY IT AGAIN SAM RECORDS BIUS-3023.(n.d.).

60. Both featured on the album *Surveillance and Punishment*.

61. Song "Beat and Scream" [text in English], on Borghesia, *Escorts and Models*.

62. Song "Police Hour," on Borghesia, *Resistance*, PLAY IT AGAIN SAM RECORDS BIUS-1038 (n.d.).

63. Quoted in Erjavec and Gržinić, *Ljubljana: The Eighties*, p. 47.

64. Regarding the Slovenian rock scene more broadly, see Gregor Tomc, *Druga Slovenija* (Ljubljana: Krt, 1989), especially pp. 116–123.

65. Interview with Furio Radin and Vlasta Ilišin, researchers at the Institute for Social Research, Zagreb, 26 June 1987.

66. Interview with Siniša Škarica, program director of Jugoton, Zagreb, 24 June 1987.

67. Telephone interview with Peter Lovšin, leader of Falcons and editor of *Gram*, Seattle-Ljubljana, 21 June 1991; and interview with Peter Lovšin, leader of Falcons and former editor of *Gram*, Ljubljana, 26 March 1992.

68. The first issue was dated 2 October 1992.

69. These are detailed and discussed in Ramet, *Balkan Babel*, pp. 101–102.

70. Ibid., chapter 5, especially pp. 89–92.

71. Song "Hrvatska mora pobijediti," on Psihomodo pop, *Maxi Single za Gardiste*, CROATIA RECORDS MS-D 2 03553 3 (1991).

72. *Politika—International Weekly* (Belgrade), 18–24 April 1992, p. 16.

73. *Bosanski Pogledi* (Sarajevo), 5 September 1991, p. 22.

74. Interview with Peter Lovšin, leader of Falcons, Ljubljana, 26 March 1992.

75. *Vreme*, 27 April 1992, p. 19.

76. *Novi Vjesnik*, 23 August 1992, p. 7A.

77. Miha Štamcar and Jani Sever, "Mitingaš v Sloveniji" [interview with Rambo Amadeus], *Mladina* (Ljubljana), 17 March 1992, p. 29. Regarding Rambo Amadeus, see also *NIN*, 5 June 1992, p. 34.

78. *Politika ekspres* (Belgrade), 16 June 1992, p. 17.

79. In addition to being a rock musician, Karaljić was also a comedian with his own show on Sarajevo Television. In September 1989, he devoted an entire show to warning, albeit through comedy, of the risks of ethnic hostilities, partition of the country, and war. For a recent article that contains some mention of Karaljić, see *Politika ekspres* (Belgrade), 10 May 1992, p. 12.

80. Such as the popular group Overflow from Koprivnica. See the report in *Heavy Metal World: Novine za ljubitelje heavy metala*, October 1992, p. 8.

81. Howard S. Becker, *Outsiders: Studies in the Sociology of Deviance* (New York: Free Press, 1963), as quoted in Paul H. Shapiro, "Social Deviance in Eastern Europe: On Understanding the Problem," in Ivan Volgyes (ed.), *Social Deviance in Eastern Europe* (Boulder, Colo.: Westview Press, 1978), pp. 6–7.

82. On Czechoslovakia, see "Tschechische Rockmusik als Seismograph für gesellschaftliche Alternativen," *Osteuropa* 35, nos. 7–8 (July–August 1985).

83. For example, see Gregor Tomc, "Punk and Protest in Slovenia," *Across Frontiers* 3 (Fall 1986), pp. 26–28.

84. Shmuel N. Eisenstadt, *From Generation to Generation* (New York: Free Press, 1956), as cited in Frith, *The Sociology of Rock*, pp. 25–26.

85. Frith, *The Sociology of Rock*, p. 198.

Whoever Doesn't Listen to This Song Will Hear a Storm

Goran Bregović in an interview with Sabrina Petra Ramet

RAMET: Bijelo dugme has often been referred to as "the Beatles of Yugoslavia" by rock critics Darko Glavan and Dražen Vrdoljak and others. How did Bijelo dugme achieve this special position?

BREGOVIĆ: Our big advantage is that we are really *Yugoslav.* There is a Yugoslav character to our music. But by the same virtue, our music is a little bit too rude and too primitive for the outside world. It is natural for Yugoslavia. Our music is as Western as Yugoslavia is—which means not too Western, because this is still the Balkans, and in some ways we are still very far away from Europe. So you can say we are a rock 'n' roll band, but we are popular in the way that a country western band would be in the United States. You can hear our songs in the pubs, for instance. Folk singers even sing my songs.

RAMET: Bijelo dugme is sixteen years old. That makes it one of the oldest rock groups in Yugoslavia.

BREGOVIĆ: Yes, we created Bijelo dugme in 1973. Our first three records were made in England, in George Martin's studio. He was in fact the Beatles' producer. It was a time when we had enough money for things like that, and at that time we didn't have very good studios in Yugoslavia.

RAMET: When did you start playing rock 'n' roll yourself?

BREGOVIĆ: Around 1967, at age seventeen, I was playing in Italy and elsewhere. Then for a while I had a band called Jutro [Morning]. I spent five years in the West, which is enough. Now I would like to go to the East. But they don't want me.

RAMET: Why not?

Interview with the leader of the Sarajevo rock group Bijelo dugme (White Button), Sarajevo, 14 September 1989.

Goran Bregović of Bijelo dugme, 1986. Photo courtesy of Vladimir Bajac.

BREGOVIĆ: Because of politics. So we have never played in the USSR. The Soviet cultural attaché here was always negative. Because we always have treated political themes in our songs. My songs are always a bit anti-communist.

RAMET: Can you give me an example?

BREGOVIĆ: I can give you an example from our domestic politics. When the problems with the Albanians in Yugoslavia started [in 1981], we made a song in Albanian—which was quite daring. And for a few years we would hoist black and red colors at our concerts, and satirize the similarity of naziism and communism.

Basically, I think rock 'n' roll in communist countries has much more importance than rock 'n' roll in the West. We can't have any alternative parties or any alternative organized politics. So there are not too many places where you can gather large groups of people and communicate ideas which are not official. Rock 'n' roll is one of the most important vehicles for helping people in communist countries to think in a different way. So for that reason I think rock 'n' roll is more important for people in the Eastern countries than for people in the West.

RAMET: The traditional cultures are different too.

BREGOVIĆ: Of course. And that means that there is a basic difference between our way of thinking and the Western way of thinking. And that in turn means that the same words mean very different things in the East and in the West; they have different resonances.

RAMET: What about the evolution of Bijelo dugme? How has the music evolved?

BREGOVIĆ: Our evolution was in fact something like the evolution of the Beatles. Remember, they started with "She loves you, yeah, yeah, yeah" and finished with Oriental effects, political songs, the satirical *White Album,* and all these songs at the end. We also started with songs about love and now sing mostly about politics. The central fact of our life is that there are Serbs and Croats and they don't understand each other. They will finish with war. It will be 1941 all over again. We are heading in the same direction. You can see this even in music. Serbs and Croats have their own songs, which are more important for them than any "Yugoslav" songs. Last year I put together their two national hymns in a single song, and when I played this at some recent concerts, it resulted in small wars. The Croatian hymn "Lijepa naša" and the Serbian hymn "Tamo daleko"—I put these together, under the title "Lijepa naša." Not to take sides, of course.

They started a campaign against me in both the Serbian and the Croatian press and wanted to take me to court because of it. We had a Serbian church choir singing the Serbian anthem and characteristic Croatian singers from Dalmatia singing the Croatian anthem. It was too much for them. But when it came down to it, they couldn't initiate proceedings against me, because there were no grounds for prosecution. The case would have been thrown out of court, and they knew it.

But really, all of this feuding between Serbs and Croats is just ridiculous. It's the same language.

RAMET: **You said the song produced "small wars."**

BREGOVIĆ: It was heavy. At a few concerts it was really terrible.

RAMET: **So are you still playing the song?**

BREGOVIĆ: Yes, I still play it, because I think it's silly to think in that way.

RAMET: **Why do people react so strongly?**

BREGOVIĆ: Well, you should know that these hymns—"Lijepa naša" and "Tamo daleko"—were forbidden in Tito's time. But since Tito's death, people have been singing these songs in public. It reflects the rise in nationalist feeling in the country.

RAMET: **So your song could be taken as a critical commentary on the national revival.**

BREGOVIĆ: Exactly.

RAMET: **Why did you call your group "White Button" [Bijelo dugme]?**

BREGOVIĆ: Because our first album had a song in which we sang, "If I could be a white button, I could always be close to you and you would not be aware of me." The record jacket showed a white button on a girl's blouse, riding on her chest.

RAMET: **You spoke yourself of Yugoslavizing rock music, and other people have given you credit for this as well. Do you think you may at the same time have been Westernizing Yugoslav young people?**

BREGOVIĆ: I think so, yes. At the beginning the communist authorities were constantly harassing us, because rock music was too Western for their tastes. We started with a bizarre image. We even wore dresses and earrings at the beginning. It was a bit strange for many Yugoslavs. Some of the newspaper journalists wrote articles saying they would like to cut off our ears altogether. Before us, rock 'n' roll was considered a youthful pastime which students would engage in while at the university, and then after university, they were expected to give it up and live like all "normal" people. But now you can hear rock music even when you go to the supermarket to buy your food.

RAMET: **Tell me some more of your early development as a musician.**

BREGOVIĆ: I wasn't really young when my career took off. I was in my fourth year at the university when I made my first record. I had been a professional musician from age fifteen and when I returned from the West I was twenty; then I started to attend the university. But I never finished university, because I sold my first 100,000 records.

RAMET: **What were you studying at the university? Music?**

BREGOVIĆ: No, I was studying philosophy and sociology.

RAMET: **In April 1976, you were supposed to go to New York, but then the tour was canceled. What happened?**

BREGOVIĆ: Those very aggressive Croatian emigré organizations sent us death threats. They were threatening to kill us.

RAMET: Why?

BREGOVIĆ: Because we think of ourselves as "Yugoslavs," not as Croats. That was the basic reason, I think. The emigré Croats don't approve of people who feel Yugoslav. But I'm from a mixed marriage myself. My mother is Serb, my father is Croat. And there are millions of people like that in Yugoslavia. So we never actually played any concerts in America.

RAMET: Where has Bijelo dugme played aside from Yugoslavia?

BREGOVIĆ: We have played in Poland and Bulgaria, but that was basically because I hoped that they would be stepping stones to Russia. I want to play in Russia. We also played at a festival in France in 1985.

Actually, we were once in Moscow, and we are really quite popular in Russia. We sell our records on the black market there. We were scheduled to play a big concert in Moscow in December 1985. Bajaga [another Yugoslav rock group] was playing before us, but the police stopped the concert before we could play, because people were breaking things. There was a huge crowd, maybe 400,000 people. So again, our concert was canceled.

At one time, I hoped to market a record of Russian groups here in Yugoslavia. (I have my own record company, Kamarad.) But it's very difficult. I even talked with some government ministers about the record project, but it's not easy.

RAMET: Beginning March 26, 1976, there was a series of articles in NIN [the Belgrade weekly] by Sergij Lukač, attacking Bijelo dugme. Who was Lukač, and why these attacks?

BREGOVIĆ: At that time, they thought we were too Western. Lukač himself is very well known in Yugoslav journalism. He is a professor at the University of Belgrade and writes a lot. Our image made him nervous, I guess. It was too loud for him perhaps. Too Western. But this article had some weight, because it was *NIN,* the most important magazine in Yugoslavia, which is always close to the official line.

RAMET: So did that have any consequences for Bijelo dugme? Were any concerts canceled?

BREGOVIĆ: No. They can't do that. We were already too strong for them. But at Jugoton, where we were recording our records at the time, they became sensitive to our lyrics and just cut out sections of our tapes and discarded them. So on our early records you can find some very strange things, where the music suddenly jumps, because a section has been removed by our "conscientious" editor. There was one song, for example, where I sang that Jesus Christ was a bastard. They didn't like that. So they spliced that line out and threw it away.

RAMET: So they protect religious groups too.

BREGOVIĆ: They protect *everything* here.

RAMET: When I talked with [rock journalist] Dražen Vrdoljak in Zagreb, he made a point that there is a big problem in Yugoslavia for rock music gener-

ally, that there are basically six different recording networks and if a group is established in Zagreb, it is easy to operate there but difficult to operate elsewhere. But Bijelo dugme is much more popular than most groups. Have you had this kind of problem in any way?

BREGOVIĆ: Now we do. It started with Slovenia. Their radio stations stopped playing music from outside Slovenia. So we started playing less and less in Slovenia. And now there are big problems between Serbia and Croatia. Many of the rock bands see themselves in national terms; they see themselves as Croatian groups or as Serbian groups. We are one of the last truly Yugoslav rock bands. But oddly, the Yugoslav idea is starting to become unpopular in Yugoslavia. Yugoslavia doesn't mean anything anymore.

RAMET: When was the last time you played in Slovenia?

BREGOVIĆ: Three years ago, I think. At that time they were already starting to become very self-centered and so I started a small campaign to get on Slovenian television. It is the one and only time when I have done something like that. But it was necessary, because some of the biggest Yugoslav stars could not get on Slovenian TV. The Slovenes are really very nationalist.

RAMET: What about Yugoslav audiences today?

BREGOVIĆ: They are all aggressive. It's a recent phenomenon, about two years now. But they are really aggressive, like at football games. They bring national flags of Serbia and Croatia. There's a lot of violence. At a few places you had to worry for your life.

RAMET: Have you addressed this issue of national aggressiveness in any of your recent songs?

BREGOVIĆ: Yes. I opened my last record with a small song about the war. We sing,

When the war starts,
What we gonna do,
You and me, baby?
Will we cover ourselves in a blanket
and kiss each other 'til it's over?

I think there will be war in Yugoslavia. It will be a stupid war.
On another record (in 1987), I opened with a song which went like this:

Spit and sing, Yugoslavia …
Yugoslavia, on your feet and sing.
Whoever doesn't listen to this song,
Will hear a storm.

I used to open all my concerts with this song. We had 20,000 people at the concerts and they would all get up and sing along.

RAMET: I thought you were playing concerts of 100,000.

BREGOVIĆ: Not any more. When we played big concerts like that, our fans would destroy the stadiums. So now we play to somewhat smaller audiences.

Anyway, a few months later, when millions of Serbs took to the streets carrying Slobodan Milošević's picture, they were singing this song, "Spit and Sing." They sang it in Serbia, in Vojvodina, everywhere. Because this is a song which can frighten the politicians: "Whoever doesn't listen to this song, will hear a storm."

On the same album, we also included a song in which Svetozar Vukmanović-Tempo, the old partisan hero and communist politician, sang a partisan song with a choir of children from an orphanage. It was a very sad song, an old war hero singing with these children. He was a real war hero.

RAMET: How did people react to that?

BREGOVIĆ: There were many strange reactions. Some people liked it. Others thought it was not good. Certainly it was strange for a war hero to be singing with a guy like me. And in this context, Vukmanović-Tempo was making a statement against the communists. Not every criticism is necessarily in the lyrics themselves; criticism can come in the format as well.

RAMET: A final question: What do you see as the future of rock music?

BREGOVIĆ: For me, the future of rock music, not just in Yugoslavia but in the world, is ethnic music. Some really fine rock records in the last few years are really close to ethnic music, like Paul Simon, like Peter Gabriel, like U-2. They all draw upon ethnic elements. I am doing this too, and I have been doing this from the beginning. After all, there is no point just copying American rock 'n' roll.

RAMET: Thank you for this interview.

STEPHEN ASHLEY **7**

The Bulgarian Rock Scene
Under Communism (1962–1990)

I N HIS SPEECH at a human rights conference in Paris in June 1989, organized by the Fondation du Futur, Bulgarian sociologist Petko
Simeonov[1] spoke about the problems of instituting democracy in a pe-
ripheral and isolated European country such as Bulgaria, where more
than 60 percent of the population had never been abroad and fewer
than 1 percent had mastery of a major Western language. Noting that his
country's contacts with even its Balkan and communist neighbors were
at a symbolic level throughout the postwar era, Simeonov said that
modern values had penetrated Bulgaria only in a distorted and misun-
derstood manner and had failed to overcome the legacy of mass poverty
and ignorance that had been preserved by four decades of communist
party rule.[2]

This dramatic presentation of the nation's political and intellectual
problems will serve as a useful introduction to an analysis of the history
of rock music under communism in a country where it was perceived as
essentially a foreign product to be copied and imitated but rarely to be
created anew. The ingrained sense of inferiority that long hampered
Bulgaria's rock musicians was demonstrated at a concert that I attended
in the Universiada Hall in Sofia in late 1980. The country's leading group,
the Shturtsi (Crickets), protested a decision by officials to turn on the
houselights during its act by departing from the agreed-upon program
of original, Bulgarian compositions and playing a medley of Beatles and
Rolling Stones classics. The clear implication was that no Bulgarian music would have adequately expressed the group's sense of outrage and
defiance.

One consequence of this overpowering foreign domination was that
until the end of communist rule in 1990, the domestic rock market was
split into two very unequal parts. The first consisted of an elite that had
direct access, through travel, family connections, and the possession of

hard currency, to Western concerts, discotheques, records, tapes, videos, magazines, stereo equipment, and musical instruments. For the second group, the vast majority of the Bulgarian population, especially those living in the countryside and small towns, rock music rarely amounted to more than listening to domestic and foreign radio broadcasts and copying tapes and records brought into the country by members of the elite, who were thus able to shape public taste. In spite of efforts in the 1960s, 1970s, and 1980s, Bulgarian rock musicians failed to create a sizable domestic industry that could supplant the popularity of Western music. Bulgarian talent and enthusiasm were repeatedly obstructed by party opposition to rock music and by the limited technical and material base in the country. Even today, Bulgaria has no popular record industry worthy of the name,[3] has very few concert facilities, and is largely ignored by foreign performers of any stature.[4] Rock journalism scarcely existed before 1989 but is nowadays flourishing, albeit at a modest level of expertise and with a strong bias against domestic musicians and singers.[5]

Young Bulgarians seem nevertheless to attach a huge significance to this imported and barely assimilated culture, seeing it as a symbol of both modernity and youthful rebelliousness. As Juliana and Klaus Roth pointed out in their recent, stimulating article "The Heritage of Rural Culture in Bulgaria,"[6] the process of modernization in postwar Bulgaria has been extremely uneven and has often remained confined to superficial or external changes that did not much affect interpersonal relations, patterns of thought, or political behavior. A parallel might be drawn with the reaction against Ottoman Levantine cultural norms in the midnineteenth century, a very visible feature of which was the *alafranga* fashion, which consisted of little more than changing clothes, table manners, and furniture.[7]

The same obsession with outward appearances may be seen in the career of the group Tangra, which in 1984 was entirely reconstituted by its leader, bass guitarist Konstantin Markov, in a bid to provide Bulgaria with its first new wave group. Imitating the clothes, haircuts, and production sound of the British group Duran Duran, Tangra achieved huge popularity in 1986, with its second album. Its title track, "Be What You Are (Badi Kakavto Si)," did not in fact advocate (stylistic) originality but merely implored young Bulgarians to copy Western tastes in dress and music. Such pleas have, however, been eagerly accepted by a young audience that perceives rock music as a badge of European sophistication and rejects Bulgaria's rich tradition of vocal and instrumental folk music as symptomatic of a *selska,* or backward and insular village culture.[8]

Another feature of Bulgaria's uneven postwar development, which the Roths highlighted in their article, is that informal groups (meaning loosely structured associations of friends) gained a huge importance in everyday life. These groups did so partly because they helped to pre- serve a limited degree of personal privacy under communism and re- sisted the most intrusive powers of the totalitarian Bulgarian state. Among the young, these informal groups tended to define themselves by a shared musical taste. During the early 1980s, the authorities voiced a growing concern about the imperviousness of such groups to ideolog- ical manipulation and the adverse effect they were having on the work of the Komsomol. This culminated in bizarre and totally unsuccessful legislation toward the end of 1985 that imposed a 9 P.M. curfew on teen- agers, made the wearing of school uniforms compulsory even on week- ends, ordered schoolteachers to conduct house-to-house checks on their pupils, and decreed that discotheques be converted into "centers for ideological education." None of these draconian measures were suc- cessfully implemented and all lapsed on the demise of the communist youth movement.

As the Roths observed, Bulgaria's informal groups have proved to be an extremely conservative force in national culture because by defini- tion they sought to isolate themselves from fresh influences and relied on jointly accepted values for their internal cohesion. The ubiquity of such groups explained, in part, the extraordinary longevity of musical trends in Bulgaria. For instance, the British beat groups of the early 1960s, such as the Beatles and the Searchers, which had inspired Bulgaria's first groups—Bandi's Boys (Bandaratsite)[9] and the Silver Bracelets (Srebarnite Grivni)—continued to exert a strong influence throughout the late 1960s and early 1970s. It could be heard as late as 1980 on the Shturtsi's third album (*Twentieth Century*). Similarly, the "progressive" rock music of groups such as Britain's Gentle Giant and Italy's PFM, which reached its peak of popularity in the West in the mid- 1970s, continued to be played well into the 1980s by Bulgaria's first syn- thesizer band, FSB (Formatsiya Studio Balkanton).[10] Articles published in the Bulgarian press from 1988 described how the "hippie" craze had survived to the present day and still had hundreds of adherents, albeit of a diluted, Bulgarian version of the cult of peace and universal love. This long survival of hippie culture in Bulgaria may be linked with the strong undercurrent of interest in spiritual matters and occultism as well as with a rejection of the militarism of communist society.

Young Bulgarians' adulation of Western music has, by no means, been indiscriminate or unselective. During the past three decades, successive generations have shown a steady preference for direct and uncompli- cated styles of rock music as well as for melody and melodrama. Bulgarians have tended not to favor Western artists who relied on musi- cal virtuosity, complex or philosophical lyrics, or outrageous effects; nor have they responded well to performers who focused on predominantly Western issues, such as the unemployment of young people in the 1970s and 1980s. For reasons that are not entirely obvious, the most popular Western musicians in Bulgaria have tended to be British and have included the Shadows, the Beatles, and the Rolling Stones in the 1960s, Deep Purple, Uriah Heep, and Queen in the 1970s, and Duran Duran, Depeche Mode, and the Pet Shop Boys in the 1980s. By 1990, U.S. performers had noticeably pulled ahead in popularity, however, with Madonna, Michael Jackson, and Prince being especially revered. (Following the fall of the communist dictatorship, the same poster shops that previously sold portraits of Marx and Lenin were selling photographs and portraits of pop stars, printed on the same paper, with the same ink and often in layouts identical to the old propaganda pictures.)

Because of the long-standing power of an entrenched mafia of lyric writers, Bulgarian rock songs have only begun to address the real concerns of the domestic audience since 1988, when the impact of Soviet glasnost began to be felt. After approximately 1986, a new generation of Bulgarian rock musicians emerged that was bolder than its predecessors and won permission to perform entirely original compositions often on controversial subjects. This privilege was never allowed to the major established groups of the 1970s and early 1980s, such as the Shturtsi, FSB, Signal, Diana Express, and Tangra, whose creative contribution to their songs was effectively restricted to composing and arranging music to lyrics by officially endorsed writers. Although Volen Nikolaev and one or two others possessed undoubted talent and tried to write songs that had some meaning, like the Shturtsi's "Twentieth Century," most of the mafiosi were content to pen sugary ballads or empty, pretentious pieces, such as Tangra's "The Lead Soldier" or Signal's "Eternal Crossroads."

The new groups of the mid-1980s, however, started to tackle ecological issues, to sing about AIDS and drug problems, to protest the powers of the communist bureaucracy, and to reflect the frustrations of young Bulgarians at their lack of personal and economic independence, their limited career expectations, and their conflicts with their parents.[11] Among such exponents of Bulgaria's generation gap were the punk group Control (Kontrol), which in 1989 became the first nonprofessional rock group to issue a record on the state-owned Balkanton label, as well as numerous heavy metal, hard rock, and new wave bands, most of whom have yet to make records or give concerts in large arenas. As might be expected, those new artists that have made important breakthroughs in their careers, such as Trio Milena or the hard rock group Agate (Ahat), have tended to be among the least provocative. Their comparative lack of passion and willingness to compromise with the communist authorities is well illustrated by the blandness of Milena's eco-logical song "Not That Way, This Way" on the composite album *Koledari-87*. It might be added that Agate accompanied the Bulgarian delegation to the World Youth and Student Festival in Pyongyang, North Korea, in August 1989.[12] (Milena's career took off after the fall of commu-nism, when she became a proponent of the democratic opposition and threw off her inhibitions and most of her clothes to become a strident Bulgarian version of the American singer Madonna.)

Ever since its inception in 1962, when the brothers Dimitar and Ivan Milev formed Bandi's Boys, Bulgarian rock music has been held back by the lack of concert venues in the country, the difficulty and expense of acquiring instruments, the lack of recording studios, and communist party patronage of the pop music (*estrada*) "mafia" and its "lemonady" groups like Tonika SV, Tramway no. 5, and Kukeri.[13] Despite the fre-quency of protests in newspapers by both musicians and the public, es-pecially in the mid- to late-1980s, when the central press became less hostile to rock music, many of the obstacles still remain.

In fact, the economic downturn since 1989 is threatening the success of the ambitious new groups and solo performers that have emerged since 1986. The weekly *Literaturen Front* observed on 13 November 1986 that even after twenty years of existence the Shturtsi had still not man-aged to acquire adequate rehearsal facilities. FSB, which formed in 1976, did not give a concert in Bulgaria until 1 February 1983 because it took the group that long to procure the instruments and equipment to repro-duce its electronic studio sound on stage.[14] The group Impulse provides an excellent example of how the fortuitous acquisition of hard currency might determine the success of a musical career. Impulse was founded by keyboard player Iliya Kanchev in 1981, after he had inherited a large sum of money from an aunt in Australia. It owed its initial breakthrough to the fact that the group actually owned extremely expensive, state-of-the-art instruments.

That there are so many obstacles to the emergence of new talent helps to explain why two groups—the Shturtsi and FSB—dominated Bulgarian rock music during the 1970s and 1980s and even today seem to be facing no noticeable decline in popularity. The veteran group Shturtsi, founded in 1968, over time evolved in the direction of a heavy metal sound, and the group acquired a reputation for writing songs with insidious meanings. In October 1980, when it performed at the Universiada Hall in Sofia, it almost provoked a riot with one song, "Wed-ding Day," which was introduced as a rock and roll lament for the loss of freedom. The song's melody was closely modeled on the Beatles' "Back in the USSR." In 1982, another leading group, Signal, was banned from public appearances after a concert in Burgas, during which—it was claimed—it had aroused "excessive excitement" among its fans. The soul singer Vasil Naydenov created consternation by avowing his ambition to be "the Bulgarian David Bowie." And Kamiliya Todorova, the winner of the 1980 Golden Orpheus contest, defected to Greece in 1983 and has since resumed her career with the Virgin Record Company in London.

The Shturtsi, after numerous conflicts with the authorities in its first decade, became so well established with the public in the final years of communism that even the Ministry of the Interior's weekly newspaper, *Anteni*, was driven to write in 1988 that it had been an irreparable loss for Bulgarian culture that the group had so often been forced to make compromises to survive and had released only six albums in its entire musical career.[15] These albums have, however, followed an impressive musical evolution, as the group has steadily expanded its repertoire and discovered an original identity, breaking away from its early, slavish imitation of the Beatles. In 1988, in honor of the group's twentieth anniversary, the Shturtsi were the subject of Bulgaria's first full-length rock music film, *Twenty Years Later,* directed by Pancho Tsankov.[16] In a later section of this chapter I describe the involvement of the Shturtsi in Bulgaria's democratic revolution in 1990 and 1991.

FSB, both because its members were protégés of the state recording company and because they preferred instrumentals to songs, never had the same conflicts with Bulgarian officialdom and therefore won greater privileges sooner. Its seventh album, *FSB Live,* was the first live rock album to be released in Bulgaria and the eighth, *I Love You This Much,* was the first to be digitally recorded. In 1988, FSB achieved the supreme breakthrough by becoming the first Bulgarian rock musicians to record in the West, which they did at Jose Feliciano's studio in Los Angeles.[17] Such plaudits will guarantee that, in spite of the energy of the new bands from Varna, Ruse, Plovdiv, and elsewhere, Bulgaria's popular, established stars will, like their Western counterparts, continue to be a force on the rock scene for the foreseeable future.

EARLY REGIME HOSTILITY

The accolades for the Shturtsi and FSB notwithstanding, the regime's earliest reaction to rock was hostile—and, on the whole, it remained hostile for more than two decades. In the 1960s, there were frequent calls for a ban on the broadcasting of Western pop music. But the publication of hundreds of pejorative articles and even the holding of two special conferences by the Committee on Art and Culture (in January 1966 and May 1968) had little impact on the popularity of such Western bands as the Beatles, the Rolling Stones, and the Doors. Nevertheless, the communist authorities did not relent in their propaganda against rock music, which continued unabashed throughout the early and mid-1970s.

Attitudes became more flexible after July 1978, however, when, in a letter to the Komsomol, Bulgarian leader Todor Zhivkov criticized the pop music program offered by Bulgarian radio and seemed to sanction the greater accommodation of young Bulgarians' true taste. By 1980, Radio Sofia had introduced the twice-weekly program "Musical Scale," which featured a pop chart compiled from the postal votes of listeners. A greater selectivity was shown in the broadcasting of Bulgarian music. Censorship remained tight, however, and certain Western artists (such as David Bowie) were banned outright. Nevertheless, in 1980 "Musical Scale" went so far as to vote "Another Brick in the Wall," by the British group Pink Floyd, as Bulgaria's most popular song that year. And in 1982, Tina Turner, then planning her comeback, was invited to give a series of concerts in Sofia.

By 1983, the authorities had begun to rethink their position once again. On 4 November, the newspaper *Narodna Mladezh* warned that Western music would denationalize Bulgarian youth and it advocated a strengthening of central control over discotheques and radio. A decree of 17 February 1984 increased the powers of the Committee on Art and Culture to regulate Bulgarian pop music and outlawed the unauthorized recording of music tapes. At the same time, an intensive campaign was started about the quality of the "musical and tonal environment," which provided an ideological dressing to the party's increasingly futile efforts to monitor and control young people.

Georgi Dzhagarov, then vice-president of the State Council and Chair of the Standing Commission on Spiritual Values, defined the musical and tonal environment as anything that formed or stimulated people's tastes in music. Every melody heard on the radio or television, on tapes and records, in concerts, at the theater, in cafes, or in restaurants—in essence, any source of music—was seen as part of this environment.[18]

Investigations carried out by the Center for Sociological Information to the Central Committee (CC) of the Bulgarian communist party, the Committee for Art and Culture, and the State Committee for People's Control found that on Bulgarian radio and television, as well as at public places of entertainment, Western music (including Western classical music) predominated by far. Less than one-third of the music broadcast over Bulgarian radio was Bulgarian in origin. In addition, Western music was played most intensely at prime time, when the greatest number of listeners tuned in. Still more alarming to the Standing Commission on

Spiritual Values were television programs that were "almost totally dominated by Western pop music."[19]

A plethora of articles appeared on the subject. For example, in the aforementioned interview, Dzhagarov used strong language to condemn Western influence in music:

> This kind of music preaches bourgeois morality and anarchy, it rouses hatred and glorifies violence, it provokes hysterics and drives one to despair, it promotes a cult of pornography and criminality, and it undermines morals and aesthetics. ... The whole country has been disquieted by the muddy stream of musical trends sweeping away all the true values of music.[20]

Discussing musical life in Bulgaria during 1981, Aleksandar Raychev, chair of the Union of Bulgarian Composers, explicitly said that immediate measures were to be taken to purge alien influences from Bulgarian culture.[21] Kiril Kosev, earlier head of the central political department of the Bulgarian Army and leader of a group attached to the Standing Commission on Spiritual Values, claimed that the musical and tonal environment in Bulgaria was increasingly losing its national characteristics and was therefore undergoing "deideologization." According to him, "the most subversive and imperialist powers, under the leadership of the United States, have undertaken a universal crusade against socialism. It is an ideological war fought in all fields of culture, including music."[22] Dzhagarov conceded, in contrast, that rock had a "pleasant sound, that could not easily be [forgotten]" but attributed this to the bewitching effects of Western propaganda. In his opinion, the Americans were experts on influencing the Bulgarian public. He said that the Americans tried to promote their "make-believe" democracy by exporting progressive music that supposedly proved their tolerance.[23]

The preponderance of Western music was also troubling in light of a party directive dating from 1971, according to which half of all music broadcast or performed in public should be Bulgarian. Just one-quarter was allowed to be devoted to "the famous names of the world of pop music" (meaning Western stars). But it was almost impossible to follow the directive because of the lack of Bulgarian popular music. Despite the fact that Bulgaria produced about 300 popular songs annually, the quality was too low to satisfy the public.

The party was in favor, as of 1984, of reviving Bulgarian folk music and encouraging better Bulgarian popular music, but the fact that the state was nearly out of funds to support such efforts left little hope for much progress. Even Bulgarian jazz, a genre that attracts a small but loyal group of musicians, found little state support. It was implicitly suspect, anyway, because of its Western roots, and jazz musicians were left to make do with the few antiquated instruments that were available. The exceptional émigré Milcho Leviev, whose career is based in the United States, received no exposure before the democratic revolution in 1989 and 1990.

To diminish the influence of Western music magazines, the Komsomol started to issue and distribute its own bulletin about disco music.[24] The purpose of the bulletin was more than obvious: to convince young people of what was good music and what was bad music. Efforts were made to transform discotheques into centers for ideological education, where political information and dancing existed side by side. The results were far from encouraging: The number of guests fell 50 percent between 1980 and 1984.

Meanwhile, in the early 1980s, some young Bulgarians started to come under the influence of punk culture. By 1983, many young Bulgarians sported spiky hairstyles, dyed their hair bronze, and adorned their clothes with safety pins. The journal *Uchitelsko delo* observed that the punks were aggressive, rejecting communism with contempt and sneering at conformist Bulgarians as "idiots."[25] Other informal groups (such as rockers, heavy metal fans, and disco fans) were less prone to violence but were almost as impervious to party propaganda. The disco fans devoted their energies to acquiring the newest Western fashions, rockers were preoccupied with motorbikes, and heavy metal fans were busy profiteering on the black market. Yet Bulgarian punks remained an amorphous group. As *Uchitelsko delo* noted, "In no way are our punks identical to their London prototypes. The same is true of all [our] other youth cults, for they do not have the opportunities for socializing that would allow them to develop into a genuine movement."[26]

SUBVERTING THE DISCOS

The first Bulgarian discotheque was set up in 1971 by students of Sofia University in a basement club. The number of discotheques increased steadily; by 1978, there were more than 300 and by 1983 more than 450 throughout the country. Although the weekly journal *Anteni* had early on complained about their lack of political purpose, the overwhelming majority of these discotheques remained strictly commercial establishments that often escaped proper government scrutiny. For example, although regulations forbade the private ownership of discotheque equipment, *Anteni* reported (in 1978) that eight out of ten discotheques in the coastal resort of Zlatni Pyasatsi (Golden Sands) depended on private equipment.[27] In fact, the ownership of lights, turntables, speakers, and microphones was effectively a prerequisite of employment as a disc jockey.

Although suggestions were made in the 1970s that discotheques should be overseen by a "unified coordinating agency" responsible to the Committee for Art and Culture and the CC of the Komsomol, nothing was put into effect. This was largely a result of the ambivalence of the authorities, who at once disapproved of discotheques and sought to control them.

The aforementioned attempt by the Komsomol after 1984 to influence the musical repertoire through the publication of a regular bulletin proved to be the prelude to a new government campaign to transform discotheques into centers for ideological education. The new regulations governing the organization, financing, and musical and political program of discotheques was published in August 1985.[28] A single national body, the National Commission for Discotheques, was established under the aegis of the Committee for Art and Culture and the CC of the Komsomol to oversee the implementation of the reform. On the local level, district and town branches of the commission were to be established, and each discotheque was to have its own council in charge of the program, finance, and discipline.

Discotheques were to cease to be "noisy," "primitive" places and were to become forums for the propagation of political ideas and a place where young people could meet "the representatives of other generations, leading figures of our society, and scientific and cultural workers." The program was to consist of music and dance as well as commentaries, lectures, debates, and interviews; the music played was to be "predominantly Bulgarian." Any Western items were to be approved by a number of government bodies, including the Committee for Art and Culture and the Bulgarian Association for Tourism and Recreation as well as by the CC of the Komsomol. Turkish and Gypsy music were not mentioned in the regulations, which suggests that they were completely proscribed at that time.

Smoking and the serving of alcohol were to be banned from discotheques, and the level of noise and the style of the decor were to be strictly regulated. All disc jockeys were to undergo special professional training and would have to be personally responsible for the program and answerable to the district commissions. Discotheques were to be classified into four categories and could charge an entrance fee of no more than two leva. Special regulations would, of course, apply to the discotheques for foreign tourists, which would not be allowed to admit Bulgarians. The Bulgarian government also tried to regulate young people's clothing fashions and artistic tastes.

In September 1985, regulations concerning so-called idle young people were devised to prevent them from taking time off after school, vocational training, or military service and thus delaying their entry into the work force. In October, tough disciplinary measures were introduced in secondary schools to improve classroom behavior and to combat truancy. The 9 P.M. curfew on young people under the age of nineteen was introduced at this point.

That it would prove difficult to guarantee the full implementation of the regulations was made obvious by the fate of similar centralizing decrees. The very complexity of some of the rules, such as those that governed the categorization of discotheques, suggested that there would be problems of interpretation. Moreover, as many as five authorities were given control over various aspects of discotheques: the Committee for Art and Culture, the Komsomol, the Central Cooperative Union, the Bulgarian Association for Tourism and Recreation, and the Ministry for the Production of and Trade in Consumer Goods (which has since been absorbed by the Ministry of Trade). The conflict of their interests quickly militated against the success of the new measures.

A series of articles appeared in *Rabotnichesko delo* in January 1986 that highlighted some of the problems that had arisen.[29] Nikolay Dobrev, the president of the National Commission for Discotheques, admitted that many establishments had been converted into bars or restaurants so that they could continue their profitable alcohol sales. The Bulgarian Association for Tourism and Recreation had estimated that of the scores of discotheques under its control, only nine were suitable for conversion, whereas the Ministry of Trade had offered only 38 establishments, of which some had previously been operating as children's snack bars. The Central Cooperative Union did not submit its recommendations. Of the 450 or more discotheques functioning before August 1985, therefore, fewer than 47 had in fact been transformed into ideological centers, and a number of districts (including Sofia, Shumen, Haskovo, and Kardzhali) had been left without any "discotheques of the new type."[30]

Problems arose over the shortage of equipment, the lack of acceptable music and videotapes, and the supply of adequate quantities of snacks, specifically sandwiches, fruit juice, and yoghurt. It had also proven difficult to recruit disc jockeys and to establish an efficient system of inspection to guarantee the observance of the regulations. Where "discotheques of the new type" had been created, they had proven unpopular with older teenagers and had been forced to rely on the custom of fourteen- and fifteen-year-olds, who often could not afford to pay an entrance fee, which had therefore been waived.

A CALL FOR LIBERALIZATION

A remarkable article published in the Bulgarian communist party daily, *Rabotnichesko delo*, on 24 July 1988, offered a strong defense of informal youth groups and hard rock music and sounded a call for liberalization. Quoting Todor Zhivkov's recommendations to the July 1987 CC plenum, it called for a dramatic liberalization of official policies toward young people in general that would permit independent clubs and associations and uncensored performances of all types of rock music (including heavy metal) by both amateurs and professionals in concerts and on television and radio.

Just previously, the dismissal of sociology professor Stoyan Mihaylov as CC secretary for ideology and culture had been widely interpreted in the West as a blow to the more liberal elements of the Bulgarian communist party, who were sympathetic toward Mikhail Gorbachev's policy of glasnost. (In view of subsequent career moves, it seems hard to believe that Mihaylov could ever have been considered a proponent of reform. In the June 1990 elections, he was elected as an independent MP on a platform of defending traditional Marxism. However, by the standards of 1988 he might have been a liberal.) Mihaylov's dismissal seemingly took effect in March 1988 (his last public engagement was on 18 March) but was not formalized until 20 July, when the first Bulgarian communist party CC plenum of 1988 ratified his dismissal and left hardline Politburo member and CC secretary Yordan Yotov in sole charge of ideological policies. Shortly thereafter, the editorial staffs of two newspapers (the trade union daily, *Trud*, and the Writers' Union weekly, *Literaturen Front*) were purged in a bid to restrain grass-roots pressure for openness in the Bulgarian media. The expulsion of former Artists' Union chairman Svetlin Rusev from the Central Committee was also seen as a strike against liberals in the Bulgarian communist party.

But these personnel changes could not halt the rising pressure for cultural liberalization—including in the sphere of rock music. In an earlier article in the Fatherland Front daily, *Otechestven Front*, the philosophy professor Vasil Prodanov had warned that without both careful handling by the authorities and significant political liberalization in Bulgaria, the informal youth groups might develop into a nexus of opposition to communist rule.[31]

The *Rabotnichesko delo* article of a year later entirely supported Prodanov's plea for tolerance and concluded with a series of recommendations that would revolutionize party policy toward hard rock music and informal youth groups. It called, in short, for official acceptance of heavy metal and punk music and for the relaxation of youth club regulations to abolish membership schemes, drop entrance charges, and permit a more diverse range of nonpolitical and recreational activities. The authors proposed that television and radio allot more time to hard rock music and encourage amateur Bulgarian groups. It advocated the establishment of a national rock concert agency to organize performances throughout Bulgaria on behalf of professional, semiprofessional, and amateur musicians. Lastly, it called for the improvement or construction of facilities for performing rock music in every region of the country.[32]

The article was written jointly by Dragomir Dakov, a thirty-one-year-old staff reporter, and economist Mariana Mihaylova. Nothing in their earlier careers had suggested that either had a particularly liberal outlook or was likely to challenge the party. Mihaylova has, in fact, written a number of propagandistic articles attacking leading Western economists; in 1986, she reported for *Rabotnichesko delo* on the international conference in Warsaw and wrote an article entitled "The Role of Propaganda in the Struggle Between the Two Sociopolitical Systems."[33]

One of the striking features of the article by Dakov and Mihaylova was its readiness to cite the opinions not just of experts on youth policy but of the rock performers themselves as well. They also cited the opinions of sociologist Dr. Petar-Emil Mitev, who had frequently argued in the press for a more tolerant approach toward trends among the young. (Later he emerged as the leader of the "Bulgarian Road to Europe" faction in the communist party and briefly figured in its Supreme Council in 1990.)

URIAH HEEP ON TOUR

In August 1988, the British heavy metal band Uriah Heep gave fourteen concerts in Bulgaria, including concerts in Varna, Burgas, Ruse, Gabrovo, Veliko Tarnovo, Shumen, and Vratsa. The climax to the tour came on 11 August, when the group performed before a crowd of more than 10,000 fans in the Akademik stadium in Sofia. As several Bulgarian newspapers remarked in advertising the tour, Uriah Heep was at that time the best-known Western rock group ever to perform in Bulgaria.[34]

Although Uriah Heep had long ceased to be a major attraction in the West, the Bulgarian public responded enthusiastically to its tour. Part of the reason for the enthusiasm was that in the early 1970s the group had won a very large following in Bulgaria, which had been rivaled only by another British hard rock group, Deep Purple. The popularity of the two groups was also enhanced when, in the mid-1970s, the keyboard player Mitko Shterev, of the leading Bulgarian band Diana Express, devoted an entire album to his adaptations of their music.

Bulgarian fans reportedly paid 15 leva for tickets to the concert in the Akademik stadium on 11 August. This sum was large in a country where the average monthly wage was approximately 220 leva. An eyewitness reported that the concert had been attended by every age group between five and fifty; indeed, some young parents had gone with children on their shoulders. *Sofia News* reported that Uriah Heep had been well received by "teenagers brought up on punk and Madonna."[35] During the group's performance, fans repeatedly went up onto the stage to give flowers, waved banners saying "We've Waited So Long," and at times made so much noise that they drowned out the group's music, which was poorly amplified.

The tour received a good deal of press coverage; the group's photograph and a short account of its history were even published on the back page of the Bulgarian communist party daily, *Rabotnichesko delo*.[36] The literary weekly *ABV* even printed an interview with the singer Mike Box, under the title "Rock Blessed by Dickens," together with a letter from the group that urged readers to "keep on reading and keep on rocking."[37]

RECENT TRENDS

During the second half of the 1980s, largely as the result of the efforts of a British independent record company, Hannibal Records, Bulgarian folk music acquired a cult following throughout the West. The breakthrough release was a compilation disc, *The Mystery of Bulgarian Voices*. To the great surprise of its promoters, it entered the British top twenty album charts, a feat quite unequaled by any other East European folk music recording. Part of the record's success resulted from the vogue for world music that had been fostered by Paul Simon's album *Graceland*. But the Western audience was also intrigued by the unfamiliar vocal quality revealed on the album.

The most remarkable tracks were by a trio of elderly women from the village of Bistritsa (near Sofia) who performed under the name of Trio Bulgarka. They featured prominently in the concert tours that were subsequently set up to promote the album and successive anthologies that were also marketed under the title "The Mystery of Bulgarian Voices." Another beneficiary of the vogue for Bulgarian music was the clarinetist Ivo Papazov, who is as much a jazz musician as an exponent of traditional Bulgarian music. The huge state companies that the communist regime ran at much expense for so many years also participated in the boom. The Western audience was not sufficiently aware of the differences between their blander, modified renditions of folk favorites and the more authentic performances of amateurs, quite a number of whom made their way into the compilations promoted by Hannibal Records and other companies.

By 1988, a number of top rock musicians had spoken out in support of Bulgarian folk music and suggested that its almost oriental tones and rhythms could influence the mainstream Western music scene. *Sofia News,* the foreign-language weekly published by the Sofia press agency, featured an interview with former Beatle George Harrison, who was shown in a photograph alongside Trio Bulgarka. Harrison was quoted as saying that he had been so impressed by traditional Bulgarian music that he now listened to little else. Linda Ronstadt was another Western star who gave her seal of approval to the trend. But the Western artist who made the first and greatest effort to adapt musical influence from Bulgaria was the eccentric and reclusive genius Kate Bush. Her album *The Sensual World,* released in 1989, featured three tracks on which Trio Bulgarka sang backing vocals. Of these, perhaps the most successful is "Rocket's Tail," which has both Bush and her Bulgarian collaborators engaging in the vocal dynamics and wails that had so impressed the West. On all three tracks, Trio Bulgarka sang backing parts in Bulgarian, which gave a weird, alienated feel to the songs. Kate Bush's album was received with virtual rapture in Bulgaria and the state record label, Balkanton, began at once to release her earlier work. Previously, Bush had been regarded with outright suspicion by the music censors because of the mystical subjects and esoteric styles that characterize her work. It has yet to be seen what influence she will have on the Bulgarian rock scene. Although a number of writers and performers had tried to incorporate folk rhythms and motifs in rock music and even sing about folk rituals and beliefs, until *The Sensual World* there had never been anything akin to the musical crossover achieved on the track "Rocket's Tail."

The main attempt to synthesize folk music and rock music was made in the 1970s and early 1980s by the Gypsy keyboard player Mitko Shterev and his group, Diana Express. However, in striving for a mixture of the two styles, Shterev had lost a lot of the excitement and force of rock and had veered toward the middle-of-the-road ballads that, he knew, would pass by the censors with minimal difficulty. A rather less bland synthesis was achieved by the Shturtsi on a few of its albums. The most successful songs are on the album *Musketeers' March,* the group's last before the fall of dictator Todor Zhivkov at the end of 1989. "Rhythm in Pink," for instance, is a hard rock version of a folk tune, and "Tom Thumb" (Pedya Chovek) turns to a folk story for its subject. On neither track, though, do the Shturtsi use any traditional instruments, such as the *gaida* (bagpipes), the *kaval* (flute), or the *gadulka* (the rebec, or one-stringed violin). Nor does it in any way alter its Western-derived vocal style. Perhaps the best of its folk-tinged hard rock numbers is the song "Enyovden" (Midsummer's Day), on the 1982 double album *The Taste of Our Time.*

Released as a single, it topped the Bulgarian chart (compiled from listeners' requests to Radio Sofia) for weeks on end during summer 1982.

One fact that could promote a more successful synthesis of traditional music and Western rock is the complete disappearance of censorship following the political revolution of 1989 and 1990. Bulgaria was relatively slow to join the anticommunist revolt throughout Eastern Europe, probably because of the weakness of the native dissident movement. However, the day after the fall of the Berlin Wall, on 10 November 1989, the decisive event took place. Todor Zhivkov, the village-born head of state and party who had ruled Bulgaria since 1954, was ousted in a coup d'état. The precise details of the plot will perhaps never be known, but it seemed that the move went ahead with the backing of both the Soviet leadership and the Bulgarian army. Zhivkov was replaced by his former foreign minister, Petur Mladenov, who quickly handed the party leadership over to Aleksandar Lilov, a former ally of Zhivkov's late daughter, Lyudmilla, who had been purged from office in 1983 because of his evident ambition and greater liberalism. Together with the former foreign trade minister, Andrei Lukanov, who became prime minister in February 1990, Lilov installed a far more liberal regime that, under the pressure of public expectations and events elsewhere in Eastern Europe, found itself obliged to introduce a multiparty democracy in spring 1990.

Four days before the coup, the environmental pressure group Ecoglasnost organized the first mass protest in Bulgaria for more than forty years, since the consolidation of one-party rule by the communists. Although ostensibly the march had been called to support an ecological petition, it turned into a mass rally for democracy, attracting over 4,000 people, a huge number by Bulgarian standards. Immediately after the coup, the film director Anzhel Vagenshteyn organized a further and much larger prodemocracy rally. Within a matter of weeks, protesting became almost a way of life in Sofia, as hundreds of thousands of people tasted the novelty of street politics in what had previously been Eastern Europe's most placid state.

It quickly became a matter of routine for musicians entertainers to perform at these rallies. As might have been expected, rock musicians were to the fore, but none more so than Kiril Marichkov, the leader of the Shturtsi. He threw his lot in at once with the Union of Democratic Forces when it was formed by leading dissidents in the first week of December 1989. The Union of Democratic Forces quickly established itself as the chief opponent of the ruling Bulgarian communist party. It was a coalition of groups and parties, including Social Democrats, Agrarians, Greens, and religious rights activists.

One episode in which Marichkov was prominent was the "human chain" protest around the National Parliament in mid-December 1989.

The parliament had convened in session, so it was generally believed, to abolish the subclause in the constitution that guaranteed the leading role of the communist party in public affairs. However, when the amendment was put before the assembly, the chair of the parliament, Stanko Todorov (a leading Zhivkov aide and former prime minister), objected that it was unconstitutional. He pointed to an obscure provision elsewhere in the 1971 constitution, stipulating that a full month had to elapse between a constitutional amendment being tabled and voted by the deputies. In anger, thousands of people, including a large number of students from the nearby university, formed a chain around the parliament building and threatened not to let the deputies leave until they had abrogated the party's leading role in the state. The human chain protest lasted more than a day and was organized by a small committee that included Marichkov. He also arranged entertainment to boost the morale of the protesters. One month later, in January 1990, the subclause and another provision asserting the dominance of the working class were deleted from the constitution.

Subsequently, the Shturtsi performed regularly on behalf of the Union of Democratic Forces. When the country's first free election since the war was held on 10 and 17 June 1990, Marichkov was elected to parliament as a deputy representing his native Haskovo region. During the fall, there were even rumors in Sofia that he might be appointed Bulgaria's ambassador in Germany, but these came to nothing.

The Shturtsi were by no means the only rock musicians and singers to support the anticommunist opposition: The overwhelming majority of the music business endorsed the Union of Democratic Forces. One of the opposition's most effective preelection posters showed almost a hundred musicians and actors waving the Union's blue campaign flag. Prominent on the poster in the very center of the front row were soul singer Vasil Naydenov and ballad singer Lili Ivanova, whom most Bulgarians had long regarded as a darling of the regime. Other singers who backed the opposition included Margarita Hranova, Bogdana Karadocheva, members of Tangra, and Milena Slavova of Trio Milena.

The Union of Democratic Forces also published and sold cassettes of political rock songs to boost its electoral chances, both before the June 1990 poll and before the second postcommunist election in October 1991. The cassettes featured many of the singers and musicians who had performed at rallies, including Lili Ivanova and some newer names, such as the Poduene Blues Band, whose contribution, "Communism Is on the Way Out" (Komunismut se otiva), was one of the most popular tracks. Both cassettes featured the Union of Democratic Forces' rally song, "45 Years Is Enough! The Time Is Ours" (Vremeto e nashe! 45

godini stigat), which was sung by a large choir of artists in imitation of such Western ventures as the Band Aid initiative for Africa in 1985.

The stance taken by the music business was evidently a source of deep embarrassment to the former communists, who, in an attempt to improve their public image, had changed their name to the Bulgarian socialist party in preparation for the elections. Failing to win any Bulgarian stars to their platform, they concluded their campaign with a huge rock concert in Sofia, staged almost exclusively by Western stars. This bizarre event was mounted with considerable assistance from the Czechoslovak-born newspaper magnate Robert Maxwell, who provided funds and campaign materials to both sides during the campaign. The two main acts that appeared were the Jamaican vocal group Boney M., which had enjoyed enormous popularity in Eastern Europe during its heyday in the early 1980s, when it was marketed as the voice of the Third World and as a genuine collective enterprise, and the British singer Samantha Fox. Fox, who owed her success in the West more to her figure than to her voice, performed a few of her disco hits, including "Touch Me! I Want Your Body!" Later, in a newspaper interview, she claimed that the concert had been nonpolitical and she had not been paid any high sum to appear. It is hard to estimate if the concert had any impact on the socialists' campaign. In the ensuing vote, they lost heavily in Sofia but captured 52 percent nationwide, giving them 211 of the 400 seats in the new Grand National Assembly. By September, they had formed a new cabinet, again led by Andrei Lukanov. However, the socialists' success resulted more from the votes of the elderly than from the support of the young.

The Union of Democratic Forces had, in any case, replied to the socialist party's concert by organizing its own concert on 8 June, the final day of campaigning. Two Western stars again topped the bill—Art Garfunkel and Dan Seals (formerly of the early 1970s duo Seals and Crofts, who had had hits with "Dust on My Saddle" and "We May Never Pass This Way Again"). Although it is impossible to estimate the size of the crowd that attended, most observers agree that it exceeded half a million people. A BBC reporter in Sofia, covering the election, claimed that in excess of a million attended this final Union rally. In any case, there seems little doubt that it was the largest meeting ever held on Bulgarian soil.

It is still too early to gauge how strongly Bulgarian rock music will develop under a democracy. The serious plight of the economy will undoubtedly cause a good deal of difficulty for performers, particularly in releasing records and staging concerts. It will take many years to rectify the lack of recording facilities. However, provisions allowing independent recording studios to open and independent promoters and managers to work will boost the domestic scene enormously.

It is ironic that the immediate impact of the collapse of the communist regime in November 1989 was to limit the opportunities for domestic performers. The long-standing regulations rationing radio airtime between Bulgarian and foreign musicians were scrapped with the result that Western rock stars achieved a virtual monopoly in record programs. Part of the reason for this shift in preferences was that disc jockeys saw little reason to play inferior domestic copies once the foreign originals had become available. Another factor was that Bulgarian radio was anxious to explore the previously forbidden catalog of Western music. Artists that had been an anathema under the dictatorship, like the heavy metal superstars Iron Maiden and AC/DC, the sexually ambiguous David Bowie, and punk originators the Sex Pistols and the Ramones, became the staple force of Bulgarian programs. Moreover, the public was swept by a mania for things Western and a revulsion against everything connected with the communist era and Bulgaria's decades of subjugation by the Soviet Union. Request programs were equally dominated by Western music. The sole exceptions were for the Shturtsi and other groups that had openly sided with the new democratic parties.

The climate of tolerance allowed new and young Bulgarian groups to adopt more outrageous and controversial styles than had ever been available to their predecessors. Heavy metal enjoyed a particular boom, with fan clubs sprouting up throughout the country. One of the most active was the Annihilator Club, for followers of "thrash metal," which organized concerts and promoted literature and record exchanges in Sofia. In 1991, the first rap groups began to perform and broadcast.

Another long-suppressed club that formed openly in late 1989 was a Beatles fan club, which attracted scores of members too young to have been alive before the group split in 1970. The club organized commemorations of the fiftieth anniversary of the birth of John Lennon in October 1990. It also began to agitate for a permanent monument to the Beatles to replace the so-called John Lennon Wall on Patriarch Evtimi Street in downtown Sofia. This wall, part of a public building, had been covered with painted graffiti since the early 1980s, most of it honoring the Beatles, John Lennon, or the ideal of world peace. In the record exchanges that began to be set up as legal businesses under the auspices of Decree no. 35 on private and cooperative enterprises, original recordings by the Beatles commanded the highest, often preposterous, prices.

The popularity of the Beatles was again proven in late November 1990, when students pioneered a nationwide rebellion that culminated in a successful general strike against Andrei Lukanov's socialist government. At the height of the confrontation with the former communists, students occupied more than fifty colleges and universities, and on 28 and 29 November they blockaded streets in the vicinity of Sofia University in an effort to paralyze transport in the capital. The students adopted Paul McCartney's song "Let It Be" as their anthem, playing it on the hour, every hour, on loudspeakers on the sidewalk. On 29 November, Bulgarian radio joined the general strike (more than half of its journalists had walked out at its start on Monday, 26 November). The radio demonstrated its solidarity with the students, miners, oil workers, and other strikers by playing prolonged programs of Beatles music, including the portentous "Let It Be."

Undoubtedly, the emotional impact of Bulgaria's fresh and unmediated encounter with Western rock will have a tremendous effect on the country's young for many years to come. As to whether this will promote anything more than a more energetic and immediate imitation of foreign trends remains to be seen. Although Bulgaria has its own domestic sources and traditions that Western artists, such as Kate Bush, have endeavored to exploit, as yet those traditions have held little interest for domestic rock musicians.

Mainly because of its poverty, poor infrastructure, and small size, Bulgaria is unlikely to win a more prominent place in concert itineraries. A major problem is the lack of a convertible currency, a handicap that may not be overcome for several years, even though the national money, the lev, can be used to purchase U.S. dollars inside Bulgaria.

For these reasons, it would be wrong to expect a boom in domestic music that will have anything more than local significance. Nevertheless, it cannot be doubted that the climate, both financially and artistically, will be more propitious during the 1990s than at any other time since the Milev brothers started out in 1962. The dead hand of communist party supervision has been lifted. Also gone is the bizarre propaganda, whose effect was only to make the rock genre more appealing to Bulgaria's young.

The middle-of-the-road or "lemonady" artists who thrived during the 1970s and 1980s, such as Tonika SV and the Kukeri, are unlikely to lose their popularity altogether. Nor is the entrenched mafia of songwriters likely to be ousted too quickly. These people have established strong networks of personal connections that will continue to serve them. They will undoubtedly modify their styles, perhaps to become more risqué, perhaps to modernize their favored acts. It should not be forgotten that Milena Slavova, the nation's current favorite rock singer, began her career as a member of the Kukeri.

The very best that Bulgaria produced under the communists will survive in people's memories, but hardly with the appeal it once held. The Shturtsi's early recordings may now sound too derivative and pallid, but among the group's later releases are several songs that could remain favorites, such as the hard-driving "Midsummer's Day" and the subtle lampoon of Soviet domination, "Wedding Day." The group's great handicap is that, unlike a writer or an artist, it had no opportunity to store up secret works and banned recordings. The same is true of other bands that attempted to escape the draconian restrictions imposed by the censors. Signal, Tangra, FSB, Trio Milena, and Diana Express all had their moments of resistance, timid though they usually were. Perhaps in the future people will continue to talk about legendary groups like the punk Tip Top, which never performed in public and never released recordings. This is all a question of what might have been. What actually was cannot begin to compensate the possible loss.

NOTES

This chapter draws heavily from my previous reports on the subject, written while I was a staff member of Radio Free Europe, Munich, from 1985 to 1990. Some material was also contributed by George Slavov of Radio Free Europe.

1. Petko Simeonov, a founding member in 1988 of the dissident Club for the Support of Glasnost and Perestroika, is a leader of the small nonparliamentary Liberal party in Bulgaria. He was the campaign manager for the Union of Democratic Forces during the parliamentary elections in June 1990 and represented Plovdiv, the country's second city, in the Grand National Assembly until October 1991.

2. For a fuller account of Simeonov's speech, see Bulgarian Situation Report, *Radio Free Europe Research,* 29 June 1989.

3. During the 1980s, the state recording company Balkanton released an average of six Bulgarian and eight foreign rock music albums each year. Virtually no singles were released, and the only Bulgarian rock music chart was one compiled from listeners' votes by Radio Sofia, which is subjected to rigorous ideological censorship. Since November 1989, more foreign albums have been released on license. Also, the censorship laws were effectively scrapped, allowing the Bulgarian public access to the full range of world rock music. This resulted in Radio Sofia devoting hours (if not days) of airtime to the neglected hits from the West that had been denied approval by communist censors.

4. Tina Turner, who gave a series of concerts in Sofia in 1982, three years before the success of the album *Private Dancer* resurrected her career in the United States and Western Europe, is probably the most prominent Western rock musician to have performed in Bulgaria. The veteran British heavy metal group Uriah Heep made a Bulgarian tour in 1988, as is described in the text. In 1990, Art Garfunkel and Bonnie Tyler performed in Sofia.

5. *Ritam,* a monthly magazine that focuses largely on heavy metal, was created in early 1989. Since then, two other publications have been launched—*Rok bulevard* and *Meridian-Rokshou.* Regular articles on rock music have also started

to appear in other publications, such as the cultural weeklies. One problem is that the writers make little effort to promote domestic performers.

6. Juliana and Klaus Roth, "Das Erbe der bauerlichen Kultur und die jüngsten Reformen der bulgarischen Landwirtschaft," *Südosteuropa* 38, no. 6 (June 1989).

7. *Alafranga* meant, literally, "in the Frankish [i.e., West European] style."

8. *Rabotnichesko delo*, 26 June 1989.

9. Bandi's Boys, which included the future leader of the Shturtsi, Kiril Marichkov, on bass guitar, were founded by the brothers Dimitar and Ivan Milev in 1962. Bandi was Dimitar Milev's nickname in school.

10. FSB originally consisted of a core of three musicians—Rumen Boyadzhiev and Konstantin Tsekov, who both played keyboards, and Aleksandar Baharov, who played bass guitar. Other musicians joined them on a temporary basis to record albums and give concerts (outside Bulgaria). The group expanded to a permanent five-piece ensemble in 1979.

11. *Sofia News*, 27 April 1988.

12. *Puls*, no. 19 (9 May 1989).

13. The word "lemonady" (*limonadov*) is in current use as a term of abuse among young Bulgarians who despise the empty, romantic ballads favored by such performers as Tonika SV (a group that allegedly was run by the Ministry of the Interior).

14. Heinz Peter Hoffman and Yordan Rupchev, *ABV na Popmuzikata* (Sofia: Muzika, 1987), p. 182.

15. *Anteni*, no. 31 (3 August 1988).

16. *Narodna Kultura*, no. 4 (22 January 1988); and *Sofia News*, 7 December 1988.

17. *Tvorchesko-Stopanski Kombinat Balkanton: Programa 1989* (Sofia: Balkanton, 1989), p. 48.

18. *Literaturen Front*, no. 4 (26 January 1984).

19. *Narodna Armiya*, 11 May 1983.

20. *Literaturen Front*, no. 4 (26 January 1984).

21. *Rabotnichesko delo* (30 December 1981).

22. *Narodna Armiya*, 11 May 1983.

23. *Literaturen Front*, no. 4 (26 January 1984).

24. *Otechestven Front*, 13 January 1984.

25. *Uchitelsko delo*, 20 March 1983.

26. Ibid.

27. *Anteni*, 16 August 1978.

28. *Darzhaven Vestnik*, no. 66 (23 August 1985).

29. *Rabotnichesko delo*, 6, 7, 9, and 10 January 1986.

30. *Puls*, no. 4 (28 January 1986).

31. *Otechestven Front*, 24 July 1987.

32. *Rabotnichesko delo*, 24 July 1988.

33. *Rabotnichesko delo*, 26 December 1986.

34. Uriah Heep was formed in 1970. The group named itself after the villain in Charles Dickens's *David Copperfield*, partly in response to centenary commemorations of the novelist's death. The group enjoyed great success in the United Kingdom throughout the early 1970s, performing a rather unadorned but me-

lodic style of heavy metal rock music, often set to mystical or esoteric lyrics. Perhaps its most famous songs are "The Wizard," "July Morning," and "Easy Living." The group's popularity declined with the rise of punk and new wave rock music in the late 1970s, but Uriah Heep failed to benefit from the heavy metal revival of the late 1980s, which has been led by groups such as Iron Maiden, Whitesnake, and Bon Jovi. That Uriah Heep was able to mount a successful tour of Bulgaria showed that the Bulgarian communist party had finally abandoned its attempts to exclude Western hard rock music from Bulgaria.

35. *Sofia News,* 31 August 1988.

36. *Rabotnichesko delo,* 8 August 1988.

37. *ABV,* 30 August 1988. In its previous issue, *ABV* had published a long extract from Tina Turner's autobiography, *I, Tina.* See *ABV,* 23 August 1988.

NICK HAYES **8**

The Dean Reed Story

The twentieth century has often fooled us.
—Yevgeny Yevtushenko

D EAN REED, the American superstar of the East, had his annual winter getaway vacation in the communist variant of the Club Med
winter spree. Every holiday season since the mid-1970s, Dean Reed took
a week's spa and cross country ski break at a party lodge outside of
Moscow. There, he was *the American* invited to mix with the Soviet
smart set of the communist party and their favorites in the pop arts.

The Colorado native could cut it on any ski trail. Zipping through the
forest trails, he once almost collided with an elderly comrade whose
memory, if not his sense of the passing of time, was sharp:

"John Reed," he exclaimed!

"*Net*, Dean Reed," Reed replied.

"*Net, vy* (you're)—John Reed."[1]

The confusion had occurred frequently in Dean Reed's visits to the
USSR. And why not? This Reed looked the way we wished the original
communist Reed had looked. Dean Reed had the looks to match Warren
Beatty's role in *Reds*. John Reed didn't have it. An American in East
Berlin, Dean Reed had also embraced the communist East. On CBS's "60
Minutes," Mike Wallace extended the metaphor in 1986 to suggest that,
like John, Dean Reed was becoming a prisoner of the communist sys-
tem.[2] Disillusioned with the communist system he had once embraced,
Dean Reed had come to resent his entrapment and had started making
moves to return to his native land.

Six weeks after the Mike Wallace report, the press could complete its
metaphor. On 12 June 1986, Dean Reed died under suspicious circumstances in East Berlin. Every report of his death picked up the lead. The
American expatriate had become disillusioned with the communist system and longed to return home. A suicide. Or perhaps the sinister forces

of East Germany wanted to stop him. Perhaps his death was not a suicide or an accident, as the East German press had reported. Perhaps someone stopped him from making it to Checkpoint Charley ...

Perhaps. But, there were at least two flaws to the comparison of the two Reeds. History was not repeating itself. The press was. The media wanted to play the Dean Reed story as a rerun of Warren Beatty's *Reds*, with the change that this Reed was to be cast as a farce. The second problem was that the story was wrong.

DEAN WHO?

"Dean *who?* Right? Who's Dean Reed? That's what you want to ask me." Dean Reed used this opener in interviews with the American press. He would steal the reporter's first question with a disarming sense of humor that let the interviewer know that Dean Reed already knew that if his reputation had preceded him, it had arrived as a joke.

The Western media that picked up the Dean Reed story in the 1970s and 1980s liked to play it as the pop joke of the Cold War. The Soviet press routinely heaped public praise on the American, but the private view often corresponded to the Western opinion.

The more knowledgeable in the USSR were more skeptical. The television journalist Vladimir Pozner said of Reed: "I once said to him. Look! How come I took a class in high school in New York on American folk music and I know Pete Seeger and never did anyone mention you?"[3]

The real story of Dean Reed had all the banal and the beautiful of the best Hollywood script. Dean Reed was an actor/singer of enough talent to make it in the American pop scene. He ditched that life for fame and radical politics in Latin America and later for fame and love in Eastern Europe. The real meaning of the Dean Reed story is that if you're a pop star in the East or West, they'll kitsch you in the end. Dean fled the commercialization of American culture in the age of excess only to fall into the trap of communist kitsch in the era of stagnation. And he knew it.

Born in 1938 in the high plains of eastern Colorado, Dean Reed had the looks and athletic prowess in high school to compensate for an otherwise bitter home life. His father, Cyril, was a Goldwater Republican who tried and tried without success to make it out of the depression that held on to the Colorado plains well beyond the 1930s. His mother, Ruth Anna (later Ruth Anna Brown), was a schoolteacher; she left his father for California and later for Hawaii, where she became a feminist activist. After graduating from high school in 1956, Dean had a full ride on an athletic scholarship to the University of Colorado. He gave it up after two years and decided to head West. But he had no money. He then tried a stunt: He bet the town boosters that he could race and beat a team of mules across the continental divide. He got $200 for winning the race. With the prize, he bought an old Chevy and headed for Hollywood. A hitchhiker he picked up on the way gave him the telephone number of a contact at Warner Brothers.

The telephone led to Paton Price and the Hollywood Left. Blacklisted in the McCarthy era, Paton worked as an acting coach for Warner Brothers. A former roommate of Kirk Douglas and a pacifist from Texas, he had refused the draft in 1940 and went on to protest his confinement in a conscientious objector camp. He ended up waiting out the war years in a cell at Danberry with Dave Dellinger as his cellmate. When Dean Reed arrived in Los Angeles, Paton's acting class became his family. One of his classmates, Jean Seberg, the future star of *Bonjour Tristesse* and *St. Joan,* would remain a close friend and confidante of Dean until her tragic death in 1969. Paton Price became a surrogate father for the boy from Colorado. In every crisis of his life, Dean Reed would turn to him for advice and support. Reed was there in 1983 when Paton died of cancer.

"When I showed up in Paton's class, he knew I was totally naive," Reed recalled about their first meeting. Like his classmate Jean Seberg, Dean Reed picked up radical politics as well as acting from Paton. Dean also learned something else. "I was a virgin!" Reed went on, "and Paton told me that to act I had to know my sexuality and one of the first things Paton did was to get me laid."

The boy from Colorado was a quick study. In 1955, Dean Reed landed an acting contract with Warner Brothers and a recording contract with Capitol Records. In 1961, his hit single "Our Summer Romance" made it on the top ten and he appeared on Dick Clark's "American Bandstand." He was under consideration for the lead in *Spartacus*. Dean Reed was making it.

As the fan mail poured in, Warner Brothers and Capitol Records noticed that Reed received an unusually high number of letters from Latin America, where "Our Summer Romance" ran higher on the charts than any other American hit, including the best from Elvis. Warner Brothers concluded that it had a shot at making Reed into the King in Latin America and sent him on a promotional concert tour.

Throughout Central and South America, Dean Reed played before enthusiastic audiences in stadiums and clubs. What Dean Reed found in Latin America was not merely the mass adulation and the stardom he craved. At the time, he wasn't doing too bad on that score back in the United States. In Latin America, Reed encountered mass poverty and oppression such as he had never seen, and what is more important, the cheers of the Latin fans made him believe that his songs could make a difference. When he returned, he told Paton Price that he was leaving the United States for Argentina, where he had been offered a job as the host of a Buenos Aires television program.

Arriving in 1962, Reed mixed politics and rock into a sensational career in Latin America for the next half decade. He delivered a series of hits that dominated the Latin charts for the next three years; at the same time, he mixed with the communist party and the radical Left. In 1966, he had an affair with a Soviet actress who was in Buenos Aires as part of a Soviet delegation. He accepted her invitation to come to the Soviet Union.

In November of that year, Dean Reed, dressed in denim blues and wide bell-bottoms with red, white, and blue flairs, arrived in Moscow. Billed as the first American rock singer to perform in the USSR, Reed sold out Moscow's Variety Theater, where he went through three encores, twenty-five minutes of sustained applause after that, and the hands of screaming fans who grabbed and tried to tear a bit of his clothing as he beat it to the exit.

The call to the East was there, but Reed returned to Buenos Aires only to discover that political pressure had forced Argentine television to take him off the air. In 1970, he performed in Chile at rallies on behalf of the communist party and Salvador Allende. In protest of the war in Indochina, he burned the U.S. flag at the entrance to the American Embassy in Santiago. The gesture earned for him a deportation order by the Chilean government. It also earned him the permanent admiration of Pablo Neruda, who met Reed as he boarded the plane and returned his American flag. The Nobel laureate also gave him a copy of a poem dedicated to Reed that included the following lines:

> The American flag has the blood of Vietnam on it.
> But Dean Reed had cleansed it.
> Let us return it to him.[4]

By 1970, Dean Reed had to divide his time between radical causes in Latin America and making a living in Italy. Together with his first wife, Patty, an American and former Miss Universe turned actress, Dean Reed had first gone to Italy in 1967. He would play in Italy on and off for the next half decade in eight spaghetti Westerns with the likes of Yul Bryner and Clint Eastwood.

In 1971, he fell in love with and eventually married photographer Vivka Wiebke from East Germany. Married in 1975, he moved to East Berlin with Vivka. She had contacts in the East German film industry who showed an interest in his prospects as a filmmaker. At the end of 1975, he directed and starred in his first film, *Blood Brothers*, a story of the Ute uprising. For the next three years he worked on his dream project: the film *El Cantor,* based on the life of Victor Jara, the Chilean singer and activist incarcerated in 1973 and presumed to have been murdered by the Pinochet regime. Dean Reed wrote the script, directed, and starred as Victor Jara.

While working on the film, he met the star of the East German screen, Renate Blume. Renate became his third wife and the passion of the last decade of his life. "I live in the German Democratic Republic, not because I'm an expatriate, but because of Renate, for reasons of love, not politics," Reed later explained about his decision to settle in East Germany."I can work in any country, but my wife can have her career only here in the GDR."

This was probably true for Renate, and Dean *could* have had other careers elsewhere. But only in Eastern Europe could Dean Reed have had the career that was to be his for the next decade. Since 1972, Dean Reed had been packing stadiums across Eastern Europe with throngs of fans chanting *"Din Rid! Din Rid!"* He recorded thirteen albums, which together sold over 10 million copies. His personal correspondence documented a first-name relationship with virtually every leader of the Warsaw Pact. In 1979, Moscow honored him with the Lenin Prize. In every interview, Reed would note with pride that he was the only American ever to have received the Lenin Prize.

The ties to home still bound him. He retained his American citizenship and with it the right to travel as he pleased. He kept in regular touch with his mother and a daughter (Ramona, from his first marriage) who lived in California. He brought his second wife to Los Angeles to meet Paton in 1975 and from there to visit his longtime friend in Minnesota Marv Davidov, a peace and civil rights activist.[5]

In November 1978, en route to give a concert in Havana for an international socialist youth festival, Dean took a detour to visit Marv Davidov in Minnesota and plug the film *El Cantor.* Marv apologized that he would miss the screening of the film because he expected to be arrested the next day in a protest against a power line that cut across the farms of nearby Buffalo, Minnesota. "I want to be arrested with you," Dean replied.

Eighteen people, among them longtime activists, local farmers, and Dean Reed, were incarcerated in the Wright County jail in Buffalo, Minnesota. Dean announced the first night that he had some friends who could turn on the political pressure. The locals were cautious. Dean Reed's friends were not exactly what Minnesota farmers wanted for allies. But finally they agreed. The sheriff, shaking his head in amazement, brought in the first one. The first telegram in protest of Dean Reed's incarceration arrived from Yasir Arafat. Others came from Erich

Honecker, Gustáv Husák, and even a copy of a telegram sent by Andrei Gromyko to President Carter.

The ploy worked. What would have been a story for the local news became an international media curiosity. Within three weeks, a sympathetic judge acquitted Dean Reed, together with the other eighteen protesters, of the trespassing charges. Yet throughout fall 1978 letters and telegrams continued to pour in while the press in the Soviet Union and Eastern Europe heated up its campaign for Dean Reed's freedom. *Komsomolskaya pravda* published a letter from a high school class in Chelyabinsk in the Urals: "We are indignant about the arrest of Dean Reed. We demand his liberation. Freedom to Dean Reed. Freedom to all political prisoners in the United States."[6] The Buffalo incident gave Dean a new slant in the Soviet and East European press. His name joined the litany of Angela Davis, the North Carolina Wilmington Ten, Leonard Peltier, and others whose human rights the Soviet press defended in the face of American oppression.

The *New York Times* called him "the Johnny Cash of the Iron Curtain." His rock and folk videos were a popular and regular feature of Soviet and East European television entertainment. His next film *Sing, Cowboy, Sing* (1981) was a box office success throughout the Warsaw Pact. Yet the superstar of the East kept up his ties on the other side. On invitation from Daniel Ortega in October 1985, Reed gave a concert in Nicaragua in protest of the Contras and U.S. policy. Taking a risk, he returned the same month to Chile. He performed the songs of Victor Jara in Santiago and was beaten by Chilean soldiers who broke up what had turned into an anti-Pinochet rally. Vernon Bellecourt, a leader of A.I.M. (American Indian Movement), had accompanied him on the tour. With Bellecourt's encouragement, Reed started working on a film on the 1973 uprising at Wounded Knee, South Dakota. The project was a joint GDR-Soviet production called *Bloody Heart*.

In November 1985, he returned to the United States to promote a 1985 documentary portrait of his life, *An American Rebel,* produced and directed by Will Roberts. He screened the film and gave concerts in Minneapolis and Denver.

In early December, Dean Reed returned to East Germany. By February, he was working on location in the Crimea for his film on Wounded Knee. He complained to friends back in the United States that the project was stalled. For the first time, the Soviet partners balked. He repeatedly argued with his East German producer, Gerhardt List. He returned to East Berlin in the spring to work out some production and financing problems. On the evening of 12 June, he left home to drive to the television studios to meet List. Five days later the East German police reported that they had found his body clothed in a lined overcoat with his American passport in the pocket. Reed had drowned in less than a foot of water in the nearby lake (Zeuthener See) that he had often swum across for exercise.[7]

The East German press described the death as a tragic accident. In August, the Soviet television news *Vremya* profiled the life of the American and concluded that Dean Reed died of "unnatural causes and the circumstances are still under investigation."[8]

TAKE A SWORD

"Take a sword and cut it around me on every side," Reed said in 1985. "There are no strings attached. I'm a puppet of nobody. I don't belong to any party." The winner of the Lenin Prize did not have a party card. The only political organization he belonged to was the World Peace Council in Helsinki. Since his days in Argentina, however, he had been keeping company with communists and professing his support for socialism.

Reed's faith in socialism, however, was born not from a strong belief in the "advanced socialism" of the Brezhnev era but from a loss of faith in the United States in the age of the Vietnam War and military intervention in Latin America and the Third World. The conversion experience came in Latin America. "You can't live there for five years, if you have eyes and a conscience, without changing," he said. "They have these dictatorships against the will of the people only because the U.S. government supports them financially, militarily, and politically. That was a great shock to a boy from Colorado, and I began to change."

OK. But years later didn't the winner of the Lenin Prize ever suspect that the Brezhnev Doctrine was not exactly in force in Eastern Europe by popular mandate? Privately, Reed often expressed contempt for the corruption and privileges of the communist party elites. Publicly, he lived their life-style. If he had reservations about the conditions of socialism in Eastern Europe and the Soviet Union in the Brezhnev era, he kept them to himself. There were a few remarks to the U.S. press in 1985. In a television interview in November 1985, he rejected Soviet socialism as a model for anyone (except perhaps the Soviet people) and advocated that the future of socialism would involve the discovery by each nation of its own socialist path. There was a significant gesture in East Berlin. In July 1985, together with the American folk singer and activist Larry Long, Reed gave a concert in East Berlin that included a few numbers in defense of Polish Solidarity. The gesture brought a reprimand from Erich Honecker.

His occasional remarks in the socialist press implied that the American in East Berlin was a political expatriate. Not quite so, Reed explained.

I'm a U.S. citizen and a resident of what you call East Germany, what I call the German Democratic Republic. I live in the German Democratic Republic not because I'm an expatriate, but because of Renate—for reasons of love, not politics. I haven't defected or asked for asylum. But my wife is East Germany's most famous actress and she speaks only German. Besides English, I speak Spanish, Italian, and German, and I can work in about any country, but my wife can have her career only in the GDR.

Reed didn't even want the label "protest singer." His repertoire included some politically oriented standards—"We Shall Overcome," or in its Spanish version as "Venceremos," and his own "We Are the Revolutionaries." The rest, the majority, were simply love songs, rock, and country because, as he liked to say, "politics is only a half truth and I want people to laugh and to cry, to inspire them to continue, which is often difficult, and to give them knowledge." Unless you count the Robin Hood motif in his Italian remake of *Zorro,* only *El Cantor* and the unfinished *Bloody Heart* stand out among his films as decidedly political. Reed would always describe himself as an artist first but one who accepted "my obligation to use my art and fame for world peace and social justice."

Dean Reed had his own recipe for mixing politics and art. It was part Hollywood Left, part Pete Seeger, and part Wobbly, but in the Warsaw Pact it was mixed into an American entrée for the cultural diet of communist kitsch in the heydays of Brezhnevism. At his best, Reed was acutely sensitive to the plight of the underclass of Latin America and brave in the tradition of the best of the American antiwar movement when he protested American military intervention in Vietnam and Latin America. At his worst, he was conveniently blind to the plight of Eastern Europe and opportunistic in courting the powers that were in the Eastern bloc.

The real Dean Reed, Paton Price's orphan in Brezhnev's bloc, was a displaced person from the late history of the Hollywood Left. Reed's genuine politics were irrelevant to the Soviet and East European youth who desperately wanted to believe that the folk-rock cowboy from Colorado was giving them a taste of something close to the real rock Americana. His politics, moreover, were somewhat useful to communist regimes from East Berlin to Moscow. So why not let them have Dean Reed?

THE DEAN REED PHENOMENON

The Dean Reed phenomenon demonstrated that the hunger for American pop culture was so extreme in the East that they were willing to accept substitutes. From the *stilyagi* (style-conscious faddist) to the *khippi* (hippie), the communist world responded to the hunger of its young for American rock by assuring them that if their hunger could not be controlled, then at least it would not be satisfied on communist terms. How convenient that Dean Reed existed. Otherwise, he would have had to be invented. Reed benefited from this starvation diet that had preceded his arrival in Eastern Europe. They were ready for anything that walked in denim and sang.

Then, into the Eastern bloc walked the actor/singer looking like he had just stepped off the set from *Giant*. To his credit, Reed evinced a warm and simple directness, a natural gregariousness, a lack of pretension as well as sophistication, and classic western American good looks that fed into Eastern Europe's fondest stereotype of the American. And he could act, perhaps only as a B-grade actor to some, but then this script didn't require much. And, he could sing—not the best, but good enough.

Listening to Dean Reed records is like listening to someone singing in the shower—a lot of zest, energy, and exuberance delivered in a slightly flat and occasionally off-key voice. But then, that was part of his charm and appeal. The amateur voice was compensated for by energy and sincerity that threatened no one and gave Eastern Europe a performance that might have been at a state fair bandstand or at sing-along night at the local college.

The communist regimes had an obvious use for the political remarks of the hero of the Buffalo jail in the years when Washington was heating up its campaign over human rights abuse in the Warsaw Pact. The incident in Minnesota came four months after the trial of the human rights activist Anatoly Shcharansky. Moscow had moved toward a harder line on dissidents, and bracing against the negative publicity to come from the West, the Soviet media searched for its angle on the human rights story. It picked up Ambassador Andrew Young's remark that there were "hundreds, perhaps thousands of political prisoners in the United States." A Soviet television crew and an *Izvestya* reporter had followed Reed to Minnesota, where they found the copy they were looking for. From Washington, TASS announced that Reed's only crime was his "active struggle in defending the rights of political prisoners in the U.S." Within a week of Reed's arrest, the labor paper *Trud* prepared Soviet readers for a long wait for their hero's release but gave them hope: "It is possible to throw the singer in jail, but impossible to put handcuffs on his songs. ... Numerous friends of Dean Reed believe that he will overcome his ordeal and come out of it even stronger, with new songs of struggle and solidarity."[9] Of course, he did come out of it—in three weeks. As for the new songs, well, the following New Year's Eve television program broadcast live from the Hotel Rossiia included a video from Dean Reed thanking the Soviet people for their support and then singing "This Land Is Your Land."

The heat over Dean Reed stayed on. Throughout the year, guides for a USIA (United States Information Agency) exhibition of American culture reported facing confrontations in every Soviet city on the tour with angry Russian fans who demanded to know why the USIA was not playing or displaying Dean Reed records. If American militarism refused to recognize its own son, the Soviet people did. In spring 1978, before the incident at Buffalo, Minnesota, Reed had already received the Champion of Peace Medal from the Soviet Peace Committee. What better gesture next than to award him the Lenin Prize for Art, which came in May 1979!

The Soviet media hype of Dean Reed's "active struggle" on behalf of political prisoners played into the hard side of the U.S. image in the Soviet Union in the 1970s and early 1980s. The Dean Reed video of "We Shall Overcome" that rolled into the Soviet central television's program "Peace and Youth" provided the b-roll for *Vremya*'s frequent interviews with Leonard Peltier in prison or reports on Angela Davis's speeches.[10] At the same time, Reed, the winner of the Champion of Peace Medal of the Soviet Peace Committee, fed into the soft side of that Soviet image of "progressive" and peace-loving America. A decade of Dean Reed's songs had prepared the way for the early 1980s Soviet hype of the Soviet-American peace crusades that brought to the Soviet television screen the play *The Peace Child* or the making of Samantha Smith.

Hard or soft, the specific political tags attached by the Soviet media to Dean Reed were far less important than the cultural politics of the Dean Reed phenomenon. His music was mellow in the extreme. His mixture of folk, folk-rock, and rock oldies came off as an exercise in soft rock hootenanny prepared especially for communist tastes. Everything that communism had found repugnant in Western rock, from Beatlemania to metal and punk, was conspicuously absent in the Reed sound. It could not have been by accident that Reed was the first American rock singer invited to perform in Moscow (in 1966). In that year, the Ministry of Culture had authorized the creation of the vocal-instrumental ensembles (VIAs). These soft rock groups, such as the Happy Kids (Veselye rebyata) of Moscow or Leningrad's the Singing Guitars (Poiushchie gitary), were to feed the Russian appetite for rock with wholesome music. In that year, Minister of Culture Ekaterina Furtseva had leaked rumors that Moscow might invite the Beatles. But instead Moscow got Dean Reed. Moscow could still control which Western rock groups could perform there and what the local national groups could play. As long as Moscow could not suppress the craving of its young for rock, then let them eat kitsch. Thus Dean Reed was the foreign complement to the music of the VIAs. He was the musical image in the American mirror to the bubble gum rock of Prague's Karel Gott or Leningrad's Valery Leont'ev. If the socialist youth could believe that Dean Reed was the best of American rock, then the message was that kitsch was inescapable in both West and East.

In the end, the Dean Reed sound went the way of the kitsch that failed in the Soviet Union and Eastern Europe. There was more behind his popularity than could have been ascribed to some clever political ploy or to the cultural politics of the Brezhnev Doctrine in music. But, unfortunately for Dean Reed, there was also much more behind his popularity than he could satisfy. For over a decade in virtually every communist capital in Europe, Reed had sellout crowds of wild and hysterically devoted fans. He gave them his all but they wanted more.

Even as Dean Reed climbed to the top of Soviet pop in the late 1970s, Soviet tastes were switching to the real thing. B. B. King toured in 1978, hitting the USSR about a month after Dean's liberation from the Buffalo jail. Earlier in 1978, ABBA released an album on the Melodiya label and Boney M. had played in Moscow.

The real thing was also being made at home. Reed had a mass popular following but no influence on rock music. The decade of Reed's popularity coincided with the coming of age of Russian rock, for example, but if you mention his name to Boris Grebenshchikov, Sergei Kuryokin, or Mike Naumenko, you'll get only a laugh. By the time of his death in 1986, glasnost was already opening up more competition inside the socialist cultural world and letting in a wave of U.S. and Western pop culture that would have made it a bit tough for Reed to stay on the top of charts east of the Elbe.

Images of the United States were also changing in the Soviet media. Dean Reed videos were still a regular feature of Soviet youth programming. But on *Vremya*, stories about Leonard Peltier and Angela Davis were on the wane. In Soviet television, the producer of "Peace and Youth" and "16 and Older" had already sensed by 1986 that Dean Reed videos wouldn't cut it much longer and had started to search for other rock video material from the West.[11]

SAY WHAT YOU WANT

"Say what you want, but my life has been unique," Reed said, summing up his life in 1985. Most of the Western media chose to speak of him with a sneer. Yet Reed's list of admirers was impressive: Paton Price, Jean Seberg, Martin Sheen, Kirk Douglas, Pablo Neruda, and others.

Reed had hoped that his reputation would stand on his achievements as an artist. As for his music, Reed was always reasonably candid. Never trained as a singer, Reed knew that "there are thousands of singers in America who are younger than I, better looking than I and who can sing better than I. ... I shall never be of commercial quality for the normal American." He took his acting more seriously, however. So did some others. *El Cantor,* for example, picked up a few favorable reviews in the West German press. For his critics to demonstrate that Reed was not a great artist showed their mastery of the obvious. They might as well have proven that Lee Majors would not stand the test of time in comparison with Marlon Brando. More important, they missed the point of Reed's career.

As a singer, an actor, or a director, Dean Reed did not have the makings of an artistic genius, but he did have a shot at being a star. What made the Dean Reed story unique was not his political radicalism. Others, from Jane Fonda to Vanessa Redgrave, had that radicalism plus successful acting careers in the West. What made Dean Reed unique was that he was good enough to make it in the American pop scene, that he was making it in the early 1960s, and that he gave up a good shot at commercial success in Hollywood for a long shot at art and revolution in Latin America.

The chance for a pop comeback was still there. Into the early 1980s, agents courted him for the daytime soaps. In 1985, he had solicited help from friends in Hollywood and received a few favorable replies. But, as he said, "I'm not going to sing for Coca Cola. ... I want to work in my own country, the United States, but I also want to keep my dignity and my ideals."[12] He was going to give it a try in fall 1987. He had plans for a book on his life, a concert and lecture tour in U.S. colleges and universities in conjunction with Will Roberts's documentary film on Reed—*An American Rebel*—and hoped that a new generation of student radicals of perhaps "thirteen million" would be ready for him.[13]

What made the Dean Reed story tragic was that in the Eastern bloc he ended up playing the roles for communist kitsch that had made him despise and flee the commercial kitsch of the West. Why did he accept it? The temptation of virtually limitless opportunities to make the films or records he wanted was irresistible. Besides, he did have millions of fans at his disposal across half of Europe. *El Cantor* was not bad. *Bloody Heart* might really make it. And, finally, he was forty-something. Should he throw the life of a superstar in the East away on the chance that Hollywood was ready for an aging pinko cowboy? Why not hang on to what he had and hope for a niche in the U.S. university circuit come 1987?

In the offices of U.S. embassies and consulates and the U.S. press corps across the Soviet Union and Eastern Europe, the mention of Dean Reed's name brought out snickers. It was easy to take cheap shots at Dean Reed at a cocktail party but never to his face.

For fun, Dean Reed liked to jump motorcycles. He still did fifty push-ups, a hundred sit-ups, and pumped iron every morning. But he was forty-seven. The first triumphant tour of South America was twenty-five years behind him. He had his regrets. Most men in their forties do. Paton was dead. His third marriage was on the rocks, but this time he was holding on. The tan came from a tanning bed. He dyed his hair. He had his doubts about what he was doing. Who doesn't? He died.

"And I still miss him," said Marv Davidov, a peace and civil rights activist for more than thirty-five years, shaking his head and not hiding a few tears at the mention of Dean Reed's name.

NOTES

1. Unless otherwise cited, all direct quotations from Dean Reed were taken from interviews conducted with him by the author, 6–13 November 1985, Minneapolis/St. Paul, Minnesota, in conjunction with a television interview and profile of his career broadcast on KTCA-TV Twin Cities Public Television, 8 November 1985. Subsequent short portraits and interviews with Dean Reed were broadcast as part of an eight-part documentary series "Channel 3 Moscow" aired in 1985–1986 by KTCA-TV. Biographical information on Dean Reed can be found in Hans Dieter Brauer, *Dean Reed* (Berlin, 1980); and in probably the best portrait of him, in *Novoe russkoe slovo*, 6 July 1986.

2. The program segment on Dean Reed was broadcast on 20 April 1986.

3. Interview with Vladimir Pozner, St. Paul, Minnesota, 5 June 1986.

4. Letter of Pablo Neruda to Dean Reed, 3 September 1970. See also *La Nacion*, 3 September 1970.

5. Information on the incident at Buffalo, Minnesota, and corroborating background details on information from the interviews with Dean Reed were taken from an interview with Marv Davidov, Minneapolis, Minnesota, 20 June 1986.

6. *Komsomol'skaia pravda*, November 1986.

7. The questions surrounding Reed's death remain unanswered. The first East German report suggested that Dean Reed had taken some medication for a cold and apparently became drowsy while driving. The report claimed that Reed had a minor accident, stepped into a lake to refresh himself, passed out, and drowned. Rumors abound. One suggests that Reed had a gay lover in Prague (remember what Paton had said about being an actor), had tested HIV positive, and committed suicide. Another suggests that the Contras or Pinochet had motives for pre-empting his return to the United States the next year. The best clues point in the direction of his marital problems. Renate's responses to the press and early information were frequently false and erratic. Gerhardt List took charge of meeting

family, friends, and journalists who came to East Berlin to seek answers. He also had the connections to the East German media that might explain why the police report came five days after the death together with a press release about a "tragic accident." By that time, Russell Miller of the *Sunday Times* was already close to the story. Dean Reed was probably murdered. What is certain is that no one in the East German police or, for that matter, in the U.S. State Department was or is concerned enough to investigate further. For an account of the suspicious circumstances surrounding his death, see *Rolling Stock*, no. 12 (1986).

8. Interview with Vladimir Dunayev, Washington, D.C., 8 August 1986. The *Vremya* report was broadcast on 10 August 1986.

9. *Trud*, November 1978.

10. The b-roll is the videotape shot outside the studio, used to set the mood.

11. Interview with Edvard Sagalyev, Moscow, 3 December 1987. Sagalyev was at the time senior producer/editor, responsible for youth programming, which included *Peace and Youth* and *16 and Older.*

12. Letter to Dixie Lloyd quoted in *Rolling Stock* no. 12 (1986).

13. Ibid.

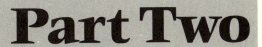

Part Two

The Soviet Union

SABRINA PETRA RAMET
SERGEI ZAMASCIKOV
ROBERT BIRD

9

The Soviet Rock Scene

> *G. G.: It's only cultures that, by accident or good management,*
> *bypassed the Renaissance that see art for the menace it really is.*
>
> *g.g.: May I assume that the USSR would qualify?*
>
> *G.G.: Absolutely. The Soviets are a bit rough-hewn as to method,*
> *I'll admit, but their concerns are absolutely justified.*
> —**Glenn Gould,** *The Glenn Gould Reader*

WHEN ROCK MUSIC first sprouted in Soviet soil in the mid-1960s, it was largely imitative of Western rock, that is to say, U.S. and British rock. Soviet authorities reacted with hostility and scorn. But rock music provided the essential underpinning for an emergent youth counterculture that has become stronger and much more heterogeneous over the years. By the late 1980s, under Mikhail Gorbachev, rock music had won broad acceptance by the authorities. The Gorbachev regime allowed the old distinction between "official" (approved) and "unofficial" (proscribed) bands to lapse and dramatically loosened the once tight censorship of rock lyrics.

There were probably several hundred professional rock groups in the USSR by 1987, with 160,000 amateur rock groups in the Russian Soviet Federal Socialist Republic (RSFSR) alone.[1] *Moskovskii komsomolets* put the number of rock groups in Moscow province at more than 1,500 but added that roughly a third of these were "not recommended" (this estimate was made in 1984, prior to Gorbachev's accession).[2] In addition, there were by that time "thousands" of discos in the USSR, 90 percent of them with dance floors. In Uzbekistan, for example, there were already 115 discos by 1984.[3]

In this chapter the growth of the rock scene in the USSR will be traced, with examination of the evolution of official responses, discussion of

181

the internal heterogeneity of the Soviet rock scene, and probing of the diversity of views to be found in the official press. Also explored are some of the differences between "official" (professional) rock groups and "unofficial" (amateur) groups in the USSR, insofar as this classification was a factor in rock music until 1988, and the politics of rock music. Finally, we hope to provide in this chapter a broad survey of the Soviet rock scene generally. The emphasis here is on Russian rock, but specific sections are devoted to the Baltic, Central Asian, Siberian, and Far East rock scenes. Discussion of rock trends in Ukraine and Belorussia is omitted here because these areas are covered in other chapters.

THE EARLY YEARS

The initial rock impulses in the West (Chuck Berry, Elvis Presley, and others in the 1950s) found essentially no resonance in the USSR. A Soviet version of the zoot-suiter (or *stilyaga*) made an appearance in the mid-1950s, prompting the satirical magazine *Krokodil* to commission a song parodying the *stilyaga*.[4] And the new music, heard at the Sixth World Youth Festival, held in Moscow in 1957, shocked some Russians.[5] But in the history of Soviet rock and roll, the Beatles marked the beginning of an era, just as much as in the West. Alexander Gradsky, a veteran of the Moscow rock scene who formed the group Tarakany (Cockroaches) in 1963, recalled his reaction upon hearing the Beatles' music for the first time in 1963: "I went into a state of shock, total hysteria. They put everything into focus. All the music I'd heard up to that time was just a prelude." Another rock figure (the founder and curator of the Beatles Museum in St. Petersburg), Kolya Vasin, commented: "The Beatles ... [were] something heavenly. I felt blissful and invincible. All the depression and fear ingrained over the years disappeared. I understood that everything other than the Beatles had been oppression."[6] By the mid-1960s, groups imitative of the Beatles were appearing in the Soviet Union, typically singing U.S. and British songs in English or writing their own songs in English.[7] Although there was initially a strong tendency to see English as the natural language of rock, some bands began writing and singing songs in Russian as early as the mid- or late 1960s.

The Nikita Khrushchev leadership was extremely conservative where the arts were concerned, and Khrushchev himself personally disliked both jazz and rock. In late 1962, he addressed the subject while visiting an art exhibit in Moscow. "I like music a lot," he said, "and often listen to it on the radio. I even went so far as to carry a little Japanese radio around in my pocket. ... [But] take these new dances which are so fashionable now. Some of them are completely improper. You wiggle a cer-

tain section of the anatomy, if you'll pardon the expression. It's inde-
cent."[8] Music, like art, Khrushchev thought, "should ennoble the individual and arouse him to action."[9]

Many in the West were likewise alarmed, in the 1950s and early 1960s,
by the sexual side of rock music.[10] But they were not in a position to de-
clare a binding "party line" on the new music. In the USSR, by contrast,
the reaction of the Soviet leadership was to attempt just that. Leonid
Ilyichev, head of the Department of Propaganda and Agitation from 1958
to 1962 and CC secretary in charge of ideology from 1961 to 1965, joined
his chief in denouncing the "cacophonous" music and "outlandish
yowlings" of foreign bands, which they viewed as linked to the class interests of the Western bourgeoisie and inherently subversive.
Khrushchev's preference was for "melodious music with content, music
that stirs people, ... that summons people to exploits."[11]

The accession of Brezhnev and Aleksei Kosygin to power brought
some changes in Kremlin policy. John Dornberg said that Kosygin, for
one, liked "cool jazz."[12] And more particularly, the authorities gradually
realized that rock was exerting a powerful attraction on the young.
Toward the end of the 1960s, a new approach emerged. Rock could not
be dismissed. Hence it had to be placed under surveillance, censored,
sanitized, and in some instances quarantined, as if it were an infectious
disease. Characteristic of this approach was the creation of a beat club
at Moscow's Melody and Rhythm Cafe in 1969 by the KGB. The
Komsomol was the ostensible sponsor of the club, but despite extravagant promises, the club actually produced very little and disbanded after a year, when the KGB had obtained hefty dossiers on club members.[13] Rock music was also becoming a serious art form by the end of
the 1960s and began to be discussed seriously as a form of counterculture.[14]

At the same time, Soviet officialdom sponsored the creation of a
clean-cut group called "Happy Guys" in 1968; the group's basic message
was that the world (at least the USSR) is fine. This came at a time when
American youth were listening to protest songs by Joan Baez, hearing
Bob Dylan advise "Everybody must get stoned," and turning on to the
heavier sounds of Cream and Led Zeppelin.

Throughout the history of Soviet rock, trends from the West, especially the United States, have exerted a powerful influence on Soviet amateur and professional musicians, an influence often first felt in the
Baltic republics. It is difficult to overestimate the tremendous impact
that Andrew Lloyd Webber and Tim Rice's rock opera *Jesus Christ
Superstar* had on the Soviet rock scene. Smuggled in immediately after
its release in the United States in 1971, the record influenced both Soviet
musicians and the millions of teenage rock fans. Although both the im-

port and production of *Jesus Christ Superstar* were banned almost at once, several musical groups attempted to stage underground productions of the opera. One of the first was staged by students of the Vilnius Conservatory in Lithuania in 1973. There were other unofficial productions in the mid-1970s in Riga, Leningrad, and Moscow. The authorities were sufficiently dismayed by the opera that when the Czechoslovak rock group Flamingo came to Riga in 1976, authorities compelled the group to drop a song taken from that opera from its concert repertoire. And performances by British rock star Elton John in Leningrad and Moscow in 1979 galvanized Russian youth, with fans paying as much as US$350 for tickets on the black market.[15]

In the mid-1970s, attempts were made to channel music tastes by having the Komsomol establish its own network of disco clubs and then supervise the programs. About that time—in 1975, to be exact—the first Soviet rock opera, "Orpheus and Euridice," by Aleksandr Zhurbin, was staged with official permission.[16] Authorities reserved the right to approve rock groups. Approval ("official" status) meant that the group was officially registered with either the state concert agency (Goskontsert) or the Bureau of Concert Bands. These organizations issued permits specifying how much money the band was authorized to draw for each performance (on a scale ranging from R 90 to R 140 per concert). A registered group had to have its program approved by the cultural affairs section of the local City Council, which is to say that both its music and its lyrics had to be approved prior to performance. In practice, the leader of the group had to report every month and present a schedule of the songs the group planned to play during that month. Approval of the given songs was valid for one month only.[17] Unapproved groups were not prevented from performing, but they were unlikely to be hired at any clubs or hotels (state monopolies), and because they were not officially recognized, their members had to take full-time jobs elsewhere to avoid being branded "social parasites"—a fate that could entail prosecution and assignment to compulsory labor. Yet it is interesting to note that at the Tbilisi rock festival in 1980, officially unrecognized groups (Aquarium, Autograph, Time Machine, and Magnetic Tape) took the top prizes.

"Unofficial" status did not, of course, exempt groups from supervision or scrutiny. Iurii Shevchuk, leader of DDT (Leningrad), recalled that he was called in by the KGB on many occasions and was told that he should write lyrics appreciative of official politics.[18] This kind of treatment was, of course, not unique to DDT.

Because Melodiya recorded only officially recognized groups, there was a great stimulus to private recording and to the creation of a black market in rock records and tapes. The black market was dominated first almost exclusively by Western rock, with the Beatles long remaining one of the items in greatest demand. However, starting in the late 1970s, privately taped recordings of underground Soviet rock groups gradually overtook Western imports in popularity. Melodiya released its first Beatles record in 1980, but in limited quantities. More recently, in 1986, Melodiya released a two-record set, *Best of Beatles.*[19] Soviet young people were known to have paid as much as R 100 for a single record of their favorite group. Very few could afford to pay that much, however. Only in 1986, after a Los Angeles musician (Joanna Stingray) smuggled tapes of four Leningrad rock groups out of the country and released a two-record album of their songs in the United States, did the Soviet authorities give a green light to Melodiya to record hitherto disapproved groups like Aquarium, Alisa, and Cruise.

The authorities hoped that the formation of disco clubs within the framework of Komsomol and the requirement that licensed DJs complete a certain amount of ideological training would ensure that the clubs would stick to official guidelines. But they soon found that DJs were often selecting music not with the aim of instilling higher virtues in their listeners but with the idea, as *Komsomol'skaia pravda* put it, of creating a feeling of ecstasy in the dancers.[20] Early in the 1980s, discotheques were required to register with the authorities, and in 1982 they were explicitly forbidden to play music that had not been approved in advance. At the same time, amateur rock groups were ordered to join the Association of Musical Groups, which would supervise their repertoires. By 1984, during the general secretaryship of the highly conservative Konstantin Chernenko, Komsomol "commandos" were raiding places where black marketeering in forbidden recordings was taking place, confiscating some 536 records in one such raid. The following year, the secretariat of the Central Committee of Komsomol established young people's "musical patrols" to conduct "musical raids" for the purpose of weeding out "low-grade music in places of public relaxation." The Komsomol was especially interested in recruiting for these patrols young people with foreign language ability so that they could translate the songs and verify their ideological tone.[21]

DIVERSITY OF VIEWS

In 1981, *Muzykal'naia zhizn',* a publication that tended to support rock music as a legitimate art form, identified three broad approaches to disco music in the USSR, namely, to view discotheques as places for the spontaneous creative activity of young people, as the cultural products of professionals, or as places in which the ideological education of young people can and should be promoted.[22] These corresponded, respectively, to lax, liberal, and conservative points of view. The "lax" point of view was difficult to articulate and even I. Kormiltsev, a member of the unofficial and "unrecommended"[23] group Urfin Dzhus, expressed skepticism about the consequences of too much spontaneity. As he put it in interview with *Literaturnaia gazeta*, "Without analysis, without links with social organizations, without reflection on what we are doing, one may not work. Spontaneity only causes damage."[24]

However, a number of publications had clearly been "liberal" with regard to rock music and disco. This group would include *Muzykal'naia zhizn'*, *Moskovskii komsomolets*, *Smena*, *Yunost'* (a youth magazine), *Klub i khudozhestvennia samodeiatel'nost'* (published in Moscow), the Lithuanian magazine *Nemunas*, as well as *Sel'skaia zhizn'* to a limited degree. *Krugozor*, the organ of the Melodiya recording company, began running features from time to time on rock as early as 1965, above all on Western rock groups, such as ABBA, Boney M., the Beatles, and Joan Baez, and various rock groups in Eastern Europe. *Klub* started to publish a similar column in the late 1970s, devoting attention to the developing Soviet rock scene. Several local newspapers, such as *Sovetskaia molodezh* (published in Riga) and *Znamya yunosti* (from Minsk) also featured regular rock columns. Their discussions of musical trends both domestic and abroad tended to be factual, to point out both positive and negative phenomena associated with the rock scene, and to emphasize aesthetic rather than the social aspects of rock music. One representative of this approach was music critic Artem Troitsky (later to become head of music programming on Russian television), who produced, for example, a very balanced, basically factual article about the Rolling Stones in 1982.[25] Other liberal critics included Anatoly Pereverz'ev, Arkady Petrov,[26] Ivan Makarov, and Valter Ojakaar.[27]

At the other end of the spectrum were *Molodaia gvardia*, *Sovetskaia Rossiia*, *Sovetskaia muzyka*, *Sovetskaia kultura*, *Krasnaia zvezda*, and until recently, *Pravda*, all of which adopted a hostile attitude toward rock music, typically treating it as a Western "plot" to undermine Soviet society. *Komsomol'skaia pravda* once figured among conservatives. It was only toward the end of the 1980s that it agreed to admit rock composers into its ranks and to include discussion.

The Union of Composers has also figured among conservatives, refusing until recently to admit any rock composers into its ranks or to include discussion of this genre in the agendas of its meetings. One of the reasons for this hostility was that the leading figures in the union feared that allowing rock composers into the organization would change the balance of power within the union and ultimately propel them out of the seats of administrative power.[28] By 1987, however, two supporters of rock music (Rodion Shchedrin and Yuri Saul'skii) had been elected as secretaries of the union.

The KGB likewise figured as a conservative voice, tending to view rock music as a medium for Western cultural and political influence. The KGB carefully monitored tours by Western rock stars, and judging from a 1987 speech by the head of the KGB, Viktor Chebrikov, the KGB seemed to think that rock stars play a role in nudging the population "into the position of criticism, demagogy, and nihilism."[29]

The Main Political Administration (MPA) of the Soviet Army and Navy took a similar position. Charged with the supervision of recreation and leisure activities in the Soviet military, the MPA was one of the most conservative and anti-Western agencies in Soviet officialdom. It is therefore not surprising that the MPA always took an extremely hostile line, in its official organ, toward Soviet rock groups. In 1982, for example, after the Leningrad group Blue Guitars had been on tour in Afghanistan to entertain Soviet occupation forces there, *Krasnaia zvezda* published a letter from ten military personnel, five of them lieutenant colonels, who reproached the group on both ideological and artistic grounds.[30] Less than six weeks later, the same newspaper published a notice to the effect that the

> artistic manager and director of Moskontsert I. N. Safonov and Secretary of the Party Committee B. V. Poliakov have sent a reply to the editors ... admitting that criticism directed against the Blue Guitars was "correct." ... The Blue Guitars have been scratched from the planned tours abroad and their scheduled performances in Moscow have been canceled. Administrative action has been taken against the director of the ensemble.[31]

The newspaper asked whether stricter standards might not be advisable for the repertoires of all musical ensembles, including those sent to entertain Soviet forces.

The MPA's attitudes toward rock music evolved to some extent, however. Whereas it would not have considered the use of the electric guitar or the modern percussion set in military orchestras in the 1960s or early 1970s because these instruments were associated with rock music, in the course of the 1980s the MPA began to allow these instruments in soldiers' and officers' clubs for use in playing soft rock (mostly of a patriotic character). Zvezdochka (Little Star), created in the Baltic military district in 1972, is one of the first examples of a rock band allowed to perform in servicemen's clubs.[32] By 1990, there were hundreds of groups similar to Zvezdochka. Yet the MPA remained uncompromisingly hostile to heavy metal; one military officer accused heavy metal bands of being "pro-Zionist."[33] After the August 1991 coup, the new Russian army was to become free of political administration, although the extent to which this has really occurred remains unclear.

The major concern of the MPA officials was that rock music can serve, in part, as a channel of dissent. As Colonel V. Roshchupkin put it, "After changing punk or metal fan clothing for the military uniform, such young men don't immediately change their ideological and moral beliefs. ... It takes a lot of determined work on the part of the propagandist [to counter the effects of heavy metal]."[34]

More recently, the National Bolsheviks and other nationalist groups took advantage of political liberalization to become more visible. The nationalist movement's major spokesmen, the writers from the "villagers" group as well as critics from the magazines *Nash Sovremennik* and *Molodaia gvardiia*, traditionally have taken extremely negative positions toward rock and roll. Although they have viewed rock as a vehicle of Western "corruption," they have also opposed endeavors to incorporate Russian folklore or folk idioms into the melodic or stylistic components of rock music.[35]

Prominent in this circle is the chauvinistic group Pamyat (Memory). It has been overtly hostile to all kinds of rock, which it sees as a uniformly corruptive influence from the West. At a 1987 meeting of Pamyat's members, as reported by *Komsomol'skaia pravda*, the atmosphere was frenetic:

> D. Vasiliev speaks: "The USSR State Committee for Agitation and Propaganda is sewing political labels on us. If this doesn't stop, we will have to resort to the criminal code's article on slander. A stream of cosmopolitanism has engulfed the mass news media. Rock groups are Satanism; they pledge allegiance to Satan!" ...
>
> V. Shumsky runs onto the stage from the audience. He ... proclaims: "We are for Leninism! What was destroyed was destroyed by the hands of Satan!"[36]

Although *Moscow News* has attacked Pamyat's members as intolerant extremists and *Izvestiia* has fretted about its racism and called for Pamyat to be "disciplined,"[37] the group nonetheless finds some sympathy in Soviet official circles. For example, some high-ranking members of the USSR Union of Writers were openly sympathetic to Pamyat. In May 1987, at a meeting of the union, several speakers addressed the subject of rock. Whereas some (such as Andrei Voznesensky and Viktor Rozov) spoke in defense of rock music, others attacked it. Among the latter was Sergei Mikhalkov, author of the Soviet national anthem and vice-president of the Soviet Academy of Pedagogical Science, who said:

Now let's talk about these infamous bands. I am utterly convinced that this is not just innocent dance music. This is a plague, which unfortunately cannot be cured at this time. This is the moral equivalent of AIDS and we cannot find any remedies for it. This is not just music. This is a medium by which our young people are being drugged. This is the turf on which everything can grow, starting with drug-addiction and prostitution, and finishing with high treason and criminal offenses. I don't think we should ban rock music but ... this is a ravine into which our young boys and girls are sliding.[38]

His colleague, Vladimir Krupin, a writer close to Pamyat, agreed and told the same meeting: "Even drugs may not be as dangerous as this music, because this music calls for violence, killings, and riots. And our TV actually encourages this behavior."[39]

Official opinion is not entirely polarized, however. Occupying a middle ground are *Innostrannaia literatura*, which is more balanced in its treatment of Western trends, and *Literaturnaia gazeta*, which is generally antirock but on aesthetic grounds rather than on the social and political grounds favored by the conservative group.

The contrast between liberals and conservatives can be well illustrated by contrasting an article by Aleksandr Zhitinskii (1987) with an article by D. Ukhov (1982). Zhitinskii understands rock in part as a social phenomenon reflecting the breakdown of value consensus (especially between generations). Hence for Zhitinskii rock is less a musical trend than a "position," a "way of feeling."[40] (This is, in fact, a distinctly Russian way of viewing rock music, and Russians have been known to insist that a band treat "serious" themes if it wishes to be considered a "rock" group. Otherwise, if the lyrics are light, the group is considered an *estrada* group.) Through rock—Zhitinskii continues—young people protect themselves from the falsity, hypocrisy, and stereotypes common to Soviet culture. They use rock to address moral conflict. Zhitinskii thus criticizes those who do not concede any serious meaning to rock and underlines that since the beginning of the 1980s Soviet rock has become more "native" (hence, less Western).[41]

Ukhov, by contrast, claims that rock music is 90 percent "bourgeois" and asserts that in its 30-plus years of development, rock has not created anything of musical or aesthetic value and has not managed to become either art or music.[42]

Until recently, the conservatives seemed to be dominant. Their antipathy toward the genre is in part a matter of politics, in part a matter of generational gap, and generally stems from a fear that rock music encourages escapism, skepticism, passivity, glorification of the West, and the spread of fashions and behaviors that are independent of party control.[43] Yuri Andropov, a modernizer and reformer in many respects, was a conservative on rock; in 1983 he warned of "ideologically and aesthetically harmful" groups with "suspicious repertoires."[44]

The high level at which rock came to be discussed is striking. In 1983, for instance, members of the CPSU Central Committee listened to V. P. Vinogradov explain that disco music induces daydreaming. *Sovetskaia Rossiia,* reporting the session, argued that disco music uniformly produces the desire to rest or to entertain oneself and kills the motivation to work. Viewing this as a self-evident bane, *Sovetskaia Rossiia* reproached the Komsomol organization for having failed to stem the tide of disco and punk.[45] Along similar lines, *Molodaia gvardia* fretted that "regular exposure to such sounds [as the Western rock group Kiss] gradually crushes the consumer of this music beneath itself."[46] *Komsomol'skaia pravda* claimed, in a 1984 issue, that the spread of rock in the USSR was the product of "Operation Barbarossa Rock 'n' Roll," a plan supposedly drawn up by "a special agency" of NATO to undermine the Soviet Union.[47]

Sovetskaia kultura, organ of the CC CPSU, likewise toed the conservative line and blasted "disco, rock and other varieties of pop music" for their "primitive associations and poverty of imagination." It warned that the pacifist sentiments, encouraged by some rock songs, are "not conducive to the strengthening of revolutionary vigilance and class consciousness" and surprisingly urged that socialist realism be taken as the standard whereby to judge musical and artistic products.[48] But if some rock was being criticized for pacifism, other rock groups were condemned for propagating a cult of violence, and yet other groups were chastised for sheer irrelevance. In the article already mentioned, *Molodaia gvardiia* quotes from the song "Banana islands":

> *Here are some bananas,*
> *Here's a whole forest of them.*
> *Here are some bananas,*
> *but nobody is eating them ...*
> *Not life, but banana paradise.*

"Now the reader may well ask," *Molodaia gvardiia* comments, "what's so bad about that? The fact is that this is a flight from itself, from life, society, country, time, into a saccharine-sweet fairyland."[49]

The liberal critic Troitsky was one who publicly disputed this. In the course of a roundtable discussion in 1983, he offered a challenge to the one-sided conservative assessment and suggested that new wave rock, rather than being symptomatic of "spiritual emptiness," is "more cheerful and more humane" because of its emphasis on melodiousness and on concrete lyrics.[50] *Yunost',* in publishing the proceedings from the roundtable, allowed the musicians participating to express their affinity for Miles Davis, the Mahavishnu Orchestra, Steely Dan, the Beatles, Led Zeppelin, Santana, Aquarium, the Police, the Rolling Stones, and even Stravinsky and Prokofiev. The result is a discussion that focused more on the music per se than on its supposed social effects. Similarly, *Literaturnaia gazeta,* in a 2,400-word article, hailed the production of Aleksei Rybnikov's rock opera *Yunona and Avos* in 1981 as a "significant event."[51]

Given the long, unresolved debate between party conservatives and liberals, the resultant policy was not always consistent. On the one hand, it was possible to open a city rock club in Leningrad in 1981 that claimed some 500 members and 60 affiliated rock groups by late 1986: The club sponsors an annual rock contest, which is how Aquarium, Kino, Alisa, Auction, and Jungle—all initially unofficial groups—first attracted attention.[52] Melodiya had issued some fourteen disco compilations by early 1985.[53] And in early 1986, the USSR's first rock music "laboratory" was opened, on the initiative of the Inter-Union House of Amateur Creative Work and the Moscow City Committee of Komsomol. Finally, the Union of Composers undertook to consider the possibility of establishing a recording firm specifically geared to young people's music, and *Argumenty i fakty* cautiously floated the idea of opening "rock music theaters" in Moscow and other cities.[54]

On the other hand, there was resistance to liberalization on the part of some elements in the establishment, who wanted to maintain "vigilance." For example, Katya Surzhikova, a Russian pop star who liked to perform while scantily clad, was told to add to her wardrobe.[55] Later, in 1985, police broke up a small gathering on the fifth anniversary of the death of Beatle John Lennon, and—on a separate occasion—broke up a Moscow concert by Bajaga and the Instructors, one of Yugoslavia's most popular rock groups, because they objected to seeing the audience dancing and singing and hence "losing control."[56] In 1984, moreover, the Ministry of Culture issued a document imposing a ban on the playing of certain music, in any form, within the city limits of Moscow and enumerated 106 groups that are "not recommended." More specifically, the document listed 68 Western rock groups and artists whose music should be banned, including Kiss, Nina Hagen, the Sex Pistols, AC/DC, Black Sabbath, Alice Cooper, Pink Floyd, the Talking Heads, Van Halen, Patty Smith, Elvis Costello, and Depeche Mode. The document also listed 38 Soviet "unofficial" groups that "propagate ideals and currents alien to our society," including Alliance, Gulliver, Zigzag, Tennis, Rest Area, Nautilus Pompilius, Urfin Dzhus, Winter Garden, Aquarium, Kino, Lucifer, and Pig. And needless to say, conservatives voiced opposition to the proposal to create a recording firm specializing in rock music.[57]

LYRICS AND POLITICS

Whereas American youngsters are notorious for their general indiffer-
ence to lyrics, in the republics of the former USSR both the rock musicians and their listeners seem to place a greater premium on the words.
Not surprisingly, rock lyrics drew most of the official criticism and contributed to the troubles that long plagued rock in the Soviet Union.

Although instrumental jazz and various forms of modern avant-garde
music had been viewed at times with suspicion by the authorities, none
met with such open hostility as rock music. Aside from the sensually
rhythmic music, the authorities were also offended by the outlandish
costumes and abrasive language and manners of the musicians. Where
the lyrics were concerned, the authorities grumbled, in the early stages,
because the songs were generally performed in English—which some of
them could not understand and which, besides, was the language of the
West.[58] Later, when most of the songs were written and performed in
Russian, the authorities fretted that the words were inconsistent with
socialism. The first original lyrics performed in Moscow may actually
have been sung not in Russian but in Polish—the work of an early 1960s
group known as the Roaches that was composed of Polish students
studying in Moscow.[59] The first original Russian songs were most likely
those performed by the Moscow groups Sokol and Skomorokhy, although they were very amateurish and largely imitative efforts.[60]

According to the official cultural policy enforced by leaders from
Khrushchev to Chernenko, song lyrics were supposed to evoke
optimism, youthful energy, and positive emotions in general. If they
dealt with love or any human emotion, they had to be absolutely
straight and proper. No deviations from the officially puritan and sexless
guidelines were permitted. As already mentioned, the lyrics of official
groups had to be approved by the local government authorities before
they could be performed, and if they were to be published, they also had
to be approved by the censorship office, GLAVLIT. Official groups were
required to join the Bureaus of Musical Groups established in every major city. These bureaus strictly regulated the number of Western songs
that may be performed. Most Soviet rock songs, of course, did not deal
with political topics. Like their Western counterparts, Soviet rockers
sang above all about love, passion, alienation, and the frustrations of
life. Some Soviet rock songs were simply dancing tunes.

The political character of the more substantive lyrics can best be illustrated by contrasting those sung by official groups with those sung by
unofficial (and hence unsupervised) groups. In the 1970s the well-
known official group Samotsvety produced a patriotic song, "Our

Address Is the Soviet Union," which is still performed today (albeit sarcastically):

The railroad car wheel dictates to us
Where we'll meet tomorrow.
My telephone numbers
Are ... in different towns.

Refrain:
The heart is aching, the heart is caring.
The postal cargo is being packed.
Our address is not a house or a street.
Our address is the Soviet Union.

You, telegraph dots and dashes,
Look for me at the construction projects.
Today what is important is not my personal life,
But the reports of the work day.

Refrain.

We are with the guys who are sensible.
We are where the posters say, "Ahead!"
Where the toiling country
Sings the good, new songs.

Refrain.[61]

The text is unreserved in its patriotism. There is not even a hint of doubt about any aspect of Soviet reality. On the contrary, the society is described as moving *ahead*.

The song "Experimenter of upward-downward movement," by the unofficial group Alisa, provides a strong contrast, with its only slightly obscured mockery of Marxist dialectics:

Experimenter of upward-downward movement,
He is looking in the direction of the goal
He set for himself.
He knows the answer, he is perfectly alert.
He is breaking the path for other
generations.

Experimenter of upward-downward movement,
He is forming new models of consciousness.
He is perfectly shaven, prim and proper.
He is carrying his brick to the altar of the
universe.

Experimenter of upward-downward movement,
He sees space where I see [a] wall.
He knows the answer, he is sure of his idea.
In every process he reaches the bottom.[62]

It was a sign of the times that Alisa was eventually allowed to make a video of this song and show it on Soviet television.

Samotsvety, by then renamed Plamya, was also responsible for a panegyric to socialist progress, focused on the All-Union Komsomol Construction Project, the Baikal-Amur Railroad (BAM for short).

The rails are nearly
Cutting through the taiga,
To the ocean,
Through the blizzard.

Refrain:
Be merry, guys.
It fell to our lot
To build the railway,
Or BAM for short.

The rails stretch,
The wires buzz.
To the ocean
The trains will go.[63]

Alisa, by contrast, was less impressed with "socialist progress."

All of a sudden, I see something coming my way,
But I can't figure out what it is
No matter how hard I try.
It looks like a tractor, like a nuclear reactor
And also somewhat like a squeezed lemon.
It is white like a hospital, birds are scared of it.
It is strong as a safe
It is slimy like a jellyfish
It is of no use like a burden
It is moving among flowers and different types of grass.
What are you? What the hell are you?
And it answers me: I am your juice squeezer.[64]

Or take the theme of social engagement. The same Samotsvety endeared itself to the authorities in 1984 with a song entitled "Stop Mr. Reagan!" in which it described the policies of the U.S. president as leading to inevitable "global catastrophe."[65] The song was played at a peace concert organized by the Leningrad Komsomol and held in Moscow's

Dynamo stadium. Other groups such as Dialog, Zemliane, and Voskresenie took part in the concert as well, contributing songs with "positive" political themes.

By contrast, the heavy metal group Cruise's song "The Average Man" speaks of social estrangement, of being submerged in and by society:

Yes, I am faceless, I am an average man,
I am the result of scientific synthesis,
In my totally normal head
There is no room for thoughts or doubts.[66]

One of the best-known rock protest songs is "The Calm," first sung by the Moscow rock group Time Machine in 1978:

My ship is a creation of able hands,
My course is a total disaster,
But just let the wind pick up
And everything around will change,
Including the idiot who thinks otherwise.
An answer ready for every question,
Might has always made right.
But no one believes
That there's no wind on earth,
Even if they've banned the wind.[67]

As a result of this song, the group was disqualified from the competition at which it had dared to sing this song.

Soviet authorities, as we have already mentioned, preferred buoyant optimism in lyrics, but in the early 1980s the Latvian group Perkons took up social themes often with great frankness. In one song, the group sings of a drunkard and his bride (the latter symbolized by a white flower). The relationship is damned from the start, but the white flower has been tainted so that no one else will ever want her.

Black earth, black skies,
Black lake, black evening.
Nothing good can come of this.
It comes quietly like the devil.

Black waves in this lake
bear a white flower on their crest.
At the edge of the lake sits a drunkard.
When he returns home,
the sun will not yet have risen.
He will talk to himself
And no one will listen.

And no one will ever pluck
the flower in the lake.
The drunkard's bride tries
to make herself white again.[68]

Unofficial groups were not the only ones to discuss topical issues. Alla Pugacheva, long the best-paid pop singer in the USSR, has addressed the theme of pacifism.

Tell us, birds, the time has come.
Our planet is a fragile glass.
Virgin birch trees, rivers, and fields,
all this, from above, is more delicate than glass.
Can it be that we shall hear from all sides
the farewell sound of crunching crystal?[69]

Finally, we should mention the satirical use made by various heavy metal and new wave groups of officially approved texts or, in the case of Igor Beleov, of certain poems by Karl Marx.[70] This tendency has been given the name "Sov-retro." Groups such as Cement (from Riga) and Funny Pictures (from Moscow) have taken song texts from the 1940s, 1950s, and 1960s and set them to new music, often with surprising effect. Typically they perform in "original epoch costumes." It is inconceivable that an audience could fail to be amused to hear Cement sing the following lines, which were once taken seriously:

The stars have filled the heavens
Like schools of fish around the full moon.
When I come home, your eyes,
Like two fish, will come to see me.[71]

Other group leaders have adapted poetical works previously published in the Soviet Union. The unofficial group Winds of Change (now defunct) prided itself on singing gloomy poems by Leonid Nikolaevich Martynov (b. 1905) and Robert Burns (the latter in an approved translation). The group's members added to the effect by pointedly refraining from smiling during performances. When authorities challenged them on their lyrics, the band leader pointed out that they were culled from approved publications.[72] Another rock group, the Estonian group Raja, took Estonian poems from the late nineteenth and early twentieth centuries for its texts. But in this case the tactic was less successful. Two of these songs were suppressed by Soviet authorities on grounds of Estonian nationalism. In another case, two of Raja's previously approved songs were banned when the songwriter fled to the United States.[73]

Official "Sov-rock" bands presented a clean-cut appearance, performing in neat attire and sticking to musical and textual banalities that were often composed for them by the Union of Composers. The best known among this group of bands was Happy Guys, which was amply supplied with the best equipment available through official channels but was often instructed to add deadwood to the ensemble to give jobs to the sons or cousins of certain influential persons: Needless to say, the instruments of these pantomime actors were not plugged in.[74] Other "Sov-rock" groups have included Samotsvety (Precious Stones), Singing Hearts, Flame, and Skomorokhy. In late 1986, the domination of the "Sov-rock" bands began to come to an end, as heavy metal and new wave bands steadily acquired legitimacy, and with it the chance to make records, go on nationwide tours, and be interviewed in the press. In this context, Soviet society became ripe for musical experimentation, and new possibilities opened up. Time Machine's leader, Andrei Makarevich, put it this way: "Why should one limit oneself in this field? It's like being forced to use only certain letters of the alphabet."[75]

The clean-cut look has also been satirized—most notably by the Estonian group Kontor (Office), whose members played at the 1982 Tartu rock festival clad in 9-to-5 business suits and singing a mix of retro-swing and a version of new wave that seemed indebted to the Talking Heads. At the other extreme is the song "Grey Dove," sung by Zvuki Mu (the Sound of Music):

I'm dirty, I'm exhausted.
My neck's so thin.
Your hand won't tremble,
When you wring it off.
I'm so bad and nasty.
I'm worse than you are.
I'm the most unwanted.
I'm trash, I'm pure dirt.
But I can fly![76]

Where instrumentation is concerned, it is interesting that in the earlier stages of the development of Soviet rock musicians eschewed ethnic and traditional instruments, and people who made use of accordions and balalaikas in rock performances were scorned for "inauthenticity." It was only after the Beatles and other Western groups began to introduce exotic oriental instruments (beginning with the sitar) into their music that Soviet groups decided that the traditional instruments might be adaptable for rock after all. The first reaction among some Soviet rock musicians was to try to obtain sitars of their own; only later did they turn to traditional Russian instruments. The pioneers in this area were

*Zvuki Mu. Copyright © 1989 Warner Bros. Records. Photo by E. Basilia.
Reprinted by permission.*

Pesnyary and Siabry from Belorussia,[77] Yalla from Uzbekistan, and Ariel
from Cheliabinsk. The authorities generally approved of this development, though there have been some hot debates about whether traditional songs ought to be given modernized renditions.[78]

ROCK IN CENTRAL ASIA

Rock music has spread to every corner of the USSR, including the traditionally Muslim republics of Central Asia. Here, as elsewhere, the support for rock music is strongest among urban youth. Discos began to
make their appearance in the region in the mid-1970s, and by 1984
Uzbekistan alone had 115 and Tashkent was said to have a thriving disco
scene.[79]

The Central Asian rock scene actually consists of two parallel rock
scenes: a local Russian-language rock scene, catering to local Russians
and other Europeans, and an indigenous-language rock scene, catering
to the ethnic Muslim peoples of the region. As a general rule, these
bands (whether Russian language or indigeneous language) are several
years behind Moscow and Leningrad in picking up musical trends.
Among local-language bands, there has been a tendency for rock musicians to incorporate ethnic musical elements into their music. For ex-

ample, Natalya Nurmukhamedova, a Tashkent vocalist, uses some ethnic instruments in her performances, which also make use of some
traditional rhythms. Or again, the band Yalla, from Uzbekistan, has
tried, since the late 1970s, to combine hard rock with ethnic music. The
band includes two to three guitarists, a drummer, and several traditional Turkmen instruments.[80]

In Central Asia, as elsewhere, the early and mid-1980s saw repeated
calls for attention to the supposed educational functions of music and
disco centers.[81] In 1985, for example, Marat Qwanyshbekov, senior in-
spector of the Kazakhstan Ministry of Culture and responsible secretary
of the republic Coordinating Methodological Council for Disco Clubs,
was subjected to public criticism for allowing discos under his jurisdic-
tion to diverge from ministry guidelines. He responded by promising to
see that those clubs would do "their part to educate the workers in the
spirit of communism and to raise aesthetic levels."[82] There were also, at
that time, repeated complaints that Central Asian discos were playing
far too much Western music—indeed, in some cases evidently, exclusively Western music.[83]

ROCK IN THE BALTIC REPUBLICS

If rock music in Central Asia is several years behind the Moscow and
Leningrad rock scenes, rock music in Estonia and Latvia has traditionally been ahead of Moscow and Leningrad. Indeed, a number of Western
rock trends, including breakdance and punk, entered the USSR originally via Estonia.

As in Central Asia, however, the heavy immigration of Russians into
the area has made for the presence of two parallel rock scenes, divided
along ethnic lines. Interestingly enough, a 1987 poll taken among
Estonian and Russian young people in Estonia found that in their listing
of their fifteen favorite rock groups (whether domestic or Western)
Estonians and Russians agreed on only three groups: ELO (number 7
among Estonians; number 14 among Russians), the Swedish group
ABBA (number 8 among Estonians; number 15 among Russians), and
the Beatles (number 9 among Estonians; number 6 among Russians).
The Estonians' list was headed by the groups Rok-otdel', Karavan, and
Rein Rannap's Ruja. Similarly, Estonians and Russians overlapped in
only three cases in their respective lists of their fifteen favorite vocalists:
Tynis Miagi (number 6 among Estonians; number 8 among Russians),
Alla Pugacheva (number 7 among Estonians; number 1 among Rus-
sians), and the Italian singer Andriano Chelentano (number 13 among
Estonians; number 6 among Russians).[84]

The similarity of the Estonian and Finnish languages has long allowed Estonians to turn to Finnish radio and television for news, and this gave them a distinct advantage in terms of information over other peoples living in the USSR. It also accounts, at least in part, for their greater speed in assimilating Western musical trends. Punk hit Estonia in the 1980s and built up a certain following among young teens. Authorities reviled the trend and in the mid-1980s forced the Estonian punk band Propeller to disband, on charges of nihilism.

Later, Estonian rock musicians gave Moscow more substantial headaches. Rock music, they showed, could be put to work in the interests of local nationalism. And indeed, at the end of the 1980s, Estonians spoke of a "singing revolution," harnessed to the expanding horizons for political expression and growing aspirations for independence.[85] Alo Mattiisen, leader of the Estonian "medieval rock" group In Spe, contributed to this trend with his "Five Patriotic Songs," which, although set to a heavy rock beat, show their roots in Estonian folk and choral traditions. In one of these songs, Mattiisen sings,

I was born Estonian, I am now Estonian,
And it is Estonian I shall remain.
Being Estonian, proud and good
Free as my grandfather was,
Yes, truly free, as my grandfather was.[86]

In the open atmosphere produced by Gorbachev's policy of glasnost, from 1986 to 1990, Estonian singers eagerly took up long-taboo themes. "Naturally, the first time you are allowed to say such things, you want to say them as loudly as possible," said Mati Brauer. As Estonians stretched their political limbs for the first time in forty years, they cast a wary eye at their Russian "big brother." Riho Sibul, lead vocalist for Estonia's popular band Ultima Thule, put the idea into song:

I bow down deeply
To my big and powerful brother
I'd go to pieces
Just so that I could show you
As Vaino did, as Kogan can,
I'll take all troubles away.

And from deep in my heart I am grateful
Oh, and songs of gratitude will flow from me.

. . . .

Big brother, show yourself to me
So that I may thank you.

You're a big man, so why do you feel
As though, really, you were small?
It's the little ones who get overshadowed.[87]

Sibul's sarcasm in this song is unmistakable and gives expression to decades of deep frustration with Russian domination.

And in Latvia, where there have been a number of fascinating musical innovations in the rock genre, rock has long divided into soft rock and punk factions, with almost nothing in between.[88] Local rock groups include Perkons (discussed earlier), Minuet (a group headed by Latvian symphonic composer Imant Kalninsh, which stirred some controversy in 1977 with a song calling on the older generation to leave young people in peace[89]), and Jumprava (a heavy rock band that dressed up in neo-Roman uniforms for a rock opera entitled *Black Power*). As in Estonia, rock music in Latvia has become wed to nationalist currents—as demonstrated at a 1987 rock concert in Riga at which young people shouted, "Soviets out! Free Latvia!"[90]

In Latvia, rock groups often emerged under the sponsorship of prosperous collective farms, which begat patrons of the arts. These collective farms purchased equipment for the bands and provided them with rehearsal space.[91]

As for Lithuania, the rock scene was very slow to develop there. Indeed, Troitsky wrote in 1987, "nothing at all was happening in Lithuania, the third and largest of the Pribaltic republics."[92]

ROCK IN SIBERIA AND THE SOVIET FAR EAST

The origins of Siberian rock are unclear, but it was not until the early 1980s, with the appearance of Ufin Dzhus and others, that rock in Siberia was recognized as a force to be reckoned with. By 1989, Siberian cities such as Sverdlovsk and Tiumen were considered to be the new centers of Russian rock, surpassing Moscow and Leningrad in both the quantity and quality of groups playing the local scene.[93]

Rock in the East is marked by a certain extremism of form and textual content, with anarchist punk groups constituting a large part of the scene as a whole. This can perhaps be attributed to the traditional hardiness and independence of the Sibiriaki. It would seem, however, that it also has something to do with the predominance of industrial urban areas, the usually horrible environmental and economic conditions of these regions, and the presence of far more conservative authorities.

The first Siberian musician to emerge onto the nationwide scene was Aleksandr Bashlachev, who left his native Cherepovets for Moscow and

Leningrad in 1984. He had been involved in the local scene in Cherepovets, which has always been quite active.[94] Bashlachev's texts are very highly regarded for their combination of traditional bard poetics, antigovernment polemics, and his sense of spiritual freedom:

Through heat and cold we walked a long time.
We suffered through everything and remained free.
We fed on snow and sticks and stones.
And we grew level with the bell towers.

If there are tears, that means we didn't mind spilling the salt.
If there's a feast, that means we didn't mind wasting the sweets.
The bell-ringers, with their black blisters,
Tore the nerves of the copper speaker.

But with every new day the times change.
The cupolas have lost all their gold.
The bell-ringers wander around the world.
The bells are all broken and cracked.

Well, why now are we walking all around
On our own field, as if we were in the underground?
If they haven't cast us a bell,
That means that this is the time of little bells.[95]

Bashlachev's death by suicide in 1988 robbed Soviet rock of its most original talent to date.

Bashlachev's form of native Soviet rock is today performed by such groups as Chai-f (Sverdlovsk) and Kalinov Most (Novosibirsk). They are mostly concerned with the regeneration of prerevolutionary cultural icons and themes, rejecting the Soviet period wholesale. Both of these bands are known throughout the former Soviet Union for their distinctive Russian sound and staunch model principles.[96]

One also finds in Siberia a proliferation of hard-core punk and experimentalist bands. There are Survival Instructions and Cultural Revolution (both from Tiumen), Civil Defense (Omsk), Yanka and BOMZh (both from Novosibirsk), and Uncle Go (Baurnaul), to name but a few. Before her death in 1991, Yanka was by far the most highly regarded of these artists on a national level. These bands were universally militant in their opposition to the Soviet regime (or in fact to any form of authority) and retained clear antibourgeois positions. This stance has led to some confusion at a time when the threat of "going official" has been replaced by the threat of commercialization, and most of these principled bands rejected any offer to participate in either state-run or commercial studios. The more experimental punk bands (such as Civil Defense) often make use of various bits and pieces of Soviet culture (socialist-realist poetry, political speeches, patriotic songs, dissident literature, and so on) for the creation of concrete music. Often such icons are simply incorporated into the texts of songs. The following song by Civil Defense utilizes the socialist-realist classic "They Aren't Born Soldiers" by Konstantin Simonov:

> *A holy place is never in emptiness.*
> *With an extra body they pile the foundation pit.*
> *With a red rag they wrapped the catafalque.*
> *With a dashing song, they drowned out evil and grief.*
>
> *They aren't born soldiers*
> *They die soldiers.*
> *They aren't born soldiers*
> *They die soldiers.*
>
> *A holy place is never without an enemy.*
> *With a polished butt—at random.*
> *In a still not shot-through great coat—straight on!*
> *With a dashing march drowning out all stupidity of furious ...*
>
> *They aren't born soldiers*
> *They die soldiers.*
> *They aren't born soldiers*
> *They die soldiers.*[97]

This militant anti-Soviet song is typical of the Siberian punk genre, and one can see what difficulty these groups will experience with the loss of a clear enemy. Whereas many Soviet groups are currently performing at benefit concerts in support of various causes (the environment, democracy, nationalism), the punk groups have been losing some momentum. Survival Instructions broke up in 1989, partly because of such pressure. Civil Defense is presently inactive; its leader, Yegor Letov, has been producing 1960s-style psychedelic music.

This is not true of all Siberian groups, of course. Nautilus Pompilius, hailing from Sverdlovsk, has consistently rated as one of the top three groups in the Soviet Union. Its mix of political songs, violent love songs, and sarcastic humor has made it a master of the Soviet rock form.

The Soviet Far East witnessed similar trends in the evolution of rock. The two best well-known groups in the Far East are Nick Rock-n-Roll with Koba[98] (Vladivostok) and Eastern Syndrome (Magadan). Out of all rock performers, Nick has perhaps experienced the most difficulties with the authorities; he spent a year in a Simferopol' psychiatric hospital on trumped-up charges of fascism.[99] His song "Old Woman" is a punk standard around the country:

He used to have hard luck,
Now he's a stupid fuck.
We've got a new life—
That's real cool.
Soviet power is a prison,
But where've you taken your old man?
Be happy, old woman, make your old man happy.
Soviet power is a pain in the neck.[100]

Eastern Syndrome became known in Moscow after its 1990 appearance at the festival Syrok, where it made by far the most powerful impression.

The rise of Siberian and Far Eastern rock was accompanied by the appearance of official and semiofficial institutions such as rock clubs and studios. By 1989, most midsized cities had some kind of club for bands to play at and avoid charges of "parasitism." Novosibirsk had both a semiofficial rock club and a private studio for the sponsorship of new bands. The political climate, however, remained such that Civil Defense was forced to seek sponsorship at the Leningrad Rock Club. The local rock club in Cherepovets helped a local promoter, Zhenia Kolesov, to organize a festival in January 1990; it refused his request to dedicate the festival to the memory of Sasha Bashlachev, who in the end was not even mentioned. The tribute to Bashlachev was held in Leningrad.[101]

GORBACHEV AND ROCK MUSIC

With Gorbachev's accession, official policy toward rock eased dramatically. Within six months of his coming to office, Moscow opened its first rock recording studio and Boris Grebenshikov of the group Aquarium was accorded respectability in the press. In 1987, Michael Jackson's video "Billy Jean" was featured on a Soviet TV game show, and American rock videos became a regular feature on Soviet television. In an important move in spring 1986, the conservative Pyotr Demichev was relieved of his post as minister of culture and replaced with Vasilii Zakharov; by 1991, Nikolai Nikolaevich Gubenko, the director of the liberal Tagan'ka Theater, was minister of culture. The notorious conservative V. Shauro was replaced with the more open-minded Yuri Voronov as head of the CC Department of Culture—signaling a conscious break with the past. The Gorbachev era also saw the staging of the USSR's first-ever charity rock concert, in May 1986, and breakdancing likewise was officially endorsed "in the name of a healthy lifestyle and in the spirit of sports."[102] Heavy metal has also been accepted by the establishment; the band Cruise was given a recording contract with Melodiya.[103] Even the once-staid Institute of International Affairs in Moscow played host to a heavy metal rock festival (in January 1987).

Yet Soviet authorities remained ill disposed toward punk, which was gaining a visible following above all in Estonia and Siberia. The punk movement evidently notched a significant following among Estonian high school students, but is by no means restricted to that milieu. In February 1986, *Pravda* devoted twenty-eight column inches to excoriating the punks for "something bloodcurdling in their eyes."[104] And the Estonian punk group Propeller, which, inter alia, had recorded a song in which the members screamed, "No!" over and over against a primitive beat, was forcibly disbanded by the authorities.

The rock scene was an early beneficiary of Gorbachev's policy of glasnost. Previously unofficial and even banned groups such as Aquarium and Bravo received official recognition and support. By 1988, Melodiya began releasing "real" rock albums. The All-Union rock festival received official sponsorship. Radio and TV stations now feature rock music on a daily basis. In 1987, former underground bands were allowed to organize a Rock Laboratory and amateur groups were granted permission to advertise their concerts. And with Gorbachev, and subsequently Yeltsin, at the Kremlin, rock performers have been coming to Moscow almost as often as to any other major city in the world. This influx also permitted Soviet cultural authorities to stage rock events as "peace" concerts and gain propaganda mileage. In addition, in a rather important symbolic gesture, authorities dropped the terms *official* and *unofficial* in 1987 and now refer to *professional* and *amateur* groups.

With the newly intensified political situation, 1991 saw the rise of the political concert. Although politically motivated concerts had occurred before—for instance, a 1990 concert in defense of the environmentally threatened Lake Baikal—they had attracted neither the top musicians nor a large attendance. In April 1991, however, the top bands from around the country (DDT, Auktyson, Brigada S, Nautilus Pompilius, and others) converged on Moscow for a "Rock Against Terror" concert.[105] In August 1991, this event was followed by a concert in Moscow to celebrate the defeat of the coup.

Glasnost led to a proliferation of independent music publications and, more important, of independent management and recording facilities. By 1991, approved journals such as *Rok-Ada, Rok, Davai-Davai,* and a Russian edition of the West German *Metal Hammer* were being sold in Moscow. Moreover, underground journals, such as Moscow's *Urlait* (later *KontrKultura*), *Sdvig*, Leningrad's *RIO*, and Novosibirsk's *Ensk* were enjoying the new press freedoms and expanding readership. Besides these main journals, thousands of connected fanzines were initiated throughout the country. At the same time, companies such as

Aprel, BSA (Riga), and *Erio* were attempting to sign artists on to recording contracts.[106] Alisa released a live double album directly through the Leningrad record factory, completely by-passing middlemen.[107] Management, until recently the preserve of the large rock clubs and rock laboratories, has also become a commercial prospect for some.[108] None of these new journals or record companies can compete with the old, official bodies (such as *Komsomol'skaia pravda* among press outlets and Melodiya among recording companies) in the scope of their activities, but they offer valuable opportunities for the independent minded and expand the range of what is available to the public.

Soviet rock performers, including Alla Pugacheva, Boris Grebenshikov, Sergei Kuryokhin, Brigada S, Rondo, Stas Namin Group, Zvuki Mu, Gorky Park, and DDT, have been able to come to the United States recently for concerts and recording sessions. In late 1988, moreover, Melodiya Records released a special album of songs by Paul McCartney, prepared by the ex-Beatle exclusively for sale in the USSR.[109]

It became clear that Gorbachev's administration wanted to include rock music in its program of cultural liberalization. The alternative would have been to let the Soviet younger generation, which had already acquired a taste for Russian rock, revert back to Western-only rock. That would have been reflected, for example, in an increase in the audience for Voice of America's popular music programs and John Peel's show on the BBC, for which Soviet authorities clearly had no stomach. Hence even heavy metal came to be accepted in the USSR. In a 1987 press conference for foreign journalists at the Soviet Foreign Ministry, Aleksei Kozlov, saxophonist and composer for the jazz-rock group Arsenal, sang the praises of heavy metal rock, which he viewed as a channel for young working-class Russians to work out their resentment toward more affluent members of Soviet society.[110]

That there was resistance to the new policy on rock has already been indicated. In May 1987, for instance, a joint session of the USSR Ministry of Culture and the secretariat of the USSR Union of Composers discussed the state of music in the Soviet Union. According to a report in *Sovetskaia kultura,* session participants expressed deep concern about rock groups, focusing on the "absence of ties with national musical roots and the imitation of what are far from the best examples of Western musical art."[111] Later, in November 1987, Soviet writers Yuri Bondarev, Vasilii Belov, and Valentin Rasputin sent a letter to *Pravda* expressing alarm at rock music's "druglike ability to warp the minds of defenseless adolescents" and urging more wholesome standards.[112]

Yet even then it was unimaginable that conservative forces could successfully roll back liberalization in the cultural sphere. Official tolerance of rock counterculture in Moscow and Leningrad, and elsewhere for that matter, had reached the point where relaxation became impossible to reverse without unacceptable social costs.

RECENT DEVELOPMENTS

As the Soviet political order steadily eroded in the late 1980s, the once-potent cultural controls slackened and long-standing taboos shattered. The once-puritanical Soviet Union seemed to be entering into a delayed sexual revolution. In this spirit, a 1991 article appearing in Leningrad's *Megapolis-Express* said, "We are proud of our Soviet breasts and asses and sexual acts, and exclaim joyfully, at the top of our lungs, that we have our own, home-grown erotica."[113]

Twenty years after its American premier, *Jesus Christ Superstar* (the rock opera created by composer Andrew Lloyd Webber and lyricist Tim Rice) finally came to Russia, playing to packed houses at Moscow's Mossoviet Theater. The Soviet production added some original touches, having Jesus Christ make his entrance dressed in a black leather jacket and riding a motorcycle borrowed from the local Soviet militia, and dressing the Pharisees in dark business suits with red armbands, recalling the traditional attire of the communist party leadership atop Lenin's tomb each May Day and 7 November. When these "pharisees" appeared, the Moscow audiences greeted them with loud snickers.[114]

The failure of the August 1991 coup attempt and the subsequent collapse of the Soviet Union at the end of the same year only finished off the old cultural order, opening up the country more totally to Western rock influences. Just a few weeks after the failed coup, the Texas heavy-metal rock group Pantera played, alongside AC/DC and Metallica, to several thousand screaming Soviet youngsters at a one-day concert in Moscow. It is true that by 1989 Ozzy Osbourne, Bon Jovi, and Motley Crue had already been allowed to perform (to a full house) in Moscow's Lenin Stadium. But in 1989 one would not yet have expected to find rock graffiti on public walls; by 1991, this had become commonplace, with inscriptions of "AC/DC" being an especial favorite.[115]

Since then, segments of the Russian heavy-metal scene have become associated with right-wing politics and xenophobia. The *Wall Street Journal*, in a 1993 article, cited a Moscow-based market researcher who estimated "that one-fifth of Russia's 20 million young adults are attracted to the increasingly intolerant views of hard-line nationalists and that the figure is growing."[116] Politicians on the right have been quick to draw conclusions about the potential utility of heavy metal rock, whose adherents often leave concerts and start overturning cars and breaking the windows of local non-Russians' houses. Vladimir Bondarenko, deputy chief editor of the ultra-right-wing newspaper *Dyen* (Day), has talked of forging an "alliance" with the Russian heavy metal rockers and recently launched a regular back-page column, entitled "Rock—The Russian Resistance."[117] The column has given coverage to sundry Russian heavy metal bands, including Exorcist and Death Vomit (described as two of Russia's "raunchiest" heavy metal bands).[118] Also symptomatic of this trend is the adherence of former DK drummer Sergei Zharikov to the National Radical Party, a white-supremacist organization; thirty-seven-year-old Zharikov, who speaks of his admiration for Louisiana politican David Duke (a former Ku Klux Klansman), is the party's "youth adviser." And Vasily Boyarintsev, the owner of Davai-Davai, Moscow's best-known heavy metal record store as of 1993, adorns his office with posters of Adolf Hitler and Saddam Hussein and dreams of a right-wing takeover in Russia.

Sergei Troitsky, alias Spider, is the leader of Korrozia Metalla, one of the best-known of Moscow's new generation of heavy metal bands. Twenty-six-year-old Spider equates the heavy-metal music of his band with political action. "Russian society is getting more and more angry," Spider opined early in 1993. "It's something like Germany during the Weimar Republic, before Hitler came to power."[119] Spider's recipe for the present situation is spelled out in his song "Kill the Sunarefa" (*Sunarefa* being Russian slang for dark-skinned non-Russians). "When the beastly mugs come down from the mountains," says Spider, "Russian guns should shoot them."[120]

In this incarnation, Russian rock is now light-years away from its early, more innocent forms. Indeed, there is nothing automatic about the social content of rock music. It is a medium open to diverse uses, and—Marshall McLuhan notwithstanding—the message conveyed by any particular rock artist stands quite apart from the rock medium as such.

CONCLUSION

Several conclusions are in order. First, it was above all the authorities who made rock music a political issue in the USSR. Most rock songs written by Soviet bands were politically innocent, just as they are in the United States, and dealt with themes such as love and sex and the trials of growing up. Conservative figures in the cultural establishment react not only to the lyrics, however, but also to the music, attire, and language of the performers, all of which they may consider subversive.

Second, the factional element in the formation of policy toward rock music closely mirrors that in other policy spheres. In fact, rock music was clearly just one part of a much broader context in which liberalizers and conservatives face each other. For this reason, liberalization in the realm of music closely paralleled liberalization in other areas. In an earlier era, for instance, jazz music benefited from Khrushchev's "thaw," just as rock music has benefited from glasnost and the postcoup situation.

And third, after going through a long incubation period of imitation of Western models, rock music in the Soviet Union has now come of age and is developing autonomously, though certainly not in isolation from trends elsewhere in the world. The Soviet rock scene is richer and more diverse than ever in the past.

Until the end of the 1980s more independent-minded bands in the USSR by and large shunned official status, and there was a clear dichotomy between creative but insolvent bands like Kino and commercially successful but artistically vapid bands like Happy Guys, with some gradations around the extremes. Now official recognition is irrelevant. Could the depoliticization of rock be the kiss of death for Russian rock musicians, who have always viewed political protest as a central part of their role? This question is very much on their minds. Rock without protest somehow just isn't the same. As Aquarium's Boris Grebenshikov mused in 1987, "The best way to hear rock 'n' roll for the first time is when it's illegal."[121]

APPENDIX:
PROFILES OF THE MAJOR RUSSIAN-LANGUAGE
ROCK GROUPS PLAYING IN THE USSR IN THE 1980S

It is difficult to produce a definitive list of the most popular rock groups in the former Soviet Union because of the general lack of statistic taking done there and also because of ethnic fracturing, which makes for a number of parallel rock scenes, especially in the wake of the failed coup of August 1991. The existing readers' polls conducted by some youth newspapers are not too reliable because they tend to favor local groups that are relatively unknown to outside the given local community. For example, participants in a poll reported by the Latvian newspaper *Sovetskaia molodezh* in its 4 July 1987 issue gave 34 percent of their votes to Spetsbrigada, a group almost unknown outside Riga. Melodiya also conducts polls, but its findings seem to reflect its rather conservative recording patterns rather than actual audience tastes. A 1987 Melodiya survey reported by TASS (in *Sovetskaia molodezh*, 8 August 1987) claimed that the two most popular records were *Epitafia*, by Leningrad folk singer Aleksandr Rosenbaum, and *Just One Minute*, by Happy Guys. The following list, given in alphabetical order, thus reflects in large part the subjective impressions of the authors.

Alisa. Based in Leningrad and led by the riotous "Dr. Kostya," Alisa plays musically innovative hard rock. Lyrics include political satire. Alisa was included on the two-record set *Red Wave,* which was released in the United States by Los Angeles rock singer and promoter Joanna Stingray in summer 1986, and has subsequently released several albums in the USSR as well.

Aquarium. Founded in Leningrad in 1972, Aquarium was long constrained to play underground but eventually acquired official status, shortly before this status ceased to have the same meaning. Aquarium was the most popular band throughout most of the 1980s and is still a dominant presence, thanks in part to band leader Boris Grebenshikov's imaginate lyrics and the group's solid rock beat. In 1988, Melodiya released Aquarium's first commercial album, and in 1989 Grebenshikov released an album (*Radio Silence*) in the United States, sung in English and Russian.

Aria. Formed on 18 February 1986 in Moscow, Aria includes former members of Alfa, Art, and Black Coffee. A heavy metal band, Aria has already won first prize in three rock festivals and has thousands of followers throughout the former Soviet Union. The group is known mostly through its homemade tapes, but it eventually signed a contract for the release of an album by Melodiya.

Auktsyon. Auktsyon made its debut in 1986, with a theatrical rock show, and later became the foremost avant-garde Russian rock band. Its humorous texts, which usually address the depravity of everyday life, are laid onto intricate synthesizer and guitar-based music. The group includes Oleg Garkusha, a full-time "showman," and a full-time dancer on stage at all time. The group has traveled extensively throughout Europe and came to enjoy particular success in France.

Autograph. Based in Moscow, Autograph received some publicity in the West after its appearance via satellite during the "Live Aid" concert in 1986 and during its tours of Western Europe and Canada in 1987. Lead guitarist/composer Aleksandr Sitkovekstky is obviously influenced by the early music of the British group Genesis. Formed originally in July 1979, Autograph acquired official status in 1980. It won the 1983 All-Union Estrada Competition and often toured in both the Soviet Union and abroad. The early compositions by Autograph were in an art-rock style, but it currently plays new wave rock.

Bravo. Led at one time by singer Ivanna Anders, Bravo combines the intensity of punk with elements of 1950s-style boogie and rockabilly. The group also played 1930s swing and futuristic rock. Its first album was released by Melodiya in 1987. Ivanna Anders has since quit Bravo, changed her name back to Zhanna Agurazova, and released a record on the Riga label, BSA.

Brigada S. Led by the energetic Igor Sukachev, Brigada S was one of a number of bands promoted by Soviet rock impresario Stas Namin. Based in Moscow, this boogie/scat band sang some songs in English and played in Seattle in 1989. At the end of 1989, Sukachev left the group, which reorganized itself under the name Brigadiers. He subsequently returned to the fold, and Brigada S has recently performed at concerts in Tallinn and Moscow. Sukachev has acted in six films.

Cement. Based in Riga and led by vocalist Andrei Yakhimovich, this group has a truly unique repertoire. It consists almost entirely of the arrangements of the primitive "socialist realist" songs written in the 1950s and early 1960s. Cement plays these songs in new heavy metal or new wave arrangements and an overly expressive manner that makes a complete mockery of the literal messages of these songs.

Center. Based in Moscow, this new wave group is one of the most controversial bands from a musical point of view. Formed in the early 1980s and led by Vasilii Shumov, Center combines new wave with elements of early 1960s Soviet rock 'n' roll. Shumov is now married to a Parisian and has had records released in the USSR, France, and the United States (on Joanna Stingray's Red Wave label).

Chai-f. From Sverdlovsk, Chai-f was founded in 1984 by singer-songwriter Volodya Shakhrin. Shakhrin writes honest, anthemlike songs, based on a combination of rock, folk, and bard music. U2 is probably the closest Western analogue. Chai-f has not yet had a record released, and Shakhrin has not yet given up his day job as a construction worker.

Cinema (Kino). Based in Leningrad, Kino was included on the two-record set *Red Wave* released in the United States by Joanna Stingray. Stingray married Kino's lead guitarist, Yuri Kasparyan. Kino was widely considered the second most popular band in Leningrad (after Aquarium) after hitting superstar status in 1989 and had an early album released on Melodiya. But lead singer Viktor Tsoi died in a car accident in August 1990, and the group has since disbanded.

Civil Defense. Founded in 1985 by Yegor Letov, Civil Defense was perhaps the foremost punk band in the USSR. Noted for its prolific recording schedule, as well as its anarchism of the soul, Civil Defense has recorded more than twenty-five albums (distributed on *magnitizdat* [illegal tapes]), including fifteen in an experimental series named "Communism." The passionate Yanka Diagileva, from Novosibirsk, often joined with members of Civil Defense to perform under the name the Great Octobers. However, Yanka's career was cut short by her suicide in May 1991.

Cruise. A heavy metal band, Cruise has been featured on Moscow television and signed a recording contract with Melodiya.

DDT. Originally formed in 1980 in the provincial town of Ufa, this popular band was forced to move to Leningrad. DDT plays hard rock with some ethnic influences; its lyrics are often bitingly satirical. Lead vocalist Iurii Shevchuk has acquired a reputation as something of a poet. The band has visited the United States on several occasions and played in Los Angeles in summer 1990. DDT has had one record released on Melodiya (as of June 1991) but is planning the release of five more as well as two solo albums by Shevchuk.

DK. DK refused to register with any Soviet club and rejected Gorbachev's conciliatory line. DK prided itself on "subversive" and "outrageous" music and developed a national cult following. Widely credited with being musically innovative, DK sang of sexual deviance, broken homes, corruption, and alcoholism. Lyrics were written by drummer/vocalist Sergei Zharikov, who later emerged as the leading proponent of antisemitism in rock. DK recently disbanded and Zharikov has become youth adviser to the National Radical Party, an extreme right-wing group.

Nautilus Pompilius. A new wave band from Sverdlovsk, Nautilus Pompilius is known for its imaginative and provocative lyrics. Russian rock critic Artemy Troitsky judges that the group is "probably the best Russian band" outside Moscow and Leningrad. Nautilus Pompilius has had several albums released by Melodiya and has also shot a film.

Polite Refusal. Led by Roman Suslov, this jazz-rock band was founded in 1985 in Moscow. The group tends to perform avant-garde jazz compositions with a heavy reggae influence. Suslov's lyrics are sometimes reduced to psychedelic scat. It has had one album released on Melodiya.

Popular Mechanics. Based in St. Petersburg, Popular Mechanics incorporates noninstrumental effects (such as banging trash can lids) in its particular variant of jazz-rock. Several of the members of Popular Mechanics are graduates of the music conservatory, including the group's creator, Sergei Kuryokhin, who is also an accomplished solo pianist.

Strange Games. Formed in 1982 by Aleksandr Davydov and the two Sologub brothers, Strange Games was one of the first Soviet bands to assimilate the music and stage presence of new wave music. It was featured on Stingray's *Red Wave* album and eventually had a record released on Melodiya in 1988. The group broke up in 1985, splitting into two bands: Games and Aria (see earlier description).

Televizor. Created in late 1983, Televizor is part of the St. Petersburg scene. It is best known for its defiant song "Get Out of Control," which was banned at the time. This new wave band is similar to the Smiths or to Bauhaus. Televizor played in Rome in 1988.

Time Machine. Based in Moscow, Time Machine was formed in 1971 and now enjoys status as a "living classic." Predictably, some of the younger generation view Time Machine as convention bound and old fashioned. That notwithstanding, the band, led by singer Andrei Makarevich, has become one of the most influential and controversial rock groups in the country. Time Machine was unofficial for almost a decade, acquiring official status only in 1980. Since then it has toured almost every major city in the Soviet Union, recorded a number of movie soundtracks, and become a familiar feature on Soviet television. In spite of this, Time Machine performances were banned several times during Chernenko's brief rule (1984–1985). The group's musical style combines classic rock with elements of Russian folk traditions.

Va-bank. Founded by Sasha Skliar, former diplomat to North Korea and guitarist for Center, Va-bank ("Go for All") is, as of mid-1991, one of the most popular Moscow groups. Va-bank plays humorous punk without any explicit political message. The group members belong to the Moscow Rock Laboratory. Va-bank is

Pyotr Mamonov of Zvuki Mu. Copyright © 1989 Warner Bros. Records.
Photo by A. Petropavlovskavo. Reprinted by permission.

signed to the French division of Warner-Chappell Records and has an album released in Finland.

Zoopark. Led by Mikhail "Maik" Naumenko, Zoopark is a rockabilly band with heavy influences of Lou Reed and T. Rex. Maik's descriptions of Soviet life were considered to be especially honest and true to life. Zoopark has had albums released on Melodiya but has practically stopped performing in recent years.

Zvuki Mu. Once forced to play underground, this Moscow band gave its first performance in February 1984 and released an album in the United States in 1989. Lead vocalist Pyotr Mamonov projects himself as an eccentric schizophrenic, and he once defined his lyrics as "Russian folk hallucinations."

NOTES

The original version of this chapter was written jointly by Sabrina Ramet and Sergei Zamascikov and was published in *Journal of Popular Culture* 24, no. 1 (Summer 1990). Sabrina Ramet at that time wrote under the name Pedro Ramet. Robert Bird was co-opted into the project in 1991 and provided necessary updating and polishing of the chapter, which included a new section on rock in Siberia and the Far East. Sabrina Ramet undertook the final updating of this chapter. In preparing the revisions and updating for this book, the authors also enjoyed the research assistance of Elizabeth Grygo. The authors wish to thank the International Studies Program of the Henry M. Jackson School of International Studies, University of Washington, and program director Joel Migdal for extending a small grant to pay for Ms. Grygo's services.

1. *Sovetskaia molodezh* (Riga), 16 April 1987. See also V. Tarbakov, "Razvlekaia prosveshchat'," *Komsomol'skaia zhizn'*, no. 1 (January 1983), p. 24.

2. *Moskovskii komsomolets* (Moscow), 12 September 1984.

3. Yu. Tomilin, "Disko: Novye problemy, kotorye ne novy," *Muzykal'naia zhizn'* (Moscow), no. 13 (July 1982), p. 21; and William Fierman, "Western Popular Culture and Soviet Youth: A Case Study of the 'Muslim' Regions," *Central Asian Survey* 7, no. 1 (1988), p. 19.

4. *New York Times*, 8 May 1955.

5. S. Frederick Starr, "The Rock Inundation," *The Wilson Quarterly* 7, no. 4 (Autumn 1983), p. 59.

6. Both quoted in Artemy Troitsky, *Back in the USSR: The True Story of Rock in Russia* (Boston: Faber and Faber, 1987), p. 23.

7. Georgi Tolstiakov, "Sowjetische Rockmusik in den 80er Jahren," *Sowjetunion heute*, no. 8 (August 1985), reprinted under the title " 'Magnitisdat' contra 'Melodija'—Die unkontrollierte Rockmusikwelle in der UdSSR," *Osteuropa* (Aachen) 36, no. 2 (February 1986), p. A102.

8. Nikita Khrushchev, 1 December 1962, in Priscilla Johnson, *Khrushchev and the Arts: The Politics of Soviet Culture, 1962–1964* (Cambridge: MIT Press, 1965), p. 102.

9. Ibid., p. 103.

10. For a fast-paced treatment of rock music in the United States, see Loyd Grossman, *A Social History of Rock Music* (New York: David McKay, 1976). See also John Orman, *The Politics of Rock Music* (Chicago: Nelson-Hall, 1984), especially chapters 1, 4, 11.

11. Johnson, *Khrushchev and the Arts,* pp. 109–110, 111, 175.

12. John Dornberg, *Brezhnev: The Masks of Power* (New York: Basic Books, 1974), p. 202.

13. Starr, "The Rock Inundation," pp. 65–66.

14. D. Ukhov, "Rok-muzyka vzgliad iz 80kh," *Innostrannaia literatura* (1982), p. 228.

15. *Washington Post,* 23 and 30 May 1979; and *New York Times,* 29 May 1979.

16. Tolstiakov, "'Magnitisdat,'" p. A93; and *Argumenty i fakty* (Moscow), 6–12 May 1986, trans. in Joint Publications Research Service (JPRS), *USSR Report,* no. UPS-86-035 (28 July 1986), p. 50.

17. Vlastimir Nesić, "Rock u SSSR-u," *Reporter* (Belgrade), 14 June 1985, no. 947, p. 40; and Aleksandr Glukharev, professional Soviet rock musician from 1976 to 1986 and former member of Happy Guys, in interview with Sabrina Petra Ramet, Dover, New Hampshire, 28 February 1987.

18. Interview by Sabrina Petra Ramet with Iurii Shevchuk, leader of the Leningrad rock group DDT, Altadena, California, 25 June 1990.

19. The set consists of songs from the mid-1960s albums *A Hard Day's Night* and *A Taste of Honey.*

20. *Komsomol'skaia pravda,* 7 April 1984.

21. "The Nature of Official Documents Concerning Control of Vocal/Instrumental Groups and Discotheques," trans. from *Arkhiv Samizdata (Radio Liberty Research),* 18 October 1985, by Antonia Lloyd-Jones, in *Survey* 29, no. 2 (Summer 1985), pp. 176–177.

22. "Disko-dilemmy," in *Muzykal'naia zhizn',* no. 18 (September 1981), p. 22.

23. Recommendations of the All-Union Scientific-Methodological Center of the Ministry of Culture (1 October 1984), smuggled out and reprinted in *Novoe russkoe slovo* (New York), 2 October 1985.

24. *Literaturnaia gazeta,* 5 December 1984.

25. A. Troitsky, "Rolling Stounz," *Muzykal'naia zhizn',* no. 16 (August 1982), p. 23.

26. See Arkady Petrov, "'Tartu-82': Parad molodezhnoi estrady" [Tartu 1982: Parade of young people's entertainment], *Muzykal'naia zhizn',* no. 15 (August 1982).

27. See Valter Ojakaar, *Pop-Muusikast* (Tallinn: Eesti Raamat, 1983).

28. See interview with Gennadii Gladkov in *Smena* (Moscow), no. 15 (1986).

29. *Pravda,* 11 September 1987.

30. *Krasnaia zvezda,* 4 December 1982.

31. *Krasnaia zvezda,* 13 January 1983.

32. The history of Zvezdochka was discussed in the *Sluzhu Sovetskomu Soiuzu* program on Moscow Television, 6 September 1987.

33. Lt. Col. V. Roshchupkin, "Ob'ekt diverii-molodezh'," *Kommunist Vooruzhennykh Sil,* no. 16 (1987), p. 85.

34. Ibid., p. 86.

35. Anatoly Doronin and Arkady Lisenkov, "Chto proku ot 'roka' " [What use is 'rock'?], *Molodaia gvardiia* (Moscow), no. 5 (1986), pp. 214–231.

36. *Komsomol'skaia pravda*, 22 May 1987, trans. in *Current Digest of the Soviet Press* (CDSP) 39, no. 21 (24 June 1987), p. 3.

37. *Moscow News*, as cited in *The Economist* (London), 11 July 1987, p. 51; and *Izvestiia*, 13 August 1988.

38. *Literaturnaia gazeta*, 6 May 1987.

39. Ibid.

40. Aleksandr Zhitinskii, "Muzyka neposlushykh detei," *Teatr*, no. 2 (1987), p. 64.

41. Ibid., pp. 652–663.

42. Ukhov, "Rok-muzyka," pp. 229, 232.

43. For more discussion of these points, see Pedro Ramet, "Rock Counterculture in Eastern Europe and the Soviet Union," *Survey* 29, no. 2 (Summer 1985).

44. Quoted in the *Christian Science Monitor*, 4 April 1986.

45. *Sovetskaia Rossiia*, 19 August 1983.

46. Doronin and Lisenkov, "Chto proku," p. 215.

47. *Komsomol'skaia pravda*, 16 September 1984, trans. in *CDSP* 36, no. 37 (10 October 1984), pp. 4, 5.

48. *Sovetskaia kultura*, 16 April 1983.

49. Doronin and Lisenkov, "Chto proku," p. 224.

50. *Yunost'* (Moscow), no. 5 (May 1983), trans. in *CDSP* 35, no. 34 (21 September 1983), p. 7.

51. *Literaturnaia gazeta*, 25 November 1981.

52. *Leningradskaia pravda*, 19 January 1986.

53. *Billboard*, 12 January 1985.

54. *Argumenty i fakty*, 6–12 May 1986, p. 37.

55. Reuter News Agency (23 August 1983).

56. Sasha Dragich, manager of Bajaga and the Instructors, in an interview with Sabrina Petra Ramet, Belgrade, 13 July 1988; and Associated Press dispatch, 8 August 1985.

57. *Komsomol'skaia pravda*, 10 November 1985.

58. Grisha Dimant, émigré Soviet rock musician, in an interview with Sergei Zamascikov, Los Angeles, 22 February 1987; and Anatoly Mogilevsky, émigré Soviet rock musician, in an interview with Sabrina Petra Ramet and Sergei Zamascikov, New York, 27 February 1987.

59. See Sim Rokotov, "Govori! Illiustrirovannaia istoriia otechestvennogo roka" [Speak! An illustrated history of domestic rock], *Yunost'*, no. 6 (June 1987), p. 84.

60. Ibid., pp. 84–85; and *Sovetskaia molodezh'*, 18 July 1987.

61. The authors are indebted to Irina Rabinovich for the translation of this song.

62. This song is included on the album *Red Wave*, produced by Joanna Stingray of Los Angeles in 1986. The authors wish to thank Stingray for permission to quote from her translation.

63. See note 61.

64. See note 62.

65. Cited in M. Sigalov, "Disko-panorama: Kollektiv," *Komsomol'skaia zhizn'*, no. 4 (February 1984), p. 27.

66. Quoted in ibid.

67. Quoted in Troitsky, *Back in the USSR,* p. 42.

68. Translated from Latvian by Sergei Zamascikov and Daina Birnbaums, from the album *Vel ir Laiks,* released in Hamburg, West Germany, in 1984.

69. Quoted in Dusko Doder, *Shadows and Whispers: Power Politics Inside the Kremlin from Brezhnev to Gorbachev* (New York: Random House, 1986), p. 226.

70. Michael R. Benson, "Rock in Russia," *Rolling Stone,* 26 March 1987, p. 20.

71. *Sovetskaia molodezh',* 11 April 1987.

72. Sasha Lehrmann, lead singer of Winds of Change from 1967 to 1970 and member of Happy Guys from 1972 to 1975, in an interview with Sabrina Petra Ramet, New Haven, Connecticut, 28 February 1987.

73. After a few years, the songwriter returned to the USSR, but the songs in question remained under ban. Rein Rannap, keyboard player for Raja from 1971 to 1984, in an interview with Sabrina Petra Ramet, Rome, 9 June 1987.

74. Source cited in note 72.

75. *Sovetskaia molodezh',* 18 July 1987.

76. Quoted in Troitsky, *Back in the USSR,* p. 118.

77. Re Siabry, see the interview in *Sel'mashevets* (Gomel), 29 July 1983.

78. The Russian nationalists, for example, who have never liked rock music, strongly protested any use of folk melodies in rock music. See, for example, Doronin and Lisenkov, "Chto proku."

79. William Fierman, "Western Popular Culture and Soviet Youth: A Case Study of the 'Muslim' Regions," *Central Asian Survey* 7, no. 1 (1988), p. 19.

80. Oleg Babinov, specialist in the sociology of music, in an interview with Sabrina Petra Ramet, Seattle, 18 June 1990.

81. *Turkmenskaia iskra,* trans. into Serbo-Croatian in *Politika,* 3 September 1980.

82. *Madeniyet Zhane Turmys* (Alma Ata), no. 12 (December 1985), p. 7, trans. in JPRS, *USSR Report,* no. UPS-85-063 (7 August 1985), p. 10.

83. *Yosh Leninchi* (Tashkent), 26 January 1985, p. 2, trans. in JPRS, *USSR Report,* no. UPS-85-050 (14 June 1985), p. 77; *Yosh Leninchi,* 7 August 1985, p. 4, trans. in JPRS, *USSR Report,* no. UPS-85-078 (5 November 1985), p. 138; and *Yosh Leninchi,* 22 February 1986, p. 2, trans. in JPRS, *USSR Report,* no. UPS-86-027 (13 June 1986), p. 61.

84. N. P. Meinert, "Po vole roka," *Sotsiologicheskie Issledovaniia,* no. 4 (1987), p. 91.

85. Peter Riggs, "Baltic Rocks," *Whole Earth Review,* no. 65 (Winter 1989), p. 56.

86. Quoted in ibid., p. 61.

87. Quoted in ibid., p. 62.

88. Ibid., p. 63.

89. Mark Yoffe, "Hippies in the Baltic: The Rock-and-Roll Era," *Cross Currents* 7 (1988), p. 169.

90. *Die Welt* (Bonn), 20 January 1987, p. 5.

91. Troitsky, *Back in the USSR,* p. 86.

92. Ibid., p. 87.

93. For accounts of the Siberian rock scene, see especially the quarterly

KontrKul'tUrA (issued in Moscow since 1990); the journal *DVR* (Vladivostok and Moscow) covers the Far East.

94. See the interview with Sasha Bashlachev in Aleksandr Zhitinskii, *Puteshestvie Rok-Diletanta* (Leningrad: Lenizdat, 1990), pp. 205–208.

95. Aleksandr Bashlachev, "The Time of Little Bells." Translation by Robert Bird. *Tret'ia stolitsa* (The third capital), 1985; also on *Vremia kolokol'chikov* (The time of little bells). Melodiia, 1989, C60 27923 004.

96. Chai-f has recently been casting its gaze on Europe. See *Komsomol'skaia pravda*, 12 May 1991.

97. Yegor Letov and Grazhdanskaia Oborona, "They Aren't Born Soldiers." Translation by Robert Bird. *Nekrofiliia*, 1987.

98. "Koba" was Stalin's usual name in young adulthood.

99. See S. Gur'ev, "Delo No. 666," *KontrKul'tUrA* 1, no. 1 (March 1990), pp. 155–161.

100. Nick Rock-n-Roll and Lolita, "Old Woman." Translation by Robert Bird. *Pechal'nyi ulichnyi bliuz* (Sad blues of the street), 1990.

101. Zhenia Kolesov, Soviet rock promoter, in an interview with Robert Bird, Cherepovets, 12 January 1990.

102. *Noorte Haal* (Tallinn), 11 May 1986, quoted in Toomas Ilves, "Youth Trends: Breakdancing in, Heavy Metal in Trouble," *Radio Free Europe Research*, 29 August 1986, p. 6. See also Vadim Kiryukhin, "Breik umer! da zdravstruet breik!" *Ogonëk*, no. 43 (25 October–1 November 1986), pp. 19–21.

103. Joanna Stingray, rock singer and promoter, in an interview with Sabrina Petra Ramet, Los Angeles, 7 May 1987.

104. *Pravda*, 10 February 1986.

105. See O. Pshenichnyi, "Rock protiv terrora kak vysshei formy ugriumosti," *Komsomol'skaia pravda*, 2 March 1991, p. 6. Also *Komsomol'skaia pravda*, 5 April 1991 and 9 April 1991.

106. See *Komsomol'skaia pravda*, 21 March 1991, p. 4, and 10 April 1991.

107. *Komsomol'skaia pravda*, 6 March 1991, p. 4.

108. Chai-f was recently signed to a new organization, *Notrek*, which promised to send the group to Europe. See *Komsomol'skaia pravda*, 6 May 1991.

109. *New York Times*, 12 January 1989.

110. *New York Times*, 9 January 1987.

111. *Sovetskaia kultura*, 12 May 1987, trans. in JPRS, *USSR Report*, no. UPA-87-005, 12 June 1987, p. 77.

112. *Pravda*, 9 November 1987, trans. in *CDSP* 30, no. 45 (9 December 1987), p. 26.

113. Quoted in *International Herald Tribune* (Paris), 5 September 1991, p. 1.

114. *Los Angeles Times*, 13 August 1991, p. H6.

115. *New York Times*, 29 September 1991, p. 3.

116. *Wall Street Journal*, 18 February 1993, p. A5.

117. Ibid., p. A1.

118. By Adi Ignatius, in ibid., p. A1.

119. Quoted in ibid., p. A5.

120. Quoted in ibid., p. A5.

121. Quoted in Benson, "Rock in Russia," p. 144.

MARIA PAULA SURVILLA **10**

Rock Music in Belarus

We never had it easy
We resisted with pride the pain
You can sell your house and clothes
But can you sell your mother?
—Volha Ciarescanka
on a poem by Larysa Hienijus[1]

R OCK MUSIC in Belarus[2] shares two general characteristics with rock movements in other contexts: (1) It provides a venue for generational frustrations and (2) both the music and the musical event often provide settings for the expression of political frustrations, a concept common to many Eastern European rock movements.[3] In this chapter I outline Belarusian rock in relation to one recurring idea found in much of this music, that of identity. This approach illustrates the strong relationship that exists between traditional and contemporary expressive forms and the political, social, and cultural issues of today's Belarus. With this overall theme in mind, we consider the creative and performance choices made by several Belarusian groups and musicians.

IDENTITY AND MUSICAL CHOICE

The importance of identity in the creative process is not a contemporary nor even a recent phenomenon. Identity assertion and national consciousness have been consistent sources of motivation in Belarusian indigenous expression and have strong foundation in the perception and use of traditional expressive forms. Throughout a turbulent history, music has served as a medium for the expression and definition of cultural values as well as for the preservation and interpretation of history and experience. All of these—expression, definition, preservation, and interpretation—are key elements in the perception of self, community,

219

and nation. Traditional poetic and musical repertoires not only articulate ideas of liberty, identity, and national consciousness, but some of these repertoires are, in themselves, symbolically and practically viewed as part of that expression. That is, it is not only what these songs say but what their usage and differing function has come to imply for Belarusian audiences. Many of the mainstream contemporary musicians who express a musical philosophy often stress that national and cultural identity inform their creative motivation in some way.

Jocelyne Guilbault has written: "Music offers the audience a gamut of attitudes to take and beliefs to adopt."[4] Certainly the potency and significance of national consciousness varies among performers and audience members. By extension, contemporary musicians may have different reasons for choosing and/or evoking traditional Belarusian repertoires. In making these choices, these musicians consistently express certain perspectives: They identify themselves with their cultural identities, they recognize and are motivated by the iconic significance of traditional musics, and, most evident, they encode a *Belarusianness* into their own compositions and performances. In this sense Belarusian rock can be considered a contemporary extension of that identity-conscious element that is strongly associated with Belarusian cultural and artistic expression.

The music and the groups described in the following sections have been chosen because of their role, overt or implied, in the expression of this identity. They have also been singled out because of their popularity and because of the kinds of commentaries written about them by Belarusian rock journalists. Through this approach we should gain a better understanding of contemporary musical choices and of the ways in which fans and critics perceive the Belarusian rock scene.

THEME, LANGUAGE, AND TRADITIONAL REFERENCE AS COMPONENTS OF BELARUSIAN ROCK

What is meant by Belarusian "rock"? Before examining the details of this music movement, the subtleties of this label should be understood. It is a label that, on the one hand, specifically prescribes the choice of language in performance and, on the other hand, embraces a vast assortment of musical, instrumental, and performance styles. Language, in particular, is a key criterion of Belarusian rock.

In the most recent anthology of Belarusian rock, *Praz rok prizmu*, (Through the Prism of Rock), Miensk-based rock journalists Vitaut Martynienka and Anatol Mialhuj stress the distinction between "Belarusian rock" and "rock in Belarus." It is a distinction based primarily on language choice: Only rock sung in Belarusian is labeled Belarusian rock.[5] That language is an indicator of identity is in itself a truism. In the Belarusian context, the issue of language choice is tied directly to the idea that Belarusian rock *should* express a cultural rootedness. The presence of this cultural qualifier has much to do with the reaction to official attitudes about rock music and about indigenous languages in the then Soviet Union.

Within the Soviet system, government legislation defined the means of production for state-approved music through controls over repertoire, band membership, and the approval of performance spaces. *Official* bands received recording contracts (with Melodiya) and state stipends for music created and performed under strictly enforced censorship. Under this legislation Russian-language music was favored for publication and distribution. Thus, cultural products were systematically homogenized through a Soviet ideology that financially and practically discouraged the development and production of indigenous cultural expression that evoked a non–Soviet nation identity.[6]

The official preference for Russian-language rock was an indicator of language policy on a much larger scale. This is evident in the concerns voiced by many republics since the beginning of Gorbachev's perestroika. These concerns included access to native language in education, the arts, government, business, and daily life. The lack of linguistic freedoms in Belarus was outlined in a 1987 document to Gorbachev. In this "Letter to Gorbachev," writers, artists, and musicians[7] emphasized, among many issues, the considerable "civic courage"[8] required to speak Belarusian in the workplace, the unequal status of Belarusian-language publications, and the lack of Belarusian-language education:

> The status of Belarusian in the BSSR [Byelorussian Socialist Soviet Republic] is quite clearly shown by book-publishing policy ... the proportion of *belles-lettres* published in the republic in Russian rose from 89.9% in 1981 to 95.3% in 1984. Virtually no films are produced in Belarusian. There are about 15 theatres in the republic; only three are Belarusian. Belarusian is almost never used as a working language or in official correspondence in Party organizations, or in local and national government.[9]

At the time that these concerns were being openly expressed, the Belarusian rock movement was experiencing significant growth. Musicians and groups that chose to use Belarusian suffered certain official disadvantages. In interviews and in their writing, musicians and journalists reacted to the limited access to recording studios, instruments, and performance opportunities. Musician Lavon Bartkievic stressed that the Soviet recording monopoly Melodiya and official television programs such as the "Rasnisniaja posta" of the central TV provide questionable venues for Belarusian recording groups. Miensk rock journalist Anatol Mialhuj wrote, "Until now [1989], Belarusian rock has been developing practically without any material basis: lack of rehearsal space, unorganized concert activity, lack of studio equipment and a complete absence of our own recording industry. But times change."[10]

Since the 1991 coup that led to the breakup of the Soviet Union, the ground rules have certainly changed. Belarusian is once again the official language of Belarus,[11] and at least on the legislative level, the issue of language is more comfortably a part of the public sphere. Nevertheless, the legacy of past legislations and of official limitations on linguistic and cultural freedoms is clearly a central consideration in the rock music movement. This is evident in the comments made about rock groups.

As a member of the jury of the National Festival of Popular Music held in Navapolack, Bartkievic singled out two particular groups in a way that illustrates the link between language and musical expression: "I loved two Belarusian rock groups. I emphasize Belarusian. They were Dream (Mroja) from Miensk and Local time (Miascovy cas) from Navapolack. It's good that our Belarusian language lives with them in their soul."[12]

Musicians such as Bartkievic contribute attitude as well as music to the contemporary music scene. In addition, language as part of a musical construct is seen to contribute a distinct "melodiousness, a spirit" to the music.[13] This conception is shared by musicians from other republics. Andrej Makarevich of the Russian group Time Machine stated: "Want it or not, the melody of the language in which we were raised leaves an imprint in our conscience and, from there, on all we do."[14]

The audiences of Belarusian groups are not compartmentalized because of language choice or national distinctions. Rather than limiting the scope of prospective audiences, Belarusian rock groups have entertained audiences in "Russia, Lithuania, Poland, and Bulgaria."[15] Likewise, groups from other areas are judged by their respective sensitivity to their own roots. Thus, language as an indicator of cultural grounding becomes a criterion for the consideration of rock music from other areas. In a political system devoid of linguistic freedoms, the practical choice of language is not always an easy one. Choosing to perform in Belarusian was and remains a powerful statement of intent. At the obvious practical level, Belarusian rock musicians support and encourage the use of the Belarusian language for performer and audience alike. Because of the restrictive climate of the recent past, to sing in Belarusian was and remains a symbol of rebellion, a self-prescribed means of support for what is still being called a "contemporary Belarusian identity renaissance."[16] Another aspect of expressive and creative choice involves the use of traditional musical and textual sources.

SOURCES

Traditional repertoires often play a significant role in the expression of national and community sentiments. In Belarus, the symbolic and literal meanings associated with traditional music are both recognized and utilized by rock musicians to inform their contemporary performance. The centrality of rural/traditional repertoires in the urban context is linked in part to academic trends in the Soviet system.

Much official and academic attention was given to ethnographic materials prior to and during the Soviet period. Since the late nineteenth century, scholarly energies have been geared toward the collection and documentation of musical and poetic repertoires throughout Eastern and Central Europe. Within the ideologies of the Soviet system, collection was partially encouraged as a strategy for political strength: Folk repertoires were systematically cataloged and analyzed on modern instruments as a contemporary musical mirror of a Soviet society united in work as well as in expression. The collection of these songs partly maintained the flow of rural repertoires in the urban setting.

Beyond the academic treatment and cataloging of this music, the people themselves continue to celebrate, mourn, and understand their life events through and with music making. Music offers a means for the expression of shared experience on many levels: for individuals, for the community, and in a broader sense, for the nation as a cultural community. Much before the advent of recent expressive freedoms, music was a vehicle for the expression of cultural identity. This expression is achieved either openly or symbolically as part of the words, in the anthemlike status and effect of certain pieces, or in the overall perceived ties between this repertoire and Belarusian identity.

Together with the importance of traditional music and texts, the absence of industry-defined musical categories has affected the perception of folk music in contemporary Belarusian performance. Western listeners have a more defined sense of popular music genres because of distinctions developed by media sources and various rock/social movements. In Belarus, traditional music is not a marginalized style in comparison to rock. The centrality of the folk repertoire is best expressed in the description of rock as "contemporary young urban folklore."[17] As some of the following sections illustrate, the traditional element appears in many forms—from being performed intact on modern instruments to somehow being incorporated into new compositions. In the early emergence of Belarusian popular music, experimentation and language issues were most evident in the music of the Piesniary (the Songsters).

The consistent beginnings of the Belarusian rock movement took place in the mid-1980s, but the conscious creation of indigenous forms of contemporary musical expression (i.e., rock) was a part of the preceding decade. The Piesniary are a group of professionally and classically trained conservatory musicians who in 1969 began to perform and experiment with Belarusian traditional repertoires and to sing exclusively in Belarusian.[18]

The Piesniary were one of the leading VIAs (vocal-instrumental ensembles) of the 1970s.[19] VIA has several designations. One designation is related to the type of ensemble: "ten musicians in the line-up (rhythm section, two guitars, organ, some horns, and a couple of singers, often with a tambourine)."[20] For some, VIA is a derogatory term, a means of labeling the music of government-sponsored ensembles and separating their perceptions of rock as antiestablishment. VIAs were considered the government's official compromise with contemporary music in the face of a growing youth and rock movement. In such cases, the music has been described as follows: "limp Russian-language covers of melodies from American hits and Russian pop hits with soft electric sound."[21] Although the Piesniary include the instrumentation described earlier, their musical style and repertoire overshadow the generic definition of the VIA.

The early work of the Piesniary was framed by a self-declared intent to produce a specifically Belarusian contemporary music. Drawing from traditional folk repertoires, the group intended that its music would retain the same Belarusian character and longevity as the sources from which it was drawn. The following quote explains the members' perception of the communicative power and the longevity of traditional song: "Folk songs never die to a nation. We don't want to write hits that will last several weeks, we want to take part in something that will last forever in the minds of the people."[22]

What made the Piesniary equally identifiable with a Belarusian contemporary music was its early commitment to sing in the Belarusian language. The Piesniary were one of the first groups to become popular throughout the former Soviet Union despite its language and repertoire choices.[23] Moreover, this group had widespread impact because it was in the unusual position of enjoying the status of an official band, which meant that its music was widely disseminated through professionally produced recordings. What the Piesniary began on a mass-media scale was the association of *contemporary* music performance with cultural assertion. Music was a means through which language and cultural style could emerge into the public sphere at a time when other venues for this kind of expression were limited.

The issue of language, which clearly defined the image of this band in the 1970s and early 1980s, did not retain its significance for all members of the group. Singer Lavon Bartkievic left the group in the early 1980s. At the time, in reaction to its popularity across the Soviet Union, the group had begun to sing in Russian. For Bartkievic, this contradicted the intent of its original language choice, so he pursued a solo career. He stated, "But what happens in reality? Once they [the Piesniary] have become professionals and 'national artists' of Belarus, they abandon Belarusian songs. ... As far as I am concerned, I am a Belarusian and I will sing Belarusian songs, traditional and modern."[24]

This statement illustrates the differing and changing attitudes toward such creative options as language choice. More important, it serves to underline the importance of a philosophy of expression for certain performers—a philosophy that clearly describes the importance of culturally "marking" their musical expression through language.

The early approach of the Piesniary, dubbed by some as the "Belarusian Beatles," was to recontextualize traditional folk repertoire with contemporary sounds. Eventually, as the group's style matured, it settled upon a highly syncretic style, a rock fusion that combined jazz, traditional, classical, rock, and pop sounds.[25] For example, wooden flutes, violin, dulcimer, and hurdy-gurdy share a soundscape with electric bass, guitars, keyboards, and drum sets. Its recording of the traditional song "Pierapiolacka" (The Little Quail) is a typical example of its musical approach:

The little quail's head aches.
The little quail's hands ache.

You are my, You are my little quail.
You are my, You are my little one.

The little quail wakes early.
The little quail wakes early.

The quail's husband is old.
The quail's children are young.

The children cry, they ask to eat,
The children cry, they ask to eat,

The little quail has no bread to give.
The little quail has no bread to give.

This folk song is an allegorical lament that describes the life condition of a Byelorussian woman during the period of serfdom. (In Belarusian the diminutive form is used as both an expression of affection and to describe the young. In this song, *pierapiolka* occurs as *pierapiolacka;* the adjective for "old," *stary,* becomes *starenki;* the word for children, *dzietki,* becomes *dzietacki;* and so on.) The styles included in this performance are derived from sources that, in Western perception, would be considered polarized, that is, incorporating flute cadenzas with classical violin variations as well as rock ballad style with jazz fusions.

The Piesniary explore the piece through a complex arrangement. The arrangement is divided into sections by the clear pauses between each treatment of the melody. For this reason, it is possible to discern the direction of experimentation and dramatic development in this arrangement. The first two statements of the melody in the Piesniary's version of "Pierapiolacka" do not include text. The group emphasizes the traditional roots of the melody through the use of traditional instruments: flute, dulcimer, and violin. As an underlying drone supports the echoing treatment of the melodies, the listener is prepared for the stylistic and textural layering to come. Separated from the formal needs of the text, these instrumental sections contain the rhythmic manipulation of the traditional melodic material. These manipulations show that the Piesniary go beyond the simple addition of modern instruments by exploring the musical substance of the group's chosen repertoire.

As the piece progresses, the instrumentation and countermelodies become increasingly elaborate. In the most elaborate section, melodic improvisation is key. Near the end of the piece, an ostinato played by the electric bass provides the framework for a series of complex improvisations including electronic keyboard and blues-style organ. It is at this point that the Piesniary deconstruct the text. Until now, the sections with lyrics have been sung to follow the original text despite the underlying instrumental experimentation. The repetition of the textual refrain by the background voices is punctuated by a solo voice wailing an improvisational line on *"Tyz maja, tyz maja pierapiolacka"* (You are my, you are my little quail). The improvisational fury of this section peaks as the number of interacting voices increases. Suddenly, the song cuts off to silence, releasing the accumulated sonic tension. It is at this point that the final statement of the melody is played on a solo flute, recalling the traditional style and sound of the very first statement of the melody. The Piesniary consciously manipulate the traditional material from the first hearing of the melody and thus immediately imply the new interpretation of a traditional folk form on melodic, rhythmic, and stylistic levels.

The popularity and availability of the Piesniary set the stage for later perceptions of the Belarusian rock scene. Rock journalists and commentators have been and continue to be significant actors in shaping the image of this rock movement.

ACCESS AND ATTITUDES: WRITING ON ROCK

In a music industry devoid of mass market commercialism, journalists directly affect the popularity and audience perception of rock musicians. The most available sources of information for fans are youth publications: *Red Change* (Cyrvonaja Zmiena), *Water Source* (Krynica), and *Youth* (Maladosc). In addition to having sections devoted to music, these publications offer a cultural melange of poetry, literature, visual arts, and criticism. Mainstream treatments of rock music contain little distinction between established arts and rock as expressive media. Rock is considered by many as a contemporary art form with its own mode of intellectual expression.

Contemporary rock critics prescribe and describe the nature of a performer and that performer's music in authentic terms. Here, authenticity is based on a recognition of folk roots through the use of the national language, folk metaphors and iconography, and direct musical quotations from the poetic and musical folk repertoire. Language and folk elements inform the variety of themes in the music, such as the love song, the overt political rebellion song, social commentaries, and reflective songs about the "belonging" of the listener. From this perspective, music is not only seen as a means for description but as a means to inform the listener and the community as well. In a milieu where the response to rock music is intelligent listening, musicians and critics consider a good audience to be open to the communicative intent of the music. Irina Pond described rock music in the Soviet Union as "an outlet for personal beliefs and political concerns, not for escapism and thoughtless entertaining."[26]

Although Belarusian rockers are gaining public popularity and the interest of non-Belarusian critics, official media sources have not reflected their popularity. Belarusian journalists lament the obvious lack of attention given to indigenous, Belarusian-language groups by the general media. In his article "Their Day Will Come," Miensk journalist Martynienka writes about the underlying tendency to ignore Belarusian rock in favor of Russian-language groups from Belarus.[27] These groups, represented by the Golden Middle (Solobaya seredina) and Vaykhanski's Band, are dubbed "the intellectuals of Belarusian rock" and as such incorrectly receive representative status for the Belarusian rock movement.[28] Moreover, Belarusian television and radio reflected the monopoly of programming from Moscow and Leningrad. Despite local Belarusian radio and video productions in local studios, many programmers continue to follow past practices and choose from central broadcasts. Martynienka further comments that beyond criticism, critics fail to ask obvious questions when dealing with the rock movement; that is, they are not concerned with its support structure and its linguistic impact on a youth population that had been limited to Russian-language schools.[29] Thus, the circumstances for an identity-assertive rock movement in Belarus have been less than nurturing.

Official treatments of rock-related activities continue to draw limitations rather than encourage development. In the case of rock journalists Martynienka and Mialhuj, such official attitudes directly affected their attempt to publish a book about rock music in the Soviet republics and Belarus in particular. Motivated by the promise of perestroika, these authors presented their manuscript to the publishing houses in Miensk only to be turned away. The reasons given varied from full publishing agendas to disinterest in the subject. Like their interpretation of rock music in Belarus, Martynienka and Mialhuj's book describes the role of Belarusian contemporary music as a reflection and an inducer of Belarusian identity and nationalism. The authors suggest that this element, along with the Belarusian-language text, affected the reception of their manuscript.[30] One of the results of such difficulties is that the rock movement has had to employ imaginative methods of disseminating the music, of publicizing groups, and of organizing both live and broadcast concerts for the Belarusian audience: through underground distribution, the duplication of recordings produced on cassettes, and the organization of Belarusian rock concerts in unofficial spaces (including neighboring Poland).

Rock music as a mainstream form of expression nurtures a multifaceted audience. Although some fans place less importance on the Belarusian element in the rock music they listen to, supporters of a Belarusian rock movement seem to consider such responses as uninformed. In his article "Musical Prospect" (Muzycny praspekt), Felix Aksencau writes: "In today's conditions, non-commercial art cannot survive for a long time."[31] For Aksencau, contemporary bands that avoid mimicking musical trends are presently the exception. The increased search for mass popularity and a Soviet and post-Soviet brand of commercial success has encouraged a situation in which "rock culture becomes more and more commercial and loses its integrity, its artistic value."[32] According to this critic, the noncommercial bands of the past, typically underground groups, are increasingly harder to find.

The brand of integrity demanded of rock music has much to do with the intent of the music and the performer. Uladzislau Achramienka stresses the importance of judging Belarusian rock on what could be called the sincerity of performance: "At the present time, rock music is part of a materialistic period. For me, rock begins when a person appears on stage, someone who has something to tell (it doesn't matter with what—even a balalaika). That is, not to say what is [allowed], but to say that which he arrived at by himself."[33]

The concerns voiced by rock critics relate to their commercial view of rock in the Western rock scene. Much of the criticism about rock music and youth draws upon a negative interpretation of American standards of musical meaning and fan enthusiasm. Some writers see the negative influence as the "ideological corruption" of Western commercialism, specifically the recording industry and its role in supporting the empty adoration of image-seeking youth.[34] Such attitudes certainly reflect the effects of official attitudes toward emerging rock cultures and seem to be directed toward the behavior of fans rather than toward the Western rock music that unofficially trickles into Eastern Europe through underground means.

And yet, fans often write to the music commentators to request personal information about their rock idols. Many trends in fan devotion reflect those found in Western rock circles: fashion fads, teen idols, and group loyalties. Rock paraphernalia—those objects that identify the fans and attach them to a particular group and motivation—are not officially produced for audience consumption. Young listeners manufacture their own pins and labels as signifiers of their tastes and loyalties. In general, this face of rock enthusiasm is not viewed negatively as long as the *communicative intent* of the music remains intact. Image seekers and "Western emulators"[35] are missing the point.

When a fan of the group Magistrate (Mahistrat) commented that she liked the way Ihar Sakalouski played with the mike and the way Ihar Nikanovic continued to play despite the fact that his guitar strap broke, Nikanovic responded: "After one month of hard preparation for the program, the preparation of equipment, the choice of texts and rehearsals, here is our thanks: They liked the fact that my guitar almost fell out of my hands. There is not a single word about what we sang, why and how."[36]

Audience members and prospective fans come into contact with their favorite groups at concerts, through recordings, and through rock-club encounters. Rock clubs, such as Rhythm (Rytm) and Niamiha (established in Miensk in 1986),[37] provide a place to access the music and to interact with those who make it: "Such clubs allow us to organize encounters between live musicians, and live fans of their work."[38] Groups such as Bonda, Twins (Blizniaty), Dream (Mroja), and Magistrate (Mahistrat) have actively participated in discussion sessions with their fans.

Journalist Anatol Mialhuj suggests that these clubs play an important part in the support of homegrown talent, through access to equipment and the distribution of Belarusian material. This support is considered particularly important because of the abundance of foreign recordings available compared to domestic ones: "Here we don't speak exclusively of youth records. In the record stores of Belarus one can find records in every language, even Turkish and Finnish, but you will find little in Belarusian."[39] Most recently, cooperation between the youth center Krynica and the music center Aryjentur has resulted in the increased distribution of music by Belarusian rock groups.[40]

It is interesting that within this system of evaluation and distribution some groups emerged on the rock scene in ways reminiscent of Hollywood success stories. Martynienka recounts the "discovery" of the group Bonda in 1984:

> On our way to the ... studio we met two youngsters we did not know. They said they were musicians and when they heard that we were going to the TV studio they asked whether they could come and see. Once in the pavilion, they said: "We have a tape with us, with two songs. Do you want to hear it?"
>
> "It's lucky you didn't ask right away for a recording contract," said the director. "If we have time we will have a look, in the meantime just wait." ...
>
> We all loved the video of the Twins (Blizniaty) produced for the TV show Hospitable Court (Hascinny dvor) and nearly forgot our promise, when the director asked: "OK, where are those boys?"
>
> The next moments exceeded all our expectations: the rich sound of a strong guitar wave carrying in a secure and proud fashion the wonderful melodicity of our Belarusian language. ... I felt like hugging these boys who were humbly waiting for the reaction of the specialists.
>
> "Wait there is another song. All our program is in Belarusian, but there is nowhere for us to record it." We heard the first words of what has become the super-hit "Father is right" (Tata maje racyju). The group was Bonda and the boys' names were Ihar Varaskievic and Siarzuk Kraucanka.[41]

Again journalist Martynienka stresses the importance of language choice for rock bands belonging to the Belarusian rock movement—groups such as Blizniaty, Bonda, and Mroja (Dream), Rej, Rokas, Miascovy cas, and Juras Bratcyk.[42] Journalist Adam Lobus names three bands, Ulysses (Ulis), Dream (Mroja), and Bonda, as the "circle leaders" in the movement that supports the Belarusian language as the "state language of our rockers."[43] He stresses that of the twelve best groups out of the forty-three that performed at the 1990 festival Three Colors=The Belarusian Variant, seven sang in Belarusian. The language used second most often was English.

Although some expressive freedoms have improved in recent years, musicians and rock critics see present opportunities for the development of Belarusian rock as less than favorable. Mialhuj writes that the tendency in the past to preach "a restrained patriotism that is based on a cosmopolitan and not on a national framework, has produced a youth audience that, in some cases knows little about their homeland, their culture, and their history."[44] There is also concern that Belarusian audiences will become desensitized about their roots because of easier access to Western rock music. Nevertheless, Western rock is also important to the rock scene in Belarus. The same magazines that devote space to homegrown talent are filled with information on concert tours, contemporary Western artists, and important veteran performers. Rock music from other republics is treated with similar attention. What seems to concern those in the rock music movement of today's Belarus is that among all of that production the energies of Belarusian groups and a Belarusian style not only be heard but also recognized as such, as Belarusian.

STYLE IN TEXT AND MUSIC

The result of Belarusian and Western influence is heard in the conscious blending or layering of musical styles: the selection and manipulation of a sound through stylistic, textual, and melodic quotation. Rather than dominating the defining trends in this rock, these choices impart significant impact by informing and punctuating the musical performance.

In Belarus the term *rock* functions as a terminological umbrella for a varied grouping of contemporary music styles that include hard rock, heavy metal, punk, and "bard rock."[45] Beneath this rock umbrella, Belarusian performers coexist despite the variety of performance styles.

The multiplicity of accepted rock styles becomes evident in the surveys of popularity for contemporary musicians. Voters in the 1988 Miensk survey of most popular foreign artists revealed the top three choices: Michael Jackson, Bohdan "Dancyk" Andrusisyn, and Peter Gabriel.[46] While the first and third choices are familiar to those who listen to mainstream Western popular music, the folk-bardic style of New York–based performer Dancyk lies outside Western definitions of rock. Dancyk's performances include an acoustic sound and a repertoire based upon traditional Belarusian folk songs.[47]

The first Belarusian rock festival, Three Colors=The Belarusian Variant (Try kolery), held in Lida in 1989, included a section for "bard stars." In terms of Western counterparts, these musicians parallel the folk singers of 1960s America with their solo performances and acoustic guitar accompaniments. Rather than reacting to an American trend, such singers are contemporary examples of the traditionally strong bardic tradition found in Eastern European countries. The Russian Vladimir Vysotsky is the most well known in the West; he has counterparts in many republics, including Belarus.

Siarzuk Sokalau Vojus, from Novapolacak, is a Belarusian bard who enjoys continuing popularity. Dancyk (Andrusisyn) has called him the Belarusian Bob Dylan: "He doesn't have a good voice, and doesn't play guitar very well—but he is monumental."[48] He is well known for his poignant poetry, which he sings to acoustic guitar accompaniment. Vojus's texts illustrate the tone of nation-conscious expression. They are blatant expressions about historical exploitation and cultural destruction. For example:

> *This was a far and fearful time*
> *When from the shoulders heads were flying*
> *When they were destroying for the hundredth time in a row*
> *Our memory, our language*
>
> *Who were the masters of events*
> *Witnesses, denunciations, forms, files*
> *Pretending to be friends,*
> *Informer to the chief of police*
> *Somebody's destiny, because of them is nothing,*
> *Their own is everything.*[49]

Contemporary bards, thought of as musical poets, have an extensive legacy of Belarusian poetic tradition behind them. As sources for rock music texts, traditional and newly composed poetry certainly color textual style and musical result. One aspect, the consistency of Belarus as theme, has laid a strong foundation for this element in today's rock scene. Performers like Volha Ciarescanka provide contemporary settings for such Belarusian literary veterans as Larysa Hienijus, Ales Harun, and Janka Kupala. Those who compose their own words display the extent to which sentiments of identity are part of contemporary expression. The relationship between Ciarescanka's songs and national consciousness is recognized by other rock commentators. Ales Jausiejenka describes this singer as the true Belarusian "Madonna," more in the sense of "Our Lady of Belarusian Song" than comparing her to the American version.[50] Martynienka writes that the musical statements of many performers directly express a collective theme for these rock events. He cites Ciarescanka:

> *In order not to succumb to the pain of bad treatment*
> *In order not to forget his land*

In order for him to return as a man
To his own fatherland.[51]

With the importance given to language choice in Belarusian rock, it seems logical that lyrics play a large part in the evaluation of a band's music. Journalist Adam Lobus goes as far as to contrast "poets" such as Lavon Volski from Mroja (Dream) with "anti-poets" who "sing anything."[52] He labels the group Choj as "rock jesters" whose lyrics are full of punning and playing with vocables.

Ja bubu ciabie u hubu
Ti bubu mianie u hubu
Ja boli nia mahu
Ja chacu bubu u hubu

I will kiss you on the lips
You will kiss me on the lips
I just can't stand it anymore
I will kiss you on the lips.

The stylistic contrast with the lyric style of the group Mroja are clear in "He Told Me Too Much":

He told me there is too much disdain in a world
which is not worth anything
In which words disappear in the air
And where aspirations result in tiredness.[53]

Within these lyrics identity sentiments are implied through language choice, references to events, or in direct musical statement. The group Juras Bratcyk of the rock club Miensk sings:

We make our own steps in rock:
Obsessive and Burning
*Like **Lavonicha** here,*
*Or like the rhythm of **Polka Janka***
That all the people can dance.[54]

Here we have an example of the incorporation of traditional music within contemporary performance. However, we do not hear the *melodies* in this performance. This group relies on what the members recognize as the cultural associations evoked by this traditional repertoire. (Lavonicha, the national dance of Belarus, and Polka Janka, another dance in the traditional repertoire, are basic staples of Belarusian folk performance. These folk songs have dramatic effect because they are powerful musical icons of Belarusian identity.) Another example from this heavy metal band from Mahilou projects a much more aggressive tone:

Marvelous dream—
Another reality.
While I quietly did my Sisyphus-like work
in silence I had
an easy conscience.
Until when in my soul everything moved,
and a music sounded with force
To reveal how to live with you, Truth.

Refrain:
Heavy metal, heavy metal
Heavy Belarusian rock,
I will leave my sons,
This purpose in life.

Others will come after us,
But who will awake their consciences?
Will they be silent, indifferent,
Repeating beautiful chained words,
Will they sleep enough dreaming beautiful dreams?
No, they will find either a tribute, or a coffin![55]

The verse underlined reveals a clear musical agenda: the expression of a Belarusian heavy metal, the conception of this rock as a significant goal in life, and the legacy of rock to further generations.

Many groups specifically describe their role and the function of their music as having a direct influence on the contemporary consciousness of Belarusian identity. The intended concept for the rock group Ulysses (Ulis), which formed in 1989, directly reflects the relationship between this group's music and its self-expressed musical purpose. Inspired by a recent translation of the Greek classic into Belarusian, Siarzuk Kraucanka transposed Ulysses' journey into a conceptual vision/motto for the group. He explains that his group would provide a means to "travel inside ourselves" and would give Belarus back to Belarusians.[56] The concept was a popular one with journalists who saw the intent of the group carried through the "social fearlessness"[57] of its music.

It is obvious by the amount of attention given the rock music movement in Belarus that musicians, audience, and reviewers advocate a determined attitude for the success of a homegrown rock. The movement consistently defines the artistic and the national aspects of this music, whether it be heavy metal, punk rock, or bard-style performance. Although the climate of a national rock movement has been affected by trends in the official Soviet media as well as through production restrictions, performers and audience manage to interact, and performers gain support at the local level, through national rock festivals.

Despite the demand, official circumstances today do not allow for the organization of Belarusian rock festivals in the republic. In summer 1990, Belarusian rock groups and their followers gathered in Bielastoccyna (eastern Poland) for Basovisca '90, a Belarusian rock festival hosted by BAC, the leading Belarusian student organization of the area. By taking the event outside of Belarusian political boundaries, musicians and audience could indulge in Belarusian rock. The event was a huge success and has since become an annual event.[58] The irony of the situation is evident; nevertheless, the movement and its supporters continue to exhibit their determination.

There exists a growing demand for performances of Belarusian rock and for the development of a Belarusian rock industry. The meeting of these demands is considered paramount if Belarus is to produce what is described as its own expressive, free, and healthy mass culture.

MROJA: A CLOSER LOOK

Providing a written description of Belarusian rock is difficult. What does this music sound like? Beyond lyrics and language choice, what are its distinguishing stylistic elements?

Because I am assuming that readers are familiar with Western rock trends, I am compelled to use elements from these trends to describe Belarusian rock music styles. In using such comparisons I do not intend to imply that a familiarity with Western styles generates Belarusian counterparts. Although influences from Western groups surely have had an impact on musical trends, it would be a mistake to assume that Belarusian rock music is simply imitative. I have chosen to focus on the rock group Mroja (Dream) from Miensk. This group does not represent any general style of Belarusian rock music. My choice stems from its importance in the rock movement, its popularity, and the attention given its work by Belarusian rock critics.

Mroja was founded in 1981 by a group of art students from a Miensk art college (L. Volsky, vocals and keyboard; Y. U. Levko, vocals and electric bass; D. Demidovic, drums; V. Davidovic, guitar (until 1989); and V. Konev-Petushkovic, guitarist (since 1989). By 1984 Mroja had recorded an album-length cassette called *The Old Temple.* In 1984 three members were engaged in military service but the group reunited in 1986. Three albums have been produced since that time: *Sight* (1989), *Studio BM*

(1988), and most recently *28th Star.*[59] The songs treated here are from the latest release.

Mroja's music is anything but one-dimensional. Produced with a familiar instrument makeup (vocals, electric guitar, electric bass, keyboards, and percussion), the basic sound of the group reveals a facility in playing both rock and blues idioms. The lead singer, Lavon Volsky, alternates his style from a clear balladlike vocal quality to the more aggressive vocal style associated with punk rock. Vocal contrast is central to this group's approach, as is exemplified in the ballad song "Earth," in which the vocal qualities alternate between smooth and aggressive textures. In other selections, vocal backups tend toward the use of falsetto, which creates stark register contrasts with the relatively lower principal voice.

Contrast is a key word when describing Mroja's stylistic palette. That is, its style is not solely hard rock. The song "I Am a Rock Musician" begins with a misleadingly thick, chordal electric guitar solo, which through a hard rock instrumental interlude leads to a stark texture between voice and drums for the opening verses. The chorus is as follows.

> *I am a rock musician, in an established tradition*
> *These are not just words this is my position.*

The texture thickens until electric guitar, keyboards, drums, and bass all participate in the soundscape. Stylistically, Mroja's music also illustrates the influence of musical elements from traditional Belarusian musical styles.

In Mroja, musical elements from traditional Belarusian music appear as both overt references and as discreet musical quotations. They can be heard in the modal melodies; the sometimes bare, dissonant approach to harmony; and even in the final notes of a song, that is, the notes ending on the upper instead of the lower tonic, which is typical in Belarusian folk melody construction.

When Mroja uses Belarusian folk song in a directly referential way, the group reveals its capacity for musical metaphor. The song "Australian Polka" (Australijskaja Polka) is a case in point. Instead of simply allowing the lyrics to state an idea, the group successfully interrupts the strophic continuity of the song to insert a quotation from a Belarusian folk song.

As the title suggests, this song is a polka, a genre associated with the traditional repertoires of Eastern and Central European music. Mroja's selection of this genre implies several things: It continues the formal and stylistic link between contemporary music and traditional genres. More important in this case, the rhythmic and formal qualities of the polka have a poignantly ironic impact on the listener.

The polka is a celebratory genre: It invites listeners to dance. And in the Belarusian tradition, it most commonly includes lighthearted texts of romance and courtship. The text of Mroja's polka is loaded with irony; it is not about romance but about choices. Sung in the first person, it tells of a young man's struggle to decide between staying in Belarus and relocating to Australia. The need for the choice is made explicit only in the last verse of the song. However, because of the place of relocation (Australia), the informed listener immediately knows the reason for this choice.

The formal construction of the song provides a layer of meaning. Here it is informed by the traditional celebratory function of the polka genre and the irony of its use in the present context. Beyond irony, the potency of this formal choice also lies in implication: the nonreaction of much of the population to Belarus's radioactive environment, that is, the business-as-usual attitude. The celebration associated with the polka genre thus becomes a commentary on the lack of action of a powerless population. Briefly, after the 1986 Chernobyl nuclear fallout,[60] one of the solutions offered by many nations was the partial relocation of the population. Some of the offers were funded by the Belarusian diaspora, including that community in Australia. This rock polka evaluates the reasons for choosing Australia over Belarus by comparing the quality of life in each context. Mroja's polka also contains surprising musical episodes that inform the text on a dramatic level.

The text of the song includes six verses, which appear in pairs. The verses are separated by the refrain and the repetition of the introduction. Between each pair of verses, Mroja has used a different technique for incorporating style. The first of these is melodic quotation. The melody chosen for this section comes from the traditional polka repertoire. As we have already seen, Lavonicha is a significant choice because it holds iconic meaning for Belarusians. As the national dance of Belarus, it has come to produce an anthemlike response from performers and audiences alike. In the Mroja example, the symbolic significance of the song enhances the message of the text. The six-measure quotation appears after the singer says, "There they await us our fellow *ziemlaki*" (fellow Belarusians-compatriots). Thus, the Lavonicha quote functions as a musical signpost for a shared identity.

Verse 1
My friends stopped me in the club and said
What are you doing sitting here in these conditions
Better to come with us to Australia
There they await us our fellow ziemlaki

Between verses three and four, the listener hears another type of quotation. In this section the singer is comparing the downfall of Belarus to the "wonderful" things offered by Australia. The lighthearted verse ends with the exclamation that Australia gave us the group AC/DC. Suddenly Mroja moves away from the musical texture established up to this point and breaks into a sixteen-measure *stylistic* quote of AC/DC. This is achieved without interruption of the overall metrical and rhythmic feel of the song. Verses 5 and 6 are also divided by a similar device, although I am unfamiliar with the source of the quote. It appears at a time in the text when the speaker begins to make a decisive decision. Musically, the quote evokes a heroic character (according to Western musical gestures).

Verses 5 and 6

I spent a whole week in France changing my mind
My hands and my legs trembling
You already transferred yourself to a foreign land
But with conviction I told myself—no!

I am a patriot I told them at the station
I told them as well that I will soon die
I prefer our own radiation
It is worth more than foreign kangaroos.

Perhaps the most dramatic use of quotation comes at the end of the text for the Australijskaja Polka. It is at the end of the song that the speaker voices his desire to die "with our own radiation / It is worth more than foreign kangaroos." The somber nature of this decision is emphasized by a complete change in both style, gesture, and idiom. With this last statement, Mroja begins a section in an eight-bar blues form containing the last quote of the song taken from the Beatles song "Hey Jude." Rather than quoting from the beginning of a musical segment, Mroja chooses to quote from the last four bars of the melody. The dramatic effect of this final choice certainly lies in the complete change of musical character. However, the members of Mroja are also revealing their association between a tragic context, heroic choices, and the meaning they interpret in this appropriated Beatles song. This last quote, together with the others heard in this piece, stresses the importance of quotation as a technique of contemporary composition and performance. Furthermore, the combination of these gestures illustrates the conscious workings of a Belarusian rock style that is aware of its own roots, of Western trends, and of musical gesture in the construction of meaning.

CONCLUSION

In the early emergence of Belarusian popular music, the use of experimentation, the Belarusian language, and an identifiable Belarusian repertoire was interpreted as statements of nonconformity. These characteristics were aspects of a musical style that reflected and affected a contemporary renaissance that embodies what is described as a "spiritual" notion of identity and a practical notion of national consciousness. Language, themes, traditional references, and the successful amalgamation and molding of diverse styles have produced a Belarusian rock that is, in its very construction and aesthetic sensibilities and intent, Belarusian. Mroja's latest album cover, in soft dark blue, shows likenesses of the four members emerging from a rocky planetarylike surface. The design seems to embody the ambitions and the direction of Belarusian rock: From solid traditional foundations through eclectic lyrics and musical treatments, it is solidly emerging as a key component of contemporary Belarusian culture.

NOTES

1. Quoted in Vitaut Martynienka and Anatol Mialhuj, *Praz rok-prizmu* (Through the Prism of Rock) (New York: Belarusian Institute of Arts and Sciences, 1989), p. 192. Larysa Hienijus (b. 1910) is a significant Belarusian poet who endured forced labor in Czechoslovakia and exile to Siberia during WWII. For more about this poet, see Vera Rich, *Like Water, Like Fire: An Anthology of Byelorussian Poetry from 1828 to the Present Day* (London: George Allen & Unwin, 1971), pp. 295, 336.

2. The official name change of the Byelorussian Socialist Soviet Republic was recognized at the United Nations in October 1991. The new designation is the indigenous term for this nation, "Belarus." The adjective form is Belarusian, pronounced *b-ye-la-roo-see-an*. Other place names are also undergoing a transition back to the indigenous form and/or spellings. For example, Minsk is now Miensk or Mensk. For English-language commentaries on current events, media coverage, political, history, and economics, see Joe Price, ed., *Belarusian Review* (Belarusian-American Association, Torrance, Calif.).

3. Timothy W. Ryback, *Rock Around the Bloc: A History of Rock in Eastern Europe and the Soviet Union* (New York: Oxford University Press, 1990), pp. 215–216.

4. Jocelyne Guilbault, "Cultural, Social, and Economic Developments Through Music: Zouk in the French Antilles," *Canadian Journal of Latin American and Caribbean Studies,* forthcoming.

5. Vitaut Martynienka, "Their Day Will Come," *Maladosc* (Miensk), September 1990, p. 140.

6. Government policy and political ideologies about the West have also affected the importation of Western popular music. These policies, as well as those concerning language and culture, generated different levels of reaction. One reaction was the development of a sophisticated black market system through which Western popular music and the music of nonofficial bands could be produced and distributed.

7. *Letters to Gorbachev: New Documents from Soviet Belarus* (London: Association of Byelorussians in Great-Britain, 1987).

8. Ibid., p. 21.

9. Ibid., pp. 19–20.

10. Martynienka and Mialhuj, *Praz rok-prizmu*, p. 196.

11. *Literatura i Mastactva*, 16 February 1990.

12. Martynienka and Mialhuj, *Praz rok-prizmu*, p. 180.

13. Ibid., p. 184.

14. Ibid., p. 80.

15. Ibid., p. 23.

16. Ibid., p. 18.

17. Ibid.

18. Artemy A. Troitsky, *Back in the USSR: The True Story of Rock in Russia* (Boston: Faber and Faber, 1987), p. 37.

19. U.S. audiences had a firsthand encounter with this group from Belarus in 1976. The Piesniary, which had enjoyed phenomenal success in the Soviet Union, were the first Belarusian band to tour the United States and to perform that decade's version of "Soviet pop music" (ibid.)

20. Troitsky, *Back in the USSR*, p. 28.

21. Ibid., p. 37.

22. Quoted in Joe Sazyc, "Record Review," *Byelorussian Youth* 5, no. 43–44 (1974), p. 24.

23. The association of the Piesniary with the official vocal-instrumental ensembles of the Soviet administration has prompted some critics to dismiss the group's music despite its obvious popularity. See comments made by Russian rock journalist Artemy Troitsky, *Back in the USSR*, p. 34.

24. Martynienka and Mialhuj, *Praz rok-prizmu*, p. 182.

25. See *Piesniary*, produced by Uladzimir Muljavin, Melodiya 33C 60-11287-88, 1988.

26. Irina Pond, "Soviet Rock Lyrics: Their Contents and Poetics," *Popular Music and Society* 11 (April 1987), p. 79.

27. Martynienka, "Their Day Will Come," p. 140.

28. Ibid., p. 140.

29. Ibid.

30. Their book (*Through the Prism of Rock*) was eventually published in New York in 1989.

31. Felix Aksencau, "Muzycny praspekt," *Krynica*, March 1990, p. 20.

32. Ibid., p. 18.

33. Uladzislau Achramienka, *Krynica*, February 1989, p. 29.

34. Ibid., p. 9.

35. Martynienka and Mialhuj, *Praz rok-prizmu*, p. 9.

36. Ibid., p. 11.

37. Niamiha is the river that ran through the city of Miensk. It is now diverted through underground channels.

38. Martynienka and Mialhuj, *Praz rok-prizmu*, p. 11.

39. Ibid., p. 19.

40. Ibid., p. 18.

41. Martynienka, "Their Day Will Come," pp. 138–139.

42. "Juras Bratcyk" refers to a literary character created by U. Karatkievic in his *Christ Has Landed in Harodnia* (Chrystos pryziamliusia u Harodni), in which Juras is the hero.

43. Adam Lobus, "From Mroja to Choj," *Krynica*, no. 7 (July 1990), p. 18.

44. Martynienka and Mialhuj, *Praz rok-prizmu*, p. 19.

45. Ibid., p. 81.

46. *Cyrvonaja zmiena* (Miensk), 31 December 1988, p. 4.

47. *New York Post*, 2 January 1990, p. 17.

48. *New York Post*, 2 January 1990, p. 17.

49. Excerpt from "Miakki znak," which refers to the alteration of Belarusian orthography and grammar in 1933, when by Soviet decree certain typically Belarusian features of pronunciation were outlawed for written use. The intent was to bring the sonic characteristics of Belarusian closer to Russian, thus facilitating linguistic assimilation. The *miakki znak*, one of the eliminated elements, symbolizes all that was taken from Belarus. For full citation see *Krynica* (Miensk), February 1989, pp. 42–43.

50. Quoted in Martynienka and Mialhuj, *Praz rok-prizmu*, p. 190.

51. Ibid., p. 190.

52. Ibid.

53. Ibid.

54. Ibid., p. 22, my emphasis.

55. Excerpt from *The Silent Generation* (words by V. Michalovic, music by U. Kramuscanka). Ibid., p. 209, my emphasis. Sisyphus is the mythical king of Corinth who was condemned to eternally push a rock up a steep incline only to have it roll back each time he reached the summit.

56. Ibid., p. 193.

57. Ibid.

58. *Niva*, Bielastok No. 49 (1990), pp. 1, 4.

59. Record notes from *28th Star*, Melodiya C60 30401 001, 1990.

60. The total effects of the fallout are not yet known. Belarus received 70 percent of the total fallout, which equals seventy Hiroshima bombs. The medical prospects for the population are alarming, especially for the younger generations, who are more immediately susceptible to radiation-related illness. In 1991 the entire country was in some way affected by the disaster, be it by death, deformed births, loss of land, or an overall lack of medical relief.

ROMANA BAHRY **11**

Rock Culture and Rock Music in Ukraine

The phenomenon of rock culture can be compared to tooth-paste.
Once you squeeze it out of the tube, you can't push it back inside.

—**Vika,** in Toronto interview with author,
May 1990

ROCK MUSIC in Ukraine has experienced four waves since its first appearance in the 1960s.[1] The first wave of rock music, called "big beat," began in 1963 and 1964. The youth in Ukraine listened to the Beatles, the Rolling Stones, Procul Harum, and the Searchers on reel-to-reel tapes that they recorded from Voice of America or records from tourists. Of the approximately forty amateur groups in Ukraine, one of the most popular was Berezen (March), which performed in the cafe Halushky on Khreshchatyk Street. Because Berezen had a country-western folk-rock tendency and because it sang in the Ukrainian language with some of its songs based on words of Ukrainian poets, the band was accused of "bourgeois nationalism."[2] Other groups, such as Once, sang in the English language. In fact, according to rock musician and rock historian Kyrylo Stetsenko, the majority of the Ukrainian rock groups not only sang in English but copied English and American musicians, thereby mastering the new musical language and performance style.[3]

The first rock concert in Kiev, as described in *Fonohraf Digest,*[4] took place in spring 1967 in the center of the city, on Leontoych Street, in the cafe Mriia (Daydream). It was organized by Yuri Malchyk and Valentyna Lebedinets of the Komsomol (Young Communist League) and featured twelve groups. The Mriia had room for only 150 people, so 200 people sat on the roof of a neighboring building. Youths who couldn't get in

243

jammed the street and stopped the traffic on one of the main Kiev streetcar routes for four hours.[5] All the songs at this Kiev concert were in English except for five, which were in the Ukrainian language.[6] Among the participating rock groups was Once, which won first place. Once performed the songs of Buddy Holly, Jerry Lee Lewis, Chuck Berry, the Everly Brothers, Dave Clark Five, Ray Charles, and James Brown as well as original instrumentals with such titles as "When the Mosquito's Glands are Hurting" and "Thirteen Carrots for the Rabbit."[7] Another group that performed at this first rock concert in Kiev was Druhe dykhannia (Second Breathing), which sang only Beatles songs.[8]

The next concert of rock music took place in autumn 1967 on the same street where the first concert was held, next to the Volodyyzr Cathedral, and featured twenty groups. This concert was also organized by the Young Communist League.[9] The third rock concert in Kiev was held in March 1968 in the S'ome nebo (Seventh Heaven) club–concert hall of the Kiev main post office. The concert hall was filled to capacity (600).[10]

This first wave ended in 1968 with the invasion of Czechoslovakia. In the wake of the invasion, Ukrainian authorities clamped down on local rock musicians, prohibiting the use of English in performances and any imitation of Western fashions.[11] The only songs permitted were those composed by members of the Union of Composers and only Russian-language or Ukrainian-language songs were allowed. Strict censorship of all texts of songs before each concert was instituted. Rock musicians were forced either to join official state-controlled orchestras (filharmonii) or to move to Moscow, Leningrad, or Siberia, where the censorship was less strict. This emigration of rock musicians out of the republic was much worse than the policy of Russification, for it impoverished Ukrainian culture by depriving it of some of its best musicians. In almost every group in the USSR today, there is a former Ukrainian.[12] What remained in Ukraine were the official state-approved popular vocal-instrumental ensembles, which were forced to sing only in the Ukrainian or Russian language and only state-approved texts. These groups included Chervona Ruta (Red Rue Flower), Smerichka (the Little Fir Tree), Sophia Rotaru, Kraiany (Fellow Country People), Berkut, Medobory (Honey Bouquets), Trio Marenych, Arnika, Kobza (the kobza is a folk lute), Medikus, and Nazavzhdy (Forever).[13]

However, "since rock and roll always lives" and because "it had rooted itself,"[14] it sprang up again at the beginning of the 1970s, this time with such musically educated people as Kyrylo Stetsenko, Taras Petrynenko, Ihor Shablovsky, Mykola Kyrylin, and Oleksandr Blinov.[15] The names of the groups were Chervoni diavoliata (Red Devils), Enei (Aeneus), Hrono (Cluster), and Dzvony (the Bells). Most of the musicians were graduates of the N. Lysenko School of Music in Kiev. The same thing happened to these groups as to those of the previous wave. In 1975, they were forced to join the official *filharmonia*. For ten years Taras Petrynenko had to sing with the Russian groups Chervoni Maky (Red Poppies) and Aerobus (Airbus); his song "Pisnia pro pisniu" (A Song About a Song), written in 1978, could not be performed until 1988 because he was not a member of the Union of Composers.[16] These musicians, writes Kyrylo Stetsenko, used many sources for their music: "Ukrainian folk songs, instrumental folklore, classical music (Bach, Grieg, Khachaturian) and above all, 'The Beatles,' 'Deep Purple,' 'Led Zeppelin,' 'Chicago,' and the Polish groups 'Red Guitars,' 'No to co' (So What), 'Breakout,' and the Hungarian group 'Omega.'"[17]

The third wave began toward the end of the 1970s. This wave was even more integrated with world music and consisted of refined musicians who followed the traditions of the jazz-rock of Miles Davis, Mahavishnu Orchestra, and Weather Report.[18] The best representative of this third wave in Ukraine was the quartet Krok (Step), which was formed in 1979 and consisted of guitarist Volodymyr Khodzytsky, bass guitarist Vadym Lashchuk, percussionist Serhii Khmelov, and keyboard player Ruslan Horobets.[19] However, because of interference from the state, the group lasted only two years and recorded only one hour of music and one-half hour of film. Because this group was not allowed to perform anywhere, Oleksandr Potiomkin, the present-day leader of the Kiev rock group Perrön (which translates to "train platform" and is also the name of the pagan Slavic god of thunder), described how as a student, he and his friends would sit under Khodzytsky's window to listen to him play his guitar.[20] To find work, Lashchuk left for Moscow to play in the popular pop group Display and then later became the musical director of Sophia Rotaru's Chervona Ruta pop group. Ruslan Horobets, like Mykola Kyrylin, joined Alla Pugacheva in the pop group Recital.[21]

Kyrylo Stetsenko summarizes these three waves with the following statement: "And so the history of rock music in Ukraine to the mid-80s is the history of its pain and fading out. The general cultural and psychological and especially political conditions of the 70s and the beginning of the 80s were not at all conducive to the birth and development of independent rock groups, contests, festivals."[22]

The fourth wave of rock music began after Chernobyl. Coincidentally the same evening as the explosion, on 26 April 1986, the first independent rock music concert in Kiev took place at Kiev University, at the faculty of foreign languages.[23] Organized by the "Fonohraf" (Phonograph) section of the *Moloda Gvardia* (Young Guardian) newspaper, the concert featured five groups, all of which had previously been underground: Aeroport Kyiv (Airport Kiev, later renamed Broken Barricades), Syntez (Synthesis), Iks (X), Volodymyr Khodzytsky and his group, and Display with V. Lashchuk. Although no official organization provided any equipment and consequently the concert had to be play-back format, 500 people came to a hall that holds 300. The first independent concert of rock music in Kiev with live sound took place on 29 October 1986 on the Left Bank, in a club called Dnipro. Organized by "Fonohraf" of *Moloda Gvardia,* the youth section of Ukrainian TV programming, and Viacheslav Kurnashov, this rock concert was called Debut '86 and featured ten Kiev groups that had previously played only in cellars and apartments. It was here that Edem, an English-language rock group, formed in 1983 and Kvartyra #50 (Apartment #50), named after the notorious apartment inhabited by satanic creatures in Mikhail Atanas'evich Bulgakov's (1891–1940) novel *Master and Margarita,* performed for the first time in public. Although Rudiachenko was warned by the secretary of the city Komsomol that he would lose his job if Kvartyra #50 would sing the texts of its songs, the concert took place and Kvartyra #50 sang the songs. A crowd of 1,200 came to a concert hall that was designed for 800.[24]

Two months after the fall 1986 rock concert, the groups Edem and Kvartyra #50 formed the nucleus of a new Kiev rock music association called Rok-klub (Rock Club), which was formed in the Palace of Culture "Bilshovyk." Because of many managerial and administrative problems such as the lack of a distinction between professional and amateur groups, lack of material support from sponsors, and commercial and marketing problems, the association came to an end after one year.[25] An alternative association called Rok-artil (Rock Workshop) was formed in December 1987. It consisted of the groups V.V. (pronounced Ve Ve, an abbreviation of Vopli Vydopliasova, "the Wailings of Vydopliasov," the name of one of Dostoyevsky's characters); Kolezhskyi assessor (Collegiate Assessor, named after the lowest civil rank in the Russian Empire); and Rabbota Ho (the Work of Ho, a name derived from a Chinese letter that signifies fire).[26] In February 1988, Rok artilnyk held a rock concert.

Collegiate Assessor, formed back in 1981, performed in the Kiev Polytechnical Institute, where the members of the group all were studying together: Vasyl Hoidenko (vocals, piano, guitar), Hlib Butuzov, and Oleksandr Kievtsev. V.V., when formed in 1983, performed only hard rock until 1986, when guitarist and vocalist Yurii Zdorenko and bass guitarist Oleksandr Pipa were joined by Oleh Skrypka (vocals and saxophone) and Serhii Sakhno (percussion) and the group turned to ethnic punk. Both groups have recorded their works and performed widely throughout Ukraine, the former Soviet Union, as well as abroad. Collegiate Assessor traveled to Glasgow, Scotland, in 1989 and its last album was recorded by Artemy Troitsky in England in 1989 on the Eleven Meridians label.[27]

V.V. of Ukraine. Photo courtesy of Kobza International.

V.V. was included in the French TV program "Anten-2" in its video film *Soviet Rock* in 1989, and in March 1989 the band performed in Moscow with the English group World Domination Enterprise. V.V. performed in Switzerland in April 1990 and in France in April and June 1990. *Paris Passion*, a monthly publication, wrote:

> Today a second generation of musicians have been permitted to flourish along with Perestroika. In the Ukraine, the development of rock has its own strong cultural repercussions, celebrating legislation that only just recently made it legal for Ukrainians to speak their own language. So when the group V.V. sings Ukrainian folk songs in Ukrainian with the fury of the Sex Pistols (mixing cossacks and accordions with a sax, screeching guitars and crashing drums) the effects are far reaching.[28]

According to Kyrylo Stetsenko, the abundance of independent rock groups in Ukraine and the enthusiasm they evoke resemble the mass revival of 1966 to 1968, but the participants in the present-day rock revival are a completely new generation.[29]

The Ukrainian-language column "Fonohraf" in *Moloda Gvardia* reflects this gradual but inevitable acceptance of rock music and rock cul-

Accordion player of V.V. Photo courtesy of Kobza International.

ture in Ukraine. When it began on 28 September 1985, it appeared only once a month and at that time the word *rok* (rock) was consistently eliminated. In 1986 the column began to appear more frequently. It appeared nineteen times in 1986, twenty-four times in 1987, and twenty-eight times in 1988.[30] By September 1990, there were 120 issues. At this time, "Fonohraf" was the only column on rock music in Ukraine. In 1989, Alexander Rudiachenko and Alexander Yertushenko wrote and edited the *Fonohraf Digest,* an eighty-page overview of rock music in Kiev. For two years, until 1989, an unofficial hand-typed Russian-language journal, *Huchnomovets* (Loudspeaker), was put out by Rok artil in Kiev and edited by Mykola and Tetiana Yezhov. The 1989 issue no. 5 contained, for example, an interesting chronology of rock events in Ukraine from May to August 1989 and lyrics to songs by Kolezhskyi asessor (Collegiate Assessor).[31]

A particularly interesting and highly creative, as well as iconoclastic, underground magazine is *Vidryzhka* (Vomit) (subtitle: a hysterical-pathological journal), in the Ukrainian language. It is devoted to underground rock culture in Ukraine but originates from the Ukrainian community in Warsaw. Ukrainian-language rock music is discussed in all five issues. This publication also prints the texts of Ukrainian-language rock songs such as "Tantsi" (Dances) by V.V., in issue no. 1; "Mertvy, piven" (Dead Rooster) and "Narkomany na horodi" (Drug Addicts in the Backyard) by Braty Hadiukiny (Snake Brothers), in issue no. 3, and "Rok-n-rol do rana" (Rock and Roll Until Morning) and "Misku vvazhai" (Mishku [Gorby], Watch Out) also by Snake Brothers, in issue no. 4. This last issue also has an interview with Snake Brothers when the group was in Poland in June 1989.[32]

That *Vidryzhka* should be devoted to rock counterculture in general is not surprising, for in the words of Lviv rock singer Vika: "Rock is not only music. It's a social phenomenon. It is a way of thinking. It is how a person thinks. It is the person's ideas, life, way of life. One expresses one's thoughts through such music."[33]

In *Novyny kinoekranu* (Film News), critic Petro Cherniaiev writes the following about rock counterculture:

> Rock is not so much a style as a type of existence. These are people who stand apart from the official stage and generally reject everything official. … Rock culture … is a layer of spiritual life and culture. It is a social movement and a form of social protest. It is a new genre. … It is a type of religion with its own commandments, myths, saints. It is a way of life.[34]

The phenomenon of rock as counterculture in Eastern Europe and the Soviet Union has been described by Sabrina Petra Ramet[35] and also by Timothy W. Ryback.[36]

Numerous rock concerts and festivals have been held in Kiev since 26 April 1986. Kyrylo Stetsenko lists the following:[37] Debut '86; Rok dialoh (Rock Dialogue), April 1987; Fonohraf (Phonograph) '87, July 1987; Rock Club, November 1987; Rok artilnyk (Rock Workshop), February 1988; Zvezdy '88 (Stars '88), September 1988; Blitz-parad (Blitz-Parade), September 1989; Ms. Rok Evropa (Ms. Rock Europe), January 1990;[38] Lolky-palky (Fiddlesticks), January 1990; Chorna rada (Black Council of the Masses—a name from seventeenth-century Cossack Ukraine),

September 1990; and Festival of Green Art, April 1990. In 1988 the first international rock festival, called Aktsiia myra (World Action, or Peace Action), was also held in Kiev. Groups were from the USSR, Poland, Hungary, and Holland.

In addition to these rock festivals in Kiev, numerous other rock festivals have been held across Ukraine. For example, in Dnipr oderzhinsk, in the industrial heartland of Ukraine, near Zaporizzhia, a Beatles retrospective rock festival, Beatlemania '89, took place in June 1989. This festival was filmed by Yuri Tereshchenko of the Kiev News and Documentary Studio and included in his documentary on the impact of the Beatles in Ukraine and Russia, entitled *Vrubai bitlov* (Turn On the Beatles).[39] In August 1990 there was a rock festival in Berdniansk in southern Ukraine that was devoted to ecology, called Let's Save the Azov Sea. Annual rock festivals, arranged by the Komsomol (Young Communist League), have also been held since 1986 in Nova Kakhovka, a Dnipro River reservoir just south of Zaporizzhia. The most recent Nova Kakhovka rock festival took place in 1991, two weeks after the coup, and was named Rokenrol tavriisky (Rock 'n' Roll Tavriia). (Tavriia was the name of the Nova Kakhovka region and the Crimean Peninsula at the time of the Russian Empire. It was one of the nine Ukrainian provinces of the Russian Empire). The motto of this festival was, "Krashche vazhky rok, nizh zalizna ruka" (It's better to have heavy [i.e., heavy metal] rock than a steel hand).[40]

On 19–24 September 1989, in Chernivtsi, a city in western Ukraine, the Chervona Ruta[41] (Red Rue Flower) Festival of Ukrainian popular music took place.[42] This was the first republican festival of Ukrainian contemporary song and popular music. It was also the first festival in the history of the Ukrainian SSR in which all the songs had to be in the Ukrainian language, a condition specified by the sponsors of the festival (one of whom was the Kobza joint venture Kiev-Toronto Company, which has a recording studio in Kiev and has subsequently released recordings of the performers at this festival). The Chervona Ruta Festival featured primarily pop musicians and balladeer folk singers (bards), but there were some rock groups as well. The winners at the Chervona Ruta Festival in each of the categories of pop, folk-bard, and rock later toured together throughout 1990 in a series of Chervona Ruta concerts all across Ukraine and in Toronto, Canada.

The Chervona Ruta Festival and the subsequent concerts were united not so much by genre of music, because they included a potpourri of various styles, but rather by the theme of Ukrainian language and Ukrainian national revival. The festival also took place on the heels of an important historical event, the inaugural congress of Rukh (the Ukrainian Popular Movement for Restructuring), which took place 8–10 September 1989 in Kiev.[43] The organizers of the Chervona Ruta Festival and the following concerts worked closely with the Rukh movement. The concerts, as a result, had a political flavor to them.

There is no doubt that the 1989 Chervona Ruta Festival in Chernivtsi was a political and social consciousness-raising event of great historical magnitude.[44] Kyrylo Stetsenko had anticipated this in the Chervona Ruta program notes:

> The strength of popular songs lies in the fact that these songs can bring back those who have lost their nationality. The strength of these songs is to be able to uncover in the souls of these people sources of national existence which have been destroyed by foreign influences and education ... and so ... the Ukrainian song has the right to be one of the powerful and primary factors of national reawakening and education of our people.[45]

Rock concerts in Eastern Europe, writes Ramet, have often had this political quality, especially during the communist era, because the rock artists themselves take controversial stands in their music or because of the elites' undertaking, at times, to control or suppress rock performers or because the medium became especially attuned to political messages under communist rule.[46]

Ukrainian-language rock of this fourth wave began in October 1987 when the group V.V. began to sing Ukrainian-language lyrics. Most rock groups in Kiev tend to be bilingual and thus sing in both the Russian language and the Ukrainian language. This bilingualism in music reflects the actual situation of Ukrainian Russian bilingualism that exists in Kiev today. This situation resulted from long years of an official policy of Russification and the fact that the use of the Ukrainian language and a respectful attitude toward the Ukrainian language have been encouraged only since 1989—until that time, to sing only in the Ukrainian language was to be branded a member of "bourgeois nationalists" by the communist party. Now, however, the choice of what language to sing in lies entirely with the group.

Most of the mature rock groups in Kiev are bilingual, singing in Russian and Ukrainian, or trilingual, singing in Russian, Ukrainian, and English. Bilingual Ukrainian-Russian groups include Broken Barricades (Zruinovani barykady, formerly Airport Kiev), formed in the 1970s; Kvartyra #50, formed in 1986; Komu vnyz (Going Down) (a play on words for communism in Ukrainian is "Komunizm"), formed in 1988; and Perrön. Zymovyi sad (Winter Garden), formed in 1980, sings in Ukrainian and English and Ivanov Daun (Ivanov Down) sings in Russian and English. The trilingual groups include Collegiate Assessor and Tabula rasa. A multilingual approach to rock music obviously expands the creative possibilities for a musical group and makes it possible for these groups to enter the international music market. Some groups such as Edem, Aiaks, Euphoria, and Firelake sing only in English; they claim, in the words of Edem's leader Viktor Lukianov, that true hard and heavy rock or trash metal groups can be sung only in English. Groups that sing only in Ukrainian are Yuri Tovstohan (formerly with Slid, later with Step) and a newly formed group, Banita Baida (Outcast Baida). Groups that sing only in Russian (and these form the majority in Kiev) are Zahublenyi svit (Lost World), Tytanik (Titanic), Agoniia (Agony), Doktor Faust (Doctor Faust), Faeton (Faeton), Chervoni (Reds), Rabbota Ho (the Work of Ho), Park rozbytykh likhtariv (Park of Broken Lanterns), Pioner (Pioneer), E.R.S. (Electrical Power), Chervona ploshcha (Red Square), Ivanova Vis (Ian's Axis), Vodianyi lys (Water Fox), Akustychna komisiia (Accoustic Commission), Nevesela statystyka (Sad Statistics), Tsikava patolohiia (Interesting Pathology), and about thirty to forty more groups.[47]

An interesting development in rock music in 1990, as far as the language question in Ukraine is concerned, was the case of the group V.V., which was the first rock group of the fourth wave in Ukraine to sing rock lyrics in the Ukrainian language. Annoyed at the tendency of political groups to politicize art and music and in order to demonstrate its protest of being pressured by some Rukh supporters to sing only in Ukrainian, V.V. purposely sang in the Russian language as well as in Ukrainian. This confrontation culminated in the cancellation of the group's contract for a concert tour to Toronto, Canada, in fall 1990: The sponsor, Kobza, categorically refuses to sponsor any performances in the Russian language.[48]

Some rock groups in Kiev that are purely instrumental are Erotychnyi dzhaz (Erotic Jazz); Biokord (Biocord); Rok trio (Rock Trio), and Chyslo tsvirkuna (Number of the Cricket). Erotic Jazz is an experimental, new age folk-rock group of long-haired hippies who use various exotic instruments such as Tibetan chimes. This instrumental rock group traces its origins back to 1987, when it began as a theatrical group called Nul distantsiia (Zero Distance). In June 1989 it participated in the Festival of Street Theatres in Moscow and St. Petersburg and almost every rock festival in Kiev in 1989 and 1990. A group that began even earlier, in 1984, is Chyslo tsvirkuna (Cricket's Number), which was formed by poet and guitarist Yuri Storozhuk. This group performed in the first live-music Kiev rock festival, Debut '86. Soon after the festival, Storozhuk left for India, where he studied sitar and taught Russian language. In 1990, after the group had returned from travels to West Germany, Storozhuk, together with Hlib Butuzov of Collegiate Assessor, formed the group Godzadva (the name of an Indian philosopher as well as a play on words, "in one year or two"). In December 1990, Er Dzhaz, along with

Godzadva, Tabula rasa and Perrön, performed in the avant-garde Mandala Theatre in Krakow, Poland.[49]

Rock music in Lviv, the main city in western Ukraine, has a history similar to that of Kiev. The Lviv rock musicians interviewed, Serhii Kuzminsky and Mykhailo Lundin of Braty Hadiukiny (Snake Brothers), stated that in the 1970s they listened to the Beatles, the Rolling Stones, Led Zeppelin, Deep Purple, Grand Funk, the Doors, Jimi Hendrix, Uriah Heap, Janis Joplin, and Slade. They also listened to East European groups such as the Hungarian Omega, Locomotive, and Skorpion and the Polish groups Lady Punk, Y.V. (pronounced "oo veh"), DAAB, and Dezerter.[50] Vika said she was an admirer of Nina Hagen.[51] Two events of great importance in Lviv for the development of rock music were the concerts of Tadeusz Nalepa from Poland in 1976 and Czesław Niemen, also from Poland, in 1977. Lviv, unlike Kiev, has stronger ties with Poland than with Russia; this applies to the rock scene as well. (Before World War II, the city of Lviv and the province of Halychyna were part of Poland. Before World War I they were part of the Austro-Hungarian Empire.) Soon after the Chervona Ruta Festival, the Poles in Lviv sponsored a performance of rock music in Lviv at which the Polish rock groups Lady Punk, Kombi, and Papa Dance performed, as did Vika.[52]

Kyrylo Stetsenko singles out the jazz-pop group Medikus as being the most influential in Lviv in the 1960s. It was led by Ihor Khoma and also included the composers M. Skoryk and B. Yanivsky. A pop-folk group in Lviv in the 1960s that later joined the state orchestra (*filharmonia*) was the group Vatra (Bonfire). In the early 1970s, the popular groups were Prometey (Prometheus), led by Yaroslav Vidzhak; Evrika (Eurika), led by Yuri Varum; and Quo Vadis, led by Viktor Morozov.[53]

Vika began singing rock at age sixteen with Viktor Morozov at dances in Lviv in the 1970s. Their undergroup group was called Arnika. It sang Janis Joplin and Uriah Heap in English in the local police association club called Militsia (Police). When the repression increased, she worked in Russia, outside of Moscow, with a group called Labyrinth. When rock was allowed in Lviv, in 1988, she decided to sing rock in the Ukrainian language. Serhii Kuzminsky wrote her first six songs, but now she writes the lyrics and her husband, Volodymyr Bebeshko, composes the music. In Vika's words, "The officials do not want to admit that youth listens to rock music and has been listening to it already 10 years ago, not Ukrainian language rock, but rock music nevertheless."[54]

Although Ramet and Sergei Zamascikov mark 1985 as the date of official recognition of rock in the former USSR as a whole,[55] in Lviv real change does not begin until two or three years later. Rock music was officially allowed in Lviv only in December 1987. In January 1988 Lviv's first rock concert was held. Kuzminsky performed at this concert in a group called Plastychna Mistifikatsiia (Group of Plastic Mystification).[56]

The Chervona Ruta Festival held in western Ukraine was one of the major manifestations of Ukrainian national feeling in 1989. It took place one week after the inaugural congress of Rukh and at a time of growing political mass rallies and protests, and it was also held in the city of Chernivtsi of Bukovyna Province, the hometown of Volodymyr Ivasiuk, the popular composer of the songs "Chervona ruta" (Red Rue Flower) and "Vodohrai" (Fountain). After his murder in 1979, which was attributed to the KGB, Volodymyr Ivasiuk became a symbol of protest in Ukraine,[57] and his stature in western Ukraine, writes Kyrylo Stetsenko, is comparable to the stature of Volodymyr Vysotsky in Russia.[58] His funeral was attended by 10,000 people and took on the appearance of a political national rally.

Many of the performers at the 1989 Chervona Ruta Festival sang openly patriotic songs and songs with a political content—the condemnation of Russification or criticism of the economy and the Communist party. In addition, they ended or began their performances with such national patriotic slogans as "Slava Ukraini" (Glory to Ukraine) or "Slava heroiam" (Glory to the Heroes). The blue and yellow flags were numerous, as were the police (militsiia). Vika sang a song entitled "Han'ba" (Shame) about the deplorable state of the Ukrainian language and culture, and the Braty Hadiukiny (Snake Brothers), before beginning their performance, described a peaceful protest in Lviv that was dispersed by the militia, who beat the young participants. Serhii Kuzminsky ended his introduction by shouting out "Shame" and "How long are we going to suffer?"[59] In an interview, Kuzminsky stated that the Ukrainian television stations edited the performance, cutting out his speech about the police beatings.[60]

Many songs at the festival were about the second-class status of the Ukrainian language. There were calls during the performances by the performers themselves to have Ukrainian declared the official state language of the Ukrainian Republic. An example of such a song is "My zabuly vse" (We Have Forgotten Everything), by pop singer Taras Kurchyk of the western Ukrainian city of Drohobych:

We have forgotten everything
We have forgotten our native language
For which our grandfathers spilled their blood.
No. Do not judge me.
I have forgotten that which is native, which is close to me.

Snake Brothers, Serhii Kuzminsky, center. Photo courtesy of Kobza International.

A folk singer named Eduard Drach sang "Viddaite movu" (Give Us Back Our Language). After his performance the crowd demanded the reinstatement of Ukrainian as the official state language and the concert took on the appearance of a political rally.[61]

Rock singer Vika (Viktoria Vradii) commented on this phenomenon in the newspaper *Molod Ukrainy* in 1990: "The wave of Ukrainian language rock music, or to be more precise Ukrainian punk, is reaching the shore. It disturbs society and wakes into consciousness even those who appeared to be hopelessly asleep. Art is a great power. This is something even greater than a mass meeting or rally."[62] Volodymyr Bebeshko stated that whenever Vika performs, people dance holding blue and yellow flags.[63]

Some of the performers at the Chervona Ruta Festival stressed the economic problems rather than the national and language issues. The pop group Avans (Advance) from Zaporizzhia sang a song entitled "Myla mene maty" (My Mother Washed Me). It started out with the haunting melody of a beautiful Ukrainian folk song and then switched to rock rhythm and sarcasm with the words "she washed me with soap she bought with ration coupons." The lyrics of this song reflect the shortage of soap and other essential items in the economic system:

Where is the soap?
Where is the meat?
Where is the bacon?
Everything, everything is only available
with ration coupons.
Why? Because—
We're sick of everything.
You can't find anything anywhere.
There's shortage of food
What can one do?
The theory arises
that the ration coupons are
as useless as the system.[64]

Another group, N.Z. (Nezaimana zemlia, or Virgin Land), a hard rock group from Lutsk, sang a song at the Chervona Ruta Festival entitled "Vse dlia blaha narodu" (Everything for the Good of the People), an extremely angry and bitingly sarcastic criticism of the communist system. One of the singers who portrayed the officials was dressed in priest clothing.[65] The lyrics are as follows.

I gave you peace and freedom
With a class pick axe I built the Gulag prisons.
I gave you laws and rules
Red, in granite hands
Who picked you for the voice of the people?
Those who sit in high positions

Refrain:
Everything for the good of the people ...[66]

In contrast, Andrii Mykolaichuk from Uman sang pop-rock songs about drug addicts ("Narkomany") and unrequited love ("I Will Go and Drown Myself").[67] What is interesting about the latter song is that it is extremely cheerful. Pop singer Taras Petrynenko of the Kiev group Hrono (Cluster), which is closer to country-western and pop than to rock, sang about the people's opposition in "Narodnyi Rukh" (The People's Front Rukh).[68]

The Chervona Ruta Festival was not supported by the communist party.[69] Although the communist party did not prohibit the festival, it did wage a campaign against it. It is therefore not surprising that the organizers went to great lengths to justify it.[70] Kyrylo Stetsenko, author of the program notes and director of media for the Chervona Ruta Festival, quotes the following citation from *Pravda* (17 August 1989):

> Internationalism—is not the denial of the national, but on the contrary—it is the growing attention to national interests of peoples and at the same time—the defense of general human values. ...
>
> The Party sees its task in the protection of the free development of the spiritual life of all peoples of the USSR. The forms of this development must manifest themselves individually without regimentation and without controls.[71]

The article in the program notes continues:

> In connection with the necessity of raising the level of Ukrainian contemporary popular music and its popularisation, the Ministry of Culture of the Ukrainian SSR, the board of Derzhteleradio (State Radio) of the U.R.S.R., the Ukrainian Fund of Culture, the Union of Composers of Ukraine, the Musical Association of the Ukrainian SSR, the Union of Writers of Ukraine, the Ukraine Society, decided to initiate the establishment of a republican festival of Ukrainian contemporary and popular music—"Chervona Ruta" to take place once every two years. The first such festival will take place in Chernivtsi from 19–24 September.[72]

On 24 May 1989, the Taras Shevchenko Society of Ukrainian Language approved the decision to join the various other community groups, state institutions, and creative associations that organized the Chervona Ruta Festival. On 13 July, the Green World of Ukraine Society, which is affiliated with the Soviet Fund for Peace, became a sponsor.[73]

Also included in the Chervona Ruta Festival program notes is an excerpt from Ivan Dziuba's article "Do We Consider Our National Culture as a Totality?" published in *Nauka i Kultura* (Kiev) in 1988 and also in the newspaper *Kultura i zhyttia:* "The fullness of functioning of national culture requires also the development of mass entertainment genres and forms, such as various types of cabaret, popular songs and so on—that is, the youth subculture in general, the urban subculture."[74]

The communist party and government continued to criticize and interfere with the Chernova Ruta concerts that took place after the festival. Vika described how even in May 1990 posters of the Chervona Ruta concerts were being torn down by local communist party officials,[75] and Andrii Sereda of Komu vnyz described how in Zaporizzhia communist party officials scheduled parallel concerts on the day of the Chervona Ruta concerts to draw away crowds.[76] Serhii Kuzminsky described how immediately after the Chervona Ruta Festival, when the Snake Brothers performed in Drohobych, an article appeared in a local communist party newspaper. In the article, entitled "Chy vse chotko" (Is Everything O.K.?), the Snake Brothers were severely criticized for being carriers of a foreign ideology and were banned from performing in the whole *oblast* (province) of Lviv.[77] This ban continued until the successful Alla Pugacheva concert in 1989 December. However, these bans, attacks, and the boycott by the radio and TV stations have had the opposite effect of that intended, claimed all the interviewed musicians, for the ban has given them free publicity and has aroused the interest of the public.[78]

A milestone was achieved when the Braty Hadiukiny (Snake Brothers), second place-prize winner in the rock category at Chervona Ruta (even though the group's name did not appear on the program and the members were lodged forty kilometers away from the festival), were invited by Alla Pugacheva to perform a Ukrainian-language rock song at the December 1989 state-televised Moscow Christmas Concert. The Snake Brothers performed their "Rok-n-rol do rana" (Rock and Roll Until Morning), a song that Pugacheva selected, in twenty performances from 1 to 17 December 1989, one of which was attended by Gorbachev.[79] A triumph was also achieved by Vika when in January 1990 she received the prize for the best show at the International Female Rock Music Festival in Kiev.[80]

That the 1989 Christmas concert, in which the Snake Brothers performed, was televised on Soviet state television is an event of particular significance because even in May 1990 the radio and television networks, both the all-union ones as well as those in Lviv and Kiev, continued to boycott Ukrainian-language rock.[81] Exceptions were in June 1989, when Kyrylo Stetsenko interviewed the Snake Brothers on the Ukrainian television program in Kiev because they were participating in an all-Soviet rock festival in Kiev called Rok-budylnyk,[82] and in August 1989, when the Kiev Ukrainian-language television program televised the rock video "Pan Bazio" (Mr. Bazio) of the Lviv pop music and cabaret group Ne zhurys (Don't Worry).[83] Some excerpts from Chervona Ruta rock were televised as well on the Ukrainian-language program but poor-quality sections were deliberately selected, according to Andrii Sereda.[84]

Bards-balladeers and folk singers with a political and social cause have been important, particularly in Lviv and at the Chervona Ruta Festival[85] (namely the group Ne Zhurys [Don't Worry]). Ne Zhurys was the first Ukrainian group to have cassettes appear in the West (in 1988), and this group was the first Ukrainian band to tour North America widely (in fall 1989). Therefore it is important to look more closely at the texts of the songs, even though they do not belong strictly to the genre of rock. This group enjoys great popularity in Ukraine among Ukrainian-speaking Ukrainians.

Taras Chubai is the only rock and pop singer in Ne zhurys, which is more of a cabaret group; the group consists primarily of the folk singers and balladeers (bards) Viktor Morozov, Andrii Panchyshyn, and Va-syl' Zhdankin. In Chubai's song "Ukrainskyi vampir" (The Ukrainian Vampire), composed and sung by him (with words by Andrii Panchyshyn), we hear the familiar strains of Michael Jackson's *Thriller* and *Billy Jean*.

> *I am the Ukrainian Vampire*
> *I am looking for you*
> *I have unseeing eyes*
> *I am looking for you*
> *I have dog's teeth*
> *I am looking for you*
> *I have cold fingers*
> *I live in an abyss*
>
> *You are a green and stupid girl*
> *You are not my first one*
> *But my passion*
> *Will probably be your last*[86]

Sex, a subject formerly forbidden by the communist party, is also the theme of "Kama Sutra" (1989), words by Andrii Panchyshyn.

> *For the majority of the Soviet people*
> *The secrets of the East are necessary.*
> *There in the East they sit naked on nails.*
> *So what do Petro and Mykola have to learn from this?*
> *We achieve our triumphs in work and sport without yoga.*
>
> *But there are secrets of the East*
> *That would do our people a lot of good.*
> *Among these is a wise knowledge that which is called*
> *Kama Sutra.*
> *This is an ancient wisdom.*
> *This is ultimate sexual education.*
>
> *They know the Kama Sutra in Laos.*
> *The Eskimos have mastered it.*
> *Even from the point of view of the*
> *Guatemalans we are very behind in this.*
> *Because we have had no progress*
> *Since the time of the construction of the*
> *Dnipro electrical power station.*

In order to be able to take advantage of the Kama Sutra
You have to learn it from childhood.
It is best to start at school
Though its never too late.
I believe the secrets of the East
Will still serve our people.[87]

Another song, "Koroleva Mista Leva" (The Queen of the City of the Lion), was composed by Victor Morozov in 1988 for the first beauty contest in Lviv. (Beauty contests are extremely popular in Ukraine today.) The words are by A. Panchyshyn.

A Coronation in Lviv
A celebration of blue blood
Such erotic races are very unfamiliar
to the inhabitants of Lviv
Today you are the Queen
Of the city of the Lion
My God, what a figure
Not a girl, but a sculpture
Delicate hands
Long legs
Each girl wishes to be the winner

You have crystal eyes
and metal nerves
You are from a good family
This song is dedicated to you
Today you are the Queen
of the city of Lviv.[88]

Most of the songs of Ne zhurys are in the cabaret and bard style and draw their inspiration from Joan Baez, Bob Dylan, and Simon and Garfunkel.[89] They are bitingly satirical and critical of the political, economic, and cultural situation. Marta Kolomayets interviewed Andrii Panchyshyn, a bard and the author of most songs of Ne zhurys that were performed when the group was on tour in Canada and the United States in fall 1989. She wrote:

Mr. Panchyshyn is the author of such songs as "Oholoshennia" (Advertisement) which comments on the state of the Ukrainian language and "Video" which includes the words: "to have a VCR is like being abroad. Over there life is so wonderful, everyone owns a car, loads of money, a white villa and a fair-skinned woman. Everyone there dances for joy and only the blacks work."

He has also dedicated a series of songs to such memorable figures in the history of Ukraine as Lazar Kaganovich and is constantly looking for new victims to attack. He jokingly confesses that he has a special power in predicting history, citing the fact that just a few short days after he wrote a ditty suggesting that Vololymyr Shcherbytsky resign, the Ukrainian Communist party chief fell from power.[90]

Other songs by bard (folk singer) Andrii Panchyshyn of Ne zhurys are much sharper. One example is the song called "Symbols" (1989)—a reference to the 1989–1990 controversy on Ukrainian national symbols (i.e., the blue and yellow flag versus the red flag).

The Orthodox and Greek-Catholics demand the immediate rebirth of national symbols.

Refrain:
We shall raise the blue and yellow flags
Right up to the sky
Ah, what beauty!

The person who does not have symbols is an invalid. Refrain.
Today only the lackeys or the alcoholics protest against
native symbols.

Refrain.

The Papuans, Ethiopians and Poles have their flag
Only we fools do not have our own symbols. Refrain.
Our wise leadership sits in Kiev.

They love Ukraine more than the hordes of Batii
Don't worry lackeys
Drink up, you alcoholics
Until something changes here at home
We shall have no symbols

They shall ban the blue and yellow flags from above
This is the political plan of the central committee
It is so now for 300 years.[91]

The song "Slymachok" (The Snail) is one of Panchyshyn's earliest ones, composed in 1983.

There lived a snail in China
It moved along the green branches
But it got bored with the green branches of the tree and decided to
travel and see the world

He stuck out his horns bravely
And resolutely embarked on his journey
Some Chinese person found him there
And used him as a spread on his bread

The poor snail disappeared down a gullet
For you see in China, snails are a gourmet dish
But if he had lived in the USSR
He would have still been wandering about.[92]

"Militsioner" (The Policeman) (1989) is dedicated, in the words of Andrii Panchyshyn, to the "untiring defenders of order at the Chervona Ruta Festival":

I am the mi
I am the li
I am the tsi
I am the a

I am the militsioner
I used to look after cows in the village
Now I'm a chief
I have a stick that reaches down to my knees
And a black revolver

I am the mi
I am the li
I am the tsi
I am the a

I am a militsioner[93]

In the words of Ne zhurys, the police behaved aggressively during the Chernova Ruta Festival. Other songs in the group's repertoire are about glasnost, which is compared to an epidemic of proportions equal to AIDS in the song "Brekhunets" (which means "liar" but is also the popular name for the official radio program).[94]

In contrast to the folk songs of Ne zhurys, the music of Taras Chubai is all rock. In 1991, Taras Chubai formed a new rock group, Plach Ieremiia (The Wailings of Jeremiah). The satirical bard-rock songs composed by Taras Chubai to the words of Ukrainian avant-garde poet Viktor Neborak are particularly worthy of note because they are bitterly sarcastic, full of anger, and deal with one of the most widespread social problems in Ukraine today, namely, the widespread prevalence and acceptance of prostitution. Moreover, these songs are extremely popular, as Neborak himself admitted in a recent interview.[95] One such popular rock song is "Lolita," a frankly misogynist song about a female prostitute.[96] Poet Neborak admitted that the song "Lolita" and the words written by him express male aggression and anger, but he justified this by stating that the voice was not his but that of another character. This technique was in keeping with Bakhtin's carnival principle of antilyrical "mask" and "voice," which is the guiding principle of Neborak's poetry and that of his poetry theater association named "Bu-ba-bu" (Burlesque, *balahan* [i.e., farce], and *bufonada*, [i.e., buffoonery].)

Neborak continued to elaborate on this subject and stated that in the present-day situation of a total moral void in Ukraine and other parts of the former USSR, prostitution has become an acceptable business exchange.[97] This observation is corroborated by the widespread popularity in Ukraine, as in the rest of the former USSR, of the 1989 Russian-language Soviet film *Interdevushka*. In this film, Olena Yakovleva plays the character of prostitute Tanya Zaitseva, who is portrayed positively as a successful entrepreneur because she earns hard currency from Western foreigners and dresses stylishly and tastefully in expensive Western designer clothes.[98] Corruption and prostitution are not isolated to women, however: In another bard-rock song-poem, "Pan Bazio" (Mr. Bazio), sung by Viktor Morozov, Neborak sarcastically exposes the corrupt "businessman"—the pimp, who speculates and deals in many services, including women. The song describes the men who go to the service, which include a millionaire, a Ph.D. candidate, and a dentist.[99]

The Snake Brothers are a Ukrainian-language punk rock group from Lviv. The rock songs they perform that are written and composed by Serhii Kuzminsky, their leader, are particularly noteworthy. Serhii Kuzminsky is probably one of the most creative, original, and witty rock composers in Ukraine today. Published in *Vidryzhka* (Vomit) and recorded in 1989 on a home-produced audiocassette in Lviv, with the help of Volodymyr Bebeshko, were the texts of "Rok-n-rol do rana" (Rock 'n' Roll Until Morning); "Mis'ku vvazhai" (Mishku [Gorby], Watch Out), which is dedicated to Mikhail (Mishko) Gorbachev; "Narkomany na horodi" (Drug Addicts in the Back Yard); and "Mertvyi piven" (Dead Rooster). Serhii Kuzminsky describes how he composed the song "Rok-n-rol do rana" after listening to the official folk choir of Ivano Frankivsk (the *filharmonia*) singing *kolomyiky* (folk songs). He decided to compose his own satirical rock *kolomyika*, in Ukrainian urban slang and Lemko Ukrainian dialect, following the *kolomyika* rhythm but combined with rock rhythm.[100]

> *I will go to Verkhovyna to sing*
> *It is so pleasant to live in this Soviet land.*
> *Across the mountains, across the forest flew a cuckoo*
> *I will go to the propaganda headquarters and will announce*

Refrain:
Hey, there's a party, rock-n-roll
Drink, dance, have a good time!
Turner, locksmith, don't worry
We will work hard; we will build a new world
In our native USSR
   One, two, three kholera! *(literally cholera, used as "hell" or "damn")*

A cow was walking down the street
and a calf behind it
The Lemko's achieved their five-year-plan
Uncle was riding along on his bicycle
and had a flat tire
A worker and a peasant—that's a big power![101]

The remaining three verses are in the same satirical vein. The cover of
Vidryzhka (Vomit), no. 4, in which this song appears, carries on its title
the slogan "Proletari, vse chotko?" (Proletarians, Is Everything O.K.?)—a
reference to the title of the communist party article critical of the Snake
Brothers. Another song they performed at the 1989 Chervona Ruta
Festival was "Oi, lykho!" (O, Horrors!):

"O, Horrors!"
This happened at a bad time
The big war had ended
The Germans were retreating
They left their weapons behind
They left bicycles ...

O horrors!

Mykola had a bomb in his attic
It lay dormant for forty years
But in the forty-first year it exploded.[102]

Serhii Kuzminsky mixes Ukrainian Lemko dialect and urban slang
and even uses English words, for example in the song "America." The
songs "America" and "Mishku (Gorby), Watch Out," both composed and
written by Kuzminsky, were used by Serhii Bukovsky in his satirical ten-
minute documentary film *Satirical Mill No.* 24: Braty Hadiukiny (1990),
produced by the Kiev News and Documentary Studio. Bukovsky filmed
the Snake Brothers performing and satirically described current food
problems in the USSR by contrasting the long lineups in front of the
Moscow McDonald's with propaganda slogans and archival footage
from the revolutionary years.[103] "America" satirizes Soviet reality and

also the infatuation with the United States. Following are the lyrics of "America." (Boldfaced words are in English in the original.)

*When **midnight** replaces the bright day*
*And everybody is resting after **work,***
I havn't yet closed my eyes-ey-ey
*In my **dreams I'm flying to New York***

Life is very nice for us
All of us honest workers
In the Soviet system
Who thinks that even once
they would have a chance
To go to America?

Everybody

*America, **you say** to me "**welcome**"*
*I say, **Oh-yea,** America*
Will I ever sail to your shore?
*I will drive in a **car on the highway***
*I will eat at **McDonalds** and will eat hot dogs,*
*And I will meet a **fine girl***
And the police will respect me
Skyscrapers, robbers

*In **Central Park***
Prostitutes, drug addicts
*All are smoking **marijuana***
Cigarettes

Refrain:
*America, **you say** to me "**welcome**"*
*I say, **Oh-yea,** America*
Will I ever sail to your shore?

*On **Broadway** I will meet **Mick Jagger***
*And we will go visit **Tina Turner***
I will fall before her on my knees
*And we will spend **all night** together*
*She will **say** to me **bye-bye***
*And will sing a **lullaby** ... sleep my baby*
I will say, "Give me your hand
I want you to be my friend."

Refrain.[104]

In "Mishku (Gorby), Watch Out," the words are prophetic.

Everyday I walk about
the city, here and there
I see big changes
Everywhere
I'm not going to eat anymore
I'm not going to sleep anymore
Because I don't want to miss anything

Mishku, watch out
Spring is great
Mishku, watch out
It's bright like the sun
Mishku, watch out
Kholera, damn it,
Spring is calling me forward.[105]

Not all songs of the Snake Brothers are social satires, however. "Arrivederci Roma," for example, is about a jilted lover and expresses considerable aggression and violence toward the woman.

We saw each other one fall night
The leaves lay spread out on the ground
I fell in love, ready for forever
Cause both of us were joined by something true.

Refrain:
Yeah, you're my sweetheart
And I'm your greatest love
You were putting out, but I didn't want a thing.
Arrivederci Roma, Arrivederci Roma, Arrivederci Roma
See you later, See you later

The days went by, the winter came, snow blanketed the world
Remember baby, magic was in the air
And if someone asked, I'd tell them honestly
I wouldn't ask for greater happiness from God.

Refrain.

The spring came, the snow had thawed, and I found that you'd betrayed me
The dorm boys came by and told me all about it
A vicious hate arose up and swallowed me completely
I busted you in the head until I saw it bleed.

Refrain.[106]

Serhii Kuzminsky also wrote the texts to the two songs sung by Vika at the Chervona Ruta Festival—"Hanba" (Shame) and "Shaktarskyi bugi" (Coalminer's Boogie). Kuzminsky and Volodymyr Bebeshko arranged the music. Before the Chervona Ruta Festival, Vika sang with the Snake Brothers. The lyrics of "Hanba" follow.

I scream shame! But my request does not reach the altar,
I was only one, but now there are thousands of us!
Hey, we are standing in a circle!
And we stare at one another like young calves.

Refrain:
Who doesn't live, cannot die
Who hasn't fallen asleep, can't awake
Who hasn't opened his eyes, can't see anything
Behind you Morozenko, all of Ukraine is crying.

I scream Shame! To you, the general dream of human hearts
We rocked you for so many years
We thought you were a saint, but you're a whore,

Refrain.

I scream shame! To whom? to myself.
I present you with the scars on my neck from the yoke.
Children who have forgotten their native language
And I feel sorry for your young years
When we shouted hoorah to every single speech.

Again the question arises of the purity of the Ukrainian language.
Kielbasa or Kovbasa?
Who cares? As long as we have it.[107]

And in the Toronto concert, the line *kielbasa* (sausage, in Polish) or *kovbasa* (sausage, in Ukrainian) was replaced by "*kamunizm* (communism, in Russian) or *komunizm* (communism, in Ukrainian)? As long as we don't have it." Cleverly woven into the song rhythms is the motif from "Zasvystaly Kozachenky" (The Cossacks Whistled), a folk battle song.

In "Shaktarskyi bugi" (Coalminer's Boogie), a scathingly sarcastic attack on proletarian positive heroes and socialist realism written by Serhii Kuzminsky, Vika Vradii sings in urban slang and Ukrainian Lemko dialect.

I love you for your strength
And because you give me flowers

Beneath you I feel like a soldier under a tank
And when you drink, you sing:

Refrain:
Coalminer's boogie, coalminer's boogie, Oh yeh!

I saw you in the crowd immediately
Although you were dark-haired like the rest.
But in your eyes there shone such intelligence
And you sang with a hammer in your hands

Refrain.

For the youth all the roads are open
Straight to the coalmine with a pass from the regional party committee
I want to be your anthracite coal
You be my hammer

Refrain.[108]

Vika Vradii also writes the words to her own songs, and her newly released tape (since Chervona Ruta) contains songs such as "Mamo, ia durna" (Mamma, I'm Stupid), "Ne treba Stopa" (Stop it, Stopa). These songs are about male-female relations, sex and love, school, and the city life. Like Kuzminsky's songs, hers are full of humor, irony, and sarcasm. In Vika's words: "We have a lot of problems in our society, in our day to day life, in relationships with people and so forth. And so we express all these themes through our prism and we do this in an ironical way. But the people understand what we mean."[109]

The lyrics for "Mamo, ia durna" (Mamma, I'm Stupid) are the following:

You, mamma, sent me to school in Lviv
I went to college
I got fat like a cow on that scholarship
Because buns are cheap as in wartime.

Refrain:
Mamma! What am I to do?
Mamma! Gee I'm stupid.

You told me, mamma, not to go out on dates
Because the Lviv boys just want sex
So I fell in love at last with my director
He has a car but he's old as a dog.

Refrain.

I bleached my hair blonde
I shaved my legs
I have a manicure
Now during the nights I study sex
And during the day I drink coffee and smoke.[110]

Vika, who has short punk hair and dresses in punk style, torn jeans, and boots, projects toughness as well as a sense of irony and humor. She projects a new urban female role model. According to Vika, "I do not want to be pleasing. Women always want to be beautiful. I want to be accepted for who I am."[111] Vika, who is in her thirties, is married and has a teenage son. She is the only woman in the Ukrainian mass media and pop and rock cultural scene who presents a nonconformist and independent image of a woman. Vika is the only female rock singer in Ukraine today who challenges the establishment and functions as a rock singer and performer in the true sense of rock as counterculture. Nevertheless, in spite of her dynamism, unique image, creative spirit, nonconformist masculine clothing, short punk hair, and her rejection of traditional feminine beauty and makeup—and in spite of her popularity with music critics and her fans—Vika remains on the periphery of mass consciousness in Ukraine today.[112]

In contrast to Vika, the two other female pop singers in Ukraine today, Rusya (pronounced "roosya")[113] and Iryna Bilyk of the group Tsei doshch nadovho (This Rain Is for Long), are merely younger versions of older pop and folk-country singers such as Sophia Rotaru and Nina Matviienko.[114] This mimicry is not surprising, however, in a country where beauty contests in the 1990s are now "in" and where television and mass culture in Ukraine continue to be dominated by such romantic stereotypes as that maintained by the immensely popular Brazilian TV soap actress Lucelia Santos. She played the lead role of "Rabynia Izaura" (the slave girl Izaura) in the Brazilian TV serial, which was aired with great success in Ukraine in 1989 for many months and was faithfully and enthusiastically watched by millions of Ukrainians. (The serial, directed by Erodalo Rosano, was made in Brazil in 1975.) "Rabynia Izaura" is now a household name in Ukraine, as is *fazenda,* the Ukrainian pronunciation of hacienda (old Spanish "facienda")—the plantation estate where the sweetly feminine, obedient, and subservient Izaura lived with her benevolent master. Although Ukrainians now regularly refer to their dacha (country house) as "fazenda" and many Ukrainian women aspire to find benevolent masters, preferably from the West, there are those such as Vika who consciously and deliberately reject this stereotype.

Vika. Photo courtesy of Kobza International.

The pop group Avans (Advance) makes fun of the Izaura image. Composed of three female vocalists and a male vocalist from Zaporizzhia, the group has written and produced a humorous Ukrainian song and album entitled "Fazenda." The lyrics of "Fazenda" are included here:

Female voices:
  O, fazenda
  O, fazenda
  O, fazenda
  O, fazenda

Male voice:
  This foreign word is well known
  It is a part of our language now

Female voices:
  O, fazenda
  O, fazenda
  O, fazenda

Male voice:
  I close my eyes and
  I see a white house, a cow

Male and female voices:
  O, fazenda
  O, fazenda
  O, fazenda

Male voice:
  Maybe it's that hope
  How I dream about you
  Give each and every slave girl Izaura
  At least for rent
  Her own fazenda

Female voices:
  O, fazenda
  O, fazenda

Male voice:
  I would like to be Leonzio
  And to have my own pretty Izaura
  But where do I find that big shovel
  To shovel up more money

Female voices:
  O, fazenda
  O, fazenda

Male voice:
  Moo, moo, moo (imitating a cow)

Female voices:
  O, fazenda
  O, fazenda[115]

Whereas Lviv rock singers sing in the Ukrainian language, the rock singers of Kiev tend to be bilingual and sing both Ukrainian- and Russian-language songs. Komu vnyz (Going Down), a group from Kiev, sang only in Russian at first but then switched to Ukrainian in 1989 and performed in the Chervona Ruta Festival.

The Ukrainian-language rock song "Subotiv" (the name of the village where Bohdan Khmelmytsky, a hetman of Ukraine, was buried in the seventeenth century), an original composition by Andrii Sereda, was composed in 1983, before the group Komu vnyz was formed.[116] It is based on the text of a 1845 poem by Taras Shevchenko, Ukraine's most important nineteenth-century poet (and also a painter), who was born a serf and bought from slavery by the Russian tsar's family in a lottery. Shevchenko was arrested and sent into exile a few years later for the strong social criticism in his poetry. He wrote very powerful and emotional romantic visionary poetry in which apocalyptic imagery abounds. His images of blind slaves, crippled widows, raped women, bastard children, and dead cossacks rising against their exploitative masters had a profound effect on a nation of people who were enslaved and exploited, and these images contributed to the national awakening of Ukraine in the nineteenth and early twentieth centuries. Shevchenko and his poetry continue to inspire the current rock generation.

Andrii Sereda's "Subotiv" is considered by many to be musically the most original Ukrainian rock composition. The lyrics of "Subotiv" are taken from a poem by Shevchenko of the same name.

In the village of Subotiv
On a high mountain
Stands the tomb of Ukraine—
Wide and deep.

That is the church of Bohdan
in which he prayed
So that the Russian would share
Good and bad with the cossack.

Peace be to your soul, Bohdan!
This is not what happened.
The Russians were jealous
and robbed us of everything.
They are plundering the tombs
And looking for money.
They are digging out your vaults
And cursing you
And complaining
That is how it is, Bohdan.

You betrayed her
Your orphan Ukraine!
For that you get this thanks
And there is nobody
To repair that church-tomb
In that Ukraine.

Oh yes, Zenovii,
Friend of Aleksei!
You gave away everything to your friends,
And they don't even care
They say, you see, that all of this, was ours
That they only rented it
to the Tatars for grazing their horses
And to the Poles ... Perhaps this is so!

Let it be!
This is how strangers laugh
at us in Ukraine!
Do not laugh, strangers!
The church-tomb
Will break apart ... And from beneath it
Ukraine shall arise.
And she shall sweep away the darkness of slavery,
She will light up the world of truth
And the children of slaves
Will pray in freedom.[117]

When Komu vnyz performed this song at Chervona Ruta concerts, Andrii Sereda stated that the people should stand up, light candles, and sing this rock song like an anthem.[118]

Also filled with vicious sarcasm is the song of Komu vnyz called "Eldorado," based on the words of nineteenth-century Ukrainian poet V. Samiilenko.

Somewhere far away there is a country.
Clean, beautiful, proud in its happiness,
Everyone there lives happily
The bully, the bully.

They speak French there
Not only the officials, but the lackeys.
And the landlords know all languages
Except their own, except their own.
There is great freedom of word there
Everyone writes everything he knows
And the censorship is liberal too
It crosses out everything, crosses out everything.

There the writers are thanked for their work
By the government itself.
And in triumph they escort them
to Siberia, to Siberia.

All people live there
Russians, Ukrainians, Poles
And they live so peacefully—
Like dogs, like dogs.

In that country live many nationalities
A great diversity
And for that reason the country is called
One Rus', One Rus' [one Russian Empire].[119]

The members of Komu vnyz perform in tuxedos with tails that reach the floor and high leather boots. Their lead singer and composer, Andrii Sereda, has shaved his head. The overall effect of their performance is very strong. Another rock musician who has been composing and singing original renditions of Shevchenko's poetic texts is Kiev-based Oleksandr Tyshchenko and his rock group Zymovyi sad (Winter Garden).

Not all the songs of rock musicians have themes of national liberation. Some, such as the Kiev heavy metal rock group Perrön, are critical of the general socioeconomic situation. The music of this group, which imitates Western groups such as AC/DC and the Rolling Stones, is full of anger, frustration, and aggression. Oleksandr Leusenko has hair down to his waist.

The words of the song "Lyst do Toronto" (Letter to Toronto) are the following:

Oleksandr Leusenko of the Ukrainian group Perrön during performance in Toronto at York University's Glasnost and Global Village Conference, February 1991. Copyright © Wendy Rombough Szamosvari. Reprinted by permission.

What's a poor man to do? Money, kids, nowhere ...
What to buy, where to buy it?
What can I do, I've got no luck at all ...
Things fall apart, how can we live?
"Everything's normal, citizens.
Just believe in progress—Get to Work!"
Instead of glorious mighty-state Action, we get words ...

Refrain:
Where are you, where are you guys?
Where are you, where are you guys?
Brothers in Toronto. Help us!

Don't worry about us
We'll beat the hard times, and not just once.
Soon we'll have it better here than you have there.
"Everything's normal, citizens.
Just believe in progress—Get to work!
Instead of glorious mighty-state Action, we get words ...

Refrain.

What to buy, where to buy it?
What can I do, I've got no luck at all ...
Things fall apart, how can we live?
Don't worry about us,
We'll overcome our troubles, and not just once.
Soon we'll have it better here than you have there.[120]

Another song by Perrön is "Lavrentiivna," the name given to the monumental gigantic female statue with an uplifted sword (in reference to Lavrenti Beria, one of Stalin's chief Cheka [secret police officers]). It was built during the Brezhnev era and stands on the shores of the Dnipro River, overlooking the city of Kiev. The statue, which cost millions of rubles, is uniformly disliked by the whole population of Kiev and is also referred to sarcastically and pejoratively as the *baba* (broad). The words of "Lavrentiivna" are

What have we done?
We have become like women.
Today we walk under a woman's heel.
As if we did not have enough of our own,
We had to invite a foreign one
And we let her wave a sword.

They took all our money
From the future Five Year Plans
And we will not see nice apartments for a long time

Refrain:
Lavrentiivna-e-e-e-e
Lavrentiivna-e-e-e-e[121]

Another song in Perrön's repertoire is the Russian-language "Raket" (Organized Crime), which condemns these criminals with bitter anger. The hard rock song "Pyvo bliuz" (Beer Blues), in the Ukrainian language, confronts the widespread social problem in Ukraine of wife (woman) assault and alcoholism. The words are as follows:

Pig snout waits for his beer in the morning.
Eyes closed, pig snout howls at his wife,
You damned wife, God will kill you!
Where's the beer? the beer! Where's my beer?
The barrel is cracking, the hangover is driving him crazy.

Having had some beer, pig snout crawls under a bush.
He punches his wife in the face and she's burning like red calico.
Pig snout grows sick of watching Ukrainian T.V.
Having pigged out on beer, he stands stupidly totally spaced out.[122]

Another theme that appears in Ukrainian rock and pop songs is that of ecology, specifically Chernobyl. Some rock festivals have been devoted to ecology, such as the Rock-Pop Show in summer 1988 in Berdniansk and Save the Azov Sea in August 1990, also in Berdniansk, located on the Azov Sea. This festival was supported by Zelenyi Svit (Green World), an ecological association headed by Dr. Yuri Shcherbak (now minister of the environment of Ukraine) that has held numerous ecological rallies in Kiev since 1988.[123] In April 1990 there was a Festival of Green Art in Kiev at which several rock groups performed.

In the days and months following the Chernobyl nuclear explosion, Alla Pugacheva and her pop-rock group performed in Chernobyl for the cleanup crews and medical staff to boost their morale.[124] The year was 1986, when glasnost was just a word and not yet a reality and when the communist party and Soviet government were on the one hand covering up the extent of the catastrophe and on the other hand praising the heroes—the firefighters who died in putting out the fire and the cleanup crews. By 1988, the truth about Chernobyl and the extent of the radiation and sickness and death and the degree of official cover-up were becoming more apparent. Numerous documentary films that were censored in 1986 were being released, and the mood changed from a hysterical demand for information to self-examination, guilt, and feelings of apocalyptic doom.[125] Numerous rock and pop songs reflect this somber mood.

In 1988, the documentary film *Porog* (Threshold), directed by Rollan Serhienko with script by poet-bard-singer Vladimir Shovkoshytny, was released in the Kiev Dovzhenko Studio. This film focuses on the residents of the town of Prypiat, who were direct participants in these events and also received the highest doses of radiation. Among the former residents of Prypiat was singer Vladimir Shovkoshytny, whose bard-rock songs, poetry, and comments provide the sorrowful narrative of this film. Shovkoshytny, a Russian-speaking Ukrainian, sings in the Russian language about the people of Prypiat:

We are birds of one nest
But we have been dispersed
Our sorrowful star shone over quiet Prypiat

This reference is to the biblical passage of the Revelation of Saint John the Divine that refers to a great falling star called "Wormwood." "Wormwood" in Ukrainian is "chornobyl." Immediately after the accident, people were referring to this biblical passage as a prophetic warning. In *Porog,* Shovkoshytny comments on the moral and personal aspects of Chernobyl: "The explosion that ripped off the roof of the Chernobyl fourth reactor also ripped apart our souls. It forced us to re-evaluate our values."[126] Shovkoshytny sings sad ballads about the radioactive forest, about the graves of children, about the black zone, about his abandoned empty hometown of Prypiat.

Vladimir Shovkoshytny's somber mood is repeated by another Ukrainian singer, Taras Petrynenko, leader of the pop-rock group Hrono (Cluster). In the song "Chornobylska zona" (Chernobyl Zone), Petrynenko sings, in Ukrainian:

Everything has come to nothing
This story has come to an end
The people no longer can speak
He who planted death in his garden
Now has reaped his retribution and harvest.
Our white blooded (i.e. leukemia) fear
Our black blooded humor
Has no salvation, no escape
For what unpardoned sin
Have you entered our body
Chernobyl zone?[127]

In another documentary on Chernobyl, *The Legacy of Chernobyl,* a 1991 Canada Broadcasting Company (CBC) production, Andrii Sereda, leader of the rock group Komu vnyz (Going Down) sings a lyrical lament for the victims of Chernobyl and their families:

It is time to rest
It is still night
It is still night
Sleep, my mother
It is still night
It is still night

. . . . . .

Mama
It's the end of the night
It's day
It's day
Your eyes have burnt out
It's day
Its day
God!
God look![128]

These Chernobyl songs are filled with images of death, guilt, and despair. In 1991 a record was released entitled *The Black Star of Chornobyl*, a literary and musical composition consisting of works of singer Taras Petrynenko, composer Volodymyr Huba, and poet Ivan Drach. In March 1990, the Kiev instrumental group Erotychnyi dzhaz (Erotic Jazz) recorded a composition entitled "My zhyvemo pid zirkoiu polyn, podorozhuiuchy derevom kochannia v poshukakh korinnia i krony" (We Live Under the Wormwood Star, Traveling Along the Tree of Love, in Search of the Root and the Top).

Not all songs are concerned with social and economic problems, politics, or ecology. The majority of songs are about those issues that concern youth the most—growing up, fear, anger, frustration, drugs, alienation, loneliness, fun, dancing, physical activity, physical attraction, sex, and, above all, love: love desired, love rejected, love consummated. The opening line of one of Perrön's songs is very basic in this respect: "Lie down, let's make love." The title of V.V.'s most popular song is "Tantsi" (Dancing). Most of V.V.'s songs are love songs, as is "Wild Star":

Wild restless star; Stay; Where are you falling?
And in my heart there's another star just like yours;
　　it's flying to your star.
I will catch it because I love you. I love you. Stay;
　　You are like smoke.
I will transform this night

Into a serenade
for you.

Wild, I kiss your neck, your lips, your breasts, but in my imagination
 For you are so far away
The night zephyr licks your hair; he bends the branches.
 I see. Where are you my enchantress?

And so this night fades
My serenade echoes

My wild reggae soars. Dances-soars, rushes-soars, soars-flies!
 O-O!
The trees are my fingers; the wind is my loving—
 the heavens are my strings.
I fly with the star, I fly with it through your window.
 My Zemfira, my Zemfira ... [129]

An interesting heavy metal and blues rock song by Perrön was composed and written by Perrön's singer Julius Zarembovsky before he left
the group in 1990 to go to graduate school. It is entitled "Ghost."

The moon is shining,
All is visible as if it's day,
Somewhere at night
An owl sings songs.
An evil apparition
A robber, or myself
Who knows, who
Brings you unhappiness.

Although there is light
You can't see a thing,
Somebody was here
Somebody just passed by.
The door creaks
And your heart skips a beat
Who knows,
Who will die tonight.

I do not shine
I am invincible,
You can't find me
Even for a second.
I am the one who
Brings you terror and gloom

I am invisible,
Nothing can save you.[130]

Kvartyra #50 sings a song entitled "A Person Without a Face":

I am a person without a face,
    without a face
    without a face
And for eternity
I must run
Run in a circle
In a circle without end.

Another one of the group's songs is "Tiazhelo odnomu" (It's Hard Alone). A song by the group V.V. is "Rozmova z Makhatmoiu" (A Conversation with Makhatma), and the instrumental folk-rock group Er Jazz has produced a music video entitled "A Tea Ceremony." Another instrumental Kiev group, Biokord, has also produced a rock video entitled "Aggression."

Glasnost has allowed rock music groups and culture to develop in Ukraine. Information about rock music has improved as well; for example, the regular column "Fonohraf" in *Moloda Gvardia* (Young Guardian) publishes regular "hit parades." These charts are not based on sales because production, distribution, and copyright are not yet normalized; that is, there are as yet no laws governing these activities. Therefore they are based on telephone polls and letters to the newspaper. Other newspapers also publish information on rock music groups: for example, "Klub 636" in *Komsomolskoie znamia* (Young Communist League Banner) by O. Yaholnyk, in Kiev; "Muzychnyi ekspres" in the newspaper *Prapor Yunosti* (Flag of Youth) by V. Liubchenko, in Dnepropetrovsk; "Fonohraf" in the newspaper *Rovesnyk* (Contemporary) by A. Krokhmalnyi, in Ternopil; and in 1992 "Dzerkalo" (Mirror) in the newspaper *Holos Ukrainy* (Voice of Ukraine). In addition, the journal *Novyny Kinoekramu* (Film News), edited by O. Hordii and Leonid Cherevadenko, now regularly publishes articles on rock music and rock videos. For example, there are articles on former Leningrad rock singer Viktor Tsoi;[131] an article on a film about Tsoi by Kiev filmmaker Serhii Lysenko, called "Kinets kanikul" (End of the Holidays);[132] an article on the Beatles[133] and the Beatles film by Yuri Tereshchenko; and an article on Madonna.[134] There are also regular articles on rock music now in *Nova heneratsiia* (The New Generation),[135] *Ranok* (Morning), and *Ukrainska Kultura* (Ukrainian Culture).[136] There are also popular programs on Ukrainian republican radio such as "Kontakt" (Contact), hosted by Veronika Makovii and Olexandr Vasyliev; "Blitz"; "Vechirnia studio" (Evening Studio); and

"Kontrasty." There are also TV programs on rock music: for example, Ukrainian TV has "Video mlyn" (Video Mill), "Hart" (Energy), "Vechirnyi novyny" (Evening News), and "Vechirnyi visnyk" (Evening Herald).

Rock concerts continue to take place. Chervona Ruta No. 2 was held in Zaporizzhia August 1991.[137] A rock festival Rock 'n' Roll Tavriia was held in Nova Kakhovka August 1991.[138] A rock concert was held in the town of Borodianka of Kiev Province in June 1992 with performances by Andrii Mykolaichuk, Oleksandr Tyshchenko, and a rap group.[139] In Kiev in 1992 the concert Vernisazh-92 was held. Its rock program featured Vika, Iryna Bilyk, Oleh Laponohy of Tabula rasa, V.V., Oleksandr Tyshchenko, and new groups such as Kiev's Opalny prynts (Opal Prince) and Mertvy piven (Dead Rooster) and Taras Chubai with his new rock group Plach Ieremiia (The Wailings of Jeremiah).[140] In addition to these rock and pop concerts, a July festival of folk musicians and bards-balladeers, Oberih '92, has been taking place annually in Lutsk in western Ukraine. Here the bards Vasyl Zhdankin from Kiev, Stas Shcherbatykh from Ivano-Frankivsk, Mariika Bermaka from Khadrkiv, and Oleh Pokalchuk from Lutsk continue to perform with great success.

Recording studios are also being formed. In addition to the joint venture Kobza, there are numerous independent studios such as Fonohraf (Phonograph). Noteworthy among these is Audio-Ukraine (a former branch of Melodiya), which has released numerous cassettes and recordings, described in the March 1992 issue of *Ranok* (Morning) magazine.[141] These recordings include the pop-rock *Display;* the pop group Avans with its collection entitled *Na fazendi* (On the Hacienda); Taras Petrynenko's *I Know How It Will Be;* and Rybchynsky and Gennadii Tatarchenko's rock opera *Belaia Vorona* (The White Crow), on which they had been working since 1986.

In 1990 Kobza sponsored the groups Vika, the Snake Brothers, Zymovyi Sad (Winter Garden) with Oleksandr Tyshchenko, Komu vnyz (Going Down), Taras Petrynenko, and Hrono (Cluster). In 1992, Vika again toured Canada and the United States.[142] Many of the groups are touring neighboring Poland and other countries of Europe.

Problems continue to exist in the music industry in Ukraine, in spite of the fact that censorship has been lifted, information is allowed, and independent studios and rock music groups are allowed to exist. This new freedom has given rise to unfamiliar problems. There is as yet no widespread system of restaurants or nightclubs that hire music groups to perform. Independent restaurants and nightclubs, previously forbidden, are now only beginning to develop and it will take some time before they become commonplace. Now, still, rock groups often find that the only place where they can perform is at a concert. Also, progress is hampered by shortages and poor quality of technical equipment in independent studios and difficulties in communication and publicity (very often a result of the severe shortage of paper). Original recordings are usually made on tape. Another serious problem is that copyright law for individual works of art, including musical recordings, does not exist. Individual independent musicians and their independent producers therefore have no legal protection against pirating, which is a widespread and acceptable practice in Ukraine. It is hoped that this situation will change once laws protecting private enterprise, copyright, and the market economy are in place and functioning.

At the present time, however, the market system is not functioning and there is widespread anarchy and chaos in the society as a whole. This confusion is reflected in the instability of the rock groups and recording studios, which keep regrouping and changing or appearing and disappearing at an alarming rate. Most musicians and their managers lack not only the skills of the music industry, that is, production, marketing, and distribution, but in many cases lack even a basic understanding of business concepts. As the initial enthusiasm and joy of ideological freedom wear off, the economic realities and responsibilities begin to appear and the frustration begins to set in. Oleksandr Yevtushenko expressed this mood very well in *Muzyka* (Music) when he commented on the high prices for the Kiev Vernisazh concerts—"25 Karbovantsi [25 rubles] for one ticket!"[143] Not used to a market system, many musicians and journalists still speak about subsidies from benevolent sponsors, that is, writes Anatolii Holovko, "charitable support for the most talented performers who will be able to pursue creative goals without commercial directions. The future will reward those who give such support."[144]

As far as originality of rock and pop music in Ukraine is concerned, Anatolii Holovko admits, "Unfortunately that which we listen to or look at is a repetition of the past or an attempt at copying second rate examples of European pop-music."[145] Actually, there is little originality in youth rock counterculture in Ukraine. The rock and pop music scene is heavily if not entirely dominated by Western, specifically American, influence. The appetite for North American rock music and videos is presently unsatiable. The commercial video salon business is booming. (A salon is a room or small theater for group screenings, not a rental store.) These thousands of new video salons all over Ukraine—in cities, small towns, and villages—screen American movies that are mostly second rate (horror or pornography) and American rock videos.[146] The impact of the videocassette recorder, like its predecessor, the tape recorder, is revolutionary. However, there is hope that eventually original rock music will appear. The musicians certainly do not lack wit and in many instances laugh at their society and stand aside from it, which is, after all, the essence of counterculture.

The experiments of Serhii Kuzminsky and Vika Vradii in combining rock music and punk sound with folk *kolomyika* rhythms in a satirical fashion are interesting and original. The original rock music renditions of Taras Shevchenko's poetry by Andrii Sereda and Oleksandr Tyshchenko present interesting creative directions. A direction to be developed also is the combination of rock with jazz, and in Ukraine today there are numerous excellent jazz musicians. A particularly interesting phenomenon is the creation of bard-rock, an original style of rock music that is very popular in Ukraine and the rest of the former Soviet Union. Bard-rock in Ukraine is manifested in the music of bard-balladeers and several protest folk singers—Viktor Mokozov, Andrii Panchyshyn, Taras Chubai. According to Artemy Troitsky in his latest book published in Moscow in 1990, *Rok muzyka v SSR* (Rock Music in the USSR), bard-rock is so far the only original Soviet contribution to the vocabulary of universal rock music. Troitsky writes,

> The influence of serious poetry and especially the bard song (V. Vysotsky, A. Galich, B. Okudzhava) on Soviet rock of the mature period (from the end of the '70s), is no less signficant than blues music on American rock. It has influenced all Soviet rock groups of all styles, including punk. The particular significance of bard-rock is that it preserves not only the supremacy of the poetic text, but also the compositional and melodic structure of the bard song. Often the compositions of bard-rock are formed according to the principles of ballads and romances. ... A formative influence on bard-rock was also the graceful English folk rock and the Bob Dylan sound of the '60s.[147]

APPENDIX:
PROFILES OF MAJOR ROCK GROUPS
IN UKRAINE, 1986–1991

Instrumental Only

Erotychnyi Dzhaz (Erotic Jazz), Kiev Oleksii Oleksandrov plays flute, piano, percussion, vibraphone, and marimba and sings vocals; Andzei Pozdin does vocals and guitar; Victor Krisko plays violin; and Oleh Barabash plays guitar. Their first album was recorded by Fonohraf in March 1990 and entitled *My zhyvemo pid zirkoiu polymn podorozhuiuchy derevom kochannia v poshukakh korinniia i krony* (We Live Under the Wormwood Star, Traveling Along the Tree of Love, in Search of the Root and the Top). Performed in Fonohraf 89; Iolky-Palky (Fiddlesticks), January 1990, Kiev; Khazabuky (or Khai zavzhdu bude Kyiv—Long Live Kiev), April 1990; Festival of Green Art, April 1990; Festival of Ecology, 1990,

Lithuania; Wild Fields, December 1990, Krakow, Poland; and France, 1991. Produced the rock video "Tea Ceremony," Kiev, 1990.

Biokord (Biocord), Kiev   Formed in 1989 by guitarist Mykola Bykov, an architect. First performance on 7 January 1990 at Iolky-Palky in Kiev. Members are Mykola Bykov (guitar); Volodymyr Velychko (guitar); Ihor Morozov (keyboards); Oleksii Shmatok (percussion). Play structural rock and recorded *Rok ot serdtsa* (Heartbeat) March 1990 with Fonohraf. Also performed in Chorna rada (Black Council of the Masses) in September 1990 with additional members: Oleksandr Darov (percussion) and Oleh Sokolov (bass). Produced rock video entitled "Aggression."

Rok-trio (Rock trio), Kiev   Roman Surzha (guitar); Anton Kotsar (bass); Dmytro Pidluskyi (drums). First performed in March 1987 at Rok-dialoh (Rock Dialogue) in Kiev, in Budynok khudozhnyka (Artists Building). Tape recordings include *Bumerang* (Boomerang), March 1987; *Skhid i zakhid* (East and West), July 1988; *Brutto* (Bruto), February 1989, by Fonohraf, with pianist Victor Karasyk; *Pro shcho z toboiu ne hovoryly* (We Talked About Everything), May 1990.

Chyslo Tsvirkuna (Cricket's Number), Kiev   Formed in 1984 by Yuri Storozhuk (guitarist and poet). One of the founders of Ukrainian underground rock. Performed first on 29 October 1986 at Debut '86 in Kiev. Then Storozhuk left for India, where he studied sitar and taught Russian. Members of the group are Oleh Putiatin (bass), Ivan Davydenko (piano), and Dmytro Pasichnyk (drums). Stylistically modal jazz-rock. Cassettes include *Troiie v chovni* (Three in a Boat), 1987; *Zasady tsvirchannia* (Basics of Cricket Cheeping), 1988; *De Ne Blukaiut Khmary* (The Clouds Wander Everywhere), by Fonohraf, Kiev, in June 1990. Has performed widely across Ukraine. In 1989 visited Germany. In 1990 Storozhuk and Hilb Butuzov (ex-Collegiate Assessor) formed Godzadva.

Ukrainian-Language Rock Groups

Banita Baida (Outcast Baida) (presently renamed Viy), Kiev   Name is from the drama by P. Kulish, *Baida, Kniaz' Vyshnevetsky* (Baida, Prince Vyshnevetsky), St. Petersburg, 1885, which has the line "The King has called me a banita— 'outcast' in Poland and Ukraine." Formed in spring 1989. Viktor Nedostup (poet, singer, pianist); Dmytro Dobryvechir (bass); Taras Boiko (guitarist); Vitalii Klimov (guitarist); and Mykola Radionov (percussion). First performed 6 October 1989 in Kiev at festival Chortova diuzhyna (Devil's Dozen). Also performed in Iolky-Palky in January 1990; Khazabuky in April 1990; Vyvykh (Sprain) in June 1990 (Lviv); and Chorna rada in September 1990 (Kiev). In September 1990, recorded the cassette *Parochka ptakhiv* (A Pair of Birds). Dmytro Dobryvechir and Viktor Nedostup have now regrouped into the rock group Viy.

Braty Hadiukiny (Snake Brothers), Lviv   Founded in Lviv in 1988 from the two groups Group of Plastic Mystification and Orchestra of Grandpa Mazai. Serhii Kuzminsky, the lead singer, writes the lyrics in Ukrainian urban slang and also plays keyboard. Other members are Andrii Partyka (guitar); Mykhailo Lundin (drums); Oleksandr Hamburg (bass); and Ihor Melnychuk (synthesizer). Recorded the tape *Vsio chotko* (Everything Is O.K.) in Lviv in a homemade studio, spring 1989. They performed at Holosieve '88, November, in Kiev; SiRok (Raw Alternative Rock), February 1989, in Moscow; Rok zabava (Rock Dance), April 1990, in Kiev; and Chervona Ruta (Red Rue Flower), 1990, in Toronto. Kuzminsky also wrote the lyrics for Vika's "Hanba" (Shame) and "Shakhtarskyi bugi" (Coalminer's Boogie). The Snake Brothers received second prize for rock at the Chervona Ruta Festival (September 1989, Chernivtsi) and also performed in the Moscow December 1989 and 1990 Christmas concerts run by Alla Pugacheva. According to the readers of "Fonohraf" in *Moloda Gvardia* (Kiev), the Braty Hadiukiny (Snake Brothers) were considered "the discovery of 1989." Their style is a mixture of white reggae, Ukrainian punk, and Lemko pop. Recorded by channel 47, Toronto, at Chervona Ruta. Also featured in the film *Satirical Mill No. 24*: Braty Hadiukiny by Serhii Bukovsky. Available in video series *Ukraine in the* 1990s, volume 3, Satirical Sketches (Kiev Glasnost Films, Inc., Toronto). Audiocassette recordings of *Braty Hadivkiny* by Kobza.

Komu Vnyz (Going Down), Kiev Founded in 1988. Andrii Sereda (vocals and synthesizer); Viacheslav Makarov (guitar); Serhii Stepanenko (bass); Viacheslav Maliuhin (guitar); Ievhen Razin (drums). First performed at the Kiev rok-klub Festival in June 1988. Voted "the discovery of 1988," according to readers of "Fonohraf" in *Moloda Gvardia,* Kiev. Their style is hard art with elements of neofolk. They performed at Rock for Peace, October 1988, in Kiev and Bila Tserkva; Holosieve '88; Fonohraf '89, June 1989, in Kiev; KYROK; Chervona Ruta, September 1989, in Chernivtsi; Rok-Front-Perebudovi (Rock-Front for Perestroika), September 1989, in Nova Kakhovka; Chervona Ruta, May 1990, in Toronto; Let's Save the Azov Sea, September 1990, in Berdniansk. First Russian-language tape recorded in March 1989. Second Ukrainian-language tape recorded in spring 1990. The songs "Subotiv," "Eldorado," and "Do Osnovianenka" are on *Rock Musicians* tape by Kobza. Toronto concerts, 1990. Recorded by CTV, channel 47, Toronto, at the Chervona Ruta Festival, 1989. Appeared in 1991 CBC documentary film on Chernobyl. Audiocassette recordings by Kobza studio.

Slid (Step), Kiev Formed in 1986 by guitarists Yurii Tovstohan and Ihor Zavhorodnyi, both of whom had performed previously with official singers such as Mykola Hnatiuk. Ihor Lykhuta is percussionist in this group. The quartet first performed at the festival Molodizhne perekhrestia (Youth Crossroads), February 1987, in Kiev. Also performed at Molodizhne perekhrestia II, October 1987, Kiev; and New Year's Show in December 1988. Slid's first album, *Shliakh v chasi* (Path in Time), was recorded February 1989. The group has fallen apart, but leader Yurii Tovstohan has been continuing solo, for example at KYROK, June 1989, in Kiev; Chervona Ruta, September 1989, in Chernivtsi; First Festival of Green Art, April 1990, in Kiev; and Let's Save the Azov Sea, September 1990, in Berdniansk. Filmed by Ukrainian State Television.

Vika (Vika), Lviv Lead vocalist Vika Vradii sang originally with Viktor Morozov in the 1970s in a group called Arnika. Then she sang in the group Labyrinth, near

Moscow, in which she imitated Suzi Quatro, Janis Joplin, and Uriah Heep. For one month in 1989 she sang with Braty Hadiukiny (Snake Brothers), and just before the Chervona Ruta Festival she formed a new group—Vika, which received first place in the rock category at the Chervona Ruta Festival. Serhii Kuzminsky of Snake Brothers composed the songs "Han'ba" and "Shakhtarski bugi." Vika received first prize for best show at the Ms. Rock Europe (International Female Rock Music Festival), January 1990, in Kiev. Performed in Toronto at the Chervona Ruta Festival in May 1990 at the Diamond Club and appeared on Toronto TV. Her songs are on the *Rock Music* Kobza tape, and in 1990 she recorded her song "Mamo, ia durna" (Mamma, I'm Stupid) in the Kiev Kobza studio. Her husband, Volodymyr Bebeshko, plays bass guitar and is her song arranger. In summer 1992, Vika toured Canada and the United States with her rock group. Filmed by channel 47, Toronto, at the Chervona Ruta Festival, 1989.

V.V. (Vopli Vydopliasova), Kiev Founded in 1986. The name is taken from a character in the Dostoyevsky story *The Village of Stepanchikovo*. The skeleton of the group already existed in 1983 with Yurii Zdorenko, who does vocals and plays guitar, and Oleksandr Pipa, who plays bass guitar. At first they played hard rock, but then they were joined by Oleh Skrypka, who does vocals and saxophone, and Serhii Sakhno, who used to do percussion (now it is Oleksandr Komisarenko from Apartment #50). The French TV program "Anten-2" included V.V. in its video films *Soviet Rock* and *Rock Around the Kremlin*. In March 1989 V.V. performed in Moscow with the English group World Domination Enterprise and in April 1989 performed in Kiev with the U.S. "hard-core" group Sonic Youth. V.V. was named the most popular group in Kiev in 1987. Its first cassette, *Tantsi* (Dances), was recorded in fall 1988 by Fonohraf in Kiev. In December 1989 V.V. performed in Poland, where it recorded an album consisting of twenty-four new and old songs. The group performed in France in April and June 1990 and in Switzerland in April 1990 and 1991.

Zymovyi Sad (Winter Garden), Kiev Founded in 1980. Members are Oleksandr Tyshchenko (composer and lead vocalist); Volodymyr Mykhalchenko (drums); Ihor Zavhorodnyii (guitar); Viktor Slinchenko (bass); and Oleksandr Vorona and Serhii Krutyk (synthesizers). During the Brezhnev years the group was forced to perform in cities of Russia and the Far East. To celebrate its return to Ukraine, the group performed the premiere of its rock symphony "Dolia" (Fate), 10 May 1988, in Kiev. The composition, which is twenty-two minutes long, is based on the words of poet Taras Shevchenko. The style of the group is art-rock. The group has performed widely across the USSR in Kishinev, Vilnus, Volgograd, Krasnodar, and Tashkent. It also performed at Chervona Ruta festivals in September 1989 in Chernivtsi and in May 1990 in Toronto. In addition to Ukrainian-language songs, the group also has English-language songs in its repertoire. In 1990 the founder and leader of the group, Oleksandr Tyshchenko, began a solo career. Zymovyi sad's four songs are on the *Rock Musicians* Kobza tape.

Bilingual (Ukrainian-Russian)
and Trilingual (Ukrainian-Russian-English)
Rock Groups

Zruinovani Barykady (Broken Barricades), Kiev Ukrainian, Russian, and English languages. The leader of the group, guitarist and vocalist Serhii Smetanin, belongs to the third generation of Ukrainian rock musicians; he began in the 1970s playing jazz-rock. From 1984, he played in the quintet Aeroport Kyiv (Airport Kiev). The others were Viktor Milman (vocalist); Kostiantin Ivliv (keyboard); Volodymyr Khalpakhchiev (bass); and Valerii Lataniuk (percussion). In fall 1989, saxophonist Hryhorii Neshchotnyi joined and the group changed its name to Broken Barricades. Perfomed in first rock festival Rock for Peace on 26 April 1986 in Kiev and in Molodizhne perekhrestia (Youth Crossroads) in February 1987; Svit muzyky i molod (Music World and Youth) in March 1988; Holosieve '88 in jazz-rock festival in May-November 1988; and in the Festival of Green Art in April 1990. The group also participated in York University's conference "Glasnost and the Global Village," Toronto, held in February 1991. Stylistically the group has moved away from jazz-rock to pop-rock. The audiocassette *Broken Barricades* was produced in Canada by Kiev Glasnost Films, Inc. (Toronto). Filmed and interviewed by Much Music (Lance Chilton) in *Kiev Pop Culture,* March 1991, Toronto.

Edem (Eden), Kiev English language. Begun in 1983, it is now a trash metal group. Performed in October 1986 at festival Debut '86. Until summer 1987 instrumental only, when Serhii Losyk (vocals) returned from Red Army service. Viktor Lukianov (bass guitar and leader); Yuri Fedorytenko (guitar); Semen Rymar (drums); and Vadym Vyrvalskyi (guitar). Fedorytenko left to form the group Akademia and then played with the new wave group Zahublennyi svit (Lost World); today Fedorytenko sings in a church choir in Riga. Edem has performed at numerous festivals: Youth Crossroads in February 1987, Kiev; Rock Dialogue in March 1987, Kiev; Day of Kiev in May 1987; Donetsk Festival of Rock Music in September 1987; Rock Parade in November 1987, Kiev; Hard Rock Days in February 1988, Riga; Metaloplastica (Metalplastic) in May 1988, Sverdlovsk; First Festival of Kiev Rock Club in May 1988; Pop-budylnyk (Pop-Alarm Clock) in June 1989, Kiev; Fonohraf '89 in June 1989, Kiev; and Trash-Metal-Drama in September 1989, Poland. The group has recorded three cassettes, the first one *Ballast,* in 1987, the second *Time of Madmen,* in 1989 (by Fonohraf), and the third in 1990 called *Golgotha.* Last year drummer Semen Rymar left the group.

Kvartyra #50 (Apartment #50), Kiev Ukrainian and Russian languages. Veterans of rock music of the 1980s who have evolved from hard rock to punk-wave. First played in October 1986 in the club Bilshovik, where a few months later the Kiev rock club was formed (with Kvartyra #50, Edem, Slid, and Tytanik). Oleh Vernytskyi (leader and vocals); Viktor Shchekotun (guitar); Oleksandr Komisarenko (who has since joined V.V.); Oleksandr Katsman (keyboard); and Oleksii Dundukov (bass; died in an automobile accident in 1988). The group performed at the following festivals: Debut '86 in October 1986, Kiev; Youth Crossroads in February 1987, Kiev; Rock Dialogue in March 1987; Fonohraf '87 in

June 1987, Kiev; Donetsk Rock Festival in September 1987; Music Ring in October 1987, Berdychiv; Ms. Rock in November 1988, Kiev, in which Victoria, wife of Oleh Vernytskyi, performed; Rock Avant-Garde in January 1989, Moscow; Pop-budylnyk in June 1989, Kiev; KYROK (abbreviation for Kiev Ukrainian-Language Rock Groups) in June 1989; and Rock-Front-Perebudovi in September 1989, Nova Kakhovka. The group was invited to Italy in summer 1990. Two tape recordings were made in September 1987: *Shvydka Dopomoha* (Ambulance) and *Holosuite za Mishel-Shnaytzer* (Vote for Michael-Shnautzer), both released by Fonohraf in May 1989.

Kolezhskyi Asessor (Collegiate Assessor), Kiev   Ukrainian, Russian, and English languages. Name comes from a civil rank in the Russian Empire. Vasyl Hoidenko (piano, guitar, and vocals); Hlib Butuzov (guitar and vocals); and Oleksandr Kievtsev (bass). First performed in 1981 in Kiev Polytechnical Institute, where they were students. The group was joined by Oleksii Ryndenko (drums). It has recorded many tape programs since 1981. Its last album was re-leased in England by Artemy Troitsky of Moscow on the British independent la-bel Eleven Meridiens. Performed in Rock Dialogue in March 1987, Kiev; Rock for Peace in October 1988, Kiev; Sirok in March 1989, Moscow; Iolky-Palky in January 1990, Kiev; Pop-budylnyk in June 1989, Kiev; Chorna rada in September 1990, Kiev. In November 1989 the group toured Scotland, where it played in a concert at the the Rooftop, taking part in the New Beginnings Soviet Art Festival in Glasgow. Its three albums, *Album for Children* (1985), *Kol Az* (Call Us, 1989), *Yadivod boit'sia Zemli* (Yadivod Fears Earth, 1989), were released by Fonohraf. In spring 1990 Hlib Butuzov founded an independent group—Godzadva. Guitar player Vadim Jurginov joined the ensemble.

Godzadva (In One Year or Two), Kiev   English and Ukrainian languages. Formed in spring 1990. Hlib Butuzov (formerly Collegiate Assessor) and Yurii Storozhuck. Performed first in Chorna rada in September 1990 (Kiev); Wild Fields in December 1990 (Poland); first tape recording, *Brydke Katchenia* (Ugly Duckling), made in August 1990.

Perrön, Kiev   Ukrainian and Russian languages. Name is derived from "train platform" and ancient Slavic god of thunder. Members are Oleksandr Potiomkin (guitar and lyricist); Oleksandr Leusenko (vocals and bass); Julius Zarembovsky (vocals); and Oleksandr Veselov (drums). They play heavy blues in which there are echoes of the Rolling Stones and AC/DC. In 1990 Zarembovsky left the group to go to graduate school. First performed in Kiev Rock Club in June 1988 and quickly reached the top five in popularity of rock groups in Ukraine. Two cas-settes were recorded by Fonohraf: *Pokhovalne Biuró* (Funeral Parlour), in December 1989, and *Bronenosetz' Potiomkina* (Warship Potiomkin), in August 1990. Perrön has performed in numerous festivals: Holosieve '88 in November 1988, Kiev; Beatlemania '89 in April 1989, Dnepropetrovsk; Fonohraf '89 in June 1989, Kiev; Pop-budylnyk in June 1989, Kiev; Rock Front-Perebudovi in August 1989, Nova Kakhovka; Hit Parade in October 1989, Moscow; Devil's Dozen in October 1989, Kiev; Bdzhola (Bee) in December 1990; Iolky-Palky '90 in January 1990, Kiev; Spring Hopes in February 1990, Vynnytsia; Rock Session in June 1990,

Kiev; Dnepropetrovsk in March 1990; Tavric Rock-n-Roll in July 1990, Nova Kakhovka; Save the Azov Sea in September 1990, Berdniansk; and Wild Fields in December 1990, Poland. York University conference "Glasnost and the Global Village," February 1991. Filmed by CBC on 11 February 1991 and by Much Music (Fax—with Lance Chilton, *Kiev Pop Culture*) 1 March 1991.

Tabula Rasa (Tabula Rasa), Kiev   Ukrainian, Russian, and English languages. Members are Oleh Laponohov (vocals and guitar); Oleksandr Ivanov (guitar); Serhii Hrymalsky (keyboards); Ihor Davydiantz (bass); and Eduard Kosse (drums). They debuted 7 January 1990 at Iolky-Palky '90 in Kiev. Also performed in March 1990 in Dnepropetrovsk; Khazabuky in April 1990 in Kiev; in September 1990 in Berdniask; and in December 1990 in Krakow (Poland). First tape recording, *Visim Run* (Eight Runes), was made in summer 1990, released by Fonohraf. Singer Laponohov was a prizewinner at the 1991 Chervona Ruta Festival in Zaporizzhia.

Chervona Ploshcha (Red Square), Kiev   Russian language. Hard and heavy. Formed by Vsevolod Tatarenko. Other members are Oleh Kulyk (vocals); Oleh Pekarovskyi (keyboards); Oleksandr Larychkin (bass); and Oleksii Shmatok (percussion). Performed in Rock-Panorama in December 1987, in Moscow; toured West Germany, summer 1989; Hard-and-Heavy in 1989, in Moscow; Festival of Green Art in 1990, in Kiev. Recorded *Red Square* on Melodiya label.

Russian-Language Rock Groups

Koshkin Dom (Cat's House), Odessa   A new wave alternative rock group that has grown out of the Odessa rock traditions of such groups as Provintsia (Provincel), Bastion, Krater (Crater), Marek i Veronika (Mark and Veronica), and Monte-Crisco. The group performed in Moscow in 1989, Leningrad in 1989, Nova Kakhovka in 1988, and Dneproderzhinsk in 1989. Kostiantin ("Kit-Cat") Shumailov (keyboards) and Maks (leader, vocalist, and composer) have moved to St. Petersburg (Leningrad).

Grupa Prodlionogo Dnia (G.P.D.) (After-Care Group), Kharkiv   Members are Oleksandr Chernetskyi (vocals); Oleh Klymenko (guitar); Pavlo Mykhailenko (bass, vocals); Volodymyr Kyrylin (percussion); and Evhen Obryvchenko (keyboards). Because of the strength of official Stalinist factions in Kharkiv, which continue to ban rock music (for example, in 1987 they officially abolished the Kharkiv rock club), the group had to go underground. As a result of opposition in Kharkiv it had to perform in Kiev, Riga, Moscow, St. Petersburg, Voronezh, Tallinn, and Rostov on the Don. In 1990 the musicians formed a new group, Rizni liudy (Different Peoples).

Dykyi Med (Wild Honey), Donetsk   This Russian-language group began in 1978. In June 1990 it recorded its first cassette, on Donetsk radio: *Mamo, my liubymo kleiity durnia* (Mom, We Like to Act Stupid). The group consists of Mykhailo Koval' (guitar, vocals, and author of texts); Serhii Fedotov (guitar and vocals); Serhii Savenko (bass); Serhii Oshovin (keyboards); and Yurii Nadravetskyi (percussion). They have performed widely in Kiev, Dnepropetrovsk, Kherson, and Rostov on the Don.

Ivanova Vis (Ivan's Axis), Kiev Guitarist Serhii Popovych (former leader of Rabbota Kho) and Yurii Mykhailychenko (present-day leader of Ivan's Axis) recorded two programs together, *Skuiovdzhene Derevo* (Messy Tree, 1987) and *Potentsia* (Potential, 1988), and then split. The group also consists of Mikhail Hudak (guitar); Dmytro Okarin (drums); and Andrii Kochnev (bass and vocals). Participated in Rok-art in March 1989, Kiev; Iolky-Palky '90 in January 1990, Kiev; Khazabuky in April 1990, Kiev; Aurora in November 1990, St. Petersburg; and a festival in December 1990, Omsk.

NOTES

1. Romana Bahry and Alexander Rudiachenko, "Rock Music in Ukraine," paper presented at York University international conference entitled "Glasnost and the Global Village," Toronto, 19–22 February 1991 (subsequently published in *Glasnost and the Global Village*, Selected Abstracts from Proceedings of the York University Conference [Toronto: York University Press]); Romana Bahry and Alexander Rudiachenko, "Rock and Roll Always Lives: The Rise of Rock Culture in Soviet Ukraine," *Compass: A Jesuit Journal* (Toronto) 9, no. 1 (March–April 1991), pp. 45–49. See also Romana Bahry, "The Satirical Current in Popular Youth Culture, Rock Music and Film in Ukraine in the 1990s," in Marko Pavlyshyn (ed.), *Ukraine in the 1990s: Proceedings of the First Conference of the Ukrainian Studies Association of Australia, Monash University, 24–26 January 1992* (Melbourne, Australia, 1992).

2. Audiotape interview with Alexander Rudiachenko, rock and pop music critic and editor of "Fonohraf," music section of *Moloda Gvardiia* (Kiev), 31 August 1990. Interview conducted by Romana Bahry.

3. Kyrylo Stetsenko, "Ukraina: Rok muzyka" and "Ukraina: Rok festivali 1986–1988," in *Rok muzyka v SSSR: Opyt populiarnoi entsyklopedii,* edited by Artemy Troitsky (Moscow: Kniga, 1990), pp. 338–345 and 345–347. These two articles provide a detailed overview of the rock groups and rock concerts in Ukraine from the 1960s to the present.

4. Serhii Povitria (pseudonym of Alexander Rudiachenko), "Sribne vesillia hirko?" in *Fonohraf Digest,* edited by Alexander Rudiachenko and Alexander Yevtushenko (Kiev: Teatralno-Kontsertny Kyiv and Fonohraf Studio, 1989), p. 11. This article provides a detailed overview of the rock groups and concerts in Ukraine in the 1960s and 1970s. pp. 11–17.

5. Audiotape interview with Alexander Rudiachenko, Kiev, 31 August 1990.

6. Ibid.

7. Stetsenko, "Ukraina: Rok muzyka," p. 339.

8. Ibid.

9. Rudiachenko, "Sribne Vesillia hirko?" p. 13.

10. Ibid., p. 14.

11. Interview with Rudiachenko, Kiev, 31 August 1990.

12. Ibid.

13. Stetsenko, "Ukraina: rok muzyka," p. 340.

14. Interview with Rudiachenko, Kiev, 31 August 1990.

15. Rudiachenko, "Scribne vesillia hirko," p. 15.

16. Ibid., p. 16.

17. Stetsenko, "Ukraina i rok muzyka," p. 341.

18. Interview with Rudiachenko, Kiev, 31 August 1990.

19. Rudiachenko, "Sribne vesillia hirko," p. 17.

20. Interview with Rudiachenko, Kiev, 31 August 1990.

21. Stetsenko, "Ukraina i rok muzyka," p. 343–344; and Rudiachenko, "Sribne Vesillia hirko," p. 17.

22. Stetsenko, "Ukraina i rok muzyka," p. 345.

23. Interview with Rudiachenko, Kiev, 31 August 1990.

24. Ibid.

25. Y. Sakhno, "Rok-klub: Sproba analizu," *Fonohraf Digest*, p. 5.

26. Ibid., p. 8.

27. Interview with Rudiachenko, Kiev, 31 August 1990.

28. Tanis Khmetyk, "Rock-a-by Gorby: Soviet Rock Breaks Cultural Barriers Both at Home and Abroad," *Paris Passion*, April 1990.

29. Stetsenko, "Ukraina i rok muzyka," p. 345.

30. Rudiachenko, "Scho to za shtuka Fonohraf?" in *Fonohraf Digest*, p. 3.

31. *Huchnomovets*, no. 5 (1989).

32. I was able to obtain only issues 1 through 4 at the time of this writing.

33. Audiotape interview with Vika, Toronto, 15 May 1990. Interview conducted by Romana Bahry.

34. Petro Cherniaiev, *Novyny Kinoekranu* (August 1990), pp. 16–17.

35. Pedro Ramet [Sabrina Petra Ramet], "Rock Counter Culture in Eastern Europe and the Soviet Union," *Survey: A Journal of East and West Studies* 29, no. 2 (Summer 1985), pp. 149–180.

36. Timothy W. Ryback, *Rock Around the Bloc: A History of Rock Music in Eastern Europe and the Soviet Union* (New York and Oxford: Oxford University Press, 1990).

37. See Kyrylo Stetsenko, "Ukraina: rok festyvali 1986–1988," in *Rok muzyka v SSSR: Opyt populiarnoi entsyklopedii,* edited by Artemy Troitsky (Moscow: Kniga, 1990), pp. 345–346.

38. *News from Ukraine,* no. 5 (January 1990).

39. Film *Vrubai bitlov* (Turn on the Beatles) by director Yuri Tereschenko, Kiev News and Documentary Film Studio, 1990. Film also includes Kolya Vasin, a Beatles fan from St. Petersburg. Film is available in video series *Ukraine in the 1990s,* vol. 10, Kiev Glasnost Films Inc., Toronto, *1991.*

40. According to Maria Nesterova ("Ukraina zhyve i spivaie," *Nova heneratsiia,* nos. 2–3 (February–March 1992), pp. 46–47), these festivals in Nova Kakhovka have come to an end but should be revived.

41. The festival was named Chervona Ruta after the title of the popular Ukrainian song composed by Volodymyr Ivasiuk, native of Chernivtsi and murdered in 1979.

42. The Chervona Ruta program (21 September 1989) lists forty-nine pop groups, eighty-one pop singers, forty-nine bands, and thirty rock groups.

43. Taras Kuzio, "Inaugural Congress of the Ukrainian Popular Front (Rukh) in Kiev," in *Echoes of Glasnost in Soviet Ukraine,* edited by Romana M. Bahry (North York, Ontario: Captus University Publications, 1989), pp. 102–108.

44. Mykola Riabchuk, "Ruta proty rutyny," *Nauka i kultura,* Akademiia nauk U.R.S.R. (Kiev), 1990, pp. 396–404.

45. Kyrylo Stetsenko, Program notes of the Chervona Ruta Festival, 21 September 1989, p. 3.

46. Pedro Ramet, "The Rock Scene in Yugoslavia," *East European Politics and Societies* 2, no. 2 (Spring 1988), pp. 396–397. (This essay is reprinted in a revised and updated form in this volume.)

47. Bahry and Rudiachenko, "Rock and Roll Always Lives."

48. Ibid.

49. Ibid.

50. Audiotape interview with Serhii Kuzminsky, lead vocalist of Braty Hadiukiny (Snake Brothers), Toronto, 23 May 1990. Conducted by Romana Bahry.

51. Audiotape interview with Vika Vradii, Toronto, 15 May 1990. Conducted by Romana Bahry.

52. Audiotape interview with Serhii Kuzminsky, Toronto, 23 May 1990. Conducted by Romana Bahry.

53. Stetsenko, "Ukraina i rok muzyka," p. 345.

54. Audiotape interview with Vika Vradii and Volodymyr Bebeshko, Toronto, 15 May 1990. Conducted by Romana Bahry.

55. Pedro Ramet and Sergei Zamascikov, "The Soviet Rock Scene," *Journal of Popular Culture* 24, no. 1 (Summer 1990). (This essay is reprinted in a revised and updated form in this volume.)

56. Interview with Serhii Kuzminsky, 23 May 1990, Toronto.

57. A. A. Zwarun, "The Day the Music Died," *Smoloskyp* 1, no. 4 (Summer 1979). (*Smoloskyp* is a Ukrainian émigré newspaper published in the United States.)

58. Stetsenko, "Ukraina i rok muzyka," p. 338.

59. Videotape of Chervona Ruta Festival, September 1989, on MTV (channel 47), Toronto. Shot on location in Chernivtsi.

60. Audiotape interview with S. Kuzminsky, 23 May 1990, Toronto. Interview conducted by Romana Bahry.

61. Videotapes by MTV, channel 47.

62. *Molod Ukrainy,* 20 January 1990.

63. Interview with Volodymyr Bebeshko, Toronto, 15 May 1990.

64. Audiocassette recording, *Pop Muzykanty* (Pop Musicians), No. 1 (Toronto-Kiev: Kobza, 1989), and MTV, channel 47 videotape. English translation by R. Bahry.

65. Kobza tape of *Pop Musicians* and MTV videotape.

66. Ibid.

67. Kobza tape, *Pop Musicians,* No. 1.

68. Audiocassette recording by Taras Petrynenko and pop group Hrono *La professiinyi rab* (I'm a Professional Slave) (Toronto-Kiev: Kobza, 1990).

69. Stetsenko, Program notes.

70. Audiotape interview with Taras Melnyk, Toronto, 14 May 1990. Interview conducted by Romana Bahry.

71. Stetsenko, Program notes, p. 3.

72. Ibid.

73. Ibid.

74. Ivan Dziuba, "Chy usvidomliuiemo natsionalnu kulturu iak tsilisnist?" *Kultura zihyttia*, no. 4 (24 January 1988).

75. Audiotape interview with Vika Vradii, Toronto, 15 May 1990. Conducted by Romana Bahry.

76. Audiotape interview with Andrii Sereda, Toronto, 14 May 1990. Interview conducted by Romana Bahry.

77. Audiotape interview with Serhii Kuzminsky, Toronto, 23 May 1990. Conducted by Romana Bahry.

78. Ibid.

79. Ibid.

80. Interview with Vika Vradii, 15 May 1990, Toronto. See also "Rock Around Europe Block," *News from Ukraine*, no. 5 (January 1990), p. 5.

81. Interview with Andrii Sereda and group Komu vnyz, Toronto, 14 May 1990; interview with Vika Vradii and Volodymyr Bebeshko, Toronto, 15 May 1990; interview with Serhii Kuzminsky, Toronto, 23 May 1990.

82. Interview with S. Kuzminsky.

83. I viewed this rock video on TV while in Kiev, August 1989.

84. Interview with Sereda of Komu vnyz, Toronto, 14 May 1990.

85. Audiocassette recording, *Bardy Ukrainy* (Toronto-Kiev: Kobza, 1989), and audiocassette recording *Konsert spivtsiv festyvaliu*, Chervona Ruta Festival (Toronto-Kiev: Kobza, 1989), feature Eduard Drach, Vasyl Zhdankin, Viktor Morozov, Andrii Panchyshyn, Oleh Pokalchuk, and Maria Burmaka.

86. Ne zhurys audiocassette tape, *Kartoteka Pana Bazia* (Mr. Bazio's File), home-produced in Ukraine. All translations of lyrics are by R. Bahry.

87. Ibid.

88. Ibid.

89. Marta Kolomayets, in *Ukrainian Weekly* (a Ukrainian émigré English-language newspaper published in New Jersey). Interview with Andrii Panchyshyn.

90. Ibid.

91. The texts of these songs have been published in Andrii Panchyshyn, *Ballads* (Toronto: Kobza, 1989).

92. Ibid.

93. Ibid.

94. Ibid.

95. Audiocassette interview with Viktor Neborak, 11 June 1992, Toronto. Interview conducted by Romana Bahry. Neborak is the author of the 1990 poetry collection *Litaiucha holova* (The Flying Head) (Kiev, 1990).

96. Ne zhurys tape *Kartoteka Pana Bazia* (Mr. Bazio's file).

97. Interview with Viktor Neborak, 11 June 1992, Toronto.

98. V. Druzhbynsky, "Interdivchynka na ekrani vi zhytti," *Novyny kinoekranu,* December 1989.

99. Ne zhurys tape *Kartoteka Pana Bazia.*

100. Interview with Serhii Kuzminsky, Toronto, 23 May 1990.

101. *Vidryzhka,* no. 4, and audiocassette *Braty Hadiukiny.* Produced in Lviv, 1989, with the help of Volodymyr Bebeshko.

102. Audiocassette *Braty Hadiukiny.* Produced in Lviv in homemade studio. Interview with Serhii Kuzminsky, Toronto, 23 May 1990. According to Kuzminsky, *Moskovskyi Komsomolets* ranked this cassette as the most popular in the USSR for 1989.

103. Serhii Bukovsky, director, *Satirical Mill No.* 24: Braty Hadiukiny (Kiev News and Documentary Studio, 1990). Ten minutes, color. Film available in video format in the series *Ukraine in the 1990s,* vol. 3: Satirical Sketches (Kiev Glasnost Films, Inc., Toronto, 1991).

104. Braty Hadiunky, audiocassette. Also videocassette *Ukraine in the 1990s,* vol. 3: Satirical Sketches.

105. Ibid.

106. Ibid.

107. Audiocassette *Vika* (Kobza: Toronto, 1990). See also MTV channel 47 video.

108. Audiocassette *Vika.*

109. Interview with Vika, Toronto, 15 May 1990. Interview conducted by Romana Bahry.

110. *Vika* tape "Mamo, ia durna" (Kobza, 1990).

111. Interview with Vika, 15 May 1990, Toronto.

112. Oleksandr Yevtushenko, "11 nevhamovna prystrast," *Nova heneratsiia,* September 1991, p. 29.

113. Anatolii Holovko, "Ukrainian Blues—tse mozhlyvo," *Nova heneratsiia,* nos. 2–3 (1992), p. 44.

114. "Veseli doshchi Iryny Bilyk," *Novyny kinoekrana,* January 1992.

115. "Pislia rabyni Izavry," *Novyny kinoekranu,* January 1990. Song "Fazenda" by Avans is on Kobza tape *Pop Musicians, No.* 1. See also new album *Fazenda* produced by Audio-Ukraine and *Ranok,* March 1992.

116. Interview with Sereda and members of Komu vnyz, Toronto, 14 May 1990.

117. Kobza tape *Rock Musicians.* All translations by Romana Bahry.

118. Interview with Sereda, Toronto, 14 May 1990.

119. Kobza tape *Rock Musicians.*

120. Recording *This Ain't No Polka* (Toronto: Kobza, 1990). The rock musicians of the group Perrön actually did visit Toronto in February 1991 to perform in the cultural and social segment of York University's conference "Glasnost and the Global Village." They were filmed by CBC (Canada Broadcasting Corporation) Evening News, 11 February 1991, and by "Much Music" City TV for a special program entitled "FAX—Kiev Pop Culture," hosted and directed by Lance Chilton. Aired 1 March 1991.

121. Video of Iolky-Palky Rock Festival (Fonohraf, 1990). Unedited footage.

122. Audiocassette *Perrön* (Kiev: Fonohraf, 1989).

123. See films: 1. Sechienko; 1. Boone.

124. Romana Bahry, "Cheinolegl Themes in Film, Music and Literature," paper delivered at American Association for the Advancement of Slavic Studies, Miami, November 1991.

125. Film *Porog,* director Rollan Serhienko (Kiev: Dovzhenko Studio, 1988).

126. Ibid.

127. Audiocassette recording by Taras Petrynenko and pop-rock group Hrono *La professiinyi rab* (Toronto-Kiev: Kobza, 1990).

128. Documentary film *Chernobyl the Awakening* and *The Legacy of Chernobyl.* Codirectors: Halya Kuekmij and Ihockobrin. CBC, Toronto, October 1991 (Toronto, Canada).

129. Audiocassette *V.V.*

130. Audiocassette *Perrön.*

131. "Nash Viktor," *Novyny kinoekranu,* June 1991, pp. 14–15. Viktor Tsoi died in a car accident 15 August 1990.

132. "Kinets kanikul," *Novyny kinoekranu,* February 1991.

133. Ludmylla Novykova, "Z legioniv Dzhona Lennona," *Novyny kinoekranu,* no. 11 (352) (November 1990), p. 18.

134. "Madonna," *Novyny kinoekranu,* no. 4 (357) (April 1991), pp. 8–9.

135. Oleksandr Yevtushenko, "Li ne vhamovna prystrast" (About Vika), *Nova heneratsiia,* September 1991, pp. 29, 30; Anatolii Holovko, "Ukrainian Blues," *Nova heneratsiia,* March–April 1992, pp. 44–45; and Maria Nesterova, "Ukraina zhyve i spivaie," *Nova henerat'siia,* 1992 February–March, pp. 46-47.

136. Serhii Betsan, "Ukrainskii molodi—ukrainsku muzyku," *Ukrainska Kultura,* No. 1, January 1992, pp. 20–21; Natalka Vasyliuk, "Lovyty rukamy tuman ..." (About Rock Group iy) (formerly Banita Baida), *Ukrainska Kultura,* No. 2, February 1992.

137. Nadia Shumak, "Chervona ruta, rozkvitai v Chernivtsiakh," *Novyny kinoekrana,* March 1992.

138. Nesterova, "Ukraina zhyve i spivaie."

139. "Dzerkalo," *Holos Ukrainy,* no. 115 (365) (20 June 1992).

140. Oleksandr Yevtushenko, "Pisenny vernisazh-92: Novyi i Midzh," *Muzyka,* no. 2 (March–April 1992), pp. 28–29.

141. "Audio-Ukraine—tse ukrainska pisnia," *Ranok,* March 1992, pp. 30, 31.

142. Orysia Hewka, "Vika Highlights Verkhovyna Rock Fest Memorial Day Weekend," *Ukrainian Weekly,* 7 June 1992, p. 10.

143. Yevtushenko, "Pisenny vernisazh-'92," p. 29.

144. Anatolii Holovko, "Ukrainian Blues—Tse mozhlyvo," *Nova heneratsiia,* nos. 2–3 (1992), p. 45.

145. Ibid.

146. O. and N. Musiienko, "Deshchopvo video," *Novyny kinoekranu,* June 1990, pp. 12–13.

147. Troitsky, *Rok muzyka v SSSR,* p. 52.

About the Book

Of the many avenues for expressing dissident viewpoints in communist societies, rock music—with its broad appeal among young people—was one of the most effective. Although there were rock groups that sang the praises of communism, other groups struck the pose of "rock rebels," assailing the system through their ribald lyrics and raucous music. Communist regimes generally had a difficult time adjusting to rock music, and some, such as those in Czechoslovakia and Romania, never did accept the new genre. Others, such as the East German government, tried to control and monitor rock by requiring musicians and DJs alike to pass tests on Marxist ideology. Other strategies included censoring lyrics, record covers, and attire; insisting on haircuts for band members; and fussing about jewelry and other adornments worn by rockers. The authorities knew that although these bands could not overthrow the state, they could sing up a storm, and, indeed, rock the state.

Bringing together some of the world's leading authorities on rock music under communism, this book analyzes the rise of specific rock groups throughout Eastern Europe and the Soviet Union, examining the broader social culture in which they operated and evaluating the political ramifications of their popularity.

About the Editor and Contributors

Sabrina Petra Ramet is associate professor of international studies, University of Washington. She is the author of five books, including *Social Currents in Eastern Europe: The Sources and Meaning of the Great Transformation* (1991) and *Balkan Babel: Politics, Culture, and Religion in Yugoslavia* (Westview Press, 1992). She is also the editor of seven previous books and has contributed articles to *Foreign Affairs, World Politics, Orbis,* and other journals. She is spending the 1993–1994 academic year at the Slavic Research Center, Hokkaido University, Japan, as a visiting fellow.

Olaf Leitner started his career as a member of the West Berlin rock group Team Beats. He came to know many of East Germany's rock performers and made a television film about the leader of the Renft Combo. By 1983, he had became music editor of RIAS Radio Berlin and a columnist for *TIP* magazine. He is the author of *Rockszene DDR: Aspekte einer Massenkultur im Sozialismus* (1983).

Alex Kan is a critic, journalist, and media consultant in St. Petersburg. His articles and reviews on Russian jazz and rock have appeared in *Jazz Forum, Ear,* and *Downbeat.* He produces and hosts a radio program on jazz and rock in St. Petersburg and also serves as the consultant/associate producer for programs on jazz and rock for Russian State TV & Radio. He has served as a translator and consultant for the *New York Times, Chicago Tribune, Washington Post,* BBC, ABC, and "McNeill/Lehrer Newshour." He serves as regular program consultant on Russia for KTCA-TV Minnesota Public Television.

Nick Hayes combines a career in the media as well as in academe. He is the regularly featured commentator on Russian affairs for the popular prime time weekly public affairs program "Almanac" on KTCA-TV Channel 2 Minnesota Public Television. With KTCA-TV, Hayes worked as the consultant and on-air commentator for the "Channel 3 Moscow" series and has served as the consultant, correspondent, and commentator for several documentaries. Nick Hayes is an associate professor and director of International Studies at Hamline University in Saint Paul, Minnesota. His articles have appeared in *Slavic Review* and *Russian History,* and he has contributed to the *Modern Encyclopedia of Russian and Soviet History.*

László Kürti teaches anthropology at the Eotvos Lorand University in Budapest. He earned his Ph.D. from the University of Massachusetts at Amherst and was subsequently an assistant professor of anthropology at the American University in Washington, D.C., before returning to his native country in fall 1992. Kürti has contributed articles to *East European Quarterly, Journal of Communist Studies, Anthropological Quarterly,* and other journals and is currently writing a book about the Csepel district in Budapest.

Stephen Ashley was born in the city of Leeds in West Yorkshire, England, in 1951. He studied at the Universities of Oxford, Edinburgh, and Sofia. His doctoral dissertation traced the rise of midnineteenth-century Bulgarian nationalism until the country's independence in 1878. In 1985, after a working career that began with short periods as a schoolteacher and a civil servant, he joined the Research and Analysis Department of Radio Free Europe in Munich, specializing in Bulgaria and Balkan relations. In 1990 he moved to the South East European Service of the BBC World Service in London, where he is now the senior scriptwriter. He has contributed chapters to several books on Balkan history and current affairs, and he broadcasts regularly in both English and Bulgarian.

Sergei Zamascikov is with the International Policy Department at the RAND Corporation, Santa Monica, California. Born in Belarus, he received his undergraduate training at the Latvian State University in Riga. After coming to the West in 1979, he studied at UCLA, worked as a broadcaster for the Voice of America, and was a host of the Russian popular music show at KCRW radio station. He lives in Santa Monica.

Robert Bird spent approximately one year in Moscow rock circles. He has translated rock lyrics and published in the Soviet rock press (*Kontrkul'tura, Ensk*). He is currently a graduate student in Russian literature at Yale University, with interests in poetry, Platonov, and Russian religious philosophy.

Maria Paula Survilla has been a lecturer in ethnomusicology and theory at the University of North Carolina at Greensboro since fall 1992. Born in Madrid of Belarusian parents, she performs on clarinet, Indonesian gamelan, and flamenco guitar. She is currently completing her Ph.D. in ethnomusicology at the University of Michigan. Under a Fulbright-Hayes fellowship, she conducted fieldwork during 1993 among Belarusian communities in Poland and Belarus in connection with her dissertation. In her dissertation Survilla examines how traditional epistemologies in Belarus have been changing as a result of political changes and ecological stress. She wrote an English introduction to the bilingual book *Through the Prism of Rock* (1989), about rock in Belarus, and has produced video documentaries on culture in Eastern Europe that have been distributed in the United States, Canada, and Belarus.

Romana Bahry (Ph.D., University of Toronto, 1978) is associate professor in the Department of Humanities and the Department of Languages, Literatures, and Linguistics at York University, Canada, where she teaches Russian literature and Ukrainian literature, culture, and language. She is a specialist in comparative and Slavic literature (nineteenth-century English-Russian-French literary relations) with articles and papers on Sir Walter Scott, N. Gogol, Leo Tolstoy, Jean-Jacques Rousseau, P. Kulish, and others as well as articles on expressionism in the theater of Les Kurbas and existentialism and the absurd in twentieth-century Ukrainian writers. She is the editor of *Echoes of Glasnost in Soviet Ukraine* (1990), to which she contributed a chapter ("Soviet Ukrainian Documentary Films"). She received a Canada-USSR Academic Exchange Grant in 1989 and Social Sciences and Humanities Research grants in 1990 and 1991 for research in Moscow, St. Petersburg, and Kiev.

Index